THE BEST
AMERICAN
MAGAZINE
WRITING

2005

THE BEST
AMERICAN
MAGAZINE
WRITING
2005

Compiled by
the American
Society of
Magazine
Editors

Columbia University Press   New York

Columbia University Press
Publishers Since 1893
New York   Chichester, West Sussex
Copyright © 2006 American Society of Magazine Editors
All rights reserved
Library of Congress Cataloging-in-Publication Data
A complete CIP record is available from the Library of Congress.
ISSN 1541–0978
ISBN 0–231–13780–X(pbk. : alk. paper)

Columbia University Press books are printed on permanent and durable
acid-free paper.
Printed in the United States of America
p 10 9 8 7 6 5 4 3

Contents

Introduction

Magazine journalists must be the profession's most superstitious members. People who work for daily newspapers and television and radio news broadcasts have a feeling of ordination about what they do (though it's getting a little shaky these days): how could the institutions that employ them possibly not exist? But anybody who has been working for magazines for any length of time knows that no magazine operates by right. Magazines rise and fall. The successes would have been hard to predict, and the failures too. Editors and writers rarely have serene, one-institution careers. It's a field where luck matters.

Magazines were the first form of journalism to appear, in the seventeenth century; even the earliest candidates for the not yet officially existent category of journalism, like Daniel Defoe's *Journal of the Plague Year* (1721), have a recognizable, magazine-story feeling. What magazines do is create communities—large ones, they hope—of people who share a set of interests and sensibilities. Their loyalty may be to a place, or a hobby, or a political ideology, or to a cultural tone, but a magazine that works has to accomplish the difficult feat of making its readers feel that it speaks to them uniquely, while also surprising them consistently enough to make each issue worth looking forward to. A magazine has to be familiar and new at the same time.

Great magazine editors have something in common with talented politicians. They pick up on an emerging note in the life of the society, shape it, amplify it, and come to exemplify it and to assemble a constituency built around it. DeWitt Wallace of *Readers' Digest* stood for the reduction of a modern society to a simpler, and more comforting form; John H. Johnson of *Ebony* for the aspirations of the emerging black middle class; Hugh Hefner of *Playboy* and Helen Gurley Brown of *Cosmopolitan* for the changing sexual mores of their respective genders; Jann Wenner of *Rolling Stone* for rock and roll as a generational touchstone; George Horace Lorimer of the *Saturday Evening Post* for the early stirrings of a national mass culture; Harold Ross of *The New Yorker* for urbanity; Henry Luce of *Time* for the vigor and scope of the twentieth century. One of the great canards of the magazine business is that everything depends on "buzz," that is, the intensity of attention paid by people in the media. Actually, everything depends on building a distinct and previously undiscovered constituency, which, in order to be big enough to support a magazine, necessarily must spread far beyond the very limited bounds of the media world. Every good magazine creates a little civilization around itself. That is a species of miracle; no wonder success in magazines feels serendipitous.

But underneath the distinctiveness of every good magazine lies a set of commonalities. Some of them are matters of business— just about everybody has an advertising-sales staff and mounts direct-mail subscription-solicitation campaigns—and some are aesthetic. Magazines, though a mainly nonfiction form, are much less dull and routine than life itself. They reprocess the world. They use every visual and textual weapon at hand to create a version of reality that is more engaging than the real thing. Much more so than in newspaper or broadcast journalism, in magazines everybody sees everybody else's work, and there is rampant cross-pollination. Good ideas spread instantly, and, with many exceptions and variations, magazines have a standard format: the cover, the newsy front-of-the-book, the culturally inclined back-of-the-book, the listings, the "well," with its longer pieces and graphically ambitious opening spreads. Within the well, one finds, again, a familiar set of forms: profiles of well-known people, investigative reports, personal accounts of dramatic experiences, guides to some consumer realm, contrarian essays.

It is easy to make fun of magazines, and magazine writing, for being formulaic. My Columbia Journalism School colleague Michael Shapiro did so memorably a few years ago, in an essay called "The Curse of Tom Wolfe: What Went Wrong for the Magazine Story." Shapiro wrote: "Think of *Anna Karenina* as a magazine story. Wonderful yarn, to be sure. But where to take it? In its extreme, The Form would suggest an anecdotal lead and nut graph that reads something like: Ms. Karenina's story reflects a growing trend among Russian women who, fed up with their aging husbands, are leaving their families, taking up with handsome young men and, when things go badly, eventually falling under moving trains . . ."

Perhaps I'm biased, having spent the past thirty-three years continuously on deadline with one magazine story or another, but I'd like to propose a more benign view of the conventions of magazine writing.

Every medium of communication mystically develops its own distinctive set of structures of expression. Top-forty radio, back when that was a more robust concept than it is today, demanded songs that were three or four minutes long, with hooks, choruses, and bridges. Online journalism was thought at the outset to be a perfect platform for long narratives but has turned out to be better suited to a kind of brief, firmly stated personal opinion that one doesn't see, exactly, in printed-on-paper publications. Commercial movies, without announcing it, have three acts. So it is with magazine stories. Yes, they tend to begin with an anecdote. They are sprinkled with "signposts" and "billboards" in which an argument is unveiled and then advanced. They have firmly conclusive endings. And they have standard topics, including, especially, the lives of well-known people.

Magazine writing is an applied, or practical, art: that is, it entails creativity but also a lot of restriction. Just as a furniture maker has to produce a chair you can sit in, a magazine writer has to work within the constraints of time, form, and content associated with magazine publication. The work can, and often does, seem to have been done by rote—but then, as in the case of the magazine writing that appears in this book, it can also operate completely within the confines and conventions of the field while feeling original, free, and unfettered. Rules and imposed conditions are not antithetical to creative achievement. Greek drama, Elizabethan poetry, and Renaissance religious and court painting would be forms so restrictive as to make artistic production impossible if complete freedom were really the necessary precondition to creativity.

It is true that once in a very long while, somebody will either figure out an entirely new way to do magazine journalism, or will execute one of the existing forms in a way that feels revolutionary—but even in those cases, it won't be long before everybody copies the innovation and it therefore becomes just another standard form. More often, magazine writing soars simply by virtue of the writer's having produced nongeneric work within a genre—having been imaginative enough to make the multiple givens of magazine writing invisible to the reader. In this book, almost every selection is a long magazine "well" piece done on the basis of firsthand reporting. Almost every piece has an anecdotal lead. Almost every piece has a lead character or set of characters, a distinctly drawn setting where the author has spent time, and a kind of plot that has been resolved by the end. Most of the selections that don't fit that description belong to another well-established magazine genre, the critical essay, and conform to that genre's conventions. There is one piece of fiction, but even magazine fiction has some elements in common with the standard magazine story, such as a relatively plain, expository tone and a setting somewhere in what readers will recognize as real life.

What makes them work as well as they do varies from piece to piece, but there are certain common elements: moral passion, investigative zeal, a particularly vivid or unusual setting, especially persistent reporting, unusually artful writing, a memorable and memorably drawn main character. It's easy to imagine a dull, poorly executed version of most of the pieces. But these pieces bring some part of the world—sometimes familiar, sometimes not—joltingly to life, and they do it on the whole not by abandoning the form but by executing it at the highest level.

Writing a magazine story is a peculiar experience. A magazine tries to build a community with its readers. A magazine writer enters into a series of oddly intimate relationships with his or her subjects, during which things that are usually impermissible go on and ordinary boundaries are violated—one gets to ask impolite questions of perfect strangers or even, sometimes, move in with them. And then, most of the time, it's over—on to the next story. Once I got a call from a tough blue-collar guy with whom I'd spent months moving around the ragged fringes of the economy and the social structure of Houston, Texas, to tell me that he'd had a sex-change operation. Didn't I want to write about him again? Well, sorry, it sounded interesting, but no. You almost never write about them again.

Magazine writing entails an unusual and exhilarating combination of reportorial, literary, and intellectual skills. Many more people want to do it than can do it well, but, oddly, not many people who can do it well stick with it for a whole career. A great magazine story is a rare artifact, even a miracle: produced under rare conditions, aimed at a dreamed-of, faithfully reading audience that may not really exist, and effortlessly transcendent of the restrictive rules of the game.

Nicholas Lemann

Acknowledgments

The collective labor of love that produced this volume began over two ice-cold days in February, when 195 top editors met at the Millenium Hotel off Times Square in New York City to start judging 1,562 entries for the 2005 National Magazine Awards. It continued on a blustery day in March, when the second-round judges convened at the Columbia University Graduate School of Journalism on the Upper West Side to pick from among the five finalists for the prizes in twenty-two categories. On a sunny afternoon in April, more than a thousand leading editors and publishers gathered at the Waldorf Astoria Hotel to watch the winners receive their "Ellies"— the Alexander Calder Elephant sculptures that are the Oscars of our industry. Tense and emotional, that is the most exciting day of the year for those of us at the American Society of Magazine Editors. But a close second is the autumn day when we get the first, freshly printed volume of this anthology, drawn from the Ellie finalists, of the Best American Magazine Writing of the year.

While the entire community of American magazines can claim paternity for the awards and for this book, a few people in particular deserve the credit for giving them birth. Foremost among them are the cosponsors of the Ellies at the Columbia "J" School, especially its dean, Nicholas Lemann, associate dean Evan Cornog, and Robin Blackburn, who every year does heroic work organizing the mountains of magazines for judging. We are indebted to the book's agent, David McCormick of Collins McCormick Literary Agency, and to our new publisher, Columbia University Press. And none of it would happen without the tireless dedication of Marlene Kahan, the executive director of ASME, who picked the seventeen stories that make up this anthology, and ASME assistant director, Andrew Rhodes.

Of course, Nick Lemann is no ordinary academic administrator. From his perch at *The Atlantic* and now *The New Yorker*, he has been one of the great magazine essay and profile writers of our time. And he is also a brilliant and generous editor, as I first learned thirty years ago when Nick, then president of the *Harvard Crimson*, edited my first major feature story for the student newspaper by making me read every word out loud to see if it made sense. We are honored that he agreed to pen the introduction. As you read the best of the best for 2005, we hope that you are touched by the special magic of magazine writing that enthralls and inspires all of us.

Mark Whitaker
President, ASME
Editor, *Newsweek*

Permissions

Permissions

THE BEST
AMERICAN
MAGAZINE
WRITING

2005

Esquire

WINNER—FEATURE WRITING

Two astronauts trapped on the International Space Station as a result of the shuttle Columbia disaster literally had only one chance to make it back to earth safely. "Home" is a dramatic and revealing story about one of the longest stays in space, the mourning for lost colleagues, and the tortured and nearly deadly journey back, told by the astronauts themselves—unusual for a notoriously silent and selfless breed of men.

Chris Jones

Home

The coffee, he thinks. The coffee's a concern.

Only one hundred single-serving pouches of instant were allotted for him on *Expedition Six,* stowed in the galley in a metal drawer with a black net stretched over its mouth to make sure the pouches wouldn't float away. But for all the care in the universe, it's been more than two months since the shuttle delivered him and his coffee to the International Space Station, and there aren't one hundred pouches in that drawer anymore.

Looking out his window at the orbital sunrise, Donald Pettit, the mission's science officer, finishes taking mental stock of the supply and decides, Jeez, this is the sort of morning coffee was made for. He puts on his glasses, pulls himself out of the sleeping bag that he's anchored to the wall, pushes his way out of his private quarters—about the size of a phone booth, in Destiny, the last link in the station's chain of modules—and finds his center of gravity. With it, he propels himself in clean, practiced movements, like a swimmer who's found his stroke, toward the other end of the station, a couple of modules and a little less than 150 feet away. There, his commander, Captain Kenneth Bowersox, and the Russian flight engineer, Nikolai Budarin, lie zipped away, still asleep. Pettit opens the metal drawer and takes out a pouch, a silver bag with powder packed hard into the bottom of it. He fills it with hot water that was once his breath and begins hunting for a straw.

Everything is always taken through a straw. Except that Pettit has learned to squeeze his coffee out of the straw in tiny, perfect spheres, which hang suspended in the weightlessness, waiting for him to bite them out of the air or, if he's feeling playful, to pinch them between chopsticks and pop them into his mouth. He does that because he can up here, and he can't down there. That's all the reason he's ever needed.

On this morning, though, he just finds a straw and a little Russian *tvorog* to eat and heads back to his sleeping bag. It's an easy Saturday, the first of February. There's some housecleaning to do—the crew's well-worn routine dictates that they'll spend this weekend unclogging filters, wiping down handrails with antiseptic solution, even mopping up the occasional coffee splatter, the tiny, perfect ones that got away. But there's no hurry. Time is the single thing they aren't running out of. They're still a month away from home.

Pettit takes a sip and watches the sun rise for the second time. It comes and goes every forty-five minutes, good for sixteen dawns and dusks a day. Even after ten weeks in space, it's the sort of thing that draws you close to the window. There are the vapor trails, too, laid on top of the United States each day like a quilt, New York to Los Angeles, Boston to San Francisco; they're Pettit's way of catching a glimpse of home even when it's shrouded in storms. But today the horizon is clear and the sun is bright, so bright that he won't notice the finger of white smoke in the wide Texas sky.

·   ·   ·

Each Saturday, at about two o'clock in the afternoon, Greenwich mean time—sailor's time, the official time zone of the station—there's a ground conference with Houston to plan the upcoming week. Usually, the voice coming out of the radio tells the crew what they already know, and they float around, puttering, keeping their ears half open for news or drama. This time is different. This time, the voice tells *Expedition Six* to stand by.

Inside Mission Control, where the space station's orbit is tracked on a giant screen at the front of the room and technicians sit behind consoles labeled ODIN, OSO, ECLSS, ROBO, and a dozen other things, a debate is unfolding. No one is sure how to tell the crew that *Columbia*, a shuttle that Bowersox has twice piloted, just came apart in the thin blue-green envelope beneath them. No one is sure how to tell them that seven friends—including Ilan Ramon, who only a few days earlier told Bowersox that he'd give his three children a hug for him, and Willie McCool, with whom Pettit had been playing e-mail chess—are probably gone, too.

Jefferson Howell, a retired marine lieutenant general and the plainspoken director of the Johnson Space Center, ends the debate when he sits down at the radio, considers his words, and bounces his voice off a satellite into the space station's dry, recycled air.

"I have some bad news," Howell says, and because it's Howell who's delivering it, Pettit and Bowersox know exactly how bad before he gets it out: "We've lost the vehicle."

Nine words. That's all. Everything else is left unspoken, and in the quiet, the blanks are left for each of them to fill in on his own. In the way the parents of missing children hang on to the faintest hope that their loved ones are just lost, not lost for good, Pettit and Bowersox wonder whether any of *Columbia*'s evacuation systems triggered, and whether any of their friends are floating down to a cloudless earth under parachutes.

Discovery of the crew's remains and a helmet on the grass later in the afternoon will push aside that faint hope for sadness.

The sadness will settle itself in.

·   ·   ·

Every so often on station, you're allowed to call home on the satellite phone, on closed channels, with the tape recorders turned off.

These conversations keep you grounded. When no one is home—when it's time for her to get the groceries or for the kids to go to soccer practice—you have to leave a message on the machine: "Hey, honey, it's me, in space." Sometimes these messages are saved and listened to in the still of the night, again and again. Nowadays, these messages are almost always saved, because she never knows when they might become all she has left.

In that way, your family has finally caught up. You've learned already, over the course of your isolation training, after having been dropped into the winters of Cold Lake, Alberta, and left stranded in the woods, that the everyday interactions of life on earth—the messages left on machines, but also the smiles and waves from school buses and the notes left on fridges and pillows—are the things you need to carry. You make room for them in your memory's permanent collection, just as you learn to forget about the things that maybe you used to keep too close: what's on TV tonight, who's going to win the American League West. You come to understand the true order of things, because you know how the universe works. Some astronauts become the first men to walk on the moon, and others burn to death sitting on the launch pad, or seventy-three seconds after leaving it, or sixteen minutes from returning to it.

And sometimes you're no longer a month away from home—you're suddenly much farther, although you're not really sure how far, because the miles are meaningless. There are times when the space station orbits the earth less than 240 miles above its surface; there are moments when Dallas is farther away from Houston than you are.

What matters, what separates you from home, is time.

After the *Columbia* memorial service is piped in from the ground—after you hear President Bush say, "Their mission was almost complete, and we lost them so close to home," and you can't help thinking that they weren't very close at all—you ring the ship's bell, mounted on a bracket in Destiny, seven times for seven astronauts. The ringing still echoing in your ears, each of you finds a corner in which to try to come out the other side of your grief. A few of the things you usually do are left undone. In the meantime, your new reality begins to sink in: You remember *Challenger*, almost twenty years ago now, and you know, in your heart, that your ride home isn't coming anytime soon.

You tell Mission Control that you're all right, that you've trained a lifetime for this, that you can hold on to your memories for another year. Maybe longer if you have to. Part of you might even believe it.

•   •   •

The muscles in the legs always go first. On earth, they're kept twitching by fighting off gravity just enough to push out of bed. Without gravity, they begin to atrophy, and the body begins emptying out like another galley drawer. At the moment *Columbia* comes apart, *Expedition Six* has a month of experiments left to conduct. It also, at that moment, becomes one: The record for Americans in orbit is 196 days; another year in space would see Bowersox and Pettit eclipsing even the Russian records for being away.

Expedition Six has become the second kind of science in space. The first is programmatic science—studies that have been planned sometimes for years, experiments in fluid dynamics or crystal growth or protein production. The second, what Pettit, Bowersox, and Budarin are now, is fluke science—the science of accident.

None of them is a stranger to it. Pettit in particular fills his free time by opening random doors in the hallways of his imagination. When he gets too good at pushing back his coffee with chopsticks, he takes a sphere of water and blows on it, curious to see what wave pattern might result. (One that lasts ten minutes, turns out.) Or he injects air inside that same sphere with a syringe, and injects water inside that air, and watches the water bounce around inside itself until it becomes whole again, winning some small battle between mass and velocity. "Saturday-morning science," Bowersox calls it.

Mostly, though, they lose themselves in their routine again. Bowersox takes over most of the by-the-book work, donning an ugly tie whenever he needs a boost. He tends the plants, makes sure the crystals don't collapse in on themselves, monitors the instruments. It's his job, and close to a full-time one, to keep the station in orbit.

Pettit, with his official workload diminishing, conducts symphonies of his tiny, perfect spheres and begins to tinker. A button comes off his $3,000 NASA-issued wristwatch, and when he finds it wedged in a ventilator two weeks later, he decides to put it back in its place. He pulls his watch's guts out, sticks them to his worktable with double-sided tape, and finds a way to make them whole again—because Pettit believes everything can be fixed in time. Everything can be built to last.

He jogs on the treadmill and pedals the exercise bike for two hours each day, trying to stave off the inevitable decay. To keep the rest of themselves going, he, Bowersox, and Budarin make a point of having dinner together, of blasting a Santana record while they heat up their chicken fajitas—tortillas are good because they don't leave crumbs floating behind—Velcro their meal pouches and containers onto their foldout table, hook their legs around the restraint bars underneath it, and sit down to eat, like they did on earth, like the family they have become: Hey, honey, I'm home, in space.

There are those who dream of falling and those who dream of flying. Bowersox always dreamed of flying. He never knew why; he just knew that if he flapped his arms hard enough, he'd lift off the ground and glide over rooftops. It was in him and he went with it. Bowersox joined the Navy, became a fighter pilot, was assigned to Attack Squadron 22, logged more than three hundred arrested landings in A-7E's on the carrier USS *Enterprise*, and finally became a test pilot at China Lake, pushing F/A-18's to their limits. In 1987, he was selected by NASA as an astronaut candidate, underwent a year of training and evaluation, lost his ginger hair, and after a five-year wait, he earned his first zero-gravity trip. Now, with *Expedition Six*, and at forty-six years of age, built low to the ground and hard to tip over, he's gone into space five times—the record is seven—but even all those flights haven't put a rest to his dreaming. The only difference is now he doesn't have to flap his arms. All he needs to do is give a little kick and he can look down on skyscrapers.

Pettit operates on a different level. By schooling, he's a chemical engineer, and with his affinity for cargo pants and his perpetual bedhead, he looks it. But by inclination, he's an explorer, only more of science than of space. Fresh out of graduate school at the University of Arizona in 1984, he landed a job at the Los Alamos National Laboratory in New Mexico. His project résumé was soon filled with things like this: "atmospheric spectroscopy measurements on noctilucent clouds seeded from sounding rocket payloads, volcano fumarole gas sampling on active volcanos, and problems in detonation physics applied to weapon systems."

He also filled up his garage after driving through a blizzard one night to an auction of surplus gear at the lab and finding himself alone in the seats. He bought everything he could stuff into his junky pickup, jury-rigged the power in his house to accept three-phase tools, and learned how to make liquid oxygen from scratch. NASA brought him onboard in 1996, not long after he'd turned forty-one but before he managed to blow himself up and cast a good chunk of the southwest into darkness.

He has since become a legend in Houston, tapped by his fellow astronauts to be the first man on Mars. The smart money began moving his way during his first weeks of astronaut training, when he raised his hand during a lecture on rocket propellants—namely, the liquid oxygen that was waiting to go off in his garage. "Do you know what color liquid oxygen is?" he asked the lecturer.

"Well, no," he replied. "I've never actually seen it. I'm not sure anyone has."

"It's blue," Pettit said from his seat at the back of the class. The rest of the students turned around to look at him. He looked back at them. "I just thought you'd be interested to know," he said.

Bowersox is the firstborn brother. He is reason and responsibility. Pettit, who has never before been in space, is the wide-eyed kid who eats his coffee with chopsticks.

Budarin is the weird uncle from Russia.

·   ·   ·

Somehow, it works—even if that, too, is an accident. Every year, NASA astronauts fill out "dream sheets," indicating what sort of mission they'd like, what's their ideal. And every year, Bowersox and Pettit would write, "I believe I'd be most effective on a long-duration mission," which was their way of begging to be sent to the space station. That shared desire was all the matchmaking they needed. From the start, they knew when to leave each other alone, when to blast Santana and do somersaults in the air. Even with the stress of their now open-ended mission, and their dwindling coffee supply, Pettit and Bowersox get along like old friends.

But they argue a few weeks after *Columbia* is lost. Someone has suggested that one of them might have to stay in space for a long time while the other is replaced by an incoming cosmonaut on a Russian rocket that would return the rescued man to earth. This proposal is known as the Avdeyev Option, named for Sergei Avdeyev, who also endured an unexpectedly long mission: He survived 379 consecutive days aboard *Mir*, the International Space Station's burned-up predecessor.

The problem is, both of them want to stay.

They've grown to like how their days unfold exactly as they want them to. They like never having to alter their routine to make room for someone else in it. They're never caught in traffic, bumped on the sidewalk, jostled on the subway, inconvenienced by the weather. They never have to take the car into the shop or shovel the driveway. They're never rushed. They're never late.

They've come to trust each other in ways they've never known before, the sort of unspoken trust that comes with the knowledge that one of you could take a hammer to a window and in fifteen seconds, the station and everything inside of it would pass into history. Once they found that, just about everything else fell into its one best place. Their lives are a strange kind of perfect, spotless and serene. Every day breaks with the promise of peace, and, with the exception of one Saturday in February, that promise is kept.

•   •   •

By March, approaching the start of month five in orbit, most of *Expedition Six*'s to-do list has been exhausted. It's one of those rare, beautiful periods in his life when Pettit really has few demands on his time and nowhere else to be. So when he finishes building a gyroscope out of portable compact-disc players to hold his flashlight for him—because he can up here and he can't down there—he starts taking pictures, more than twenty-five thousand in all. First, he aims his over-the-counter Nikon at earth, waits for night to begin washing its way around the planet, and captures the physics of twilight, the strange hospital green that fills out the evening sky in thick, rolling waves. Then, after darkness has fallen, he looks for landmarks among the power grids and river bends, and he takes pictures of home.

At first, because the speed he's traveling is much faster than the snap of his camera's shutter, Pettit's pictures turn cities into streaks of white light, like the headlights in a time-lapse photo of a busy street. He takes clearer pictures when he learns to hold open the shutter and shift his shoulders in the opposite direction of his orbit, but even his best efforts turn out blurry; he knows he's looking at New York City, but he can't make out the black rectangle of lightless Central Park or the single bulb in the harbor that is the Statue of Liberty.

Not good enough. Pettit being Pettit, he puts together a makeshift, rotating tripod out of an old IMAX camera mount, a spare bolt, and a cordless Makita drill. Pressing the drill's trigger lends his camera the perfect rotation to take pictures sharp enough to make the miles meaningless all over again.

• • •

Looking at the electric webs that are Montreal or Tokyo or Washington, D.C., you can pick out the airports you've flown into and the streets you know and the hotels you've stayed in, and you can remember if the showers were hot or whether you ate a good meal there. In the end, if you close your eyes, you can even see your driveway, and you can feel yourself easing into it, throwing your junky pickup into park and walking up to the front door, your shoes scuffling on the asphalt, your hand guided by the warm light spilling out the windows to the door.

You have people waiting for you there.

All sorts of big days have come and gone. Birthdays, anniversaries, school concerts pass you by, even though you try to keep up. At Christmas, you make a cake with red icing. New Year's is harder to get a handle on; there are no crowds or fireworks, no clock strikes midnight.

Below you, SARS breaks out in Asia, Elizabeth Smart is found alive in Utah, the U.S. invades Iraq. March makes way for April. Now it's Opening Day. Who's going to win the American League West? It's just one more of sixteen dawns and dusks a day, just one more in an endless string of orbits.

Every so often, one of those orbits passes right over home, and your kids, because they're almost old enough to know what you know about the universe, wait on the front lawn to catch a glimpse of Dad. If the timing is right—if it's dark but the night is young enough for the sun to have dropped just below the horizon, still reflecting its rays off the space station's solar panels— they can strain their necks and spot a small, steady white light coming up over the trees. They'll follow that light with their eyes as long as it takes it to cross the starlit sky, on a smooth, predetermined path that'll be carrying it over Australia in less than forty-five minutes.

One of your boys, the youngest, always chases the light, taking off down the street, hoping to cover enough ground, enough of the curve of the earth, to earn even one more second in your line of sight. And always the light disappears.

·　　·　　·

In the six years that it will take to finish stitching together the International Space Station, NASA has calculated, any single astronaut working outside its confines, connecting new modules or making repairs, will have a 1-in-800 chance of being struck by dust or a scrap of broken-down satellite. If he isn't killed by the impact, there's a greater-than-1-in-800 chance that the integrity of his space suit will be compromised and his blood will boil him to death.

Along with Opening Day, April has brought a sudden, more pressing gamble: the need to go outside. A thermal cover that protects the ammonia-filled fluid connector that helps the radiator systems cool things down—a "bootie," in astronaut vernacular— has worked loose, and with a 400 degree swing in temperature between the sun and the shade, it needs to be put back tight to limit the risk of overheating, rupture, and eventual combustion. This bootie is life.

Being the sort who pours himself into the job, Bowersox has been looking forward to the action. They walked in space once before, in January, and Bowersox hadn't wanted it to end—even after it almost didn't begin. After spending six hours wrestling into his diaper, water-cooled long underwear, and three-hundred-pound space suit, he'd struggled to open the goddamn hatch that would let him out. It had snagged on something—a piece of fabric from a strap that had come out of place, the sort of thing that on earth you'd pull away like lint but in space can "compromise the mission" and make men into satellites. Pettit, worried that Bowersox was going to break the hatch and turn their home into a vacuum, asked if he might take a swing at it. The hatch resisted him the way the driver-side door on his pickup always dug in, and he remembered, and he found his touch, and the hatch opened. The cloth tether connecting Bowersox and Pettit to each other was all that kept them from a good, strong push into eternity. And now here they are, staring into the pitch black again.

A fifty-five-foot length of steel cable is spooled near the hatch, a safety line and a leash all at once. Bowersox unhooks himself from the cloth tether and onto the cable. Next, he takes a breath, uses a handrail for leverage, swings his legs out into the emptiness, and looks down between his feet at the earth. That fifty-foot length of steel cable ties him to one of his worlds, and, in turn, to the other.

For the first time in months, Bowersox lets himself stall on that. He turns off the automatic pilot, and he takes it all in:

There's my feet. There's the earth. There's my feet, there's the earth, and there's a long way in between.

That's all the pause he gives himself, because there's work to be done.

Bowersox and Pettit have topped up their batteries and made certain that their nitrogen-thrust backpacks will fire if they need to move in a hurry, their one shot at returning to station if they lose their grip; they've run the inefficiencies out of their blood and triple-checked every rubber seal that separates them from the front pages; they've layered their gold-plated polycarbonate visors with antifog solution, but not so much that it might make their eyes sting. They've done a hundred little things to make it possible for them to do one more little thing, and they do that, too. After rerouting some power cables to one of the station's gyros, they pull the bootie back into place, keeping themselves in orbit for another day, and head back inside. They've been gone for almost seven hours. It feels, in a lot of ways, like coming home from a snowstorm, without having to stamp your boots.

In the airlock, they're coming down, exhausted, when Pettit catches the hint of a smell he can't place. It's come in with them, has embedded itself into the white fabric of their suits. It's metallic, but it's more than that. It's sweet and pleasant. It's the smell of space.

If something had gone wrong out there, had one of those rubber seals ruptured or a 1-in-800 long shot come through, it would've been the last piece of data for his brain to collect. He breathes it in again, then again. For some reason, the smell reminds him of summer.

And there it is.

During college, Pettit spent his vacations repairing heavy equipment for a small logging outfit in his native Oregon. He'd used an arc-welding torch to do it, and that torch had given off a sweet, pleasant, metallic smell.

Now here it is again. And now, for him, space smells like summer, the same summer that's greening the landscape below without him.

·   ·   ·

As the days pass, you can feel yourself changing. Not so much in the density of your bones or the fiber of your muscles—although those are deteriorating, you have already proved that, physically, men can last long enough to make it to Mars—but more in the wearing away of the calluses life has given you. It's as though all your skin has been stripped off and replaced with a fresh pink layer, except it runs deeper than that.

You decide to watch a movie. You've resisted until now, because there was always something better on outside your window, but sunrises and sunsets can get old after a few thousand ups and downs, and frankly, there just isn't much new to do anymore. Movie night it is. There are a bunch of DVDs on station—smuggled up over time—and IBM Think-Pads to gather around. On this night, the three of you decide to flip on *Tank Girl*, a cult hit among women astronauts, who have told you that if you do nothing else in space, you must watch this.

It might as well be playing in fast-forward. A man walks across broken glass, and the idea of it makes your fresh pink skin crawl. There are explosions that make you jump. There are nauseatingly bright colors and painful flashes of light; people shout too loud and fight too hard. There are tanks, and there are girls—luminous girls, with lips and breath and falling hair.

You look down at your hands, and they are shaking. Your mouth has gone dry. Your heart rate is galloping. Even after you've shut off the movie and pulled yourself into your sleeping bag, you tremble, like kids who've been told ghost stories around a campfire before lights-out.

Come morning, you've each drawn the same conclusion: Maybe you've been gone for too long. Maybe it's time to go home.

Because the earth has been spinning on its axis, and you've been spinning on yours, and now you know that you've been traveling in opposite directions for all this time, and you feel like you've never been so far away.

The voice coming out of the radio stops the drift. There is no Avdeyev Option. There will be no records set. *Expedition Six* is ordered to return. NASA has drawn out the decision, dreading the possibility of losing two more astronauts on a notoriously glitchy reentry vehicle. But if NASA waits any longer, the crew risks growing too weak to return on the only craft available.

Latched to the side of their ship is the Russian-built Soyuz TMA-1.

It's the same vehicle that was supposed to be former 'N Sync singer Lance Bass's ticket to ride back in October 2002, until he was found to be short on cash. The actual crew returned on another Soyuz, and the TMA-1 has been parked here since, just in case, like an escape pod straight out of science fiction, the bucket of bolts that somehow reaches hyperspace. Its chassis design is thirty-five years old: a greenish sphere with an insect's ass and two glass wings that pass for solar panels. Inside, the buttons are square and plastic. The onboard alphabet is Cyrillic. The cradles are made for small men, and the two portholes aren't much larger than dinner plates. But it's the only way home. And because a Soyuz's orbital life span is a little more than six months—the thing gets the hiccups if you look at it sideways, never mind bathing it in the universe's metallic exhaust—it's about that time.

So Pettit and Bowersox are about to become the first American astronauts to return home on a foreign vessel. They are also about to become the first American astronauts since 1975 to return home in a capsule, forced to put their faith in the parachute above them rather than in the landing gear below. They might have always dreamed of flying, but here, now, *Expedition Six* is being asked to fall.

They are also asked to begin packing up. It is the start of a monthlong goodbye, hard as any other. Because of the Soyuz's space and weight restrictions, the astronauts won't be able to bring home all the small things they brought up with them. There is room for only three personal effects, no more. The rest will be left up to memories.

This is most difficult for Pettit. Bowersox decides to take home his favorite pair of blue shorts, the same pair that Pettit had soaked with a wayward sphere of juice he was playing with at the dinner table, and a couple of golf shirts. The ugly tie stays. Easy, done. But Pettit is the only man in the seats at Los Alamos all over again, with only a single pocket on his low-profile white Russian space suit to fill.

He'll have to abandon his beloved tools, and, in the end, he decides to leave behind his wife's favorite necklace, which she'd dropped into his hands before he left and which he'd taken out and run through his fingers whenever he felt alone. He can buy her another one, he figures. And he can always buy new tools. What he can't replace are two long-handled spoons out of the galley, designed for digging the dregs out of the bottoms of pouches, with holes punched into their ends so they can be looped with idiot string and tied to his wrist, like mittens to a jacket. He hated those strings, so against regulations he cut them, but he fell in love with the spoons. Pettit thinks they're beautiful in their shape and utility. Perfect in their way. He'll give one to each of his two-year-old twin boys, and they'll take them along camping, eating whatever they heat up over the fire right out of the tin without ever touching the sides.

So there are the spoons, one, two. His chopsticks make three.

·   ·   ·

In an otherwise empty space behind the small-man cradles in the Soyuz TMA-1, there are soft-sided white bags that contain emergency supplies, including flares, warm clothes, water, and—because sometimes bad things happen—a double-barreled sawed-off shotgun. In the sixties, a Soyuz capsule landed off target, in rugged country, and after the cosmonauts inside had gathered their nerve, they broke open the hatch to find themselves surrounded by wolves, their breath turning solid in the cold. The men might have liked to run, but they could only crawl. Since then, every Soyuz crew packs a little something under the seat.

They don't carry much else in the way of insurance. The Soyuz's operation is almost fully automatic; it can't be controlled from the ground, and there's no override for the astronauts inside. They are, in the truest sense, passengers. After suiting up, climbing through a hatch, closing it behind them, and dropping into their formfitting seats—they lie on their backs, with their knees pulled up close to their chests—they go through a long checklist, and then they press a single button, once. That's it. For the almost four hours it will take them to get home, their fates are tied to one another and to the machine.

Bowersox, sitting in the left seat, with Budarin in the center and Pettit on the right, nods and presses that single button, exactly 160 days, twenty-one hours, and fifty minutes since they'd last felt gravity's pull. The undocking sequence begins. In their small diving bell of a capsule, sandwiched between the craft's two larger spheres—the living module and the propulsion module—a pair of monitors flickers to life in front of them. On the screens, they watch the station hatch they've just come through disappear, fast. They are folded into a vehicle with a volume of 141 cubic feet, a little more than the interior size of a Dodge Neon. They are traveling more than seventeen thousand miles per hour. Small rockets fire and drop them out of orbit, pushing them into the upper layers of the atmosphere. The weight of even the thinnest air begins to slow them down.

Their second round of separation follows. The living and propulsion modules have done their job, and they're ditched. Bowersox and Pettit each see one of the modules roll out past their windows and begin burning up.

They don't know that were everything in order, they wouldn't be able to see what they're seeing. They don't know that one of the rockets assigned to keep their own capsule stable has fired less than a second too late.

They don't know that until their monitors flash again.

The computers announce that they've pushed *Expedition Six* into a steep, ballistic descent. Instead of a gentle return to earth, they've entered an accelerated, lung-crunching dive into elementary physics. The hardware hasn't given them a choice: It's as if they've been loaded into their shotgun and fired straight into the earth.

The capsule begins to spin. There is sound and vibration, each rising in pitch. The view out their windows turns pink with plasma, then orange with flames. They learn what it feels like to ride inside a meteor. Things get warm. G forces build. Three to four to five to six. Seven to eight to nine, surpassing the limit that the body can survive for any length of time. Their teeth clench. Their spines compress. The weight of the world—more than a thousand pounds of it—sits on each of their chests. First it gets hard to talk. Then it gets hard to breathe. Russian ground control is oblivious. Everything in front of them indicates that all systems are normal. Bowersox, Pettit, and Budarin each feel their tongues getting pushed farther down their throats.

One final battle is being waged: gravity versus friction.

At last, the resistance of denser air begins winning out, slowing the capsule. They can feel the blood rising back to their faces, their tongues meeting their unclenching teeth.

Now the parachute. They are willing it to open. Bowersox begins to bristle at his lack of control. He wishes there were a big red button beside him that he could press, hard, to explode the sixteen pyrotechnic bolts that pin down the part of the capsule that holds the parachute tight. But there isn't. There's just the wait. Until, finally, what sounds like machine-gun fire echoes through the cabin, and the capsule shudders, and they feel the elastic tug of their lifelines pulled taut.

Above them, the massive orange-and-white parachute has filled out.

Below them, at Russia's Star City, where officials await the Soyuz's expected touchdown in sixteen minutes—how close to home *Columbia* was when it was lost for good—the radios crackle, then go dead.

In the silence, a few people put their faces into their hands. Everybody else looks white.

•   •   •

The heat shield strips away. The capsule vents, and the instruments get wet with condensation. There is vapor in the air. Through it and their windows, they can see the ground rising to meet them. Finally, six soft-landing rockets fire moments before impact, and the Soyuz lands upright with only a bit of a bump. Relief.

A moment later, the capsule begins bouncing across the flats, dragged along by the wind still filling the parachute. Budarin cuts it loose by pressing a button on a joystick that he wouldn't have wanted to press too soon. They come to rest on their sides, their arms hanging across their bodies, with Bowersox on the bottom of the pile. He looks out his window. All he can see is crushed grass, impossibly green. It has been that long since he's seen color unfiltered by space.

They figure they are going to land off target, but not by much, so they stay strapped in, waiting for the helicopters to arrive. They are wrong, however; they have fallen north of the Aral Sea, in central Kazakhstan, far enough off target to be out of radio range, which is why Star City is in mourning. But that's something they don't know, even after they press a button to extend a blade-shaped radio antenna. Because the capsule is on its side, the antenna plunges straight into the ground, leaving them more removed from the outside world than they had ever been up there.

Time ticks by. They grow restless and stiff.

"I think we should get out," Bowersox says to Budarin.

"Yes," Budarin says. "I think we should get out."

There are no wolves. There are only white birds and blue sky and what turns out to be the Kazakhstan steppes, stretching out for almost three hundred empty miles between them and their target. There is a good possibility that in the history of the planet, no one has been there before.

But for them, now, it feels as familiar as breath itself. They drink up the air. In space, they'd been taking in a higher concentration of carbon dioxide than they were used to, and for Bowersox, it had left him feeling a little less than himself. Now, swallowing down great big gulps, he draws in a calm that he hasn't felt in a long time but had learned not to miss.

One by one, they fall to the ground. They try to walk, but they end up crawling, because their inner ears are still in space and standing up makes them feel sick. Budarin thinks he hears cars rolling in the distance and takes out the shotgun to fire off the flares. Bowersox goes back inside the blackened capsule and tries raising someone through the wash of radio static. Pettit decides that he can make a pretty nifty shelter out of the parachute. Bowersox then retrieves the emergency beacon from behind the seats and passes it out to Budarin, who flicks it on. A satellite orbiting the earth picks up the signal.

Soon, at Star City, there are celebrations, hugs and handshakes and pats on the back. For the technicians, at least, the last of the waiting is over.

•   •   •

After a couple of hours, one of fifteen search aircraft spots you. The fat-bellied military helicopters will follow. Together, you rest in the cool of the impossibly green grass, looking up at the white birds and, beyond them, the blue sky. You smile at the thought of holding your wife and your children, of feeling the rain, of sitting down to bottomless cups of fresh-brewed coffee without having to hunt for a straw. But you also savor the silence. You savor these last honest moments of being alone. And by the time the beat of the helicopter blades thumps over the horizon and the weight of the world has found your chest for the second time in the same afternoon, each of you lets your mind loose, floating, untethered, 240 miles up into the nothingness.

Each of you is dreaming of home.

National Geographic Adventure

FINALIST—REPORTING

Through vivid first-person reporting, exhaustive historical research, and stunning imagery, Paul Kvinta transports his readers to a remote region of northern India where man and elephant are engaged in a brutal battle for habitat.

Paul Kvinta

Stomping Grounds

Despite its tremendous size, the elephant was stealthy, and Lasman Bumiz struggled to see him. It was after sunset, and in the shadowy torchlight, the ten-foot tusker possessed the seemingly magical and decidedly unnerving ability to appear and disappear suddenly. One moment he was in front of Bumiz, the next he was behind him. Bumiz was a small man, not five feet tall, but if he didn't act soon, the elephant would materialize inside the residential compound nearby, and it would be too late. So the villager sucked up his courage and did what he'd done all week—he raised his torch high into the air, unleashed a blood-chilling shriek, and rushed the animal dead-on. Bumiz drew confidence from his friends, the men sprinting alongside him, swinging axes and machetes, banging empty cooking oil tins, whooping louder than partisan lunatics at an India-Pakistan cricket match. He knew that they were all in this together, that they somehow had to repel this superior invading force. But in a split second the tusker wheeled about and lunged at them, a terrifying feint that scattered the men like billiard balls and sent Bumiz backpedaling into the darkness, scared and confused. What scared him the most, actually, what petrified him, was that he was confronting not a mighty animal, but something much greater. Bumiz was at war with a god.

All week the residents of Phulaguri, a rice-farming village in India's northeastern state of Assam, had debated how many elephants were laying nightly siege to their community. Some guessed more than a hundred. Others figured sixty or seventy. The pandemonium each night made counting impossible. What the villagers did know was that five homes had been reduced to dusty heaps of thatch and mud and that the Assam Forest Department had failed to rescue them. It was no secret, of course, what two things the migrating elephants wanted from Phulaguri: the recently harvested rice stalks—known as "paddy"—that people stored in conical stacks in their courtyards, and the paint-peeling moonshine that some of them brewed from fermented rice. For a stiff drink, elephants would blast through walls.

Desperate for solutions, someone suggested making a *puja* to Lord Ganesha. In the crowded Hindu pantheon, Ganesha is the well-loved "remover of obstacles," and he would certainly save them. So the villagers offered up bananas, oranges, and sliced coconut, touched their foreheads to the earth, and prayed for relief from this unfathomable plague. The curious fact that Ganesha has the head of an elephant struck no one as particularly ironic. Most residents made little distinction between actual elephants and Ganesha himself.

But the *puja* failed to yield the desired results, and on December 28 Bumiz and his neighbors found themselves battling the tusker. At some point amid the chaos, Bumiz sprinted ahead into a bamboo patch, a flanking maneuver nobody noticed. Later, others would only shrug when speculating as to why he had chosen this ill-advised tactic. When the tusker finally turned and bolted, the group gave chase, and that's when they found Bumiz. He was pressed deep into the mud beyond the bamboo, his teeth shattered, his eyes glazed over. The elephant had stampeded right over him. Somehow, he was still alive, and he requested water. "There was no blood," says Jimmy Gothorp, the local schoolteacher. "I think his back was broken." They loaded him into a truck, where he died en route to the hospital.

Two days later, in the Bumizes' courtyard, the dead man's four-year-old son is bawling, and his pregnant wife is tugging my arm and repeating, trance-like, "What will I do now? What will I do now?" I ask some gathered neighbors why the government shouldn't simply kill Assam's wild elephants. "No, no!" the group insists. "The elephant is still God," one man says. "Even if an elephant destroys our paddy, destroys our houses, kills our people, we must respect him as a god." They believed that because God had taken Bumiz's soul directly, they didn't need to burn his body in the Hindu tradition, a process that releases the soul. Instead, they buried him. Some villagers claimed that the tusker had returned to pay respects, that they'd seen him kneeling at Bumiz's grave. Gothorp takes me to the grave and points to an indentation in the dirt. "There," he says. "They believe Ganesha knelt right there."

.   .   .

I arrived in Assam twelve days earlier, curious about something called "human-elephant conflict," a concept that to Western ears sounds like late-night comedy material. But Christy Williams assures me it's no joke, and when we pull into a village called Da Parbatia at the start of a two-week itinerary, nobody here is laughing. On the contrary, all hell is breaking loose. "There's no organization here," grumbles Williams, pressing his way past overwrought villagers. "Someone could get killed." As director of the World Wildlife Fund's Asian Rhino and Elephant Action Strategy, Williams has witnessed elephant drives before. He has even provided fuel and firecrackers to local officials of the Assam Forest Department for this one. But what we see startles him.

Before us, a crush of seething villagers jostles at the edge of a thicket, ignoring two policemen attempting crowd control. Each time an elephant head pokes warily out of the trees, the mob surges forward, howling and cursing, banging cookware and launching firecrackers. Behind us, something resembling a block party is unfolding, with hundreds of curious onlookers from neighboring villages clogging the main road. We're standing in what was once someone's grove of banana trees, but the trees have been trampled into kindling, thanks to the unwanted visitors hiding in the thicket. Suddenly, from beyond the vegetation, explosions rip the air, and a herd of eighteen elephants crashes out of the bush and rumbles across the paddy field to our right. People run screaming in every direction. On the heels of the herd are three domestic elephants ridden by several men with sticks and smoking guns. It's the Forest Department, and they chase the herd to the other side of the field, where they are met by another scrum of fist-shaking villagers. "Great," groans Williams. "They're shifting the problem from one village to the next. That makes it worse."

We elbow our way to the road for a better view. Gazing south over the open paddy fields, we watch the fleeing herd as it zigzags toward the Brahmaputra River, stopping at angry village after angry village. Williams sighs. He's a tall man, a thirty-four-year-old Tamil from South India, eloquent and self-assured, but right now he's frustrated. "We're fighting a rear guard action," he admits, between thunderous blasts of walnut-size firecrackers. Today's conflict is merely a symptom of a greater problem, he says, one driven by habitat loss. Asian elephants are migratory animals, he explains, forest dwellers that require tremendous space. At the time of the Pharaohs, herds were found from Iraq to China, inhabiting a continuous forest belt that extended over five million square miles. Today, just 5 percent of that habitat remains. As Asia's skyrocketing human population forces herds from their last forest redoubts, the result isn't surprising—a brutal death match between man and beast. In India alone, home to three-quarters of the world's 40,000 Asian elephants, the animals have stomped or gored to death some 4,000 people in the past two decades. Meanwhile, elephant populations have mostly plummeted in the thirteen countries where they reside, a result of retaliatory killings, poaching, and accidents involving railroads and highways. Laos was once called "the land of a million elephants," but now the Southeast Asian country has just 2,500. Vietnam's population has plunged to 114.

But no place has been rocked by the conflict more than India's Northeast, especially Assam, where 5,000 jumbos roam. From 1990 to 2003, the hostilities claimed 586 people and 255 elephants. If there's a ground zero for Assam's carnage, it's the district of Sonitpur, where Williams has brought me. In one week here in 1993, elephants killed more than fifty people. Then there was the three-month period in 2001, when unknown perpetrators poisoned some thirty elephants with pesticide, one of the biggest massacres of the animal in recent history.

That mass poisoning still haunts conservationists. Could it signal an attitude shift in a people who have traditionally revered elephants? Certainly, the one great force restraining this Hindu nation from exterminating its marauding herds isn't the endangered species law. It's the nearly 2,000-year-old cult of Ganesha, the elephant-headed god, along with India's rich traditions surrounding domestic elephants. "This cultural aspect has saved elephants in India," Williams says. In Sumatra, where Williams is conducting a similar campaign, "they have no elephant culture," he says. "They've brutalized their elephants." But as he and I loiter among the angry villagers outside Da Parbatia, it's clear that feelings toward elephants in Assam are at a tipping point. If villagers continue getting hammered year after year by rampaging elephants, how long before they snap?

Williams doesn't want to find out. His team has just concluded a study that identifies critical elephant migration corridors and hard-hit conflict zones in several districts north of the Brahmaputra River, including Sonitpur. In the long term, he plans to lobby government officials to protect those corridors. But over the next two weeks, he wants to drop into the maw of the conflict, to help the Forest Department's frontline troops develop village-level strategies to protect both elephants and villagers. "We can't win this in two or three years," he concedes. "But we can have an impact."

We're still watching the herd when a commotion breaks out behind us. Approaching the road is a pair of stragglers, a massive female elephant and, wobbling thirty feet behind it, a tiny calf, no bigger than an overstuffed ottoman. Williams reckons the calf is less than a month old, and as it stumbles over the paddy field's ridges, Mom drops back for some gentle coaxing.

It's a touching scene—and for reasons that may go beyond mere anthropomorphism. Elephants live about as long as humans and exhibit some of the most advanced social structures observed among mammals. Tight-knit families composed of a mother and her offspring belong to large matriarchal herds. Elephant young spend some fifteen years learning their society's complex social behaviors, and individuals seem to demonstrate a sense of history, recalling important individuals and events. Relationships are fiercely loyal. Williams tells me a story about a mother and two calves that were part of his Ph.D. research in northern India. One calf found itself stuck on a railroad track, and the mother tried repeatedly to free it as a train rumbled toward them. Unable to dislodge the baby, she finally stood between her offspring and the oncoming train, trumpeting, trying to scare the train away. All three elephants were killed. "I've never heard of a mother being more protective of her young," Williams says.

As we watch the straggling mother and calf approach the road outside Da Parbatia, a weird energy courses through the crowd. Some people jeer. Others, seemingly delighted, call out "*Ganesh baba! Ganesh baba!*" Suddenly someone from the retreating mob slingshots a large firecracker that explodes in the mother's face, causing her to spin around in a panic. Amid the smoke and confusion, she locates her calf, and the shaken elephants amble off after the herd. Williams is livid. "I don't like seeing little calves tortured like that," he fumes. "The little thing must be exhausted."

Then, after some thought, he adds, "What are the prospects for that calf, growing up like this?"

•   •   •

The forest rangers offer me betel nut, but I beg off, and they proceed to smear betel leaves with lime paste, wrap each leaf around a nut, and stuff the wads into their mouths. "The villagers were out of hand yesterday," one ranger mumbles, chewing vigorously and then arching a bright red stream of spit across the driveway of the Forest Department's Sadar Range Office. "The elephants could have hurt someone. People should stand back and let the *kunkies* through." Kunkies are domestic elephants, I learn, and the dozen men raining betel juice around me—these unshaven, middle-aged, balding foresters with baggy eyes and teeth stained red and black—are the brave-hearts I saw riding to the rescue yesterday, the Kunki Cavalry, so to speak. Admittedly, they lack a certain swashbuckling, save-the-day aura—there's not a uniform or pair of boots among them—but they do shoo away rampaging elephants, or try to, even if villagers mostly hold them in contempt. "The people do not treat us with respect," one of them complains. "They assault us because of what the elephants do to them."

Villagers aren't the only ones who disrespect the Cav.

"My men must pay for ammunition and firecrackers out of their pockets," complains Range Officer Shahdat Ali, explaining that he hasn't received funds from the state in months. "We have only one vehicle, but we need three. How can we manage?" I'm clearly looking at a shoestring operation. Exposed wires run like varicose veins across office walls that needed paint twenty years ago. There are holes in the floor and mosquitoes in the air, and using the bathroom means stepping just outside the back door.

It's December 2003, and the Cav has already conducted ninety-six elephant drives this year. Today the men are planning a drive aimed at the herd we saw yesterday, and they prepare as for a military campaign. Huddled beneath a naked lightbulb, the group pores over faded maps. Someone produces a couple of rusty shotguns, while someone else carefully counts out shells, handling them like priceless gems. Another guy taps and shakes several handheld radios, trying to determine which ones work. Christy Williams offers one of his jeeps, without which half the Cav would be staying home. We pile into the vehicles and speed toward the Brahmaputra River, where we'll meet the kunkies.

Assam is primarily a long, flat river valley, tucked south of the towering Himalaya and split in two by the Brahmaputra, one of the world's largest rivers. In winter, when the water is low, hundreds of low-slung, narrow islands stretch for miles in the braided waterway, divided by shallow channels. "Those fishing villages are seasonal," Williams says as we gaze from the north bank at some makeshift huts on one of the islands, where men are drying fishing nets in the afternoon sun. Each summer this dreamy scene turns into a nightmare as the monsoon-swollen river leaps its banks, obliterates thousands of huts, and kills scores of people. But it also washes millions of tons of silt down from the mountains, and this nutrient-rich soil produces the tasty, riverside grasses that have lured migrating elephants for generations.

More than half of Assam's 5,000 elephants live in the forested foothills along the state's northern border with Bhutan and the state of Arunachal Pradesh. This greenbelt, a nearly unbroken string of wildlife sanctuaries, national parks, and forest reserves, parallels the Brahmaputra for hundreds of miles. Each fall and winter, the elephants migrate south across the broad plain between the mountains and the river to graze along the Brahmaputra's banks. As agriculture spread across this plain during the twentieth century, so did conflict between cultivators and migrating elephants. But full-scale war has erupted only recently, as illegal settlers have ravaged Sonitpur's northern forests, flushing herds from their last sanctuaries. These elephant armies, often a hundred strong, march across cultivated land, skirmishing with villagers and raiding the fields throughout the harvest season. For poor Assamese farmers, the loss of a harvest is devastating.

At a village near the river, we meet a man named Anwar Hussein and his nine-foot-tall *kunki*, Rajeshwari. Hussein is a *mahout*, or elephant driver, and for 3,000 rupees, or $66, a day, the Cav hires him and Rajeshwari, along with two smaller elephants and their mahouts. A dark, wiry man with a serious expression, Hussein barks a command, and Rajeshwari slowly drops to her knees, allowing a couple of the Cav to scramble aboard. The men then review their battle plan. Yesterday, they drove the eighteen-elephant herd away from a cluster of north-bank villages and onto a nearby river island. Today, they'll push the herd several miles westward down that same island, farther still from the villages. Meanwhile, a scouting party will locate a strategic spot along the north bank where the herd can be steered back onto the mainland. The goal, ultimately, is to prompt the elephants to migrate north across the plain and home to the hills.

Williams and I motor off with the scout team, and we soon pass a gleaming military truck with soldiers in pressed olive uniforms and snappy berets, a ubiquitous sight in Assam. The scene is a reminder of the other war here, a war the Indian government has no problems funding and one that exacerbates the elephant conflict. On a map, Assam is shaped like a scorpion, linked tenuously to the rest of the nation by a spaghetti-thin land corridor that noodles between Nepal and Bangladesh. Perpetually overlooked and underdeveloped, Assam and the six other states of the Northeast are a country apart from "mainland" India. The region is home to some 400 tribal groups—a Dr. Seussian jumble of ethnicities including the Khasis, Kukis, and Karbis; the Nagas and the Nishis; the Tiwas and the Tagins—that often explode in ethnic conflict and separatist uprisings. Several armed militias are currently fighting the Indian government, and some indigenous leaders have encouraged their tribesmen to relocate inside protected forests and parks to solidify their territorial claims. This deluge of settlers has devastated vast stretches of prime elephant habitat in northern Sonitpur.

"The best way to clear forest encroachers is to introduce a man-eating tiger," Williams muses at one point. He tends to say outlandish things, only half jokingly, whenever he judges Assam's political chaos and booming population to be harmful to elephants. "Maybe SARS isn't such a bad thing after all," he suggests at another time.

We're standing atop a bluff near the north bank of the river with some of the Cav, waiting for the kunkies to steer the herd back onto the mainland, scanning the wide floodplain with binoculars. As the sun begins to set, we're startled by explosions near the river. In the distance, against a palette of golds, reds, and blues reflecting off the glass-calm Brahmaputra, a legion of elephants storms across the plain in a furious cloud of smoke and dust, elephants of all shapes and sizes, legs churning, heads bobbing, ears flapping. They've crossed the river and are rumbling straight for us. "I count more than a hundred!" says Williams, binoculars glued to his eye sockets. Somehow, between yesterday and today, 18 elephants have morphed into 105. I look through the binoculars. Just behind the thundering herd rides Anwar Hussein and the boys of the Cav, hurling firecrackers and screaming like, well, wild Indians. "Amazing what three kunkies can do, huh?" says Williams.

By the time the herd rushes past us, it's pitch-dark. The kunkies backtrack for a straggler, but when they return, nobody's sure where the herd went. We drive north, fanning our spotlights, but after two hours of searching, the Cav remains clueless. The men scratch their heads and finally go home.

Somehow, they've lost a hundred elephants. It didn't seem possible.

•　　　•　　　•

I offer Rajeshwari a chunk of dried molasses, but her daughter, Nagini, swipes the treat with her trunk, prompting Hussein to swat the teenager and triggering great laughter among the assembled children. We're in the village of Kataki Chuburi photographing the three kunkies that have toiled so diligently of late. Rajeshwari just wants breakfast. Her feet are chained to those of her offspring—Nagini and Suman—but she simply reaches out with her trunk, uproots a nearby banana tree, strips the bark, and devours the snowy white center. If the forty-five-year-old elephant were still wild, she'd need at least forty square miles of forest to satisfy her colossal diet—300 to 650 pounds of vegetation daily, plus sixty gallons of water.

Hussein and two other mahouts unchain the elephants and saddle them with thick burlap pads. Then, in one graceful motion, Hussein somehow levitates onto his standing mount and positions his bare feet behind her ears. He's taking the elephants to the river for a bath this morning, and, with two dozen children in tow, the kunkies parade past the colorful adobe houses of Kataki Chuburi. Everyone nods appreciatively at Hussein and his kunki. Assamese mahouts are the Marlboro Men of India: rugged, individualistic cowboys roaming an uncertain frontier, masters of all elephant lore. They're icons of a glorious elephant culture that reaches back 5,000 years.

The earliest evidence of elephant taming appeared in the third millennium B.C., when the Harappan civilization of what is now Pakistan and northwest India produced stone engravings depicting elephants draped in cloth. Later, the Vedic texts and epic poems of early Hinduism describe kings riding fabulously ornamented elephants. More than status symbols, the animals were also the first weapons of mass destruction. The Mauryan dynasty of the fourth century B.C. employed 9,000 war elephants, the largest force ever assembled. Elephants were used to steamroll opposing infantry, although they were sometimes a terrifying source of friendly fire. When Alexander the Great attacked the forces of King Porus in present-day Pakistan in 326 B.C., Alexander's arrows so infuriated Porus's 200 elephants that they went berserk, squashing friend and foe alike.

In Assam, with its huge elephant population, knowledge about the animal was so vast that in 1734 A.D. King Siva Sinha commissioned the most comprehensive treatise on elephants ever written, the *Hastividyārnava*, "sea of elephant lore." The work is an enchanting blend of poetry, ethno-medicine, and animal husbandry. To wit:

> The elephant with a short body and tail, with a head like a broken basket, whose rutting matter smells like a mādhoi mālatī flower, should be mounted by a rider with broad chest, big ears, and with youthful vigour. In order to tame them, they should be fed with the rider's feet-dusts, mixed with smoky dusts. When they suffer from fever, three sparrows are to be placed in a cage below the elephants, and when these birds twitter, the elephants get relieved of their illness.

By the late nineteenth century, Assam had become the leading source of elephants for the British Empire, with as many as 4,000 wild elephants being captured each decade, most destined to labor in the timber trade.

Rajeshwari, Hussein's elephant, was captured decades ago, and has spent her life ever since in the company of tough men like Hussein, a mahout for thirty years. "When you're starting as a mahout, the elephant doesn't listen to your commands," Hussein explains. "You must work hard for twenty-hour days in the forest. You must sleep under the stars. You don't know where you will end up each day." As we progress through the village, we're approached by a pious-looking woman in a pink sari holding a basket of rice. Hussein stops, and the woman reverently offers the grain to Rajeshwari, who promptly inhales it. Hussein orders his elephant to kneel, and the woman smears red dye across Rajeshwari's forehead, anointing her with the sacred mark known as a *tilak*. She then presses a five-rupee note into Hussein's hand, and we move on.

Here I am seeing the cult of Ganesha firsthand; in Rajeshwari, the woman is seeing not a mere animal, but a divinity that has been revered for 2,000 years. Images of the elephant-headed, pot-bellied deity are everywhere in India today—in temples and hotel lobbies, on calendars and bumper stickers. Ganesha is a rock star.

Apart from Ganesha, however, there is little left of Assam's once great elephant culture. Christy Williams and I watch one of its last remnants: Hussein bathing his kunki in the Brahmaputra. Dismounting, the mahout strips down to his *dhoti* and orders Rajeshwari into the shallow water, where he proceeds to scrub her vigorously head-to-toe with the back of a coconut shell. The long-cherished relationship here between man and elephant began deteriorating over the past century, as 95 percent of the plain between the Brahmaputra and the northern hills was cleared for agriculture, and one sprawling elephant population fragmented into many small ones, some of them barely viable. The Indian government stanched the bleeding in 1974 when it declared elephants endangered, and it later banned logging in Assam and outlawed the capturing of elephants. A government conservation program called Project Elephant has also helped. Assam's wild elephant population has stabilized at 5,000, but, ironically, the logging ban rendered most of the state's 2,500 domesticated elephants unemployed. Many are malnourished, with owners unable to afford their upkeep, and Hussein tells me he has to supplement his modest income by growing subsistence rice and vegetables. "This whole culture will probably be gone soon," sighs Williams. "Being a mahout is hardly a worthwhile profession."

·　　·　　·

When we arrive with the Cav at the Rupajuli Tea Estate, the sleepless laborers who live and work here turn out in droves, desperate to see results. For three days, some eighty-one elephants have terrorized this place, and two homes lie obliterated at the edge of a field of Guatemala grass. Later I ask one man whose home has been destroyed how the perpetrators should be handled. He chuckles uncomfortably. "The elephant is Ganesha," he says. "We don't want to hurt him." I notice that both shattered houses reek of home brew. Apparently, for the elephants involved, the past few days have amounted to one big frat party.

Rupajuli retains a distinctly colonial air, with manicured rows of dark green tea bushes and dapper whitewashed buildings. The tea pickers lead us to a swath of Guatemala grass, a rotational crop used to increase soil fertility. This patch is the size of four football fields, with a wide path running up the middle. The grass is ten feet tall and seemingly impenetrable, but the workers assure us that the elephants are lurking in there. Judging from the bread-loaf-size droppings and the cement fence posts crushed to powder, they seem to be right. Regrettably, to save $66, the Cav is kunki-less today, which means nobody is up high enough to locate the elephants. A tea picker volunteers to shimmy up a tree, and he excitedly begins blurting out herd logistics. The Cav jumps into action. First, they creep around the right side of the field, then the left, and when their quarry eludes them, they change tactics and march straight up the middle path in a brazen show of force. Several policemen accompany us today, and these guys start chucking oversize firecrackers willy-nilly into the grass, like schoolboys. It's impossible to judge our effectiveness, but when we reach the end of the field, we spy the herd huddled beneath some shade trees just outside the grass patch. From there, it should be easy to drive them away. But then, inexplicably, someone lobs an explosive at them, and all eighty-one elephants rush back into the grass.

"Who threw that?" demands Williams, throwing up his hands. "We had them!"

Everyone starts talking at once. Intricate plans are laid. For the next two hours, the Cav blindly chases the herd from one corner of the field to another. At one point, Williams and I take a breather, and we're gazing down the center path when an elephant head suddenly pokes out of the grass. It looks carefully both ways. Finally, the coast clear, the elephant gingerly crosses the path, as if tiptoeing. Thirty comrades follow.

It's pretty clear who's winning this engagement.

By nightfall, the Cav succeeds in moving the elephants to the exact place we originally found them, beneath the shade trees. But now it's too dark to drive them away, so we pile into the vehicles and leave. When we reach the front gate, however, we're blocked by a drunk, growling mob. "Don't get out of the vehicle," Williams tells me. One of the policemen gets nose-to-nose with the leader of the crowd, a man unfazed by the cop's rifle. He's spitting mad. "Those are your elephants!" he screams. "They don't belong to us, they belong to you! Get them out of here!" People push in menacingly, but the cop stands firm. After much snarling, the crowd reluctantly parts, and we speed away.

•   •   •

Every day, cries for help stream into the Cav office. Trampled crops, smashed homes, crushed limbs, and worse—the devastation swirls around us as the villages of Sonitpur come undone. The elephants would call, too, if they could. They're taking casualties as well.

What Christy Williams fears most is a repeat of the poisoning incident of August 2001, when dead elephants first began appearing in and around Nameri National Park in northern Sonitpur. None of the carcasses had any external injuries, although there was a particularly eerie quality about most of them—they were slightly blue. Officials suspected some sort of disease outbreak, but then tissue analyses revealed something startling—the elephants had ingested Dimecron, a powerful pesticide used on tea estates. Asked by reporters how this was possible, Apurba Chakraborty, the veterinarian who conducted the postmortems, noted the elephants' "affinity for liquor" and speculated that "they were given country-made liquor mixed with the pesticide by unscrupulous elements."

"It was targeted," Williams says, noting that all the carcasses were found in a relatively small area. "Maybe someone's family member was killed by an elephant there." The culprits, whoever they were, had chosen an especially brutal means of death. Dimecron would have ravaged an elephant's nervous system before weakening its entire body and causing unquenchable thirst. The biggest challenge for the killers was masking the pesticide's smell. "It was trial and error," explains H. P. Phukan, a divisional forest officer working in Nameri at the time. "They tried fruit, food, liquor. The villagers worked to get it right."

By November the death toll had exceeded thirty, and the outcry was spreading among environmentalists and journalists around the world. Even Bollywood superstar Madhuri Dixit weighed in, urging officials to "stop this mass murder, which is shocking the world." State officials assigned a one-man commission to investigate the killings, but the Forest Department insists that uncooperative villagers undermined the effort. In the end, no arrests were made.

We hear one day that a tiny calf, not a month old, has been separated from its herd. Considering the time and place of its rescue, it's possibly the same calf we saw our first day, during the chaotic elephant drive near Da Parbatia. The vets say its chances are slim. We discuss traveling to the wildlife rehabilitation center to see the calf, but then an even more urgent call comes in from Amdenga, a village to the west.

When we arrive, the body of Birtiala Tirky is still lying on the ground in her compound, wrapped in a straw mat. The night before, a group of elephants had slipped past the men protecting the village and stormed the Tirky compound. They were attracted to something Birtiala, forty-five, kept in her bedroom, a jar of rice flour for making flatbread. When an elephant crashed through the wall, Michael Tirky pulled his wife into a corner, but Birtiala panicked and ran. Two steps out of the hut, she was stomped on. The elephant then flung her limp body across a field.

Such homicidal behavior isn't unusual, Williams tells me. It stems from confusion elephants experience while raiding. They're disoriented, scared, and hungry, and thus dangerously unpredictable.

He gently asks Michael if officials have informed him of the 20,000 rupees, or $465, the government owes him for his loss. Tirky looks at him blankly. We then back off as a solemn crowd loads Birtiala's body into an oxcart. Williams whispers to me, "It's so important to give these people something immediately. There's an anger threshold. Once it gets crossed, you start getting dead elephants."

Before they wheel the cart away, Anslem Tirky, Birtiala's grown son, stands alone before his mother's body. He buries his face in his hands and weeps.

·　　·　　·

"We have an elephantine problem," admits Pradyut Bordoloi, Assam's dapper young forest minister, in his office in the state's capitol. Nonetheless, the minister has developed a program he believes can end human-elephant conflict in the region. First, he'll establish special elephant reserves; the government has already demarcated five of these. Admittedly, they're already seriously encroached, but Bordoloi has a plan for that, something called "joint forest management." Under this philosophy, once the encroachers are removed, villages bordering the reserves will play an active management role with the Forest Department. They'll replant deforested areas with banana trees and other elephant favorites. They'll line their paddy fields with plants elephants dislike, like mustard and chilies. New economic development programs will reduce the incentive for illegal timber cutting. Villagers will feel such ownership of the reserves, Bordoloi asserts, that they'll evict returning encroachers themselves.

How will he fund this, given that his men barely scrape by now? "There are many hurdles," Bordoloi concedes. "Unfortunately, the fiscal situation in Assam is not very good."

His plan sounds great, though I'm having trouble envisioning the Cav pulling it off. The Forest Department has tried to implement ambitious plans before and failed, most notoriously in 2001, when officers tried to erect a fifty-mile-long electric "elephant fence" along the contiguous southern boundaries of three protected forests in northern Sonitpur. Elephant fencing has succeeded in other places, but only in situations with targeted goals, like protecting a specific village. Designed to deliver a 10,000-volt warning, most such fences rarely extend more than a couple of miles, and locals must participate in constant maintenance. Assam's epic barrier, in contrast, was the Berlin Wall of elephant fences, designed, apparently, to stifle what local herds naturally do—migrate south to the Brahmaputra. Worse, the fence had limited local support. "We discussed it with villagers," says R. K. Das, project overseer, "but they didn't accept it." The fence was built anyway.

The structure cost $36,000—a small fortune in Assam—and wasn't up six months before the generators and fence posts disappeared.

"We're fools," one forest officer told me. "Call us fools."

The only thing worse than the department's incompetence is its corruption. For years, officials have accepted bribes to ignore illegal logging, or have been involved in timber smuggling themselves. Bordoloi concedes he has a problem. "There are lots of allegations," he admits. "I have suspended fifty-two officials in the last two years. These people are being investigated."

On a trip to the Balipara Reserve Forest, in Assam's northern greenbelt, I see what Bordoloi is up against. Not far into this 188-square-mile area, the forest abruptly disappears on both sides of the road, yielding an apocalyptic wasteland of gnarled stumps, charred earth, and pitiful lean-tos of branches and plastic. The people here belong to the Bodo tribe, which has long battled for an autonomous homeland within Assam.

Assam has a long and dubious tradition of settling people inside its "protected" forests. But the settlements exploded in the early nineties when militant Bodo leaders started recruiting people from around the region to move here illegally in order to strengthen the tribe's bid for an ethnic homeland. From 1996 to 2001, encroachers seized a chunk of forest larger than Rhode Island, and officials today estimate that Assam's northern protected lands collectively are 70 to 80 percent encroached.

There is an acrid, burning smell in the air as we approach one of the lean-tos. Two women inside cut cabbages and eye us warily, while four barefoot children watch from atop a stump that must measure five feet across. A man agrees to talk but won't give his name. "I used to cut timber," he says, "but now I grow paddy." Until recently, he says, he had a house here. But last May forest officers and police came with a team of kunkies and bulldozed everything. It was the twenty-first time he'd been evicted from this site. "They destroy our houses, break our pots and utensils," he says. "They damage our fields."

"The idea is to destroy their economic viability so they won't return," says Anindya Swargowari, district forest officer for western Sonitpur. But despite being backed by an order from India's Supreme Court, the eviction drives ignited a political firestorm. In April 2002, a crusading Bodo legislator and his followers torched a government antipoaching camp in Nameri National Park. Though the legislator was arrested, the incident stalled the program's momentum. Today, the evictions are sporadic, and, without resources for monitoring, officials can't prevent en-croachers from returning immediately. (The whole sorry story re-minds me of another one of Christy Williams's politically incor-rect musings: "Democracy's OK," I heard him mutter at one point, "but a benevolent dictatorship might be better.")

I ask the Bodo man if he thinks his presence hurts the ele-phants.

"They are part of the forest," he states matter-of-factly, "and we live here, too." He likes Ganesha, he says, but kunkies smashed his statue of the god during the last eviction.

Basically, I'm talking to a man—follow closely now—whose elephant-headed god was destroyed by elephants attempting to reclaim the forest for elephants made homeless by the elephant-worshiping man.

There's poetic justice in there, somewhere.

•   •   •

Manju Barua is a bear of a man, with a bushy beard and a com-manding presence, and as he pours us whiskey on the porch of his bungalow, he heaps scorn on Forest Minister Bordoloi's "joint forest management" idea. "It's the beginning of the end," he says with an incongruous grin. "When it falls apart—when the forests are gone—the government can lay half the blame on the people." Barua is one of Assam's most knowledgeable ecologists and a man who has used his advisory position on India's National Board of Wildlife to write blistering letters to Assam officials disparaging their folly. It was Barua who first told the world conservation community of the poisonings in Assam. We're at Wild Grass, the lodge he owns near Kaziranga National Park, one of the jewels of India's park system, home to endangered one-horned rhinos and hundreds of elephants, and a place guarded fiercely against poachers and encroachers by proud Forest Department person-nel. It's about the only spot in Assam that draws international adventure travelers; why it can't be replicated elsewhere in the state is a tragic mystery.

This evening Barua has hired some traditional Assamese dancers to entertain his guests around a campfire. I'm not sure if it's the chanting from the performance, the shadowy light on his porch, or the whiskey, but Barua's words have an eerily prophetic quality. "What we're seeing here is the beginning of the next worldwide mass extinction," he insists. Habitat is fragmenting as fast in Assam as in any place on Earth. Crop depredation by elephants is rising. Naturally, he says, "the villager response will be to kill them." In fact, Barua reckons there's a connection between the fence fiasco and the poisonings, that encroachers north of the proposed fence feared an increase in crop depredation by trapped elephants. So they took action. "Anyone with an iota of foresight would have predicted that this fence would provoke cultivators to express their outrage in some volatile form," he says.

Barua explains that India's highly stratified society has always shunted the poor to marginal areas, to the forests and hills, forcing them to use their only available resources in an unsustainable manner. The nation's middle class condemns this behavior while demanding more wood products as they adopt consumer-driven, Western lifestyles. The Assam Forest Department can't possibly reengineer these society-wide trends, he insists, nor can nongovernmental organizations. Ultimately, solving human-elephant conflict would require all of Assam's governmental departments working to remedy several social and economic problems, including poverty and soaring birth rates. Barua chuckles at such a pipe dream and wags his finger. "The elephants will go first," he predicts. "But mark my word. People won't be far behind."

•   •   •

Christy Williams's view couldn't be more different. "We have to fight this well into the future," he says, before leaving for Sumatra for another elephant project. He appreciates the conflict's complexities, he insists, but he also believes that NGOs like the WWF can make a difference, particularly as supporters of ragtag forest departments. "Sure, some of these guys are bad," he says of the forest service. "Some are corrupt. But at the end of the day, these are the guys who have to tackle this."

These two weeks have sparked many ideas for Williams on how to reduce pressure on villagers. Early warning systems must be established. He'll buy another vehicle for the rangers we tagged along with, and he's contemplating financing several kunki teams and basing them near heavy conflict zones across Sonitpur. There's much to do.

After Williams leaves, I visit the Center for Wildlife Rehabilitation, near Kaziranga National Park. The rescued elephant calf is here, the one we heard about earlier in the week. "I've never seen a calf so traumatized," says the vet. "Usually in two or three days they snap out of it. It's been a week. He's not settled yet." The calf was only a week old when foresters found him in a trench in a tea garden, his still-attached umbilical cord bloody and infected.

"I'd give him a fifty-fifty chance," he says.

He invites me to peer through a window into an adjacent room. Inside, there's a man standing in the center of a dimly lit eight-by-eight-foot enclosure. He's holding a baby bottle, and staggering around him is the little elephant. The tyke is three feet tall, and there's a wool blanket draped over him. His big brown eyes are glassy. He walks around and around in that tiny room, and he can't stop trembling.

GQ

FINALIST—
FEATURE WRITING

"The Wronged Man" is a riveting account of a man who spends twenty-two years in prison for a rape he did not commit. The saga of Calvin Willis's precipitous fall from grace and the friendship that became his salvation might have been yet another story about a young black man lost in the system. But Andrew Corsello's masterful narrative forces the reader—one intimate detail at a time—to confront Calvin's vibrant humanity and strength of character.

Andrew Corsello

The Wronged Man

Three little girls sleep in a house. They're alone. It's a strange house, long like a shoebox and only one room wide, tin-roofed, set on cinder blocks, removed from the street by a long steep rise. The house has no toys, no television, so the girls have spent the night playing dress-up—they've all gone to sleep wearing comically large women's nightgowns. Katina is seven. She lies in her mama's bed. Her nine-year-old sister, Latanya, curls on the living room couch with their friend, Lucretia.[1] It's a dim, grimy room, littered with beer cans and lit by a single red bulb propped in the front window.

Where are their parents? The fathers—vanished. The mothers come and go at weird hours. Often they're gone all night, sometimes for days at a time. When they go, Lucretia babysits Katina and Latanya, though Lucretia herself is just a child. She's two weeks from her eleventh birthday. She's large for her age, and vaguely sad, a special-ed kid who understands others only when they stand in front of her and speak loudly and slowly. An odd drowsiness envelops her. She often sleeps from nine in the evening until three the next afternoon.

A man enters. Gently, he lifts Latanya off the couch, takes her to the bedroom, sets her down next to her younger sister, then returns to the living room.

---

[1] The victim's name has been changed.

He's not gentle with Lucretia. He puts both hands around her neck, wrenches her into the air, hurls her against the thin wall separating the living room from the bedroom. A noise flutters out of her. Katina and Latanya come half awake. They listen from their mother's bed less than a foot away. They're scared but too young to understand. Even if they did, there'd be no call to 911. The house has no phone.

The man mashes a thumb into Lucretia's throat. Then, palming her forehead with both hands, he wallops the living room wall with her skull once, twice, three times.

He says, "Shut up, or I'll kill you."

Lucretia can see him in the red light of the room. Black man. Big. A beard. Cowboy hat and cowboy boots.

Has she seen him before? Maybe.

Lucretia twists. Twists free. Bursts through the door. The block is dark except for a single streetlamp between her house and the next. She flees into its yellow cone of light. The beige nightgown she's wearing, sized for a woman and trailing behind her on the lawn, trips her. He catches up. She gets another look at him, the hulking cowboy with his hat and his boots.

He says nothing. Just takes Lucretia by both hands, the way a father might take a daughter to swing her around in circles, and boots her in the stomach. She goes limp. He carries her back into the house. Now that she's had the fight kicked out of her, he can take his time. He removes the boots, the pants. He keeps the hat on. After, he decides to leave a memento on the living room couch. A pair of boxer shorts, bunched and wet, size forty.

·　　·　　·

Eleventh of June, 1981. Dawn. Calvin Willis wakes with a start. He feels odd. Not himself. He feels *larger* than himself, as if his spirit has grown beyond the boundaries of his body. He nudges his pregnant wife.

"Debbie, something going on with me."

"Oh, Calvin," she says, smiling, eyes closed.

"Serious. I feel *good*."

He wants to explain it to her, but how? So much change lately. In the five years he's known her, she's been singing the same song. *Come home, Calvin.* Until recently, he's scattered himself around town. How could he not? At twenty-two, Calvin Willis has a gift, an ease—the guileless, guileful appeal of a man with a blessed body that he is unafraid to fully inhabit. Big Hands, they call him. Not just for the physical fact of the hands, which would look enormous on a seven-foot man, much less one standing five feet eight, but because he is, simply, a handler. A man who knows how to dance fast and dance slow, how to tell a story, how to make his friends feel they're at the center of things, afloat with him in his bubble of youth even as they're stuck in Shreveport, Louisiana, an industrial smear near the Texas border.

Yes, Calvin has always enjoyed being Calvin. Some months ago, though, the thrill began steadily growing. At first he thought he was simply being given more mojo. But soon it became clear that the voice in his head was proffering not license but conviction. *It's time to step up. Be a man.* Be a father to the two-year-old daughter he and Debbie already had, and to the son she was carrying.

So Calvin decided to take the enormous energy of his youth and his manhood, his spirit, and pour it into their life together. Step by step, he began changing things. Two months ago, he married Debbie. He started talking to God, too, like when he was a kid, giving the Old Man the play-by-play on his inner workings, in part to humble himself and in part to show he finally had something worth saying. Now they converse when Calvin is in his car, or walking down the street, or in the shower, and after they hang up, Calvin often finds himself singing.

You know, my Jesus is on the main line / Call him up sometime!

Just yesterday Calvin quit his job as a sanitation worker. He doesn't want his kids having to say their daddy rides the back of a garbage truck. He's going to become a long-haul truck driver instead. He's due to take his written test this very day.

Now, as he sits in bed next to his sleeping wife . . . a giddy feeling. The optimism he's been feeling is there, but something else is, too, a touch of the queer dark energy that's come over the neighborhood in the last few days. That business with the girl. Calvin was shocked to hear of it but not surprised; he'd believed for some time that the girl's mother, Barbara, and her next-door neighbor, Maxine, were turning tricks, that their homes were parades of junkies and strange men. He'd gotten into it with Maxine a month before. She'd wanted to know why he thought he was too good for her. He'd told her he didn't truck with no hookers.

Then, yesterday, after his last shift hauling trash, Calvin stopped by his grandmother's.

"You been on Perrin Street?" she said sternly.

One block over, where Lucretia lived.

"Nah. Why?"

"Two detectives been by looking for you."

Calvin waited all day, but the detectives never followed up.

Twenty-four hours later he's all but forgotten about that. As he sizes himself up in the mirror—the sheen of his Jheri curl; the ivory shirt cuffs that show off, by contrast, those giant languorous hands of his; the thick black belt with the nickel-plated buckle, tightly cinched around the taper of his twenty-nine-inch waist—he chats casually with his Jesus. "Don't know what you got planned for me today, Lord, but it feels big!" Yet once he's done with Jesus, he finds he can't stop talking. To Debbie. To himself. To the air.

"Somethin' different today!" he says, walking out the door. "I can feel it!"

He fires up the Dodge Colt, pulls out of the driveway. After one block he begins to feel physically uncomfortable, his whole body queasily overloaded like a sleeping limb roused to feeling. Two blocks from home he slams on the brakes. Now he knows.

"Goddamn!"

He whips the car around. Pulls into the driveway. With one hand he throws the car door open. With the other he undoes his collar. He scurries up the walk, throws the door open. Shucks his boots.

"That you, Calvin?"

Calvin snaps the belt off his waist. "*Goddamn!*" Unzips his pants as he strides past the room where his daughter still sleeps.

"Calvin, what you doin'?"

He doesn't answer. Just takes off his boxer shorts, climbs into bed and says simply, "I love you." Then slowly, serenely, with eyes wide open, ever careful of her curved belly, he makes love to his wife.

The written exam takes two hours. He schedules his road test for the following Monday, then emerges from the driving academy brimming with the calm, clean feeling that comes from taking care of business. A small voice in his head then.

One more thing to set right.

Calvin crosses the street to City Hall, where the police are headquartered, and steps up to the front desk.

"My name is Calvin Willis," he says, "and I hear y'all lookin' for me."

• • •

Ninth of June, 1981. Two days prior.

Maxine gets home first. The sun is up. Her daughters, Latanya and Katina, play in the yard. She heads for the bedroom. Lucretia's hunched in a chair with her face buried in a pillow.

Lucretia?

The girl's face is a shell, lumpy and discolored. Dried blood sheathes her neck. Maxine goes next door for a phone.

A detective named Betty Brookins arrives. What happened? Who did this to you? But Lucretia is incoherent. She keeps grabbing her stomach and breaking into hysterics.

Maxine gets Lucretia's mom, Barbara, on the phone. She's at somebody's house watching *The Price Is Right*.

"Mama," Lucretia says, when Barbara appears. "That man ugly."

At the hospital, Barbara remains with her daughter for a while. But only for a while. After a few hours she goes back to Perrin Street, where she and Maxine and a few of their neighbors start to hash things out. Fueled by grief and spite and a feral hazy sense that somebody needs to pay, they make a decision.

You'll find him one block over, they soon tell the detectives. At his grandmother's.

"This is about Perrin Street," the detective says, "and what you did there Monday night."

"Monday night?" Calvin says. "Let me lay it out for you."

He provides the details. How Debbie told him as he walked out the door that she wanted him home by midnight. How he laughed—what did it matter whether he was in by midnight or sunrise, since her big old pregnant self was going to be in bed the whole time anyway? How he hung out with his friends Gerald and Jerome until eight o'clock. How Calvin and Jerome went off and visited a couple of friends, then hit the Glass Hat Lounge around ten forty-five. How, when he stripped to his underwear, threw his pants and shirt over the dresser, and got into bed, Debbie roused, looked at the clock, saw that it was exactly five minutes to midnight, and said, You made it home, Calvin.

"Do you remember what shoes you were wearing, Calvin?"

Calvin laughs. Nothing he wears is ever an afterthought.

"Dress shoes. Beige. Leather."

"Not cowboy boots?"

"Nope."

"What about a cowboy hat? You have a hat on, Calvin?"

"Haven't worn a hat since last winter."

"You sure about that?"

"Look at me," Calvin says, pointing to his hair. "This cost me sixty-five dollars. You think I want to hide my curl? You think I want to muss it up with a *hat*?"

"That little girl knows who you are, Calvin. She knows your face."

There's an edge of fear now. This is 1981, not 1960, but it's still Louisiana, and Calvin is still a black man answering to a white detective. To help keep cool, he begins a separate and simultaneous conversation. To the detective he says aloud, evenly, "Sir, my wife is pregnant. I have a daughter. Till lately I been keeping three women on the side. I don't got to rape nobody." To his constant companion he says silently, ardently, *Sweet Jesus, I been trying to get good with you. You know that, right?*

"Would you be willing to take a test, Calvin?"

"I take any test you got."

Calvin surrenders his saliva, his pubic hair, his blood. The tests show him to be a type O secretor. Like 41 percent of black people. And like the cowboy man, whose semen has been found spangled over the size forty boxer shorts and Lucretia's nightgown, and inside her.

Forty-one percent. Thousands, *millions*, of other men standing between him and the horror on Perrin Street. It can't touch him, can it?

Of course it can, for the oldest, tritest reason of all: He's black and poor.

Calvin is charged with the aggravated rape of a child and jailed pending trial.

Seven months pass.

When Calvin was two years old, his mother took him to his grandparents' house. He was so malnourished he was covered with sores—he looked *gnawed*—and drifted from room to room like a wraith, whispering nonsense to himself.

"Give me that little boy," Calvin's grandfather demanded.

"Take him," Calvin's mother said. "I can't take care of him."

So Calvin grew up calling his grandparents, Samuel and Narlvil Newton, Poppa and Momma. The Newtons, they were as filled with God, exuberantly and tremulously, as people can be on this earth, and they taught their boy how to open his heart to God, how to talk to Him and praise Him with song.

Twenty years later, the Newtons once again stand between Calvin and the abyss.

The lawyer they hire, a man named Stacey Freeman, believes the state had no cause even to suspect, much less arrest, Calvin, and waives his client's right to a jury trial. This is an incendiary charge, after all; why bring human uncertainty and prejudice into the equation when the case—as a matter of law, of *fact*—is so feeble? Let the judge rule from the bench.

From the get-go, however, the trial is bizarre. The district attorney announces that a day after the rape, Lucretia picked Calvin's face out of a photo lineup (the police having had his mug on file from a couple of misdemeanor arrests dating to '79). Neither Calvin nor his lawyer has heard of this lineup. The DA says he himself has just learned of it. He also announces that the photo lineup has been lost. And that the police have kept no record of how it was assembled.

After the judge denies Freeman's motion to exclude, the lineup and the issue underlying it—did Lucretia actually name Calvin as her attacker and, if so, *when*—becomes the trial's central question. Problem is, nearly all the prosecution witnesses contradict statements they made to police the day of the crime—and even statements they've already made on the stand. The testimony of Lucretia's mother, Barbara, is typical: She starts by saying she'd never heard the name Willis before talking to the detectives. Then she admits she had. Then she says a detective suggested the name to her. Finally, she says that Lucretia named "Calvin" to her just before they arrived at the police station on the morning of the tenth.

Then there is Lucretia. She is, simply, a terrified child, saying "yes" both literally and effectively to whatever is being asked, no matter who's asking, and casting a veil of confusion. Even her swearing-in raises questions.

"Do you know what an oath means, when you raise your hand to tell the truth?" Judge Paul Lynch asks.

"Like when your mama tells you not to do something and then you go and do it?" she offers.

Unsatisfied, or perhaps unnerved, Lynch persists.

"What did that mean when you said that you would tell the truth?"

No response.

"You are unable to answer?"

Lucretia shakes her head.

"You are crying. Are you that upset?"

Despite this beginning, Lucretia possesses some recall about the photo array.

"[Detective Betty Brookins] showed me some pictures, and then she told me to pick the ones that didn't have a full beard," she says, later adding, ominously, "[Brookins] said pick the one who did it to you, and I said neither one of them."

In other words, the police did not ask if her attacker's face was among the photos, as they should have, but *told* her it was—and instructed her to find it. (Detective Brookins corroborates Lucretia's account, testifying that she told the girl, "I need you to pick out the one that raped you.")

Lucretia's testimony gets stranger still. Under cross-examination, she says that she was unable to pick a face from the lineup, that the name Calvin was then *suggested* to her, and that she *still* didn't pick out a face.

When Calvin takes the stand, his sense that the trial has become a joke mixes with his fear to produce a taut, edgy witness, ready to fight. After the DA launches a series of oddball questions about daylight savings time, Calvin snaps.

"Do I look like I got a hole in the top of my head?"

"I don't know what you understand," the DA says.

"Are you trying to take me for a fool?"

Calvin's account—everything from where he was, and when, to the beige shoes he was wearing—squares perfectly with the testimony of his friends, Jerome and Gerald, with whom he spent the night of June 8, and with that of his wife. But in the end, Calvin's testimony does not matter. Nor does it matter that if the testimony of Calvin's alibi witnesses is taken at face value, the scenario of Calvin as rapist *necessarily* means that he returned home at five to midnight, changed out of his beige shoes, played possum for a while next to his sleeping wife, snuck out of bed, dressed up as a cowboy, left the house, savagely raped and beat a child, returned home, hung up his cowboy paraphernalia, and crept back into bed without rousing his wife. It does not even matter that the rapist's waistline, as evidenced by his boxer shorts, is eleven inches larger than Calvin's.

None of this matters because the trustworthiest witness of all—science—has calmly pointed its finger at Calvin: "Shorts were found at the scene," Lynch rules, "and . . . semen stains matched that of the defendant. The nightgown that was worn by the victim had semen stains that matched that of the defendant."

On February 2, 1982, Judge Lynch finds Calvin Willis guilty of raping a child. On May 17, 1982, Lynch sentences him to a term no shorter than "natural life" without the possibility of parole.

"Do you have anything to say?" Lynch asks.

Calvin turns from the judge to face Mrs. Newton. He speaks in a quiet, bewildered voice.

"I didn't do it, Momma."

Narlvil Newton feels her face tightening into a mask, open-mouthed and silent, as her boy is taken away.

"Momma?" Calvin whispers, looking back, waiting for her face to move. "Momma?"

•   •   •

In all of Shreveport, young Lucretia notwithstanding, is there a human being as cursed as Calvin Willis?

There is.

Her name is Janet Gregory. She's a white woman a few years older than Calvin who walks with a limp and talks with a drawl. By her own admission she was raised among racists, though she herself has never bought into that. Prissy, as she is known, has an unusual disposition. She has an uncanny ability to sniff out liars and phonies and a corresponding inability, just as uncanny, to refrain from telling those liars and phonies exactly what she thinks of them. In other respects Prissy is strangely guarded. She doesn't like being looked at or touched by men, because men have brought almost incomprehensible pain to her life. Three months after marrying her high school sweetheart, Ralph, Prissy accidentally shot herself through the knee with his .357. Doctors told her she would never walk again. Four months later, before it became clear that Janet was tougher than anyone knew and would indeed walk again, Ralph was killed in a car wreck.

When a proper period of time had passed, Prissy agreed, at the prodding of friends, to date a man named Daryl. He picked her up in his truck and took her not to the concert he'd told her they'd be attending but to his rented trailer home. He asked her to take a seat, walked into another room, returned with a shotgun, and announced that she would be performing oral sex on him.

"I think you should just shoot me," Prissy said.

Daryl shrugged, laid the shotgun in one corner, raped her, then drove her home.

On some level, Prissy suspected that Daryl might somehow be the price she needed to pay for living and breathing when her husband had died, so for many years she told no one about what had happened in the trailer.

She did find love again, though. His name was Ferris. They married. Ferris and his dog were hit by a seventy-five-car freight train. He'd been fiddling with the radio in his truck.

Prissy is now married to her third husband. She refers to this man not as "my husband" but as "my son's father." This is because he beats and forces himself upon her. In years to come, after she secures a protective order and a divorce, people will ask about her ex, and Janet will say, "The one constant anger in my life is my son's father. I can handle whatever happened between him and me. I can handle no child support. But for my boy's whole life he hasn't had a father. And for that, I could literally rip his head off and shit down his neck." Given all that has befallen Janet Gregory, such statements carry a certain weight.

Because Janet's third husband—whom she characterizes drily, ominously, as "the one who lives"—makes no financial contribution, she works as a paralegal. In this capacity, she strikes up some remarkable relationships. One is with a death-row inmate named Wayne Felde, whom her boss represents on appeal. Janet knows Felde killed a policeman in a drunken rage, and he doesn't pretend that he didn't. But throughout his unsuccessful appeals—even after she stops working for his lawyer—she talks to Wayne Felde, writes him, visits him, lays her hands upon him during court proceedings, functions as a vessel for him, assuring him when he feels his humanity departing him that it is safe and intact with her. This is the thing about Janet. For some reason, her sufferings, rather than withering her soul, have greatly expanded it. They have given her sight into the inner lives of others and, yes, an abiding and forceful anger. Yet what she sees she tends not to judge, the energy of her rage instead being transmuted into wondering: *What is my role here?* On the day of his electrocution, Wayne and Janet speak on the phone until his time comes. "I have to go, they're here for me, I love you, I'll miss you, good-bye," he says. Janet takes out a loan to pay for his burial.

After working for Felde's lawyer, Janet finds employment with an attorney named Graves Thomas—whom Momma and Poppa Newton have hired to appeal Calvin's conviction. In May 1987, while weighing Calvin's options, Graves—one of Janet's dearest friends—goes waterskiing. After cleaning moss from the engine's propeller, he steps up to the deck, says, "Let's go!" and is struck dead by lightning.

A few months after this, Samuel Newton, Calvin's de facto father and the man whose meager salary has been keeping Calvin's legal strategies—his *hope*—alive, dies of cancer. Calvin is given leave from prison to attend the funeral. In a way, it feels like his own.

In the two years preceding Graves Thomas's death, Calvin has heard the name Janet Gregory once or twice, though he's never met her. He actually thinks she's a secretary. He does not know that there is little in this world Janet Gregory has not withstood, or how this has generated a matter-of-fact willingness—utterly bold, utterly without vanity—to think *Yes, I'll take it* to everything life shovels at her, no matter how daunting or malign. He does not know that Janet Gregory, a white woman raised to be racist and violated by two men, has been going through her dead boss's files, reading the trial transcript of a black man convicted of rape and alternately exclaiming "This is *bullshit*!" and "I cannot live with this!" and, more important, wondering, *What is my role here?*

All Calvin knows is that there are two people out of place at his grandfather's wake, and that Calvin is one of them. There are the scores of mourners in their Sunday best, silent and elegant, all black. There is Calvin, hands and ankles tautly chained to a black steel box affixed to his beltline, shuffling, clanking, eyes lowered—no longer Big Hands, no longer the man who once used his gaze to seize ownership of whatever came before him. And there is that woman, the sole white face, kneeling before his children and speaking softly. Now she's moving toward Calvin, limping, crying, backing his guards off with a ferocious glare, then hugging his neck and saying *Calvin, oh Calvin.* It's been five years since any woman—including his wife, whom he sees only at family gatherings in prison—has touched him with such intensity.

"Lady," he says, "who *are* you?"

. . .

From 1982 to 1986 the state of Louisiana houses Calvin at the Caddo Correctional Institute thirty miles outside Shreveport. Debbie brings the family every Saturday—Momma and Poppa Newton, while he's still alive; Calvin's little girl, Kesha, three years old at the time of his conviction; and Calvin Jr., the baby, born while Calvin was jailed awaiting trial—and this gives his life a semblance of reality, even as the reunions, in a noisy visitor's room full of strangers, feel formal and sterile and weird.

The visits are never enough, of course. Not even close. His need for Debbie is complex. At first he tethers his longing to his memories: of dancing with her for an hour straight the night they met; of their holiday celebrations; of Kesha's birth; of instances when the might of their physical love verged on the preposterous. But as the years pass, he comes to see that there is a difference between what he can *remember* about their relationship and the relationship itself—that the great moments of their life, though marvelous, are unconnected dots, and that what actually holds a man and a woman together are millions of tiny, unremarkable moments that cannot be individually seen or collectively explained. The moments one simply must be *there* for. So he finds himself pining for what he cannot quite remember, the nonevents, the sweet quiet nothings of being with her. There's a thing she used to do as she nuzzled his chest in bed, a peaceful rolling coo. Did she know she did it? Did she know he could feel the low little hum in his sternum? What did she mean by it? Something plain and good, he thinks now. *You're here with me. I'm here with you.*

His longing for his babies, on the other hand, is not complex. Where missing Debbie is an act, something he engages in, his need for his babies seizes and terrorizes him. There is no controlling it. He will try to numb himself, dip his mind in a gray vagueness for days at a time, but then something sharp—the ammoniac sting of industrial solvent in the mess, the cold shock of his cell's stainless-steel shitter against his haunches—will jerk him to a state of full awareness and he will freeze, clasp his son's first bib, which he keeps with him, over his eyes and say aloud, "My babies." He discovers that his desperate hunger to touch them, compounded a hundredfold by the fact that he's innocent—*he is innocent!*—is sometimes ameliorated by physical pain. One day he goes so far as to sneak into a room he's not supposed to be in. When, inevitably, a guard approaches saying, "Hey, you," Calvin calmly wraps a hand around the man's forearm, lowers himself into the man's chest, and flips him on his back. The storm comes within seconds, half a dozen guards with billy clubs, calling him nigger and bludgeoning his kidneys and shins until he no longer feels the agony of his lost children.

In 1986, shortly before being transferred 260 miles across the state to Angola prison, Calvin addresses the unspoken question hanging over the Saturday reunions. He asks the Newtons and his children for some time with Debbie. Once they're alone, he tells his wife that he aches for her, aches the way he did in his last hours as a free man, when a spirit came upon him and sent him home to make love to her for the last time. Debbie begins to cry.

"Don't say this thing, Calvin."

But he must, and she knows it. He tells her that he knows it's been hard for her. That he knows she's been working six days a week at Dillard's with double shifts on Saturdays. That he knows Kesha and Calvin Jr. now spend most of their time at their great-grandparents'. That this is no way to live. And he tells her that even though the thought of her with another man feels to him like a form of death, he knows that it must happen.

"I hate it," Debbie sobs. "I *hate* it!"

Calvin just shakes his head, folds his big hands around hers, and looks her in the eye.

"The only thing in this world that could separate us," he tells her, "is if you had a child by another man."

.   .   .

The most despised and marked man in the world is the man imprisoned for raping a child, so Calvin tells no one on the inside why he is there. To avoid anyone asking, he seeks no company and strives to keep others from seeking it in him. To hide himself in plain sight, he kills everything within him that is engaging—his ability to tell a story, to offer counsel, to make everyone around him laugh and forget. He even strips the confidence and sex from his stride, tightening it up and keeping his eyes downcast when he moves from here to there so that his body in motion suggests nothing except *Nothing to see here.*

Calvin's way of being, showing his heart to God through constant conversation while showing the world the face of a zombie, takes enormous effort. It requires psychic sustenance: the faith and love of family and of the extended community back in Shreveport. Yet after the first few months, nobody besides Calvin's family visits. Nobody writes. *Why?* Why don't all those people who once adored Big Hands stick by him?

It's not that anyone back home thinks he's guilty. Nor does their belief in his innocence lack conviction. They are thoroughly convicted people. Yet theirs is not a conscientious, do-the-right-thing kind of conviction. It's subtler, deeper, beyond righteous anger: It's conviction-as-resignation. The people Calvin grew up with *presume* that innocent black men will go to jail and that there's nothing anybody can do about it. Most are Baptists or born-again evangelicals, a handful of generations removed from slave theology, who believe that the reward for people such as them lies in the next plane and that there is little if any human agency in this world. When a right man like Calvin is shut away, their response is less *That is an outrage!* than *Ain't that a shame.*

Debbie, though, does not believe God has willed Calvin to be in prison or his community to abandon him, and she is outraged. Her anger thickens and curdles her heart until she begins to carry a conviction of her own, secret and terrible. One day when she can no longer abide herself, she tells her grandmother-in-law that as hard as it is working all those shifts at Dillard's, she's starting not to mind, because almost everyone she works with is white.

"They the only ones that been offering me kindness."

"You need to look to God, child," Mrs. Newton says.

"We got a black church on every corner in this neighborhood—where they been?" Debbie fires back. "It's a *white* church that's been bringing my kids gifts at Christmastime. My pastor hasn't even talked to me about it. I got no one of my own people I can talk to. Black people don't stick together, Momma! Now that we finally got something—'cause we free and we can work and make something of ourselves—it's like we afraid they'll take it away again, so we don't share anything with each other."

Debbie knows how a bigoted mind works, the way it assigns the characteristics of individuals to whole groups of people. *All black people eat watermelon. . . . All black people are shiftless. . . .* But as her community forsakes her family, she finds her mind and heart similarly debased—*black people don't stick together*—and the indignity of it makes her all the more enraged at what the state of Louisiana has done to their lives.

·   ·   ·

When Calvin sees that white woman whispering to his eight-year-old daughter and six-year-old son at Poppa Newton's wake, he assumes she's talking cute to them, distracting them from the enveloping sadness. He's wrong. She is making a furious and tender vow.

"Two things," she tells Kesha and Calvin Jr. "First, if you hear people saying bad things about your daddy today, don't you believe a word of it." The children nod. They don't know what to make of this woman. "Second, if I have to, I will go to my grave trying to prove he is innocent."

Indeed. After *cookie* and a few other nouns, *Calvin* is one of the first words Janet Gregory's child utters. Sometimes when his mother can't get to the phone, he'll pick up and squeal "Calvin! Calvin! Calvin!" into the receiver. In a way, "Calvin" becomes the man of Janet's fatherless house, a palpable presence by way of the legal briefs carpeting the living room floor and the Post-it–note brainstorms spackling the walls.

Just as some nurses become as expert in medicine as the doctors they work with, Janet has built an encyclopedic knowledge of criminal law. While holding down a job, attending classes in pursuit of a college degree, and singly raising her child, she researches and writes Calvin's petitions herself, picking apart the bungled photo array and the contradictory testimony at his trial. Then she shows up at the doorsteps of various Shreveport lawyers, announcing that "I've prepared this marvelous writ and I need a warm body with a law degree to sign it." Since everyone knows she's no sucker or bleeding heart, and since she's just a little bit scary, they sign.

In 1988, by way of Janet, Calvin files a postconviction application. It is denied without explanation. This kind of per curiam judgment, as it is called, is very difficult to challenge. By essentially declaring, "Because we said so," it offers a convict no legal traction, no argument to parse on appeal.

In 1989 he files a writ of habeas corpus. Denied per curiam.

In 1990 he files a second postconviction application. Denied per curiam.

The same year, he files his second writ of habeas corpus. Denied per curiam.

Again in 1990 he files for postconviction relief with the Louisiana Supreme Court. Denied per curiam.

In early 1991 he files another writ of habeas corpus in federal court. Denied per curiam.

During these years, as Janet fails to prove Calvin's innocence—fails, even, to get a court to explain his "guilt"—the two of them never lay eyes upon one another. In fact, after their first face-to-face at his grandfather's wake, Calvin and Janet don't meet in person for seven years. Janet simply hasn't the time or the money for the 520-mile round-trip from Shreveport to Angola prison. She does not travel. She does not eat out. She does not shop. She does not have a love life. She works at her job and her schoolwork, raises her boy, and files briefs.

Despite the physical distance—or perhaps because of it—Janet's relationship with Calvin takes on a teetering intensity. At first their letters and calls concern only legal matters. After a time, though, what once became clear to Wayne Felde becomes clear to Calvin Willis: that Janet knows no bounds, that she is capable of acting as a preserving vessel for another person's humanity—humanity that would otherwise stagnate or deform. Tentatively at first, then flowingly, then in a roaring geyser, Calvin reveals to Janet . . . everything. Everything he must keep hidden in Angola for fear of being killed, or worse, and everything he must keep hidden from the members of his family, who are already fragile. Only with Janet is he able to flex the humor and intelligence and libido and wrath that together form his manhood. He tells Janet about Angola, a hard-labor camp redolent of the slave plantation it once was, where Louisiana's lifers are sent to wither and die—how the place is designed not to rehabilitate or even hold men but to turn them into something less than men. He tells her how every day hurts and threatens to remove him from his self. He tells her what it's like not to see his wife and children and mother, and how the ghost of things not done haunts his conscience. He tells her about his ongoing lover's quarrel, belligerent and ecstatic, with his God. He tells her about his fevered and tearful masturbation, usually conducted without privacy. He tells her about scouring the dictionary in the prison library for new, long, strong, clean words: *phenomenon, fastidious, punctilious, omnipotent.* He tells her about performing biceps curls with law books—the only way they prove useful. He tells her about the dead-eyed cellmate who, when arrested in a nightclub, had a beer in one hand and a sack stuffed with a woman's head in the other. He tells her about seeing human beings hang themselves, puncture their wrists, overdose, anything to escape, and about human flesh getting shivved and cudgeled and fucked. He tells her about the petty and arbitrary humiliations the guards mete out: the way they give Calvin thirty days in extended lockdown for "reckless eyeballing" (failing to turn and face the wall in the presence of a female guard) and another thirty for the "aggravated sex offense" of accidentally grazing a female security guard's shoulder in passing, the way they fire rifle shots a foot above his head when he crosses an imaginary "guard line" out in the fields on work detail, and the way they cuff him to the bars of his cell for six hours just for fun and mace his eyes if he doesn't offer up his wrists the instant he's told. He tells her about being paid four cents an hour to pick cotton in the fields surrounding the prison, and how much worse this is than being paid nothing at all. He tells her what it's like watching the children of the guards, who live on the plantation grounds, grow up, and how strange it is to see young boys who once called "Hey, nigger!" to him as he worked the fields become guards themselves—*yes, that much time is passing*—with rifles in their hands and toothpicks in their mouths and absolute power over where he rests his eyeballs. He tells her he is losing his grasp on time, losing his ability to *count*, in a way; how during his first four years of imprisonment, at Caddo Correctional, time was still solid, still the bedrock of his reality, each day marked by a beginning and an end linked by a continuous line of being, but how at Angola, a place that cannot possibly be real (can it?), he has learned that a man's grasp on time is like his good health—something taken for granted until it dissolves. He tells her about the way a cell becomes a kiln in the summer, the air void of motion, 110 degrees at two in the morning, the way he will take a tin cup and splash the brown water from the tap onto the concrete floor, then lie in it face down, spread-eagled and naked, his nose and mouth filled with the ever present shit-stink bubbling up from the drain, his ears filled with the baboon shrieks of men whose consciousness has been reduced to the purely physical, saying to himself over and over, for hours on end, *I will not die in Angola.* . . . *I will not die in Angola.* . . . *I will not die in Angola.* . . .

More than anything, though, it is his anger that Calvin tells Janet about, and that he needs her to absorb and carry for him. It is his anger that debases and emasculates him most, even more than all his unspent love. It is his anger that shuts down his imagination (he does not dream when he sleeps at Angola—ever) and stills time, that turns a day into a month. And it is his anger, eating him inside-out like lupus, that threatens to alienate him from his God. *This* is the thing that cannot happen. For only in prayer does Calvin travel beyond the cast of his own umbra to perceive something other than his own suffering self. Prayer is not to Calvin what drugs or suicide are to other men in Angola—a means of escape. It is how he tunes in to the fact that he is a real person, here on this earth, living in real time, and that he is not alone. And it is only in prayer that the voice comes to him, full of mystery and hope.

You have a testimony. You must bear witness to yourself. And you will.

·　　　·　　　·

In January 1993, after a change in Louisiana law allows him to do so, Calvin obtains the initial police report on his case. It is an astonishment. In it, two detectives write that on the morning of June 9—hours after the crime—Latanya told them that a "big" man named "HARRY" [*sic*] who "had on a cowboy hat, cowboy shoes" had visited the house and left after finding only children there.

Harry. A big man. A man Latanya knew by name. Ugly. Not Calvin Willis.

Eleven years into his sentence, Calvin secures a certificate of probable cause and reappeals.

A month later, the U.S. Fifth Circuit Court of Appeals dismisses the grant—not on the merits of its argument but because of the "untimely filing by petitioner."

Untimely.

As if Calvin has had the original police report in hand for ten years and has been omitting it from his previous appeals out of . . . caprice?

He has one more shot. In October 1993 he files another application for postconviction relief; in March 1994 the First Judicial District Court of Caddo Parish denies Calvin's application. This denial is not per curiam. Reasoning is offered.

"The police report does make mention of . . . 'HARRY,' but it does not state that 'HARRY' visited the home where the incident occurred earlier that day."

This is inane: Though the detectives did not quote Latanya on when "HARRY" visited, it is patently clear she meant the day of the incident—and that this is what the detectives thought she meant.

"Because . . . 'HARRY' was not necessarily a suspect," the ruling continues, "there is no need for the court to consider [this claim]."

Catch-22: "HARRY" was never a suspect because the police report in which his name appeared never saw the light of day throughout the investigation, during the trial, and for the next eleven years.

It is over now. In legal terms, Calvin's case has been "exhausted." Janet, too, is exhausted, and stooped under the weight of anger, both her own and Calvin's. All of her heart and soul and *rightness* have been poured into Calvin's legal briefs over the better part of a decade. Countless thousands of words, all met with the same slap to the face: DENIED.

Until now there has been a distinct difference between what Janet did for Wayne Felde and what she has been doing for Calvin. What she did for Wayne was a form of palliative care; she was never going to save him. Calvin has always been different. Like Wayne, he has demanded her love but also—because the object *has* been to free him—every ounce of her intellectual fortitude. And she has failed. Now it is merely her job, as it was with Wayne, to ensure Calvin goes to his grave knowing he has been understood.

But then one day not long after his final denial, Calvin calls.

"People around here been talking about something," he says. "It's called DNA."

For a time the only sound on the line is the recorded voice that interjects every few minutes to remind her that she is taking a collect call from a prisoner. Janet knows about DNA evidence, how it has broken men out of death row. Still, something within her resists its promise of sword-through-the-knot magic. To Janet, believing in DNA—in the possibility of a force cooler and stronger than the human minds that conduct and corrupt the business of justice—is like believing in happy endings, something to which she has long been allergic.

"I need to see your face," she says at last.

Janet brings the kids and Mrs. Newton. Debbie remains in Shreveport; in the wake of Calvin's final failed appeal, she has written a series of letters explaining that she finally has the means to purchase a home. But creditors won't lend to a single mother with an incarcerated husband. She has assured him the divorce will be nothing but a piece of paper to mollify the bank. But signing it has left Calvin with a sick feeling. Maybe it's better she's not here.

Janet, for her part, now knows Calvin more intimately than anyone save God. Yet having met Calvin in person only once, seven years before, she barely knows his face. He in turn barely knows hers. Their faces—hers reveals its weathering; his, strangely, appears as fresh as the day he turned himself in—render them unrecognizable to one another. For the first fifteen minutes they do something they've never done before: small talk. Finally, Calvin addresses the subject.

"People gettin' relief from this DNA," he says.

"Let me give you a reality check," Janet says.

This is one of the reasons she has come in person; she's not sure he can survive another dashed hope. She explains that exoneration by DNA evidence is a long shot. Eleven years have passed. Even if the DNA in the rape kit and on the boxer shorts has been preserved, the DA's office might refuse to release the file.

"We need to do this," he says.

Another reason Janet has traveled 260 miles is to look Calvin in the eye, and she does so now.

"I will do what needs to be done. You know that. I will write the letters. I will talk to the police. I will raise the money. But the thing about DNA evidence is, it's . . . irrefutable."

"I know."

So she will start again, from scratch.

•   •   •

It takes nine years.

For the first four, Janet's on her own. After determining that the Caddo Parish clerk's office has preserved Lucretia's rape kit and the boxer shorts, she does what she did during the appellate phase of Calvin's case: letter-writing, calling, fund-raising. In 1998 she discovers the Innocence Project, cofounded by Barry Scheck and run out of the Cardozo law school in New York City, and submits an application on Calvin's behalf. Scheck accepts. This is big. Scheck is the country's most credible legal advocate when it comes to DNA evidence, with access to the most vaunted laboratories. He tells Janet she'll need to raise $2,500, though by the time all is said and done the bill will top $14,000.

Janet redoubles her fund-raising efforts, showing up in the offices and homes of friends and enemies alike armed with Calvin's story and a letter printed on Innocence Project stationery. She hits up clerks at the grocery store, the woman at the dry cleaner's, strangers on the street. The donations rarely top $50. She mails copies of the checks—including one for $3 from her mother's housekeeper, the most the woman can afford—to Calvin, who pens each contributor a thank-you note. (The four cents an hour he earns slinging a blade in the fields of Angola nets him about a stamp's worth of postage a day.)

She even hits up a retired prosecutor named Carey Schimpf.

"Hey, Carey, do you remember a guy you prosecuted about twenty years ago named Calvin Willis?"

Not in great detail, Schimpf says.

"Well, he was innocent. But guess what? You have the chance to redeem yourself."

Schimpf declines to contribute.

In 1999 the district attorney agrees to release the evidence to Scheck's DNA specialist, Edward Blake of Richmond, California.

Four more years pass.

Janet is adept at rage; she's known for years how to channel the two lives' worth that she carries into her legal questing. But these four more years of waiting threaten to transport her to a place where her anger consumes her. One thing keeps her on an even keel: a burly, bearded, ex-junkie, ex-alcoholic country-music guitarist and songwriter named Randy Arthur. He is, like Janet, intimately familiar with pain. Years ago, in an alcoholic stupor, he killed a jogger with his pickup truck. Now, Janet stays awake at night and listens as Randy pleads with the man's widow in his sleep, telling her how he's bettered his life and asking for her forgiveness. Randy, in short, is a person who *gets* Janet. They marry in November of 1999.

•   •   •

A change comes over Calvin in these years as he waits for his blood to speak for him. During his first fifteen years or so behind bars he often felt that every filament of his being was aligned in the service of pain, as if pain itself had designed and realized in him the perfect instrument for its expression. Over time, though—as with Janet, and perhaps because of her—the perfection of his pain has cleaned him out, concentrated and clarified him, pushed him deeper into God. Not just his own God, either. Calvin's prayer life has imbued him with a peaceful intellectual hunger; by the late nineties he has become the kind of Christian who reads the Koran and attends Muslim prayer services so as to behold the manifold nature of holiness, and who sees God in every face he encounters—even those of his guards.

On his way to the dungeon known as Camp J for yet another "reckless eyeballing" offense, Calvin turns to the guard hustling him along and asks, "Why you hate me?" Something in Calvin's tone commands the man to confront the question head-on rather than sarcastically.

"I hate you because you are the shit of the earth."

"No," Calvin says. "Why you hate me?"

"I hate you because of what you did."

"No. Why you hate me."

The guard gives Calvin a long look.

"Boy, I was *raised* to hate you," he says, walking off.

"I'm not the one you hate," Calvin calls after him. "I'm not the one."

This is Calvin Willis now. Even as he continues to suffer one of the greatest offenses a man in this world can endure, his consciousness has been multiplied. He sees *through*. It is even possible that he forgives. There is power in that. And knowledge. He knows now that he can never be repressed, only murdered.

By the time Calvin's blood reaches Blake, his life can no longer be measured in terms of time, which he's lost track of anyway—

only in terms of its crescendoing radiance. Because he finally can, he begins to take back the anger Janet has been carrying for him.

"The work you have done is good," he tells her over the phone and in letters, time and again. "*You* are good. Concentrate on that. Let your anger go."

She says she doesn't know how.

"Just give it to me," Calvin says.

It is by way of this grace that when the cruelest blow comes, Calvin can sustain it.

Late in 1999, a man on Calvin's cellblock, also from Shreveport, receives a family visit.

"I got news for you," he says when he returns. "Your wife got remarried, man! She got a *daughter*. That girl already 5 or 6 years old!"

Debbie, it turns out, did not need his signature on the divorce decree just to buy the house. Back in 1994, while Janet, Momma Newton, and the children were visiting Calvin in Angola, she was in the hospital giving birth to her daughter, Briana; Janet and Mrs. Newton hadn't thought it their place to break the news.

The one line I drew. The only thing that could separate us.

He thinks, too, about the little art-class trinkets he's sent her over the years, the toothpick houses and construction-paper Valentine's Day cards, and how childish and pathetic they've surely seemed to her, an adult getting on with her life, going on without him, a new family.

"What you gonna do, Calvin?"

It's a rhetorical question, but Calvin answers.

"Nothing, man. When you in prison you can't do nothing about nothing."

And by the time the cruelest blow comes to Janet, Calvin has already taken back the principal on his anger, assuring her by way of his manifest serenity that she is free to fully concentrate on her own burden.

Randy's years of substance abuse have caught up with him; his liver is dying. In September 2001 a donor organ matching

Randy's tissue type is located. Prissy kisses her husband before he goes under and tells him she'll be there when he gets back. But when the doctors open him up they discover his hepatic veins have turned to jelly. He bleeds out on the operating table. At the age of forty-six, Janet becomes a widow for the third time.

A group of local musicians throws a benefit; Janet has been sending her own money, along with the donations she's drummed up, to the Innocence Project to pay for Calvin's testing, and doesn't have enough to bury her husband.

· · ·

In March 2003, Janet gets Calvin on the phone.

"Hey, Calvin," she says, "you need to start studying for your driver's test."

"What you talking about?"

"There's male DNA in Lucretia's fingernail scrapings. It matches the male DNA on the boxer shorts."

"Okay."

"It's not your DNA."

Calvin doesn't say anything.

"You're coming home, Calvin."

There's something blindingly, even painfully, bright about the words, and for a moment they crush him. How could it be? How could something in the blood, a million times smaller than anything the eye can see, rout the brutality of mind and heart, as old as the species, that took his life away?

Word spreads quickly around the cellblock.

Calvin is innocent! Calvin gettin' out!

Over the next few days, the guards overseeing Calvin approach him to have a word. They do not congratulate. They do not apologize. They grin. Grin and say, each of them, the same three words.

You'll be back.

Six months pass.

No one at Angola bothers explaining to Calvin or Janet why a proven-innocent man continues to serve time. Nor do they offer any guesses as to when he might be released.

But on the evening of September 18, 2003, a journalist tells Janet that Calvin is being put on a bus at five the next morning to the Caddo Correctional Center, where he will be released. Janet has a terrible vision: Calvin greeting freedom in a neon orange jumpsuit. She runs out to buy a selection of jeans, khakis, and dress shirts, as well as socks, tennis shoes, and a belt.

The guards keep Calvin's hands and feet manacled throughout the 260-mile drive. They take a long McDonald's stop. They give Calvin nothing to eat or drink. They offer him no acknowledgement whatsoever. Inside the correctional center they unshackle his limbs, then leave without saying another word.

An officer approaches Calvin with the clothes Janet has purchased.

"Your lady friend brought these for you," she says.

Calvin stares at the shirts and pants for a while. Spiritual matters aside, he has not made a choice since 1981. He no longer knows how.

"Miss," he finally says, "I haven't worn clothes in twenty-two years. Could you pick something out for me?"

The corrections officer takes each article of clothing from the box and places it up against Calvin's frame. She picks the khakis and a plaid button-down shirt. The cling of the new socks on his ankles startles him.

"You look nice," she tells him after he's dressed. Then: "It's time."

"What do I do?"

"Leave," she says, pointing to the exit.

As he approaches the door, Calvin prays. Prays for a renewing of his mind and heart, prays to be free of whatever anger he retains, the self-inflicted wound of it. And at the instant he lays his hand upon the door and steps into the light, he receives this final piece of his deliverance; he experiences it as a hand, searing and baptismal, passing over him.

You must bear witness to yourself. And you will.

They are out there with the media, waiting. Momma Newton and Kesha and Calvin Jr., whom he hasn't seen in almost ten years. And Janet. All his loves except Debbie.

Debbie had a terrible night last night. Lying in bed next to her husband, Edward, with eyes wide open, she prayed for the trembling to stop.

Lord, keep my body still. If my husband sees my distress he'll think I want Calvin back.

Later, in the hours before sunrise, her mind went elsewhere.

I was twenty-three years old. I had the best marriage anybody could have. And then you were gone. And I couldn't talk about you. Not even with black people. My own people. And my mind went blank. For years my mind went blank. I couldn't remember you the same. I had to let you go. And I hated you. Hated you for making me need to be with other men. Hated you for not being at home. You should have been home, Calvin.

At the instant Calvin Willis, age forty-four, steps into freedom—as the 138th convict in this country to be exonerated by DNA evidence—Debbie and Edward are at Home Depot purchasing supplies for a home renovation.

Debbie sees the replay on the evening news, however: There are her children. There is Janet, God bless her. There is Mrs. Newton, eighty-five years old, unable to form words, howling as she grabs her boy. And there is Calvin, serene, poised, fielding questions.

"You know," he says, "I lost my wife."

Then he bursts into tears.

It is not over. It will never be over. Hugo Holland, chief of the sex-crimes unit at the district attorney's office, makes a concerted effort to ensure that Calvin Willis retains the stigma of child rape, unleashing a series of acid sound bites:

"Calvin Willis is not innocent. He's just not guilty."

"There is no reason whatsoever for us to ever say that the legal system made a mistake."

"[Just] because we didn't find Calvin Willis's DNA on the underwear doesn't mean that he didn't leave them there."

Hugo Holland is the least of Calvin's problems. In practical terms, as an exonerated man in the state of Louisiana, he gets nothing. Not a dime for having two of the best-earning decades of his life stolen from him, and for the loss of his family. Without Momma Newton's spare bedroom, he'd be homeless.

Yet there are myriad odder ways in which Calvin is burdened. There are, for instance, his dual aversions to making eye contact and to being touched. His old friends, who remember him as the most physically assertive and expressive of men, never know what to say when Calvin goes stiff and silent in their embraces. There is his inability to stop cleaning (he scrubs Mrs. Newton's floors, sinks, and toilets at least once a day), as if the literal and figurative upwelling of shit he battled every day in Angola has permanently imprinted his olfactory nerves. There is the way life behind bars has damaged his understanding of time. He can tell you in vivid detail, for instance, about an episode in Angola in which he brandished a coffeepot during a fight and ended up burning a layer of skin off his face, but he can't remember what year this happened, or even whether it happened in the late eighties or early nineties or mid-nineties.

So much he has unlearned. Shortly after his release, Momma Newton prepares an enormous repast. When the spread is ready, she hands him a plate and says, "You start!" But Calvin just stands there, puzzled. A minute passes before Mrs. Newton makes the realization—*the boy doesn't know how to serve his own plate*—and turns away so he doesn't see her tears.

This is Calvin Willis after twenty-two years in a box: a man of rare spiritual elevation; a child who doesn't know how to spoon food onto his own plate.

At Thanksgiving, Momma Newton gathers her kin—Calvin; Kesha and her husband; Calvin Jr. and his boy (Calvin's first grandson, Elijah, born two days after Calvin gained his freedom)—as well as Debbie, her husband, Edward, and their nine-year-old daughter, Briana. The minute she lays eyes on Calvin, Debbie becomes acutely self-conscious; where she's put on the pounds, Calvin, having been stopped in time, is as beautiful as the day he vanished.

"I know," she says, casting her eyes down. "I was a size five when you left. Now look at me."

Calvin just smiles.

"Still look good to me."

She hugs him, then asks if he's ready. When he says he is, Edward comes forward.

"I got to say something to you," Calvin says.

Edward braces himself. This has been a long time coming.

"I want to thank you," Calvin continues. "It takes a strong man to raise another man's kids right, allowing them to become who they need to become. My children are beautiful. I know you've had a hand in that. I thank you."

"Who's that man?" Briana asks her mother. "Why he make Daddy cry?"

Debbie takes her daughter aside.

"He's father to Kesha and Calvin Jr.," she explains, "but no one to you."

Briana does a lovely thing then. She runs across the living room and grabs hold of Calvin's waist. He takes her up, and the two of them talk for a while. He says the things one says to a child. Hello, missy. What's your name? How are you? But after a few minutes Briana sees something in this man, something cavernous and vast, and it amazes her. Calvin, a man who has been forced to spend half his life letting other souls carry and act upon his most fathomless passions, then watches as Briana turns to face her mother.

"Mama, this man!" she cries. "He love you!"

The New Yorker

WINNER—REPORTING

Samantha Power's story makes it impossible for us to avert our eyes from the ethnic cleansing in western Sudan. Her firm, intelligent control of her material, born of reporting of extraordinary enterprise, allows the horrors of the Sudanese conflict, and the political forces behind it, to speak for themselves.

Samantha Power

Dying in Darfur

Amina Abaker Mohammed occupies a simple mud hut with a thatched roof outside a refugee camp in northern Chad. Until earlier this year, she lived in Darfur, the western region of Sudan, where the Sudanese government is pursuing a campaign of ethnic cleansing against non-Arabs. Amina is a member of the Zaghawa tribe, one of the largest non-Arab ethnic groups in Darfur. Her village, which was burned to the ground by Sudanese soldiers and Arab militiamen, is only fifty miles from the camp, but by donkey the trip requires a weeklong journey across the Sahara, through mounds of powdery sand, up and down steep seasonal riverbeds, over gravel slopes, and around towering red-rock mountains.

Amina, who is twenty-six and Muslim, grew up in the town of El Fasher, in North Darfur. Twelve years ago, she married Haroun Adam Haggar, and moved a hundred and sixty miles north, to a farming village near the town of Furawiyah. They had six children, and made a good living growing sorghum and herding ten cows and some five hundred sheep. During my visit to northern Chad, in July, Amina told me that Arab nomads used to pass through Furawiyah with their animals, but they stopped doing so eight years ago. That was around the time that she first heard frightening stories about the *janjaweed*, nomadic Arab bandits who rode on horses and camels, and enriched themselves by stealing livestock and attacking Africans. ("*Jaan*" means "evil" in Arabic, and "*jawad*" means "horse"; "*janjaweed*" means, roughly, "evil horseman.") The *janjaweed* included local camel herders, and also nomads who migrated to Darfur from Chad and West Africa in the nineteen-seventies and eighties.

During the planting-and-harvest season, from August to November, Amina's oldest child, a ten-year-old named Mohammed Haroun, moved south with the livestock in search of grass and water. When the animals were brought back, four months later, they were ready to be sold, or used for leather, food, and milk.

In the months when Mohammed was at home, Amina recalled, she would accompany him and their animals to one of Furawiyah's two dozen wells. Amina would straddle the well, drop the bucket to the bottom, thirty feet down, and haul up the cool water; then she would empty the bucket into a trough for the animals, or into bags made of donkey hides, for storage. Mohammed would immediately follow her, sending the bucket tumbling into the darkness and using all his strength to mimic his mother's maneuvers.

By January this year, Amina told me, the townspeople of Furawiyah were on alert. The government was trying to crush a resistance movement that had emerged in Darfur, and it had enlisted the *janjaweed* as its foot soldiers. Amina's neighborhood had been inundated with family members, tribal kin, and displaced strangers, who had been driven from their homes by a combination of *janjaweed* raids and government air assaults. Many of these visitors had not stayed long. They had stopped in Furawiyah for water and quickly resumed their journey to Chad. They urged Amina to do the same. "The *janjaweed* are nearby," they said. "Leave while you still can."

Amina was no stranger to tribal killings. Five years earlier, the *janjaweed* had attacked a village outside El Fasher and murdered Africans, including two of her uncles and four of her cousins. But Amina told herself that her town would escape the violence spreading through Darfur. Unlike many towns in the region, it was guarded by policemen, who had helped fend off cattle rustlers in the past. Other villagers were less sanguine. Government helicopters had been flying overhead for three months, and some tribal leaders insisted that the Air Force was surveying the town for bombardment. They were right: soon, a military aircraft fired four rockets, two from each wing, on Furawiyah. The attack terrified Amina; although one rocket failed to explode, the others left large craters in the ground. She and her husband refused to abandon their land, but they sent all their children, except Mohammed, to hide in the mountains.

On January 31, Amina's husband was away visiting his family. Not long after dawn, when Amina and Mohammed arrived at the wells, they heard the sound of approaching planes. Fifteen minutes later, Amina recalled, the aircraft began bombing the area around the wells, where a group of her neighbors had also gathered. She and Mohammed were separated, as she fled with a few of the family's donkeys, and he tried to assemble their panicked sheep. According to Amina, dozens of people and hundreds of animals were killed in the onslaught.

In the wake of the planes came Sudanese soldiers, packed into trucks and Land Cruisers; they were followed by hundreds of menacing *janjaweed* on camelback and horseback. Most of the *janjaweed* wore turbans around their heads and mouths, so that only their eyes were visible. They carried *hijaab*, tiny leather boxes containing Koranic verses, which were meant to keep them safe from bullets.

When Amina saw the *janjaweed* approaching, she hurried the donkeys to a red-rock hillock three hundred yards away. She assumed that Mohammed had fled in another direction, but she turned and saw that he had remained at the wells, with the older boys and the men, in an effort to protect the animals. He and the others were surrounded by several hundred *janjaweed*. As the circle closed around her son, she ducked behind the hillock and prayed.

By nightfall, the sounds of gunfire and screaming had faded, and Amina furtively returned to the wells. She discovered that they were stuffed with corpses, many of which had been dismembered. She was determined to find her son, but also hoped that she wouldn't. Rummaging frantically around the wells by moonlight, she saw the bodies of dozens of people she knew, but for a long time she was unable to find her firstborn.

Suddenly, she spotted his face—but only his face. Mohammed had been beheaded. "I wanted to find the rest of his body," she told me. But she was afraid of the *janjaweed*, who had remained nearby to celebrate their conquest with a roast of stolen livestock. She gave up and carried her son's remains to the mountain where her other children were hiding. "I took my child's head, and I buried him," she told me, dabbing her tears with the tail of her head scarf. A week later, Amina took her five remaining children on the seven-day trek to Chad. The family's last surviving animal—a donkey—died upon their arrival.

. . .

Two days before the 2000 presidential election, George W. Bush met the Reverend Billy Graham for breakfast in Jacksonville, Florida. They were joined by Graham's son Franklin, the president of Samaritan's Purse, a Christian relief-and-development organization that has worked in Sudan since 1993.

Sudan, the largest nation in Africa, had been mostly mired in civil war since it won independence from Britain, in 1956. The central conflict, between Muslim government forces in the North and rebels in the South, began in 1955, abated in 1972, and resumed in 1983. Some two million people died because of the war, and many of them were Christians. The situation was deeply troubling to American evangelicals, and Franklin Graham had led an effort to raise money for victims. During the breakfast meeting, Graham told me, he urged Bush to turn his sights to the suffering of Christians in Africa. "We have a crisis in the Sudan," Graham said. "I have a hospital that's been bombed. I hope that if you become president you'll do something about it." Bush promised Graham that he would.

Sudan had already attracted an unusually formidable constituency in Washington. In the nineties, the Clinton White House imposed successive sanctions against the Sudanese government. Sudan had become a haven for terrorists—including Osama bin Laden, who had settled there in 1991—and had repressed religious minorities in the South; in addition, it had failed to crack down on a slave trade that had emerged there. Backed by Christian and African American constituencies, many U.S. lawmakers had traveled to Sudan. Senator Bill Frist, a surgeon, made several short trips there, serving as a volunteer doctor at the hospital in southern Sudan that had been bombed shortly before Graham's meeting with Bush.

President Clinton's approach was largely confrontational. In 1996, he withdrew the U.S. ambassador, citing terrorist threats against American officials. (There is still no U.S. ambassador in Khartoum.) The same year, the United States and Saudi Arabia pressured Sudan to expel bin Laden, who subsequently left for Afghanistan. In 1998, after Al Qaeda's attacks on the American Embassies in Kenya and Tanzania, Clinton ordered a Tomahawk-missile strike on the Al Shifa pharmaceutical factory, which was suspected of producing chemical weapons. (This suspicion remains unproved.) Meanwhile, the administration made little progress in curtailing Sudan's civil war. In 1999, Clinton announced the appointment of a special envoy to Sudan, but then never met with the person who filled the post.

President Bush was more attentive. He rejuvenated a multilateral peace process that had been hosted by Kenya since 1993. On September 6, 2001, he appointed John Danforth, an ordained Episcopal minister and a three-term senator from Missouri, his special envoy for peace in Sudan.

During the 2000 campaign, Bush frequently invoked the values of Midland, the Texas town where he and his wife, Laura, grew up, telling the *New York Times,* "People—if they want to understand me—need to understand Midland." Midland is home to several churches with sister congregations in southern Sudan. In November 2001, Midland hosted the International Day of Prayer for the Persecuted Church, an annual evangelical event. Some forty Midland churches participated, and many of them passed out leaflets on Sudan and devoted part of their Sunday services to the civil war and the slave trade there. A half-dozen Sudanese refugees spent the weekend in Midland and shared their stories. "They took us out of our comfort zones," Deborah Fikes, one of the event's organizers, said. "We Christians in the U.S. have to use our resources not to build bigger churches, and not to be even more concerned with being pro-life, but to show how we value life by protecting the lives that are being lost every day because of war, disease, and starvation." Midland's churches raised money for Sudanese schools, and local religious and civic leaders petitioned the White House and wrote letters to the government in Khartoum. The chief of mission at the Sudanese embassy in Washington deemed "the town of George Bush" important enough to respond personally to these letters.

In 2002, Fikes and other activists invited thirteen Sudanese exiles to visit Midland during its annual Christian-music festival, and paired them with local youths to construct two portable "Sudanese villages." The first had seven wooden huts with grass roofs, a large thatch-roofed church, and a market, modeled on that of a typical southern Sudanese town. The second consisted of six huts that had been burned or partly demolished. Fikes had ordered some plastic skeletons from a Halloween Web site and set them aflame ("with the town fire marshal on hand!"), so that they could be displayed as charred corpses. The American evangelical community's intense interest in Sudan put Danforth and the rest of the U.S. government team under considerable pressure.

The Bush administration was also aware that Sudan's oil reserves yield two billion dollars in annual revenue, although just a fraction of the oil has been tapped. (Oil was discovered in Sudan, by Chevron, in the nineteen-seventies, but it has been exported only since 1999.) These reserves, which were being exploited by China, Canada, and Sweden, were off limits to American companies, because of a 1997 executive order barring U.S. oil companies from operating in Sudan. Before U.S. companies could legally begin prospecting Sudan would have to end its civil war.

Danforth's overtures were surprisingly well received. The Sudanese government, a U.S. diplomat told me, was desperate to end U.S. sanctions and to court American oil investors, and in the wake of September 11 and the war in Afghanistan it wished to avoid being added to the administration's target list. The southern rebels, who saw that they stood little chance of dislodging the government, were also ready to negotiate.

Thanks largely to the sudden surge in U.S. involvement, the peace talks moved forward. Both sides agreed to allow the posting of a small team of civilian protection monitors. Fighting in the South abated, and Sudan's rival parties inched closer to a long-term political agreement that they hoped would end the civil war. The president, Omar al-Bashir, provisionally agreed to share about half the oil revenues with the South, and to permit Christians in the North to escape punishments dictated by Sharia—traditional Islamic law. Bashir even offered to give the South the right to secede from Sudan six years from the signing date, if irreconcilable divisions remained. In return, the rebel leader, John Garang, said he would be willing to serve as vice president in a postwar government. By December 2003, negotiators were so certain that a deal was imminent that two seats were reserved for Bashir and Garang at Bush's 2004 State of the Union address. The stage was set: Bush would delight his Christian constituency; U.S. businesses would gain access to Sudan's oil; and Sudanese civilians would stop dying. Moreover, at a time when the U.S. was isolated and mistrusted abroad, Bush would prove that he was capable of making peace as well as war—and in the process be seen as uniting Arabs and Americans, Christians and Muslims.

There was a difficulty with this scenario, however: Amina Abaker Mohammed's home region of Darfur had caught fire. At the same time that the Sudanese government was offering autonomy and oil profits to southern Sudanese, people in another neglected region, whose leaders had been excluded from the U.S.-backed peace talks, had risen up and demanded political reform and economic assistance. Just when Bashir's regime seemed poised to stop its raids in southern Sudan, it had launched a bombing campaign in western Sudan. Washington had a problem—and the people of Darfur had a far greater one.

.   .   .

Darfur, which is roughly the size of Texas, was an autonomous sultanate until 1916, when it was conquered by Britain and incorporated into Sudan. The area is topographically diverse—high desert in the north flows into lush grasslands in the south—and ethnically kaleidoscopic. It is populated by some ninety tribes and countless sub-clans. Virtually all of Darfur's six million residents are Muslim, and, because of decades of intermarriage, almost everyone has dark skin and African features. To a visitor, Darfurians appear indistinguishable.

Despite the tradition of ethnic mixing, the population has recently begun subdividing between "Arabs" and "Africans," who are known, derogatorily, as *zurga*, or "blacks." People of Arab descent tend to be nomadic, herding camels in North Darfur and cattle in the south. The three largest African tribes are the Fur—Darfur means "land of the Fur"—the Zaghawa, and the Masaaleit. The Africans generally farm, though certain groups, like the Zaghawa, sometimes maintain farms while also sweeping south with their herds during the harvest season. Competition among the tribes—for economic, not ethnic, reasons—has always been fierce, but

tribal leaders customarily resolved these disputes, and their decisions were respected by the authorities in Khartoum.

In the nineteen-eighties, however, competition for land intensified. There was a regional drought, and the expanding Sahara
began transforming arable soil into desert. The introduction of
tractors and other mechanized farming equipment fed the ambition of some African farmers. Arab herders in North Darfur
began to resent the seasonal forays of Zaghawa herdsmen into
Arab-occupied grazing areas. African farmers grew hostile to the
camel-riding Arab nomads from the north who increasingly
trampled their farmland as they roamed in search of pasture.
Arabs from countries to the west—Mauritania, Mali, Niger, and
Chad—also began flooding the region, exacerbating the feuds.
Farmers who had once celebrated the annual return of Arab nomads, whose animals had fertilized their farmland and helped
carry their harvests to market, began to impede their migrations.

Instead of intervening to defuse these tensions, Khartoum's
leaders essentially ignored them. A previous government had
weakened the tribal-administration system, in favor of state institutions that had little legitimacy in Darfur. As a result, the region
lacked a trusted system for resolving conflicts. The tribes grew
more polarized, and they began gathering arms to defend their
economic interests. Between 1987 and 1989, serious battles broke
out between Fur farmers and Arab camel herders. Some twenty-
five hundred Fur were killed, forty thousand cattle were lost, and
four hundred villages were burned; five hundred Arabs died, and
hundreds of the nomads' tents were burned. Even though a local
inter-tribal conference was held in 1989, its recommendations for
compensation and punishment went largely unheeded—leaving
outstanding grievances that would explode fourteen years later.

• • •

At 5 A.M. on Friday, April 25, 2003, a blast shook a tiny, one-
runway airport in El Fasher, the town of Amina's birth. It was fol-

lowed by six rapid detonations. Sleeping Sudanese soldiers, who were encamped in a nearby garrison, awoke and scrambled out of their barracks toward an ammunition depot across the street. Many of the soldiers, some still in their nightclothes, were picked off by machine-gun fire as they ran. Rebel Darfurian marksmen were perched high in the trees.

The attackers, members of a then obscure group, the Sudanese Liberation Army, did damage far greater than their numbers or their reputation. Employing two hundred and sixty men, forty Toyota Land Cruisers, four trucks, and mainly small-arms fire, they managed to take over a vital military outpost. Because the attack occurred on a Friday, the day of prayer in Sudan, when many soldiers are home with their families, the Sudanese military had mounted few patrols around the airport, and the rebels sneaked unchallenged onto the tarmac.

The raid, which lasted several hours, killed around a hundred soldiers. Five Antonov airplanes and two helicopter gunships were destroyed. (The government is said to have fewer than a hundred attack aircraft.) The rebels at first tried to disable the planes with haphazard gunfire; then someone shouted, "Hit the fuel tank," and the aircraft erupted in flames. The rebels also seized nineteen Land Cruisers and six trucks, and emptied several warehouses that were filled with weapons. (They almost made away with eight tanks, but they couldn't find the keys.) When the rebels left El Fasher, around midday, they had lost only nine men, and had kidnapped the head of the Sudanese Air Force, General Ibrahim Bushra Ismail, whom they released forty-five days later, after protracted negotiations with tribal leaders.

The rebel group, which was formed in February 2003, had legitimate complaints. Darfur's inhabitants felt that the region was being ignored. The Sudanese government rarely paid for road building and repair, schools, hospitals, civil servants, or communications facilities in Darfur. Those who considered themselves ethnically African were angered by the government's practice of awarding most of the top posts in the region to local Arabs, even though they were thought to be the minority there. Disgruntled Darfurians had appealed to the government to include their concerns on the agenda of the U.S.-backed peace process. This effort failed, and many concluded that, if they ever wanted to see their needs met, they would have to do what John Garang had done in the South: take up arms against the Sudanese government and try to get the world's attention.

The Sudanese Liberation Army's founding manifesto, which was posted on the Internet and circulated by hand in Darfur, invited Arabs and Africans alike to join in protesting Khartoum's "policies of marginalization, racial discrimination, exclusion, exploitation, and divisiveness." The group's objective, it said, was "to create a united democratic Sudan on a new basis of equality, complete restructuring and devolution of power, even development, cultural and political pluralism and moral and material prosperity for all Sudanese." All regions should have significant autonomy and work together under the banner of "Sudanism"—a shared identity for Arabs, Africans, Christians, and Muslims. The S.L.A. attempted to demonstrate its inclusiveness by appointing an Arab, Ahmed Kabour Jibril, to be its commander in South Darfur.

At first, the Sudanese government did not take the S.L.A. seriously, and dismissed its demands. At a rally in El Fasher on April 12, 2003, President Bashir downplayed the rebellion, calling it "acts of armed banditry." Two weeks later, after the devastating airport raid, the government decided to treat the rebels as a major threat.

•   •   •

During the conflict with the rebels based in the South, the Sudanese military had honed a strategy for combatting insurgents: the Air Force bombed from the sky, while Arab tribesmen, armed by the government, launched raids on the ground. In Darfur, the Sudanese Army needed to rely even more heavily upon local Arab militias. A majority of the Army's rank-and-file soldiers were from Darfur, and they could not be trusted to take up arms against their neighbors and kin. (Many Darfurians had served with the Army in the war against Garang's rebels.) By July 2003, the government was appealing to Darfur's Arab tribal leaders to defend their homeland against rebels whom they branded as "tora bora" (an allusion to the terrorist fighters based in the caves of Afghanistan).

Musa Hilal, a forty-three-year-old Arab sheikh, was one of the first to answer the government's call, and he soon became the co-ordinator of the *janjaweed* in Darfur. I met Hilal recently, at the Khartoum airport, outside a hangar for charter flights. It was 5:30 A.M. Hilal, who is six feet four and has an athletic, com-manding build, wore a white turban over a white lace skullcap; a pale-blue, crisply starched djellabah with a white, black-striped gossamer sash; and dark-brown loafers. Hilal's skin is the color of sand—much lighter than that of most Arabs in Darfur—and he has bright hazel eyes, long, curly eyelashes, and a faint goatee. He has the confident gait of someone who has spent his life in charge. During our encounter, he carried only two items: a wooden walk-ing stick capped with the head of a hound dog ("a gift from Switzerland") and a Nokia camera phone, which, when opened, displayed a photograph of himself on its screen.

Hilal was named sheikh of his Arab tribe, the Um Jalloul, in 1984, when he was twenty-three. He claims that his appointment was the will of the people, but others told me that he bullied his way to the title, assaulting rival contenders. Hilal long had a rep-utation in Darfur as a troublemaker who instigated skirmishes against the Fur and other African tribes, with the aim of control-ling more grazing land and amassing greater wealth for himself. But generally he enjoyed immunity. Indeed, the men under his command were notorious for the lengths to which they went to cover their trails. Ibrahim Suleiman, the former governor of North Darfur, told me that whenever one of Hilal's men died in an attack on a rival tribe he was beheaded by his fellow-tribes-men. The decapitated trunk was left at the scene, but the head was spirited away.

In the nineties, government officials tried repeatedly to have Hilal arrested. In 2002, they finally succeeded; Suleiman resorted to a tactic familiar to prosecutors of the Mafia—citing tax evasion, he detained Hilal. After being imprisoned for five months, Hilal was released on the condition that he would not return to Darfur. But, with the emergence of the S.L.A. rebellion, the government reassessed the situation, and decided to put Hilal's skills to use in Darfur. When Suleiman objected, he was fired. In 2003, with funds and arms from the government, Hilal set up a training camp near his home town of Mistiriyah, and rallied Arabs to the cause of suppressing the S.L.A. rebellion and populating the land with Arabs.

Hilal agreed to meet with me because he wanted to clear up the impression in the West that he is a *janjaweed*. When I mentioned the word, Hilal, who sees himself in regal terms, scoffed at what he considers a grave insult. In Sudan, nobody ever calls himself a *janjaweed*. Although many Africans in Darfur apply the term to any Arab civilian who carries a gun, government officials and Darfur's Arab-militia leaders, like Hilal, apply it only to the bandits—African and Arab—who have been hijacking and looting in Sudan's remote areas for decades. Western diplomats use "*janjaweed*" more broadly, to describe the Arab militiamen who have carried out much of the pillaging, killing, and raping in Darfur. These men, who receive orders on Thuraya satellite phones, have joined up with the Sudanese Air Force and Army, killing as many as fifty thousand Darfurians and destroying nearly four hundred villages. More than a million and a half people have fled from their homes—fifty refugee camps have been established in Chad, and a hundred and fifty unofficial sites have sprung up in

Sudan—but this hasn't stopped the *janjaweed*. They continue to terrorize, murdering men and raping women who dare to venture outside the camps.

"Don't you people understand what a tribal leader does?" Hilal asked, tapping his walking stick on the floor. "I answered my government's appeal, and I called my people to arms. I didn't take up arms personally. A tribal leader doesn't take up arms. I am a sheikh. I am not a soldier." I asked him about eyewitness reports that he had participated in burning and looting in Darfur. He laughed and rolled his eyes. "That is rebel gossip-speak," he said. "The *janjaweed* have taken advantage of the troubles to pillage. I've had to fight them myself, as a tribal leader."

Hilal offered to take me and two colleagues on a tour of Darfur. The Sudanese government provided the transport—a sign of how entwined he is with the authorities. We flew the four hundred miles from Khartoum to the El Fasher airport in a government-chartered plane, an old Russian aircraft that had few windows and was sweltering inside. When we reached El Fasher, Hilal was embraced on the tarmac by the Sudanese colonel in charge of border intelligence. Then we piled into a military transport helicopter; incongruously, female flight attendants were on board, as was a box of Thuraya satellite phones and a cooler filled with soft drinks. The flight attendants and the cooler made the return journey; the phones did not.

As the helicopter swept over the decimated landscape, Hilal stared placidly out the window, seeming not to notice the blackened and emptied villages below—a bleakness interrupted only occasionally by a few, presumably Arab, villages where boys still herded animals in the fields and women washed clothes and gathered firewood. But these emblems of the selectivity of ethnic cleansing were not of concern to Hilal. He wanted to show us his harmonious ties with the African tribes of Darfur.

When our helicopter landed in the town of Kala, in North Darfur, more than a thousand people rushed out to greet us. As we disembarked, Hilal turned to us and said, sarcastically, "You're in my territory now. You're in territory under the control of the leader of the *janjaweed*." A group of men strode forward, chanting "*Allahu akbar*"; they shouted praise for Hilal and shook walking sticks in the air. The women hung back and assembled in an orderly row; the collage of colors from their sarongs and scarves was blinding in the desert sunlight. A dozen or so of the women then performed a screeching song-and-dance number in Sheikh Hilal's honor.

When the welcomes subsided, Hilal led us underneath the largest tree in the semi-desert town, where we were served dates and orange Fanta. Tribal representatives rose to commend Hilal and the unity that he had fostered. "We live in harmony together in our different colors and tribes," one said. "We love each other. We marry each other. If you feel sick in one part of your body, you feel pain all over. We are like that here." Hilal, whose motions are deliberate and dramatic, tossed date pits onto a silver tray. He grew visibly impatient with the speeches and began barking commands to those around him as his supplicants droned on. "All of us have chosen a leader, the suitable man who will show us the good way," another said. "The man we have chosen is Musa Hilal. That's why we live here in peace."

I showed Hilal a recent State Department map that depicted the hundreds of villages that had been destroyed and burned by combined *janjaweed* and Sudanese Air Force attacks. The map designated destroyed villages in Darfur with small orange-and-yellow flames. Hilal pointed to Kabkabiyeh, a town in North Darfur where there had recently been a lot of fighting, and where many flames were clustered on the map. "Yes," he said, nodding. "This is where the government clashed with the rebels and aerial bombardment occurred." Then he squinted and gave the map a disapproving glance. "Many more villages have been destroyed than this!" he said. "What about Korma?" he asked. "Why is there no flame there?" I gave him my pen and urged him to demarcate his area of dominion. He drew a large triangle within which there was not a single flame marker.

Suddenly, Hilal turned toward the proceedings and cut off the elderly African man who was heaping encomiums upon him. "Let's have a woman speaker," Hilal snapped, in Arabic. Two women came forward; predictably, one was an African Fur, the other an Arab.

Hilal appears to have unlimited power in Darfur. A statement from local authorities in February instructed "security units in the locality" to "allow the activities of the mujahideen and the volunteers under the command of Sheikh Musa Hilal to proceed" in North Darfur and "to secure their vital needs." The document stressed the "importance of non-interference" and directed local authorities to "overlook minor offences by the mujahideen against civilians who are suspected members of the rebellion."

•　　•　　•

Later, in Khartoum, I met with Salah Abdallah Gosh, the head of the National Security and Intelligence Service, in his office. "Musa Hilal is not a criminal," Gosh said. Western diplomats say that Gosh is one of the principal architects of Khartoum's war in Darfur; he had never before granted an interview to a western journalist. "The non-Arabs passed the Americans wrong information. They said, 'Musa Hilal is the leader of the *janjaweed*.' But he is not. He is a leader of the Arab tribes. Musa Hilal is not a man who would burn down a village and kill the people and take their money. He is not like that. He was invited by the government to back the government Army, and he gave the people guns and leadership."

While in Khartoum, I also met with Mustafa, an eighteen-year-old from Kabkabiyeh, who had briefly trained with Hilal's militia. (He asked that his last name be withheld.) In October 2003, because of the fighting around his home town, Mustafa's school was closed. That December, he said, Hilal put out a call to young men in the area to attend a military camp in Mistiriyah, promising guns and a salary equivalent to ninety-five dollars per month. Although Mustafa is from an African tribe, he signed up; his parents were aghast. "You are going to join the *janjaweed*?" his mother said. "You are African, they are Arab. They will kill you." Mustafa, who believed what he had been told by the town recruiter, insisted that he was not becoming a *janjaweed* but, rather, was joining multi-ethnic "border forces," which would bring peace to the area.

In January, Mustafa and several hundred other youths boarded trucks that took them to the bustling Mistiriyah camp, where about five thousand fighters were said to be training. To Mustafa's frustration, they were not immediately armed. "Musa Hilal is the only one who can distribute weapons," the youths were told. Five days after they arrived, a Sudanese military-transport helicopter landed, and Hilal emerged from his tent, nearby. He presided over the unloading of twelve boxes of Kalashnikov and G3 rifles, Mustafa said, but he did not use the occasion to welcome the new cadets; instead, he returned to his tent for a feast. This time, the boys were told that they would get guns only when they embarked upon an official *mumariya*, a military mission.

Mustafa was already growing restless when some two thousand Arab militiamen returned to Mistiriyah from the field. The commanders arrived first, in eight Land Cruisers. More than a thousand men followed on horseback, with the remainder on camels or on foot. The camels were weighted down with chairs, bed frames, blankets, radios, suitcases filled with valuables—even the doors of houses. The fighters also brought hundreds of sheep, goats, and cows. The men paraded around the camp singing songs lampooning the Africans of Sudan. A few men who knew that Mustafa was African teased him, saying, "We are the lords of this land. You blacks don't have any rights here." He was told that the Arabs would be sent to attack local villages and civilians, while

Africans like him would be sent into high-risk conventional battle with the S.L.A. rebels—their ethnic kin. After two weeks in the camp, Mustafa had seen enough. He fled and has been in hiding ever since.

A week later, in South Darfur, I met Mahasin Abaker, the wife of Khadir Ali Abdul Rahman Hussein Abukoda, who was a prominent local leader of the Fur tribe. She was at home with her husband on March 27, when Hilal stormed into town wearing a Sudanese Army uniform with two stripes and an eagle. A military vehicle arrived at the front door, and Khadir was taken away. Soon thereafter, Mahasin recalled, Hilal's *janjaweed* horsemen and camel riders began looting, stripping shops and houses bare, even seizing the carpet from the local mosque. Khadir never returned home, and his wife feared that he had been killed. In April, though, Mahasin received a note from him, in which he said that he was being held by Hilal. On May 19, one of Hilal's officials sent a ransom note to the local emir of the Fur. "Concerning Khadir, if you want him released, send ten million Sudanese pounds"— four thousand dollars. "For the urgent resolution of this matter, please send the money as soon as possible. If you do not, his fate will be in your hands." The ransom note, which Mahasin showed me, was signed by the office of military intelligence in Mistiriyah. So far, Khadir's tribe has been able to raise only 7.5 million Sudanese pounds.

As Hilal's forces have expanded their zone of power, they have targeted Arabs as well as Africans. In May, some three thousand fighters arrived in the village of Khar Ramla. Witnesses told me that Hilal, this time dressed in a green camouflage Sudanese military uniform, summoned the male villagers to a meeting at sunset in a warehouse on the outskirts of the village. When the men arrived, they were surrounded by Hilal's gunmen and told that they could not leave. For the next four hours, the men heard the sound of the militiamen firing their guns and the screams of the women. The village was looted, and at least nine women were raped.

During our encounter, Hilal expressed disgust at the idea that his men would stoop so low as to commit rape, but his forces have been repeatedly accused of this crime. In February, the town of Tawilla, forty miles southwest of El Fasher, and its surrounding villages were attacked by Hilal's forces, witnesses said; seventy-five people were killed, and more than a hundred women and girls were raped—six of them in front of their fathers. A UNICEF study found that some girls were raped by as many as fourteen men. Surviving villagers told international investigators that, in addition, a hundred and fifty women and two hundred children had been abducted. Their whereabouts are unknown.

·　　·　　·

After meeting Amina Abaker Mohammed in Chad, I decided to travel, along with John Prendergast, of the International Crisis Group, to see the wells in Furawiyah where she said her son had been killed by *janjaweed* forces. In order to make our way to Furawiyah, which was in an area said to be in rebel hands, we had to cross the Chad-Sudan border illegally. The Chadian authorities had tightened up their border patrols in order to stop the *janjaweed* from crossing into Chad, to chase refugees and to loot villages. (In June, Chadian forces killed sixty-nine *janjaweed* who had attacked the village of Birak, which is four miles inside Chad.) Not surprisingly, it has proved impossible for the Chadian authorities to seal the eight-hundred-mile desert frontier. As a result, our only real challenge was scaling a steep wadi in an aging Land Cruiser. This done, we began the long, slow drive through the Sahara toward Furawiyah.

Our journey across the inhospitable terrain of northern Sudan resembled a virtual tour of the solar system: we saw the soft yellow powder of Earth's great deserts; the red-rock mounds of Mars; the volcanic gravel of Venus; the deep gray craters and gullies of Mercury. The hundred-and-thirty-degree heat, along with the terror inflicted by the *janjaweed* and the Air Force planes, had driven human life either into exile or into hiding. We felt utterly alone.

After five hours on the road, having advanced at less than ten m.p.h. and having seen only scattered camel carcasses, we suddenly glimpsed a procession of men and horses on the horizon, minuscule amid the expanse of desert. As we approached, we saw fourteen men making their way east with walking sticks in the scorching afternoon sun. Five horses hauled trailers piled high with rugs, sacks of millet, and various household necessities. The horses were so emaciated that their pelvic bones stuck out sharply.

The men were participating in a kind of underground railroad. They were Darfurian refugees, now living in tents in Chad; together, they had rented the horses and the trailers and stocked them with emergency food stores, which they were delivering to their kin who remained trapped in Darfur—those too old, scared, or infirm to make the trek. Once the refugees had emptied their load, they would travel for eight days to get back to Chad, carrying on the trailers people who wished to escape.

One of the men, Mahmoud Ibrahim Mustafa, who is thirty-eight, was making his second trip. He had already collected his two wives and seven children; now he was returning to gather his brother and sister-in-law and their seven children. S.L.A. officials claim that hundreds of thousands of people are hiding out in Darfur. Since many of them left their stores of grain behind and were robbed of their animals, they may be at risk of starvation.

The next day, as we drove deeper into Darfur, we came to the Zaghawa village of Hangala. Zaghawa villages are constructed functionally and hierarchically. The head of the household occupies a small, round stone hut, which is sealed with a conical thatched roof. The hut is around fifteen feet in diameter and sits in the center of the family compound. Around this hut are as many as seven smaller huts—one for each of the man's wives. The compound is enclosed by a fence, which is built of either straw or tree branches.

At Hangala, we found only the stone walls of the huts, which had been set ablaze. Each was filled with two feet of ashes; without their thatched roofs, the charred huts resembled beheaded figures. In the burned remains of Hangala—a village that had never had running water or electricity, and that was accessible only by following tire tracks in the thick sand—we came across the remnants of a jewelry box, a bicycle, women's slippers, and bottles of French perfume. The residents' animal and land holdings had made them comparatively rich, and this wealth had made them an inevitable target for the marauders. Of the four hundred and eighty people who lived in Hangala before the attack, we were later told, forty-six were killed. The rest are now homeless, scattered throughout Sudan and Chad.

The village abutting Hangala had been ransacked but not burned, perhaps because the attackers had wanted someplace to sleep the night of their rampage. One hut contained a child's backpack and his "Duckzilla" notebooks, which contained exercises in mathematics, Islamic studies, and Arabic. In another house, we found small packages of beans and nuts, a sign that the inhabitants had fled in a hurry, and a branding iron. As we left one of the huts, where pots had been overturned and valuables looted, we spotted three toothbrushes tucked into the thatch in the roof. Nestled next to them was a sheet of paper that had been folded into tight squares; upon opening it, we saw that it was a prayer from the Koran, urging Allah to keep watch over the family home.

Furawiyah was less than an hour's drive from Hangala, but before entering town we had to "register" with S.L.A. rebels, who manned a base on the outskirts. The S.L.A. commander in Furawiyah, a lanky thirty-eight-year-old Zaghawa wearing Army fatigues, a bright-yellow turban, and wraparound Ray-Bans, was lounging on a rug in the shade when we pulled up to the base. Under a nearby tree, unguarded, was a stack of a dozen or so rocket-propelled grenades. On his rug lay a laminated package of hot-pink pills. "They are malaria pills," the commander explained. "We stole them from the government. Everything we have we have stolen from the government." He didn't have malaria and, in this malaria-free area, stood little chance of catching it. He was just flaunting the fruits of victory.

I asked to be directed to the wells where Amina had collected water. As we drove toward them, with a local guide, we passed a large gray rocket that was partly lodged in the sand; this was the undetonated Sudanese Air Force rocket that Amina had described to me. We also passed an enormous crater, at least twenty-five feet in diameter and five feet deep, where another bomb had exploded. Antonovs are imprecise bombers, and the Sudanese Air Force crew simply heave their munitions out the planes' trapdoors. As a result, the planes have proved bad at killing S.L.A. rebels but good at bluntly wiping out civilian life.

"Here are the wells," our guide said as we pulled up to the red-rock hillock that Amina had depicted on a map she had drawn for me. I saw only more Sahara sand at the base of the rock. "What wells?" I asked. The guide kept pointing to the same patch of desert, and, frustrated, I stepped closer. There, barely visible beneath the pale-yellow sand, were the faint outlines of one large stone well and two smaller ones. This was where Amina and Mohammed had watered their animals, and where Amina had found the corpses of her slain neighbors and the head of her son. The *janjaweed* had buried the wells and their victims beneath many feet of sand. In so doing, they had not only made it more difficult for their crimes to be investigated; they had also destroyed vital water sources. Among the twenty-five wells in the Furawiyah area, only three were left unmolested—and those may soon dry up, owing to overuse.

The killers in Darfur are not always so careful. The young man who showed us the wells urged us to accompany him on a short drive outside Furawiyah. Fifteen minutes after leaving the town, he told us to park our Land Cruiser at the base of a slope and ascend by foot. The stench of decomposing flesh greeted us before we saw that rotting bodies were lying in the gullies on either side of us. There were the bodies of fourteen men, dressed in bloodied djellabahs or in shirts and slacks. Seventeen bullet casings lay scattered around them. The victims appeared to have been driven to this remote spot—the deep tread of vehicle tires was still visible— and then divided into two groups and lined up in front of the ditches. They had all been shot from behind, except for one man. His body lay not in a ditch but in the center of the slope, and one of his palms was outstretched, as if he were pleading for mercy.

．　　　．　　　．

Neither President Bush nor Kofi Annan, the secretary-general of the United Nations, spoke publicly about the killings in Darfur before March of this year, by which time some thirty thousand people had died as a result of ethnic cleansing. Thanks to the relentless efforts of Andrew Natsios and Roger Winter, two officials at the United States Agency for International Development, the U.S. government had begun attempting to deliver humanitarian aid to Darfur in February 2003. But the administration's top officials remained quiet. Cabinet members were, of course, preoccupied with Iraq, but even Washington diplomats who monitored Sudan chose not to speak out, for fear of upsetting the North-South peace process. By this time, some hundred thousand Darfurians had fled to Chad, in addition to the million or so people who had been displaced within Darfur—yet the North-South negotiations continued, as if nothing unusual were happening elsewhere in Sudan.

Last March, the U.N.'s humanitarian coordinator for Sudan, Mukesh Kapila, who had served a year there without denouncing Darfur's horrors, erupted. "The only difference between Rwanda and Darfur is the numbers involved of dead, tortured, and raped," Kapila said at the final press conference he gave before leaving his post. He told the BBC, "This is ethnic cleansing, this is the world's greatest humanitarian crisis, and I don't know why the world is not doing more about it." Kapila's statement was well timed. The following month, the world's leaders were to commemorate the ten-year anniversary of the systematic slaughter of eight hundred thousand Rwandans. Both Bush and Annan would have to issue statements on Rwanda, and the media interest aroused by Kapila's declaration made it impossible for the two leaders to avoid the subject of Darfur. In a statement on April 7, Bush condemned the "atrocities" in Darfur, saying, "The government of Sudan must not remain complicit in the brutalization of Darfur." Annan went further, raising the possibility of "military action." In May, Natsios and Winter issued a grim mortality survey predicting that, even if world leaders substantially increased aid to Darfur, three hundred thousand people would be dead by December. If world leaders ignored Sudan, they warned, a million could die.

The international media was extremely slow to post journalists to the region. Those who went tended to remain at the Chad border, for the Sudanese government often denied journalists' visa requests. But in May firsthand reports from Darfur began appearing, and the editorial boards of the *Washington Post* and the *New York Times* regularly publicized the crisis. Between April 1 and August 19, the *Post* ran twelve editorials. The *Times* ran only four, but its columnist Nicholas Kristof traveled twice to the Chad-Sudan border and wrote ten passionate columns about the atrocities.

On Capitol Hill, where interest in Sudan's oppression of Christians had always been high, members of Congress finally shifted their focus to Darfur. "We were late," Frank Wolf, a Republican congressman from Virginia, told me. "We so wanted to get peace in the South that it was like the Simon and Garfunkel song: 'A man hears what he wants to hear and disregards the rest.'" Wolf and Sam Brownback, a Republican senator from Kansas, visited Darfur in June and returned with grim refugee testimonies and video footage of torched villages. In July, Congress passed a resolution, introduced by Donald Payne, a Democratic congressman from New Jersey, to describe the killings in Sudan as "genocide"—the first time that Congress had described an ongoing massacre in such terms.

Bush's evangelical base offered full backing. That same month, Franklin Graham called the White House and told one of Bush's aides, "Just because you've signed a peace deal with the South doesn't mean you can wash your hands of Darfur." Samaritan's Purse, Graham's charity, is now transporting food aid by plane from Khartoum to Darfur. "Killing is wrong, whether you're killing a Jew, a Christian, or a Muslim," Graham told me. "I'm as concerned about what's happening in Darfur as I am about what happened in southern Sudan. It's evil. God made the people there in Darfur. For us to ignore them would be a sin." In August, fifty-one evangelical Christian leaders, representing forty-five thousand churches, called on the president to consider sending troops to Darfur to stop the "genocide."

For many African American leaders, the targeting of Darfurians on the basis of ethnicity has rekindled memories of apartheid. On July 13, Charles Rangel, the New York City congressman, and fifty protesters sang "We Shall Overcome" and were arrested in front of the Sudanese embassy in Washington. "We acted too late to save millions of Jews during World War II," Rangel said. "We didn't act at all when hundreds of thousands of innocents were slaughtered in Rwanda. We have the opportunity now to stop a genocide and we must act." Numerous other protesters were arrested in July, including Bobby Rush, a Democratic congressman from Illinois; Joe Hoeffel, a Democratic congressman from Pennsylvania; Ben Cohen and Jerry Greenfield, the co-founders of Ben & Jerry's, the ice-cream company; Rabbi David Saperstein, from New York; and four grandmothers from the Washington area.

In the end, America contributed $192.4 million in relief aid, pressed for multilateral U.N. denunciations, and dispatched Secretary of State Colin Powell to Darfur. The U.S. even compiled a kind of "Most Wanted" list of *janjaweed* leaders, who it said should be arrested and tried. No. 1 on that list was Musa Hilal.

•   •   •

Sudanese officials like Salah Gosh have developed two methods for deflecting American criticism. First, they meet every charge with a reference to the quagmire in Iraq. In Khartoum, when I asked Gosh about the Sudanese attacks on civilians, he told me that armies are made up of individuals. "In Abu Ghraib, there are violations by the U.S. Army," he said. "But the violations are not from the whole Army. The violations are from individuals. You cannot generalize." When I asked why Sudan had not complied with American demands that it disarm the *janjaweed,* he said, "The United States is facing those terrorist people in Iraq. Is it possible for the United States to disarm those criminals? Is it possible for the United States, with all of its equipment—it is a superpower—to disarm these people in one month, two years? Danforth stands there in the United States and says, 'The government of Sudan has just a few days to control the *janjaweed* and to stop those attacks.' If it's so easy, why don't you do it in Iraq?"

When I broached the prospect of international intervention, he said, "It will make things worse. People in Sudan do not like foreigners to control them. They would love to fight them. The United States should take care of the information it is building its decisions on. We have lots of cases where the United States was fooled by bad information—the bombing of the Al Shifa factory, the weapons of mass destruction in Iraq . . . We told the United States, 'We have bin Laden in Sudan. We can monitor him and divert his efforts.' They ignored our claim. We were told to send him out. What is the loss for the United States? How many people died?"

The government in Khartoum has also attempted to hide the evidence of its ethnic-cleansing campaign. It has integrated the *janjaweed* into the regular Army and police forces, pretended to arrest and prosecute war criminals, and tried to break up large camps of displaced persons.

Sudanese officials say that some eight thousand new police officers are starting to patrol Darfur. But refugees told me that they recognize many of these policemen as former *janjaweed*. Around the town of Kas, in South Darfur, where forty thousand refugees had taken shelter inside and outside local schools, the new police were visible. But it was clear that they had not been trained. One policeman, riding a camel, was wearing the navy-blue trousers of the Sudanese police and the green camouflage top of the Sudanese Army. Others were loitering in the Kas market wearing crisp blue police uniforms, but their turbans, the rifles slung over their shoulders, and their flip-flops gave them away as former *janjaweed*. In the local parlance, they had been "re-hatted."

When I met with Salah Gosh, on July 11, he said that forty-six *janjaweed* had been arrested in Darfur. A week later, a government official upped the number to sixty-seven. The state-owned media reported that in Nyala, a town in South Darfur, ten *janjaweed* had been sentenced to amputation of their right hands and left feet for their role in recent assaults. To confirm this, I scheduled an appointment with Nyala's top judge and got his permission to visit the jail on July 21. He presented me with files on the recently arrested. Seventeen *janjaweed* had been convicted so far, he said, and nineteen were awaiting trial. "This isn't just talk," he said, handing me the indictments. "This is proof." The documents were neatly filled out, and each listed the name of the prisoner and the section of the criminal code that had been violated. But when I looked more closely the papers seemed suspicious: every one of the nineteen new arrivals was said to have been processed on July 14 and was scheduled to begin trial on July 30. I made my way into the prison courtyard, where sixty-three inmates were gathered. The men who had already been convicted were sitting cross-legged on the right side, wearing mud-brown prison uniforms, and those awaiting trial sat on the left, dressed in grimy white djellabahs. The prison director urged me to question them. I asked how many had been arrested in 2004. Only four men raised their hands. Who had been accused of rape? None. Had any of them arrived at the jail on July 14? No. Had any of them even been arrested in the past three months? No. The Sudanese government was attempting to pass off criminals arrested several years ago as *janjaweed* but hadn't informed the prisoners of the ploy.

While in South Darfur, I also visited Sania Deleiba, a village south of Nyala, which was once home to four hundred and seventy-four families. In May, witnesses told me, government and *janjaweed* forces attacked, killing twelve people and looting and burning virtually all the houses. This summer, the government promised to provide monthly food supplies and an official police presence, and more than two hundred families returned. When I toured the village, residents explained that they had been unable to obtain food in Nyala or in the refugee camp in nearby Kalma. They said they thought they might still be able to plant in time for the August rains.

It is no accident that this tiny village was chosen as the site for such a pilot—or, more likely, Potemkin—program. Sania Deleiba is an easy ride from Nyala, one of the few Darfur towns with an airport, on roads that will remain passable throughout the rainy season. International dignitaries could be escorted there for short visits, and they would find battered but resilient Africans living alongside their Arab neighbors.

None of this means that Sania Deleiba is a safe place to be. When I visited, the police were scattered about the town's perimeter, but they looked incredulous when I asked if they would try to arrest any *janjaweed*, some of whom had been seen lurking on horseback nearby. "No way," one said. "We hope that when they see us they won't attack. But if they do there's nothing much we can do."

On numerous occasions, the Sudanese government has threatened to force people in the camps to go home, but the U.N. has insisted on a voluntary-return policy. As a result, in August there were a number of incidents in which masked gunmen swept into camps in the middle of the night and abducted village leaders. The leaders returned the next morning, limping and bruised, saying that their assailants had threatened to kill them if they didn't take their people home.

In Kas, the town where schools had become impromptu shelters, officials were determined to move displaced people to a nearby swampy area, where they would be separated from the town by a wadi. Several police tents had been set up in the swamp, in order to create the impression of a secure environment. But, as I talked with the policemen inside one tent, a forbidding trio of men on camelback carrying G3 rifles rode by outside. I pointed to the *janjaweed* and asked the policemen, who were African, if they would make arrests if they learned of attacks on the refugees. "We don't have instructions to arrest them," one said. "If we captured them, we would be sacked." Another added, "There are six of us here and thousands of them. They have heavy weapons and modern weapons, and we have these old Kalashnikovs. If we arrest one of them, they'll come after our families." The policemen said that the government had given each of them only one gun cartridge.

·   ·   ·

Soon after Colin Powell's visit to Sudan this summer, the government relaxed its visa and travel requirements, and the number of expatriate aid workers leaped from three dozen, in March, to nearly five hundred, in August. The U.N., which had established a food program in Darfur, expanded its scope, reaching nine hundred thousand of the estimated one and a half million in need. Nonetheless, the displaced continued to live in deplorable conditions. In the camps, sanitation was poor, raising worries about outbreaks of cholera and measles. Residents remained vulnerable to constant *janjaweed* attacks. And they still had no prospect of returning home to safety; *janjaweed* assaults on African villages continued.

Not long after Powell's visit, I went to the refugee camp in Kalma, where thirty-five thousand displaced persons have arrived just since June. New residents had taken up patches of land at the edge of the camp, and, using grass and acacia branches, were beginning the meticulous process of assembling their new homes. Some hunted fruitlessly for plastic sheeting or clothing that could shield their families during the nightly downpours. The new arrivals shared familiar tales of attacks by the *janjaweed* and the Sudanese military.

Throughout the crisis in Darfur, the government's agenda has remained obscure. Why, exactly, has it armed and funded the *janjaweed*, bombed African villages, and purged or killed so many non-Arabs? One theory holds that the slaughter and deportations in Darfur are part of a master plan that was hatched in the late nineteen-eighties, by political hard-liners, to "Arabize" Sudan. Around that time, Colonel Muammar Qaddafi, of Libya, began promoting "Arabism" as a political ideology in sub-Saharan Africa, backing armed Arab rebels in the region and fostering grander dreams of an "Arab belt." In October, 1987, twenty-three Arab intellectuals sent a letter to Sadiq al-Mahdi, Sudan's prime minister at the time. The letter, which was published in the local press, credited the "Arab race" with the "creation of civilization in the region . . . in the areas of governance, religion and language." The signatories demanded a larger proportion of local, state, and national jobs, warning, "If this neglect of the participation of the Arab race continues, things will break loose from the hands of the wise men to those of the ignorant." Soon afterward, the process of removing Africans from senior civil posts in Darfur and replacing them with Arabs began. The current assaults on Darfurians who are considered "black" are thought by some to be phase two of Sudan's Arabization plan.

A second theory, which is slightly kinder to the leaders in Khartoum, holds that the Sudanese government, which in 2002 had just agreed to grant a right of secession to rebels in the South, could not afford to placate another rebel group. To do so would have emboldened disaffected minorities throughout the vast country, ultimately unraveling the patchwork state of Sudan. The government was particularly reluctant to lose Darfur, a Muslim territory. It therefore decided to quash the rebellion, gambling that Musa Hilal and other Arab tribal leaders in Darfur, as well as Arab-immigrant fighters, would serve as reliable proxies. (In return, the Arab militias could freely plunder villages.) The Sudanese government could hardly have predicted that an obscure, inaccessible Muslim region like Darfur would become a cause célèbre in America. Nor could it necessarily have expected that, even after it had emptied out more than half of Darfur's African villages, the *janjaweed* would continue attacking so many civilians.

Regardless of whether Sudan's murderous campaign in Darfur stems from a racist conspiracy, a counter-insurgency strategy run amok, or a combination of the two, its policies deserve to be condemned. Yet international opinion has been strangely divided. Europe's lingering hostility to the Bush administration over the invasion of Iraq seems to have infected its response to Darfur. In April, at a meeting at the U.N. Human Rights Commission, in Geneva, European diplomats opposed a strong American denunciation of the atrocities, preferring a resolution so watered down that Sudan welcomed it. At a time when America had given twenty-eight million dollars to the U.N.'s Darfur relief program, Germany had given one million dollars, and France nothing.

European officials have also been unduly trusting of Khartoum's assurances that it intends to solve the crisis. This summer, Renaud Muselier, the French secretary of state for foreign affairs, argued publicly that the Americans were overreacting. He invoked recent comments of Kofi Annan, who said that the killings and purgings in Darfur were only "bordering on ethnic cleansing." Muselier told Radio France, "Kofi Annan, who is very careful in his choice of words . . . has said very clearly that this was not genocide. That is what I also believe." When asked if the atrocities in Darfur constituted ethnic cleansing, he said, "No, I firmly believe it is a civil war." The Sudan *Vision*, a government-controlled newspaper, hailed the French stand, crediting Paris with "slamming U.S. foreign policy."

The State Department has stopped short of calling the atrocities in Darfur genocide, but Pierre-Richard Prosper, the U.S. ambassador-at-large for war crimes issues, has pointed to "indicators of genocide." The campaign of massacres, rapes, and ethnic cleansing may well fit the definition of genocide established by the Genocide Convention, which does not require a Rwanda-style extermination campaign but, rather, an attempt to "destroy" a substantial "part" of a group "as such." But genocide is a crime based on intent, and pin-pointing who has acted with the goal of destroying Darfur's non-Arab groups will remain difficult unless investigators dig up the wells, examine the ravines, apprehend perpetrators, and ascertain the command-and-control relationships among Sudanese leaders, Air Force pilots, and Arab militiamen. This will not happen soon: the major powers have not established an intelligence-gathering operation in Darfur that is sophisticated enough to gauge either the death toll or the intentions of perpetrators. In the meantime, the debate over semantics has only further distracted the international community from the more important debate about how to save lives.

In late July, the U.N. Security Council passed a resolution imposing an arms embargo on the *janjaweed* and the S.L.A. rebels, and threatening the Sudanese government with "further action," such as an asset freeze or a travel ban, if it did not show substantial progress within thirty days in disarming the *janjaweed* and bringing war criminals to justice. But the Sudanese government has made it clear that it will not disarm Musa Hilal or other Arab tribal leaders. The Arab tribes have carried guns for decades, and they would never give them up. Moreover, if they did, Arab civilians could be left vulnerable to revenge attacks by aggrieved Africans.

What is most needed in Darfur is an international peacekeeping and protection presence, and this is what the Sudanese government most wants to avoid. When Britain and Australia announced in July that they were considering sending troops for peacekeeping, a Sudanese group calling itself Mohammed's Army appealed to young Muslims to fight the arriving foreigners. "We call upon you to head immediately to Darfur and dig the ground deep for the mass graves for the crusader army," one recruiting statement said. Musa Hilal, who in recent months had been lying low in Khartoum, reportedly returned to his base in Mistiriyah to begin training his troops for clashes with foreign peacekeepers.

The most realistic hope for peacekeepers comes from the fifty-three-member African Union. In April, the S.L.A. and the Sudanese government signed a temporary ceasefire, and the A.U. agreed to send a hundred and twenty unarmed monitors to Darfur. It was a hopelessly small number, given the size of the region, and those observers were slow to deploy. Moreover, the A.U. officials were limited to investigating violations of the ceasefire. They weren't supposed to combat the biggest threat: *janjaweed* and military attacks on Darfur civilians. In August, Rwanda and Nigeria agreed to send a hundred and fifty soldiers each to Darfur, and the A.U. countries are pushing for permission to send several thousand more, with a mandate to protect civilians. Sudan has thus far refused.

Although the A.U. seems likely to expand its presence, almost all the displaced Africans I spoke with in Darfur said they would trust only western forces to bring peace. African troops were too susceptible to bribes, they said, and African governments would end up siding with Khartoum, as they had in the past. "We will not return to our homes until the white people come and make us safe," Abdum Shogar Adem, a thirty-two-year-old father of three, told me at the Kalma camp in July, soon after his village had been attacked by government helicopter gunships. The western powers, however, are not likely to answer Adem's call. The United

States military is overstretched, given the occupation of Iraq, and it is unwilling to contribute troops for a peacekeeping mission. It has not even offered to equip or transport A.U. troops, which lack the logistical sophistication to deploy on their own.

The Bush administration has been admirably willing to send relief to Sudan and to condemn the *janjaweed*. But, having alienated many of its U.N. allies with its unilateralism and perceived moralism, it has been unable to rally other nations to the cause. Countries like Russia and France have exploited the U.S.'s loss of standing internationally to justify their own inaction on Sudan. Meanwhile, the administration, which views the International Criminal Court with contempt, has not urged the U.N. Security Council to refer the atrocities in Darfur to the court, although no other international institution is equipped to prosecute such crimes. In the end, the U.S. has applied just enough pressure to get humanitarian relief to many Darfurians, but not enough to persuade the perpetrators of violence to lay down their arms. Meanwhile, the seasonal rains have begun to fall, reducing the reach of international aid workers and substantially increasing the risk of cholera, dysentery, and mass death.

·　　·　　·

It is hard to view Amina Abaker Mohammed, the refugee in Chad whose son was beheaded, as fortunate. Her husband, too, never returned home, and is presumed murdered. But in certain respects her current state is preferable to that of displaced people who are still in Darfur. Although she has to worry about feeding her five children, she can feel relatively secure when she goes scouring for firewood. In Sudan, by contrast, displaced people in camps remain as fearful of *janjaweed* attacks as they were when they inhabited their villages.

Because the food that comes from aid groups must be cooked before it becomes edible, in the camps wood is a commodity as precious as millet and flour. Foraging for wood is women's work in Sudan; but, given the high incidence of rape outside the camps, families have begun sending out women who are old or considered unattractive. This does not seem to have deterred the *janjaweed*, however.

In Kas, the displaced people living in makeshift tents near the schools must venture outside town to find wood. When the refugees first arrived, they had to walk a few hundred yards into the neighboring savanna to find fuel; now, with the nearby wood used up, they must walk for as long as an hour—and that will only increase with time. Two days before I arrived, in late July, Aisha Abdullah Youssef, twenty-two, and Asha Muhammed Abd el-Karim, twenty-seven, were captured by *janjaweed* soldiers while gathering wood, and were gang-raped. When I spoke with the women, they kept their eyes fixed on the ground. Their attackers had stripped them of their clothes, and they had returned naked to the crowded camp; word spread quickly that they had been violated. As I listened to their stories, a queue formed of people who wished to share their tales of recent assault. Others pointed to reddened gashes in their feet and backs; the marks, they said, were from worms that had pierced their flesh at night as they slept on the hard earth.

I noticed a woman who was sitting nearby with a child on each side of her. She was trying to stir millet over a fire, but she had no wood and was having little luck using grass to make a flame. Both children looked extremely weak; their legs were bone thin, and pus caked around the eyes of one child. The woman, Rashida Abbas, came from Kailek, a town a few hours away; in March, Rashida said, more than a hundred men had been summarily executed there, including her husband. She had six children before the conflict, but only four had survived.

When the *janjaweed* came, Abbas told me, her oldest child, a boy, had run ahead of her. She had carried her infant on her back, and she had taken one of her girls in each hand. This hadn't left her with a free hand for either of her younger sons, five-year-old Adam Muhammed and seven-year-old Hassan Muhammed. They trailed behind as the Arab soldiers threw matches onto the roofs of the huts. An Arab militiaman suddenly grabbed the boys, and Abbas pleaded that they be released. The gunman warned her that if she didn't shut up, all of her children would be killed. She backed away as instructed, but as she did so the man threw five-year-old Adam into the fire. "Mama, Mama!" he shouted, as the flames consumed him. Hassan, his older brother, briefly escaped his captor's grasp, but as he ran toward his mother he was shot in the back twice and died instantly.

It is no wonder that Darfurians say that they will not return to their homes unless international peacekeepers are deployed to protect them. They will never trust Khartoum again.

•   •   •

As I talked with Musal Hilal in the El Fasher airport waiting room, he discussed the possibility that he and other *janjaweed* leaders could have their assets frozen and their ability to travel curtailed. "I have no assets in international banks, so that is not a problem," he said as he watched Sudanese soldiers ready our plane for its flight back to Khartoum. "But the travel ban—that would be a humiliation. I am a tribal leader. My reputation comes above anything and everything."

Hilal is aware that if the international pressure on Khartoum intensifies the government might sell him out. This explains why he courts western journalists, staging elaborate shows of African-Arab unity. But he also knows how risky it would be for the government to challenge him—even if it wanted to appease its international critics. Khartoum's leaders rely on tribal militias as their main weapon of war. And, in Hilal's case, the Sudanese government helped create him, and he knows too much.

"The government call to arms is carried out through the tribal leaders," Hilal said. "Every government comes and finds us here. When they leave, we will still be here. When they come back, we will still be here. We will always be here."

Sports Illustrated

FINALIST—PROFILE WRITING

As the Athens Games approached, nobody cared about the Olympic event of race walking. But Albert Heppner, the American son of a Holocaust survivor, cared far too much. In "Walking His Life Away," master profiler Gary Smith, takes us on a four-hour walk across the embers of one man's obsession, all the way to the railing of a mountain bridge.

Gary Smith

Walking His
Life Away

W ho knows why?
In two weeks they'll light the world's largest wick,
let some white birds loose and then start lining up
men and women from around the earth to see who can run the
fastest from here to there. The fastest down straightaways, around
curves, over barricades, through puddles, even clenching metal
sticks. Who knows why? For days you'll sit in front of your TV and
watch all of these races. Except for one.

It's the oddest and longest footrace, the one that *forbids* the
competitors to go as fast as they can—in fact, that forces them to
walk. It's the one Olympic race you'll scoff at, at first. Then ignore.

That's the race I'll be watching closest. See, I know what happened one day five months ago in the race to get to this race. I
know how much can be at stake when a man takes a four-hour
walk: Everything.

•   •   •

Al Heppner was the first race walker to arrive. He appeared just as
dawn did on the U.S. Olympic Trials fifty-kilometer course at
Chula Vista Marina, a few miles south of San Diego. His stomach
hurt. He hadn't slept. No one had ever wanted a race as badly as
he wanted this one.

The others began to materialize in the wan gray light on that Sunday in February: the race officials, the media, the walkers and their dearest friends and loved ones, along with a few dozen high school cheerleaders that the event's organizer had mustered to create noise and excitement.

No one else cared about race walking. No one else would watch men or women walk that funny walk for hour after hour. Neither the NCAA nor the U.S. and European pro track circuits bothered to hold the event. Bob Costas, NBC's Olympics host, would say that having a race to see who can walk the fastest is like having a contest to see who can whisper the loudest.

The walkers assembled for the 7:30 A.M. start. They'd all long since made it to the other side of mirth and disdain. They'd all had seven-year-olds follow them and ape their pumping arms and swaying hips. They'd all heard twenty-year-olds barrel by in rusting cars and scream *Fag!* at them on country roads. They'd all shed their need for the world's approval, attuned their ears and hearts to an inner voice. Except for one.

Al stood out. He was the five-foot-eight-inch pied piper of race walking, the twenty-nine-year-old with the munchkin's cackle who was loved by everyone in his fringe fraternity. The one so loud that other walkers would remind him to use his indoor voice. So vulnerable that he'd sob on a stranger's shoulder after being disqualified from a race. So exuberant that he'd end up on the dance floor at a postrace party, his shirt soaked, juking like no Jew ever juked, encircled by people chanting, "Go, Al! Go, Al! Go, Jiggy!" Rabbi Jiggy. That was just one of his nicknames.

"Don't *make* it happen, Al," fellow race walker Dave McGovern counseled him at the starting line. "*Let* it happen." Al nodded. He had heard it a thousand times: Patience. Stay inside yourself. Walk the first 25K slower than the last 25K. Don't try to bust open a thirty-one-mile race early. It's lethal, Al.

Only he and four other Americans—Curt Clausen, Philip Dunn, Sean Albert and Tim Seaman—had a real shot at the four-hour time necessary to qualify for the Athens Olympics. No more than three could go. They'd all trained together every day for years at the ARCO Olympic Training Center in Chula Vista.

Foremost loomed Curt, the reigning U.S. champ, the gritty U.S. champ determined to make his third straight Olympics, then return to law school. Philip, the quiet bookworm—Al turned inside out—had been Al's enemy a few years earlier, the two of them forever clashing for the third berth on national teams, but who could sustain anger at a puppy like Jiggy? Mild-mannered Sean seemed on the verge of breaking the four-hour barrier for the first time, nearly in command of his long legs and arms in this cruelly mechanical event. Tim, Al's fiery roommate at Wisconsin-Parkside, was a 20K specialist who had said he'd likely stay in the race for 30K and then pull out, use it for conditioning . . . or was he lying in the weeds, ready to pounce if he saw a chance to steal an Olympic berth at 50K?

"Go, Al!" a fan screamed as the gun sounded and the walkers took off. Who wouldn't root for him? He was the greeter at the gate, the man who popped up from his moonlighting post behind the customer-service desk at the training center dining hall and showed all the newcomers where to get their mail, their rub-downs, their grub, then helped them haul in all their belongings, thrilled to welcome one and all—Americans and foreigners, swimmers, skiers, shot-putters, shortstops—to the fantasy factory in the Southern California desert. He'd carry his lunch tray to the far table where a new arrival ate alone. He'd take the Honduran cyclist to the airport at 5 A.M., beg the outraged decathlete to make peace with the offending kayaker, concoct nicknames for them all. *Hey, V-Dub! Big John Stud, my man! What's happenin', Apples?* He turned his cramped dorm room into the campus lounge, the gathering place for field trips organized by camp counselor Al to the amusement park, beach, ball games, bars and dance clubs. He turned all these masters of abstruse and exotic athletic skills into the most unexpected thing: a family.

"You can do it, Al!" came the cries as he and the four other favorites, in a cluster, fired away from the pack. Al settled into rhythm and felt the nightmare of the 50K begin: his heart pumping hard enough to generate three to three and a half steps per second, equivalent to the rate of a one-hundred-meter sprinter, pumping even harder than a marathon runner's heart because he had to use more of his body to create locomotion and then maintain that rate for nearly two hours longer. His gait requiring a gymnast's explosive strength in the hips and hamstrings, a dancer's fluidity. The mental strain unrelenting, because if he fatigued or lost focus covering those thirty-one miles at a 7:40-per-mile clip, he could violate one of race walking's two bedrock rules and be disqualified. One rule stipulated that his lead leg remain straight from the moment of contact with the ground till the leg passed beneath his hips. Al could usually follow that one. The other one, the rule that tortured him no end, decreed that at least one foot be in contact with the racecourse—both feet could never be off the ground at the same time.

Agony loves company. That's why most 50Ks began the way this one did. The best walkers broke away and forged an unspoken pact, one man doing the hard slogging out front for a few minutes, cutting wind resistance, then dropping back and drafting behind the next leader, each man drawing psychological comfort from the group for thirty-five or forty kilometers, functioning on trust. Trust that his competitors would sustain a pace that would keep him on target. Deeper trust, in himself, that he'd have what it takes to devour them all in the jungle of the final ten kilometers.

For the first seven kilometers Al, Curt, Philip, Tim and Sean upheld the agreement. Then Curt grabbed a handful of toilet paper from a tabletop and began to surge away.

What should Al do? Stay with Curt, the race walking sages had advised him. After all, they said, he knows the 50K's secrets and trip wires the way a husband knows his wife's. Let him take you to a 3:58 finish, Al, take you all the way to Athens.

But now Curt, far too early, was pulling away. Did the tissue paper in his hand mean what it seemed to, that he was about to make a toilet stop and was speeding up to compensate for the time he was about to lose? Or could it be a ruse?

Al's competitive lust had cost him before. Once, when he was six and his father's bike moved ahead of his, he'd pedaled so furiously that he'd pitched over the handlebars and broken his arm. At camp six years later he broke his arm again, astonishing counselors who had never seen a boy dive with such fury in a friendly game of Capture the Flag. Too many times he'd been disqualified from races because he couldn't restrain his urge to go faster, faster, couldn't keep both feet on the ground.

Curt's lead increased. The race walkers all let him go, mindful of that toilet paper. Except for one.

•   •   •

No, Al, No. . . . Those who knew race walking muttered those three words as he went after Curt. They all wanted to protect Al. They all knew the story of Al and the monsoon in the 2000 U.S. Olympic Trials. They all knew how he'd had one of the three Olympic berths in the bag that day, leaning into the thirty mph winds and frigid downpour to share the lead with Curt and Andrew Hermann, opening up a seemingly insurmountable two-and-a-half-minute advantage over Philip Dunn after thirty-seven kilometers when Philip pulled a hamstring and stopped dead. How Al had slowed a little then, had lost the protection of the other two walkers and begun to shiver, then shake and finally shut down with hypothermia, watching in a daze as Philip bit back the pain and stormed past him to become the third Olympian. How Al had swooned into a race official's arms before the finish, been cocooned in blankets for an hour before comprehending the catastrophe and weeping. Then lapsed into a deeper fog, finally departing from the Olympic Training Center by mutual consent because no man that depressed could remain there.

If only Al had done what the other walkers had done before the race: put on a T-shirt beneath his singlet. But then, people were always saying, "Al, what were you thinking?" The first oven he ever owned caught fire because Al thought that he was supposed to keep oven mitts *in* the oven. One night his roommate at Chula Vista, triple jumper Von Ware, returned from a three-day road trip during a rainstorm and found all his shoes on their balcony because Al had decided to rearrange their dorm room. The balcony had no overhang. Ware's shoes were soaked, and one sneaker contained a swallow's nest with four eggs. Ware wanted to wring Jiggy's neck as the swallow dove and pecked and shrieked at them, but how could he? Al was his, and everyone else's, little brother.

Al's six-month depression after the 2000 trials frightened all of them. For half the day Al would lie in bed or on a couch, staring at floors, at ceilings, at *SportsCenter* repeats. "No, Al, no," they pleaded when he told them he was joining the U.S. Army that August.

But everyone was wrong. Boot camp jolted Al out of his depression, the Army accepted him into its World Class Athlete Program, and—bingo!—that December, Specialist Albert Heppner was back. Back in race walking, back in the ARCO Olympic Training Center, back in his old dorm room, back in the family. His old buoyant self again, leaping out of his car to dance the Electric Slide with a pretty pole vaulter on the side of the road at 2 A.M., another of those women whose relationships with Al didn't quite pan out. And now, back in the U.S. Olympic Trials, chasing his redemption, closing in on Curt in kilometer ten.

It wasn't a ruse. Curt peeled off the course and ducked into the portable toilet. Al, the man who needed people all around him, looked back. He was way out front, all alone.

•   •   •

What should Al do? The men behind him had stuck together for years, and Al was their glue. He exchanged gifts and shared holiday meals with them, played hoops in Mexico and gasped for oxygen with them during altitude training in the Andes. He was the mediator, the one who needed most to be liked . . . and yet the one who'd turn grim and silent a few weeks before a big race, torch the pace that coach Enrique Peña set for them in training, take off and turn practices into wars.

The contradiction of his two needs—for love and conquest—contorted him, confounded him, churned again and again in his training log entries: *Focus on yourself!* In how many other athletic disciplines would America's highest-ranked rivals find themselves together on a five-hour hike at the bottom of a gorge, as they did a few days after last Thanksgiving in the mountains west of San Diego, marveling as they stared 450 feet up at the Pine Valley Bridge, the highest in the U.S. interstate system? Chortling together after Al reached into a thatch of poison oak and then made matters worse, much worse, when he took a pee?

Now Al faced the second critical juncture in the race of his life, a decision that cried out for the least of his skills: calculation. He could slow his pace and rejoin the others, as the cognoscenti hoped. Or he could roll the dice, maintain his pace and his lead, begin to sow doubt in his competitors' hearts. After all, he'd left the pack and walked a sub-four-hour 50K once before, a 3:58:45 second-place finish to the late-charging Curt in the 1999 U.S. nationals. He was in better shape now, the best condition of his life, and better form too, having surprised even himself by winning the award for best technique in a race just a few weeks before.

Damn it all, he'd been beating every one of them, even Curt, in their daily training sessions over the past few weeks. Why should Al shadow Curt and settle for a second- or third-place ride to Athens when he could *win* and go in style?

Curt popped out of the john and fell in with the others. Al made up his mind. No, he wouldn't slow down and rejoin the men behind him. No, he wouldn't maintain his lead and his pace. He *accelerated* and began to pull farther away.

The numbers flashed on the website monitoring the race. The walking fraternity across the country joined the ones along the course murmuring those three words. *No, Al, no. . . .*

.   .   .

His lead swelled to thirty seconds . . . forty-five . . . a full minute! He heard his mother's squeaky voice imploring him onward. He glimpsed his father cheering him on too, no matter how perplexed the old man was. Seventy-one-year-old Max Heppner cared nothing for sports, couldn't fathom how a footrace had become life and death to *his* flesh and blood. As a child in the Netherlands he'd had to run for his life, hiding from the Nazis for three years in an attic, a barn, a windmill, a bathhouse, a chicken house.

Max lost his grandfather to the gas chambers, his father to disease and his companion in hiding—a boy eight years older than he—to a hammer blow from one of the people Max's father was paying to hide them from the Nazis. When the horror ended, he and his grief-ravaged mother washed ashore in America, where he eventually married and for fifteen years tried to live as if the Holocaust hadn't happened to him, tried to muster the only response a man could make to six million deaths: creating one new life. Finally, when Max and his wife, Evelyn, had almost given up hope, came the miracle: Albert.

Then, four years later, the wallop. Max left his wife and son, having fallen in love with a therapist who'd lost relatives to the same butchers, a woman with whom he could finally talk about the depression and nightmares from all the memories he'd buried. Evelyn turned Al over to her sister in Cleveland and sank into depression too. Nobody could say how it all affected the boy, but he didn't take it sitting down. He bounced off walls, crawled under chairs, ricocheted through stores, ran circles around his house when he returned home to Columbia, Md., a few months later.

He kept slipping out of the quiet house, finding his way into a chair at neighbors' dinners, materializing in the empty seat at strangers' restaurant tables. Evelyn took him to see a play and nearly choked when she looked up during a dance number and saw Al on stage, shimmying for all he was worth. He ended up on Howard High's pep squad, the only white boy among a flock of African American girls, bringing down the house with his hip-hop moves. Sure, depression was rampant among children of Holocaust survivors, but how could it catch that dynamo out there with the gold chain, backward cap and baggy clothes all a-flapping?

His father, by now, had found a mission. He'd joined a group of Holocaust survivors and organized an international seminar on the subject, begun delivering lectures and laying plans for two books and a movie he would produce about his family's experience, all under his new name, Amichai—Hebrew for "my people live." Al stopped staying with him every other weekend and in summers. He wasn't going to be the son of a Jewish Holocaust survivor. He was going to be a winner, baby, red, white and blue.

One problem: He had to be an athlete first. He was too short and scrawny to play the all-American sports he adored, but there was one thing, God knows, that he could do: run circles. He became one of the top three distance runners at his high school, amazing teammates when he'd run off after races to run some more, but it wasn't enough. He wasn't the best. One day when he was fifteen, he and a buddy shook with laughter at a Junior Olympics meet as they watched some little kids bobbing around the track in a most peculiar way. "I'll do that next week," Al said. "You watch."

"Bet you a dollar you'll *never* do it," said his friend. Al entered the next week's 3K race walk, drawn to the strange discipline that both released and restrained his boundless energy but seduced even more by the heft of that first-place medal draped around his neck. So what if he was the only entrant in his age group?

His relatives and neighbors were astonished and relieved. The pinball had a path. A calling, like his father. The kid who couldn't afford college had an *athletic* scholarship. The boy who had to run would walk.

· · ·

Curt veered to the toilet again. Philip and Sean, too, were wincing with stomach distress. Everyone was wrong. Al kept increasing his lead—1:30 . . . 1:40 . . . 1:45—as the halfway point blew by. His form was flawless. Out front, alone, he didn't have to struggle with his doubts or his impulse to run. Out front he commanded everyone's eyes.

This was better than the best night of his life, that magical eve in Poza Rica, Mexico, six years earlier, when Al—dead last and racked with intestinal pain in a race the U.S. team had entered solely for conditioning—defied his coach's order to stop after 30 kilometers, obeying instead the adoring cries of the female spectators who'd fallen for his baby-face grin, who waited five hours for him to finish and showered him with kisses, flowers and lollipops until security guards escorted him away. It was "a brief moment in my life," he wrote in an article, "that I will always treasure."

Yes, Al was race walking's bard. Singlehandedly, he'd solved his dilemma—what if he became an Olympian and no one ever knew?—by making *sure* people knew, by writing previews and wrap-ups of all his races, by collecting the e-mail addresses of everyone he met, nearly 500 of them, and sending his stories to them and to a half-dozen race walking periodicals and websites. The off-weeks he spiced with amusing Day in the Life of Al and His Fellow Walkers chronicles that were so well done that you'd wonder why he was walking his life away instead of spending it with all those other sports-smitten Jewish lads who couldn't jump or jack a curveball—the ones in the press box.

At last, today, he wouldn't need to clang his own bell. His triumph would be in the San Diego newspaper—who knew, might even merit a few lines in *Sports Illustrated* trumpeting Al Heppner, Olympian. An upgrade, for sure, over *SI*'s Faces in the Crowd mention of his NAIA 5K championship in 1997, laminated on a plaque that hung on his wall. Sweeter than his appearance in the "Your Portfolio" feature in *USA Today*'s Money section.

The small crowd filled his ears with the most heavenly music of all as he blew through the 30K mark: "U-S-A! U-S-A! U-S-A!" Imagine how that would sound when he marched into the magic circle on the floor of the Olympic Stadium for the opening and closing ceremonies. Oh, rest assured, everyone back home would see Al. He'd come bursting out of the stadium tunnel, high-fiving Iverson and swapping e-mail addresses with LeBron, boogying with the Swedish synchronized swimmers and twirling the Canadian gymnasts round and round. He'd be mayor of the Olympic Village by the dawn of Day Two.

Thirty-two K's down. A *two*-minute lead over Curt and Tim, with Philip, more than a minute behind them, slowing down and about to throw up. All of it, every bit of Al's obsession, worth it now: the hundred miles a week of walking, the interval training so intense that even the 10,000-meter runners marveled at it, the sleepless nights in the $5,000 oxygen tent designed to simulate high altitude and increase red-blood-cell production, the arrows spray-painted on the roads in the neighborhoods of all the friends and relatives he visited out of town to mark his fifteen-mile routes. All the exhortations plastered on his walls—GET PSYCHED!

. . . BELIEVE IT! . . . TASTE IT ALL! All the details etched into his daily racing log for years: weight, pulse, heart rate, body fat, lactic acid level, mileage, times, temperature, weather, route location, goals.

Balance? Perspective? The all-eggs-in-one-basket stuff that Jim Bauman, the sports psychologist at the Olympic Training Center, and Al's parents worried about as the 2004 Olympic Trials drew nearer and memories of his 2000 crash returned? Sure, Al knew balance was important. But not *too much* balance, because somewhere out there some unbalanced sonofabitch who lived and breathed and slept the Olympics even more than Al did was waiting to kick his balanced ass. Somewhere some guy, burrowed even deeper in a tunnel to overcome enormous obstacles and reach the Games through sheer will and wanting, was being videotaped for an up-close-and-personal profile that would make eyes mist in homes across America.

"But what happens if you don't make it this time?" his mother fretted on the phone.

"Don't worry, Ma, this time I can handle it," he replied.

"There's a million other things you can do, Al."

"I *have* to get to the Olympics, Ma."

"But it's not going to change your life, Al," Tim Seaman chimed in. "I made the Olympics, and look where I'm living—an apartment in the Mexican 'hood."

"I *have* to get to the Olympics, Tim."

They didn't understand. The dreamer had cased dreamland and found it: that one small window left ajar, that one entry for an ordinary athlete into the world's most extraordinary athletic showcase. It didn't matter that Poland's and Russia's best walkers could cover the 50K twenty minutes faster than Al ever had. It was good to want something that much. It made him feel alive. He was surer than ever in 2002 after his father, eager to be closer to his son, paid for Al to take a four-day course called Landmark Forum, a nineties incarnation of the est self-empowerment workshops that swept the nation in the seventies. Al loved it. Landmark, he told people, made him understand the reason that he hadn't made the 2000 Olympics: He hadn't *wanted* it badly enough. He hugged his dad, who flew from the East Coast to attend Al's "graduation," and he crowed, "Dad, you gave me life twice!"

Nothing could stop him now that he'd been given the green light to want even more than he'd wanted before. Not the hernia surgery in 2003. Not the decline in his performances that meant he had to give up his dorm room at the Olympic Training Center. Not a new wave of depression that began to devour him, no matter how many times he was reminded that he could keep training, working and eating at the center. Not the nights when the Prozac he took to combat the depression, possibly triggering a manic reaction, made him more hyperactive than ever, kept him up dialing friends across the world, playing video games and cleaning out his closet.

He flew to Maine to improve his custom-made walking shoes, added yoga to his regimen of walking, weightlifting and swimming. He swore off women. He vowed that he was going to bring his splintered family together in Athens. He made a sign and taped it dead center in the bathroom mirror of the condo his parents helped him buy in Chula Vista:

NOBODY WANTS IT MORE THAN ME
ATHENS 2004

He stopped taking Prozac. An Olympian couldn't possibly need such a crutch, and besides, the quest killed sadness better than any drug could. "It's just situational depression," he told people. "I'm fine now . . . . My life is like a fairy tale now."

He affixed a second sign to his wall—THERE'S NO 'I' IN TEAM, BUT THERE IS IN IRAQ—because if he didn't make the four-hour Olympic qualifying time, he'd likely lose his place in the World Class Athlete Program and might end up being reassigned anywhere.

He rose at a meeting of the track and field athletes at the training center, wearing the ATHENS 2004 sweatshirt he'd bought a year before the Games. The speech he delivered might set off alarms in other settings, but in this one it lit a blaze. "The Olympics are a precious, precious opportunity," he cried. "I'm serious as a heart attack! . . . It's a fragile opportunity, and you've got to make sure you're doing *every*thing"—his fist pounded a table—"*every* goddam thing you can do to put yourself in the best position to make that team. . . . But it's not good enough to make the team! That's why I brought this freakin' sweatshirt! My goal is not to make the team, my goal is to contend for a medal! If you guys can't see that, if you guys don't want to contend for a medal, then you guys shouldn't be here! I don't even know if I'm gonna make the team! There may be a monsoon again! I hope to God I do, but I may not. But I *swear* to God, if I make it, I'm fightin' for my country." His fist pumped. The Olympic hopefuls whooped. "I'm going to the goddam Olympics because I'm gonna try to win a medal! And I'm gonna freakin' die rather than lose!"

.   .   .

Al began to slow. Had he failed to take enough liquids and carbohydrate gels, underestimated the effect of temperatures climbing from the forties into the sixties on a course with no shade? Or was he just recovering for a kilometer or two, girding for the home stretch?

Al slowed even more. On came Curt, chewing at the gap. On came Tim, catching a second wind and deciding to go for it all. By the thirty-fourth kilometer, it was written all over Al's flesh: He'd miscalculated. At 35K, Curt and Tim went by him as if Al were planted in the asphalt.

The world around him began to whirl. He crept the next five kilometers, and then the horror of 2000 flashed before his vacant eyes. Philip, seemingly out of the race minutes earlier, stormed past him into third place . . . *again*. "C'mon, Al, go with me," Philip implored, his heart aching this time for Al. But Al couldn't. No one, until afterward, would realize how much pressure he'd heaped on himself, how much energy had been consumed by the Olympic flame that burned within him.

Curt won in 3:58:24, the only walker to slip in under four hours and qualify for Athens. Then came Tim, Philip, Sean . . . and finally Al, staggering home fifth in 4:23:52, bending over at the finish line, being kissed on the back by a race official whose heart was broken too, then staggering into a blanket that someone held open for him, sagging onto a stretcher, trembling with dehydration and disbelief that his dream had slipped away again.

·   ·   ·

Yes, Al, Yes. You still have a shot, a helluva shot, everyone at the training center reminded him. There's the World Cup in Germany in May, and if you don't get your four-hour race there, then Wisconsin-Parkside will hold a 50K and you can try again. There are still two slots open, Al! Keep your chin up! You can still go to Athens!

Al nodded, said little. He didn't tell them that there was nothing left inside him, nothing left at all. Everyone was relieved that he didn't seem quite as distraught as he had been in 2000.

His father encouraged him all he could, then left California and flew back home two days after the race. His mother remained at his condo. On the third day, he mustered a smile as he headed out the door. "I'm going to train with Tim, Ma," he called. He met Tim at the Olympic Training Center dining hall for a breakfast with California congressman Randy (Duke) Cunningham and Olympic candidates who'd received federal scholarship money to attend college and graduate classes.

The congressman had heard about the race. He rose and told a story of a silver dollar his father had given him to keep in his pocket as a reminder never to give up, and how that coin and his father's admonition had helped him survive a drill sergeant who took him to his breaking point at flight training school in Pensacola, Fla., and later during harrowing moments as a fighter pilot over Vietnam. He concluded by rolling silver dollars across the table to Al and Tim.

"That's for you to keep," said Cunningham, "to remind you, the way my silver dollar from my father did for me, never to give up."

Who knows what that silver dollar meant to Al? He left the dining hall with it, ran an easy three kilometers with Tim and 20K race walker John Nunn, then said goodbye to them and Coach Peña. It was eleven A.M. He climbed into his SUV and departed.

No one knows what filled those next eight hours. He exchanged a series of calls with his mother, promising to pick up her cousin in San Diego that evening so the three of them could eat together at seven. At five P.M. he told his mother he had to stop at the airport and pick up a friend. Instead he drove toward the mountains. There was a place he remembered.

A light mist fell. He neared Pine Valley, the gorge forty-five minutes west of San Diego that he and the other walkers had hiked down three months earlier. His mother called at 6:50 wondering what had become of him. "Sorry, Ma, the weather's bad, my friend's plane's late," Al lied.

"Please, Al, my cousin's waiting," she protested. "Can't you find someone else to wait for your friend?"

For the first time, she heard an odd ring to his reply. "Uh . . . I'll try," he said. She called again six minutes later. The cellphone, lying near his wallet, rang again and again in his car.

Al began to walk across the bridge. Cars hissed past him on the wet asphalt. Dusk pooled in the gorge below. He stopped not even a third of the way across. He wouldn't need all 450 feet.

Now that the flame was out, the rules made no sense. He looked over the railing. The emptiness went on and on. Both feet left the ground.

The New Yorker

The photos of U.S. soldiers abusing detainees at Abu Ghraib prison provoked disbelief and outrage when they were first broadcast. But it was Seymour M. Hersh who revealed the much larger and more disturbing story that the pictures couldn't tell. Terror, as Hersh showed, had indeed come full circle at Abu Ghraib.

Seymour M. Hersh

Torture at
Abu Ghraib

I n the era of Saddam Hussein, Abu Ghraib, twenty miles west
of Baghdad, was one of the world's most notorious prisons,
with torture, weekly executions, and vile living conditions. As
many as fifty thousand men and women—no accurate count is
possible—were jammed into Abu Ghraib at one time, in twelve-
by-twelve-foot cells that were little more than human holding
pits.

In the looting that followed the regime's collapse, last April, the
huge prison complex, by then deserted, was stripped of everything that could be removed, including doors, windows, and
bricks. The coalition authorities had the floors tiled, cells cleaned
and repaired, and toilets, showers, and a new medical center
added. Abu Ghraib was now a U.S. military prison. Most of the
prisoners, however—by the fall there were several thousand, including women and teenagers—were civilians, many of whom
had been picked up in random military sweeps and at highway
checkpoints. They fell into three loosely defined categories: common criminals; security detainees suspected of "crimes against
the coalition"; and a small number of suspected "high-value"
leaders of the insurgency against the coalition forces.

Last June, Janis Karpinski, an Army reserve brigadier general,
was named commander of the 800th Military Police Brigade and

put in charge of military prisons in Iraq. General Karpinski, the only female commander in the war zone, was an experienced operations and intelligence officer who had served with the Special Forces and in the 1991 Gulf War, but she had never run a prison system. Now she was in charge of three large jails, eight battalions, and thirty-four hundred Army reservists, most of whom, like her, had no training in handling prisoners.

General Karpinski, who had wanted to be a soldier since she was five, is a business consultant in civilian life, and was enthusiastic about her new job. In an interview last December with the *St. Petersburg Times*, she said that, for many of the Iraqi inmates at Abu Ghraib, "living conditions now are better in prison than at home. At one point we were concerned that they wouldn't want to leave."

A month later, General Karpinski was formally admonished and quietly suspended, and a major investigation into the Army's prison system, authorized by Lieutenant General Ricardo S. Sanchez, the senior commander in Iraq, was under way. A fifty-three-page report, obtained by *The New Yorker*, written by Major General Antonio M. Taguba and not meant for public release, was completed in late February. Its conclusions about the institutional failures of the Army prison system were devastating. Specifically, Taguba found that between October and December of 2003 there were numerous instances of "sadistic, blatant, and wanton criminal abuses" at Abu Ghraib. This systematic and illegal abuse of detainees, Taguba reported, was perpetrated by soldiers of the 372nd Military Police Company, and also by members of the American intelligence community. (The 372nd was attached to the 320th M.P. Battalion, which reported to Karpinski's brigade headquarters.) Taguba's report listed some of the wrongdoing:

> Breaking chemical lights and pouring the phosphoric liquid on detainees; pouring cold water on naked detainees; beating detainees with a broom handle and a chair; threatening

male detainees with rape; allowing a military police guard to stitch the wound of a detainee who was injured after being slammed against the wall in his cell; sodomizing a detainee with a chemical light and perhaps a broom stick, and using military working dogs to frighten and intimidate detainees with threats of attack, and in one instance actually biting a detainee.

There was stunning evidence to support the allegations, Taguba added—"detailed witness statements and the discovery of extremely graphic photographic evidence." Photographs and videos taken by the soldiers as the abuses were happening were not included in his report, Taguba said, because of their "extremely sensitive nature."

•   •   •

The photographs—several of which were broadcast on CBS's *60 Minutes 2* last week—show leering G.I.s taunting naked Iraqi prisoners who are forced to assume humiliating poses. Six suspects—Staff Sergeant Ivan L. Frederick II, known as Chip, who was the senior enlisted man; Specialist Charles A. Graner; Sergeant Javal Davis; Specialist Megan Ambuhl; Specialist Sabrina Harman; and Private Jeremy Sivits—are now facing prosecution in Iraq, on charges that include conspiracy, dereliction of duty, cruelty toward prisoners, maltreatment, assault, and indecent acts. A seventh suspect, Private Lynndie England, was reassigned to Fort Bragg, North Carolina, after becoming pregnant.

The photographs tell it all. In one, Private England, a cigarette dangling from her mouth, is giving a jaunty thumbs-up sign and pointing at the genitals of a young Iraqi, who is naked except for a sandbag over his head, as he masturbates. Three other hooded and naked Iraqi prisoners are shown, hands reflexively crossed over their genitals. A fifth prisoner has his hands at his sides. In another,

England stands arm in arm with Specialist Graner; both are grinning and giving the thumbs-up behind a cluster of perhaps seven naked Iraqis, knees bent, piled clumsily on top of each other in a pyramid. There is another photograph of a cluster of naked prisoners, again piled in a pyramid. Near them stands Graner, smiling, his arms crossed; a woman soldier stands in front of him, bending over, and she, too, is smiling. Then, there is another cluster of hooded bodies, with a female soldier standing in front, taking photographs. Yet another photograph shows a kneeling, naked, unhooded male prisoner, head momentarily turned away from the camera, posed to make it appear that he is performing oral sex on another male prisoner, who is naked and hooded.

Such dehumanization is unacceptable in any culture, but it is especially so in the Arab world. Homosexual acts are against Islamic law and it is humiliating for men to be naked in front of other men, Bernard Haykel, a professor of Middle Eastern studies at New York University, explained. "Being put on top of each other and forced to masturbate, being naked in front of each other—it's all a form of torture," Haykel said.

Two Iraqi faces that do appear in the photographs are those of dead men. There is the battered face of prisoner No. 153399, and the bloodied body of another prisoner, wrapped in cellophane and packed in ice. There is a photograph of an empty room, splattered with blood.

The 372nd's abuse of prisoners seemed almost routine—a fact of Army life that the soldiers felt no need to hide. On April 9, at an Article 32 hearing (the military equivalent of a grand jury) in the case against Sergeant Frederick, at Camp Victory, near Baghdad, one of the witnesses, Specialist Matthew Wisdom, an M.P., told the courtroom what happened when he and other soldiers delivered seven prisoners, hooded and bound, to the so-called "hard site" at Abu Ghraib—seven tiers of cells where the inmates who were considered the most dangerous were housed. The men had been accused of starting a riot in another section of the prison. Wisdom said:

> SFC Snider grabbed my prisoner and threw him into a pile.... I do not think it was right to put them in a pile. I saw SSG Frederic, SGT Davis and CPL Graner walking around the pile hitting the prisoners. I remember SSG Frederick hitting one prisoner in the side of its [*sic*] ribcage. The prisoner was no danger to SSG Frederick.... I left after that.

When he returned later, Wisdom testified:

> I saw two naked detainees, one masturbating to another kneeling with its mouth open. I thought I should just get out of there. I didn't think it was right... I saw SSG Frederick walking towards me, and he said, "Look what these animals do when you leave them alone for two seconds." I heard PFC England shout out, "He's getting hard."

Wisdom testified that he told his superiors what had happened, and assumed that "the issue was taken care of." He said, "I just didn't want to be part of anything that looked criminal."

· · ·

The abuses became public because of the outrage of Specialist Joseph M. Darby, an M.P. whose role emerged during the Article 32 hearing against Chip Frederick. A government witness, Special Agent Scott Bobeck, who is a member of the Army's Criminal Investigation Division, or C.I.D., told the court, according to an abridged transcript made available to me, "The investigation started after SPC Darby ... got a CD from CPL Graner.... He came across pictures of naked detainees." Bobeck said that Darby had "initially put an anonymous letter under our door, then he later came forward and gave a sworn statement. He felt very bad about it and thought it was very wrong."

Questioned further, the Army investigator said that Frederick and his colleagues had not been given any "training guidelines" that he was aware of. The M.P.s in the 372nd had been assigned to routine traffic and police duties upon their arrival in Iraq, in the spring of 2003. In October of 2003, the 372nd was ordered to prison-guard duty at Abu Ghraib. Frederick, at thirty-seven, was far older than his colleagues, and was a natural leader; he had also worked for six years as a guard for the Virginia Department of Corrections. Bobeck explained:

> What I got is that SSG Frederick and CPL Graner were road M.P.s and were put in charge because they were civilian prison guards and had knowledge of how things were supposed to be run.

Bobeck also testified that witnesses had said that Frederick, on one occasion, "had punched a detainee in the chest so hard that the detainee almost went into cardiac arrest."

At the Article 32 hearing, the Army informed Frederick and his attorneys, Captain Robert Shuck, an Army lawyer, and Gary Myers, a civilian, that two dozen witnesses they had sought, including General Karpinski and all of Frederick's co-defendants, would not appear. Some had been excused after exercising their Fifth Amendment right; others were deemed to be too far away from the courtroom. "The purpose of an Article 32 hearing is for us to engage witnesses and discover facts," Gary Myers told me. "We ended up with a C.I.D. agent and no alleged victims to examine." After the hearing, the presiding investigative officer ruled that there was sufficient evidence to convene a court-martial against Frederick.

Myers, who was one of the military defense attorneys in the My Lai prosecutions of the nineteen-seventies, told me that his client's defense will be that he was carrying out the orders of his superiors and, in particular, the directions of military intelligence. He said, "Do you really think a group of kids from rural Virginia decided to do this on their own? Decided that the best way to embarrass Arabs and make them talk was to have them walk around nude?"

In letters and e-mails to family members, Frederick repeatedly noted that the military-intelligence teams, which included C.I.A. officers and linguists and interrogation specialists from private defense contractors, were the dominant force inside Abu Ghraib. In a letter written in January, he said:

> I questioned some of the things that I saw . . . such things as leaving inmates in their cell with no clothes or in female underpants, handcuffing them to the door of their cell—and the answer I got was, "This is how military intelligence (MI) wants it done." . . . . MI has also instructed us to place a prisoner in an isolation cell with little or no clothes, no toilet or running water, no ventilation or window, for as much as three days.

The military-intelligence officers have "encouraged and told us, 'Great job,' they were now getting positive results and information," Frederick wrote. "CID has been present when the military working dogs were used to intimidate prisoners at MI's request." At one point, Frederick told his family, he pulled aside his superior officer, Lieutenant Colonel Jerry Phillabaum, the commander of the 320th M.P. Battalion, and asked about the mistreatment of prisoners. "His reply was 'Don't worry about it.'"

In November, Frederick wrote, an Iraqi prisoner under the control of what the Abu Ghraib guards called "O.G.A.," or other government agencies—that is, the C.I.A. and its paramilitary employees—was brought to his unit for questioning. "They stressed him out so bad that the man passed away. They put his body in a body bag and packed him in ice for approximately twenty-four hours in the shower. . . . The next day the medics came and put his body on a stretcher, placed a fake IV in his arm and took him away." The dead Iraqi was never entered into the prison's inmate-control system, Frederick recounted, "and therefore never had a number."

·   ·   ·

Frederick's defense is, of course, highly self-serving. But the complaints in his letters and e-mails home were reinforced by two internal Army reports—Taguba's and one by the Army's chief law-enforcement officer, Provost Marshal Donald Ryder, a major general.

Last fall, General Sanchez ordered Ryder to review the prison system in Iraq and recommend ways to improve it. Ryder's report, filed on November 5, concluded that there were potential human-rights, training, and manpower issues, system-wide, that needed immediate attention. It also discussed serious concerns about the tension between the missions of the military police assigned to guard the prisoners and the intelligence teams who wanted to interrogate them. Army regulations limit intelligence activity by the M.P.s to passive collection. But something had gone wrong.

There was evidence dating back to the Afghanistan war, the Ryder report said, that M.P.s had worked with intelligence operatives to "set favorable conditions for subsequent interviews"—a euphemism for breaking the will of prisoners. "Such actions generally run counter to the smooth operation of a detention facility, attempting to maintain its population in a compliant and docile state." General Karpinski's brigade, Ryder reported, "has not been directed to change its facility procedures to set the conditions for MI interrogations, nor participate in those interrogations." Ryder called for the establishment of procedures to "define the role of military police soldiers . . . clearly separating the actions of the guards from those of the military intelligence personnel." The officers running the war in Iraq were put on notice.

Ryder undercut his warning, however, by concluding that the situation had not yet reached a crisis point. Though some procedures were flawed, he said, he found "no military police units purposely applying inappropriate confinement practices." His investigation was at best a failure and at worst a coverup.

Taguba, in his report, was polite but direct in refuting his fellow general. "Unfortunately, many of the systemic problems that surfaced during [Ryder's] assessment are the very same issues that are the subject of this investigation," he wrote. "In fact, many of the abuses suffered by detainees occurred during, or near to, the time of that assessment." The report continued, "Contrary to the findings of MG Ryder's report, I find that personnel assigned to the 372nd MP Company, 800th MP Brigade were directed to change facility procedures to 'set the conditions' for MI interrogations." Army intelligence officers, C.I.A. agents, and private contractors "actively requested that MP guards set physical and mental conditions for favorable interrogation of witnesses."

Taguba backed up his assertion by citing evidence from sworn statements to Army C.I.D. investigators. Specialist Sabrina Harman, one of the accused M.P.s, testified that it was her job to keep detainees awake, including one hooded prisoner who was placed on a box with wires attached to his fingers, toes, and penis. She stated, "MI wanted to get them to talk. It is Graner and Frederick's job to do things for MI and OGA to get these people to talk."

Another witness, Sergeant Javal Davis, who is also one of the accused, told C.I.D. investigators, "I witnessed prisoners in the MI hold section . . . being made to do various things that I would question morally. . . . We were told that they had different rules." Taguba wrote, "Davis also stated that he had heard MI insinuate to the guards to abuse the inmates. When asked what MI said he stated: 'Loosen this guy up for us.' 'Make sure he has a bad night.' 'Make sure he gets the treatment.' " Military intelligence made these comments to Graner and Frederick, Davis said. "The MI staffs to my understanding have been giving Graner compliments . . . statements like, 'Good job, they're breaking down real fast. They answer every question. They're giving out good information.' "

When asked why he did not inform his chain of command about the abuse, Sergeant Davis answered, "Because I assumed that if they were doing things out of the ordinary or outside the guidelines, someone would have said something. Also the wing"— where the abuse took place—"belongs to MI and it appeared MI personnel approved of the abuse."

Another witness, Specialist Jason Kennel, who was not accused of wrongdoing, said, "I saw them nude, but MI would tell us to take away their mattresses, sheets, and clothes." (It was his view, he added, that if M.I. wanted him to do this "they needed to give me paperwork.") Taguba also cited an interview with Adel L. Nakhla, a translator who was an employee of Titan, a civilian contractor. He told of one night when a "bunch of people from MI" watched as a group of handcuffed and shackled inmates were subjected to abuse by Graner and Frederick.

General Taguba saved his harshest words for the military-intelligence officers and private contractors. He recommended that Colonel Thomas Pappas, the commander of one of the M.I. brigades, be reprimanded and receive non-judicial punishment, and that Lieutenant Colonel Steven Jordan, the former director of the Joint Interrogation and Debriefing Center, be relieved of duty and reprimanded. He further urged that a civilian contractor, Steven Stephanowicz, of CACI International, be fired from his Army job, reprimanded, and denied his security clearances for lying to the investigating team and allowing or ordering military policemen "who were not trained in interrogation techniques to facilitate interrogations by 'setting conditions' which were neither authorized" nor in accordance with Army regulations. "He clearly knew his instructions equated to physical abuse," Taguba wrote. He also recommended disciplinary action against a second CACI employee, John Israel. (A spokeswoman for CACI said that the company had "received no formal communication" from the Army about the matter.)

"I suspect," Taguba concluded, that Pappas, Jordan, Stephanowicz, and Israel "were either directly or indirectly responsible for the abuse at Abu Ghraib," and strongly recommended immediate disciplinary action.

·   ·   ·

The problems inside the Army prison system in Iraq were not hidden from senior commanders. During Karpinski's seven-month tour of duty, Taguba noted, there were at least a dozen officially reported incidents involving escapes, attempted escapes, and other serious security issues that were investigated by officers of the 800th M.P. Brigade. Some of the incidents had led to the killing or wounding of inmates and M.P.s, and resulted in a series of "lessons learned" inquiries within the brigade. Karpinski invariably approved the reports and signed orders calling for changes in day-to-day procedures. But Taguba found that she did not follow up, doing nothing to insure that the orders were carried out. Had she done so, he added, "cases of abuse may have been prevented."

General Taguba further found that Abu Ghraib was filled beyond capacity, and that the M.P. guard force was significantly undermanned and short of resources. "This imbalance has contributed to the poor living conditions, escapes, and accountability lapses," he wrote. There were gross differences, Taguba said, between the actual number of prisoners on hand and the number officially recorded. A lack of proper screening also meant that many innocent Iraqis were wrongly being detained—indefinitely, it seemed, in some cases. The Taguba study noted that more than

60 percent of the civilian inmates at Abu Ghraib were deemed not to be a threat to society, which should have enabled them to be released. Karpinski's defense, Taguba said, was that her superior officers "routinely" rejected her recommendations regarding the release of such prisoners.

Karpinski was rarely seen at the prisons she was supposed to be running, Taguba wrote. He also found a wide range of administrative problems, including some that he considered "without precedent in my military career." The soldiers, he added, were "poorly prepared and untrained . . . prior to deployment, at the mobilization site, upon arrival in theater, and throughout the mission."

General Taguba spent more than four hours interviewing Karpinski, whom he described as extremely emotional: "What I found particularly disturbing in her testimony was her complete unwillingness to either understand or accept that many of the problems inherent in the 800th MP Brigade were caused or exacerbated by poor leadership and the refusal of her command to both establish and enforce basic standards and principles among its soldiers."

Taguba recommended that Karpinski and seven brigade military-police officers and enlisted men be relieved of command and formally reprimanded. No criminal proceedings were suggested for Karpinski; apparently, the loss of promotion and the indignity of a public rebuke were seen as enough punishment.

· · ·

After the story broke on CBS last week, the Pentagon announced that Major General Geoffrey Miller, the new head of the Iraqi prison system, had arrived in Baghdad and was on the job. He had been the commander of the Guantánamo Bay detention center. General Sanchez also authorized an investigation into possible wrongdoing by military and civilian interrogators.

As the international furor grew, senior military officers, and President Bush, insisted that the actions of a few did not reflect the conduct of the military as a whole. Taguba's report, however, amounts to an unsparing study of collective wrongdoing and the failure of Army leadership at the highest levels. The picture he draws of Abu Ghraib is one in which Army regulations and the Geneva conventions were routinely violated, and in which much of the day-to-day management of the prisoners was abdicated to Army military-intelligence units and civilian contract employees. Interrogating prisoners and getting intelligence, including by intimidation and torture, was the priority.

The mistreatment at Abu Ghraib may have done little to further American intelligence, however. Willie J. Rowell, who served for thirty-six years as a C.I.D. agent, told me that the use of force or humiliation with prisoners is invariably counterproductive. "They'll tell you what you want to hear, truth or no truth," Rowell said. "'You can flog me until I tell you what I know you want me to say.' You don't get righteous information."

Under the fourth Geneva convention, an occupying power can jail civilians who pose an "imperative" security threat, but it must establish a regular procedure for insuring that only civilians who remain a genuine security threat be kept imprisoned. Prisoners have the right to appeal any internment decision and have their cases reviewed. Human Rights Watch complained to Secretary of Defense Donald Rumsfeld that civilians in Iraq remained in custody month after month with no charges brought against them. Abu Ghraib had become, in effect, another Guantánamo.

As the photographs from Abu Ghraib make clear, these detentions have had enormous consequences: for the imprisoned civilian Iraqis, many of whom had nothing to do with the growing insurgency; for the integrity of the Army; and for the United States' reputation in the world.

Captain Robert Shuck, Frederick's military attorney, closed his defense at the Article 32 hearing last month by saying that the

Army was "attempting to have these six soldiers atone for its sins." Similarly, Gary Myers, Frederick's civilian attorney, told me that he would argue at the court-martial that culpability in the case extended far beyond his client. "I'm going to drag every involved intelligence officer and civilian contractor I can find into court," he said. "Do you really believe the Army relieved a general officer because of six soldiers? Not a chance."

Esquire

FINALIST—ESSAYS

In an essay both solidly reported and deeply felt, writer James McManus puts a human face on the contentious debate over embryonic-stem-cell research. It is the face of his own twenty-nine-year-old daughter, whose juvenile diabetes is just one of the life-threatening diseases for which this promising but politically controversial research may offer a cure.

James McManus

Please Stand By
While the Age
of Miracles Is
Briefly Suspended

A damp, nasty Thursday, January 15, 2004. The President's Council on Bioethics is meeting in the downstairs conference room of the Wyndham Hotel, four or five blocks from the White House. Minimal risk-to-benefit ratios for cutting-edge medical research are what the panel is trying to calibrate. Thumbs-up or thumbs-down, live or die. It's 8:45 in the morning, day one of week three of the most crucial election year since 1932, or perhaps 1860. Not to be melodramatic.

To get a better handle on the ethical objections to embryonic-stem-cell research, I've been listening with as much detachment as possible, given my twenty-nine-year-old daughter's ongoing slow death from juvenile (Type 1) diabetes, one of several diseases likely to be cured by this research. Bridget has already undergone a vitrectomy—open-eye surgery to remove vision-blocking blood clots and scar tissue from her vitreous humor—and several rounds of laser treatment to help keep her retinopathy in check. During these procedures, she needs to remain awake while a gonioscope is held against her eye and an ophthalmologic surgeon burns her pigment epithelium about eighteen hundred times with two hundred milliwatts of light. In each eye. Victims of juvenile diabetes can go blind because their elevated blood-sugar levels cause capillaries throughout their bodies, especially in their eyes and extremities, to leak and proliferate in unhealthy ways.

But like I said, I'm trying to listen to every voice here, even that of Alfonso Gómez-Lobo, the dapper metaphysician from George-town who proclaimed half an hour ago in his lilting Chilean accent that "all of us were once a blastocyst." His point was that *no* blastocyst, cloned or otherwise, should ever be destroyed for its cells, however great the possible benefits. I wanted to say that we all were once an ovum as well, yet we don't hold a funeral every time a woman who's made love has her period. That being evolved from amphibians doesn't keep us from deep-frying frog legs and washing them down with Corona. That defenders of animal rights fervently believe that eating meat, even fish, is a sacrilege, but we don't let them dictate to Smith & Wollensky or cut off government subsidies to the beef industry. . . .

To be fair, the Bush council straddles both sides of the fulcrum: ten members on Gómez-Lobo's side, seven on mine. Each is a brilliant and well-informed ethicist, doctor, or legal scholar; nearly all have an M.D. or Ph.D or sometimes, as in the case of chairman Leon Kass, both. Today they're presenting in public the ideas they've already fine-tuned and published.

Kass, Gómez-Lobo, columnist Charles Krauthammer, and the rest of the majority argue that embryonic-stem-cell research would put us on a slippery slope toward organ farms and cloned children. Their hostility focuses on a procedure called somatic cell nuclear transfer, in which the nucleus of an ovum is removed or deactivated and replaced with the nucleus from a human donor cell. After chemicals coax the doctored egg to reproduce itself, what forms after five days is a blastocyst, a cluster of one hundred to two hundred cells, including the stem cells prized by researchers. This early-stage embryo could be used for either reproductive cloning (to make a baby that's genetically identical to the donor), which almost no one favors, or therapeutic cloning (to isolate and harvest its stem cells) to advance the field of regenerative medicine.

Chapter 6 of *Human Cloning and Human Dignity*, published by the council in July 2002, is where its members most fully address the ethics of cloning. The majority recommends, "albeit with regret," that therapeutic cloning ought not be pursued. "The cell synthesized by somatic cell nuclear transfer, no less than the fertilized egg, is a human organism in its germinal stage." Somewhat defensively, the majority adds, "It is possible that some might suffer in the future because research proceeded more slowly. We cannot suppose that the moral life comes without cost."

No one wants cloned babies or fetuses cultured in hatcheries. But the council's minority is willing to let a small number of early-stage embryos—cloned embryos as well as those fertilized in vitro and now stored in the freezers of infertility clinics, bound for the Dumpster if not donated to science—be destroyed during medical research. Why? Because only embryonic—as opposed to adult—stem cells are "pluripotent," which means they're capable of morphing into any kind of cell in the human body. These "differentiated" cells could then be programmed to replace diseased neurons, heart-muscle tissue, or insulin-producing islet cells for diabetics. Genetically compatible with the patient, they would not be rejected by her immune system. Bona fide miracle cures are what we are talking about here. Even before they're perfected, they'll dispense potent medicine—hope. But only if the president's restrictions on this research are lifted.

·   ·   ·

In the summer of 1979, Bridget was four and a half, a pink-cheeked, blond kindergartner with a respectable forehand and a new baby brother. In the upper right side of her abdomen, though, her immune system suddenly attacked the islets of Langerhans in her pancreas, inexplicably mistaking them for foreign invaders. Within a couple of weeks, almost all of her islet cells had been obliterated. Her body no longer made enough insulin, the hormone that regulates the passage of nutrients into the cells, so she couldn't process food into energy. Long before we knew what was happening, Bridget's crystal-blue eyes began sink-ing into gray sockets, her ribs protruded through her flesh, and she started walking around in a daze. At a tryout to place her into the regular or advanced group of tennis students, she failed to even get a racket on balls she would have drilled a month earlier. In words that humiliate me even more now than they did in 1979, I criticized her from the sidelines for "doggin' it."

Her pediatrician referred us to an endocrinologist, who admitted her to Children's Memorial Hospital in Chicago. Bridget began receiving insulin intravenously. Within a week, she looked and felt back to normal. The only difference was that her islet cells couldn't be revived or replaced. As any macho dad would, I fainted and collapsed on the floor as the doctor was telling us that the disease is chronic and incurable. (Dozens of people visited Bridget in the hospital, and the joke became to ask the nurses how Jim was doing.) I eventually managed to learn that the tip of one of Bridget's tiny fingers would now have to be stabbed with a stainless-steel lancet three or four times a day, allowing a droplet of her blood to be smeared across a chem strip that measured the glucose in her bloodstream; this determined the correct dosage of regular and timed-release insulin to be injected into her butt or thigh. She would no longer be able to eat the same treats her classmates' parents had packed in their Big Bird lunch boxes or served at their birthday parties. But at least Bridget was released fairly healthy from Children's. At least she had come home at all.

·   ·   ·

FULL DISCLOSURE: Even if my daughter weren't ill, I would cheer on stem-cell research with gusto. Because that's the kind of Mick I am, brother. I was raised Roman Catholic but have lived the last forty years as a secular humanist. People like me get branded atheists, heretics, ethical relativists, French, and much worse; more affectionate terms include freethinker, agnostic, existentialist, beatnik. I have faith that our bodies—brain waves and action, commerce and science, art and language and children—are pretty much all there is to us. Or all there is to me, anyway. Once my EEG line goes flat, it's gonna be all she wrote. In the meantime, my one and only life will be awful in several respects, awesome in others. Later or sooner, a crosstown bus or a Hummer will squash me like Wile E. Coyote. Either that or an organ or two will break down and I'll suffer, piss and moan not a little, then purchase the farm. I've already made the down payment.

As far as the suffering goes—when it starts, how long it drags out—I used to be confident that western medicine was riding full speed, or almost that fast, to the rescue. I pictured a rangy Asian cowgirl in a lab coat and Stetson, a bandolier of specimen vials jangling against her modest cleavage as she clutches in one hand the reins of a galloping stallion, in the other a filament delicate enough to boink a few islet cells into a failing pancreas. Not that I expect to live forever—just an extra decade or so, with a little more spring in my step. More important, I want people like Bridget to get a fair shot at their biblical threescore and ten. Our Bible-totin' president, however, has stripped my infinitely resourceful cowgirl of her most promising protocols and forced her to ride sidesaddle on a stubborn Texas mule better equipped for wagon-train duty than galloping into the future.

Many of us who were willing to give Bush a chance, who voted for Al Gore but weren't terrified at the thought of a compassion-ate conservative in the Oval Office, now feel that the president isn't much less benighted than the Muslim fundamentalists he has en-gaged in an infinitely perilous clash of theocracies. Not that Bush is a dyed-in-the-wool Holy Roller himself. No, I believe he's a cold-blooded opportunist, able and willing to pander to our least-educated citizens—and that's much, much worse. After all, if, as Gallup recently reported, only 49 percent of Americans accept Darwin's theory of evolution, that number must hover near zero among certain blocs of red-state voters. What besides *shazam* can we say to these folks? But surely we can't let them hinder the momentum of biomedical research.

Not all conservative Christians attack science and reason while gorging on their fruits—laws, markets, medicine, weaponry, energy systems, computers—but the fanatical fringe surely does. Pretending to split the difference between these folks and the rest of us, the president's "compromise" effectively amounted to a ban on embryonic-stem-cell research. Announcing his decision from his ranch in Crawford, Texas, in August 2001, he claimed that "more than sixty genetically diverse stem-cell lines already exist" and that the NIH would be permitted to fund research on these existing lines only. Three years later, however, a mere nineteen of those lines have been made available to scientists, and most are genetically limited to people who tend to use in vitro clinics—the white, the infertile, the affluent. Not that there's anything wrong with these characteristics, but researchers will need hundreds— possibly thousands—of lines to provide genetic matches for the entire population. As the White House itself acknowledges in a fact sheet on the subject, "approximately 128 million Americans" stand to benefit from this research.

Fortunately, a movement to challenge or circumvent the Bush policy is now in full swing. On February 24, New Jersey governor James McGreevey submitted a budget that would make his state the first to fund embryonic-stem-cell research. In April, the privately funded Harvard Stem Cell Institute opened with a mandate to fill the void left by the ban against federal money. On April 28, 206 members of the House—including 36 Republicans, more than a few pro-lifers among them—sent the president a letter urging him to loosen restrictions on embryonic-stem-cell research. On June 4, the day before Ronald Reagan succumbed to Alzheimer's, a similarly bipartisan plea from fifty-eight senators landed in the president's in-box. And in November, Californians will vote on the Stem Cell Research and Cures Initiative, a hugely ambitious ballot measure that would allocate $3 billion in state money for research on stem cells, embryonic and otherwise. But so far, Bush hasn't blinked.

By supporting a bill proposed by Kansas senator Sam Brownback to send scientists engaged in embryonic-stem-cell research to prison and to outlaw treatments developed in other countries using such methods, the president has made this research downright unsavory, and he's done it on purpose. Even Dr. Kass regrets that young grad students won't go into stem-cell research as readily and that "maybe there's a certain chilling effect on the field as a whole."

Whatever is motivating President Bush, his policy has about it the stench of the witch doctor. It may be the most unenlightened position, with the most negative and far-reaching human consequences, ever taken by an American president.

. . .

In the 1980s, as Bridget's mother and I researched the possibilities for a cure, we were told to supervise Bridget's diet and insulin routine as closely as possible, and to teach her to maintain it herself. This would reduce the risk of complications ten or twenty years down the road. The better her control over her blood-sugar levels at each stage of her life, the healthier she'd be when a cure was discovered. It could even affect whether she'd be eligible for cutting-edge treatments.

During the eight or nine years after her diagnosis, our well-behaved little girl dutifully followed her regimens of shots, diet, and exercise. She almost never asked me, "How long do I have to take the shots, Dad? Do you know?" Having scrutinized every syllable of the Juvenile Diabetes Foundation literature and traveled to New York and St. Louis to interview researchers, I learned—or I chose to believe—that the disease would be conquered long before Bridget developed any serious complications. What I emphasized to her was that a cure would be found by the time she got her driver's license. "Just hold on until then," I would say with a hug, "and we'll have a ginormous double celebration."

At thirteen, Bridget was an A-minus student, a not-bad cello and piano and tennis player, and the starting shortstop for the Winnetka All-Stars, our town's traveling softball team. During the daylong tournaments on baked-clay diamonds in Midwestern heat and humidity, she was usually the last player to run out of gas. We had to pack our Igloo with extra Gatorade and fruit and syringes, but by then we were used to that stuff. Bridget may have started sneaking the occasional candy bar or Pepsi with her teammates, but her overall health remained phenomenal. One mid-August Sunday, against the Deerfield Does, she snagged a line drive just behind second base, stepped on the bag to double off that runner, and ran down the runner advancing from first, completing an unassisted triple play.

·   ·   ·

Back at the Wyndham, the debate around the five-table pentagon has been framed, as it should be, in moral-philosophical terms. The tone remains cordial. Members forgo honorifics and refer to one another as Frank, Leon, Karen, "my friend." Yet the rock-bottom question persists: Should "man in his hubris" or some other entity write the ground rules for biomedical research?

Chairman Kass has written, "In leading laboratories, academic and industrial, new creators are confidently amassing their powers and quietly honing their skills, while on the street their evangelists are zealously prophesying a posthuman future." A key notion for Kass is the Wisdom of Repugnance, also known as the Yuck Factor or, as I think of it, *E*wisdom. "Repugnance is the emotional expression of a deep wisdom," he writes, referring to such things as rape, murder, incest . . . and somatic cell nuclear transfer. "Shallow are the souls that have forgotten how to shudder." But the shudder test is hardly foolproof and can lead to a slew of false positives. When Dr. Zabdiel Boylston used inoculation to thwart Boston's smallpox epidemic in 1721, one clergyman thundered, "For a man to infect a family in the morning with smallpox and pray to God in the evening against the disease is a blasphemy," language that caused bombs to be thrown into the homes of Dr. Boylston's cohorts. Whereas hamstringing researchers racing to cure diabetes makes me shudder with rage and disgust.

As a Jewish M.D. and humanities professor, Kass has no trouble pronouncing words like *nuclear* or *vekhen lo' ye'aseh* (Hebrew for "such as ought not to be done"). He hardly fits the stereotype of the born-again zealot embodied by John Ashcroft, Dick Armey, and the like. That said, his views may surprise you. Kass's seven-hundred-page tome, *The Beginning of Wisdom: Reading Genesis*, performs what he calls an "unmediated reading" of the first book of the Bible. Nature is morally neutral, but humans should not be. The "new way," according to Kass, is really the old way, and can be summarized in a single word: *patriarchy*. Man rules in this world, and woman obeys—to her benefit. From the president's point man on ethics, we read that "a prolonged period of barrenness" before childbirth is God's way of "taming the dangerous female pride in her generative powers," and that marriage as an "institution of stable domestic arrangements for rearing the young depends on some form of man's rule over woman." Again, this is no adjunct lecturer at Bob Jones University, an easier target of condescension for radical centrists like me. Nope, this is the Addie Clark Harding Professor of the University of Chicago's Committee on Social Thought, that bastion of pricey Nobelitude.

I sit down with Kass during a break at the Wyndham. Trim and energetic at sixty-five, scholarly without seeming fussy, he has a genial spirit to go with a thorough command of this complex scientific material. Much as I disagree with him, I have little reason to doubt his goodwill. I begin by congratulating him for leading such nuanced and respectfully argued discussions for and against therapeutic cloning. I also tell him up front that, mainly because of my daughter, I want the spigot open much wider than he and the president do.

He politely objects to my premise. "It's been misrepresented that the council came out in opposition to embryonic-stem-cell research by a vote of ten to seven," he says. "It did not. It came out in favor of a ban on all cloning, including the cloning of embryos." Speaking, as always, in muscular sentences and pausing for paragraph breaks, he goes on. "Congress has not declared stem-cell research illegal; it has said there should be no federal funding for research that involves the destruction of embryos." Pause. "The president found a way to fund embryonic-stem-cell research on the existing lines, which means he has liberalized the research opportunities."

Liberalized? Only if we're talking about the handful of lines he let slide in 2001 while banning federally funded work on the hundreds more lines researchers will need to succeed. But this is the schizoid position in which Kass and his boss have been in lockstep from the outset—or so I assume.

"Is it fair to say that the president appointed you chair of the council because he knew in advance you agreed with him about the proper limits of cell research?" I ask. "Or did he form his position after, or mainly because of, advice you have offered?"

"The truth is, I don't know," Kass responds. "I will say that I think it's improper to reveal conversations that we have had or to speculate on the mind of the president. I think I know what brought me to his attention. It was not my views on stem-cell research, about which I'd never written a word. I've been trying to stop human cloning for thirty-five years. The president wanted to hear a discussion of the ethical issues, to hear how one would lay out the various arguments. I think it's fair to say that I did not tell him what I thought he should do."

So it's not that the president wanted a council that would lend intellectual heft to whatever position wins red-state votes?

"Look," he says, holding my eye, "the president is pro-life. You've got to acknowledge it." He hooks a thumb back toward those of his colleagues still being interviewed. "But no previous bioethics council had anything like this diversity. It's not fair to say you've got a council that's opposed to embryonic-stem-cell research. You have some people on this council who'd be distressed to see lots of embryos destroyed before there was any proof of efficacy. I myself am very hopeful that over the next decade we will learn an enormous amount from the existing lines. The spigot is open."

"What about your opposition to in vitro fertilization?" I ask, referring to the fact that in 1971 he was speaking against it aggressively, predicting that it would lead to deformed infants. A million or so normal IVF births down the road, he's been branded everything from a "bio-Luddite" and "false prophet of doom" to "a sixteenth-century sensibility to guide us through twenty-first-century conundrums."

"I was an early critic of IVF because I didn't know it was going to be safe for children," he says. "I thought IVF might eventually lead to cloning, which it might. I had a change of heart in 1978, just when Louise Brown was born. On the question of IVF for infertility, at least if it's shown to be safe, I changed my mind."

It takes a good man to admit that. Even so, I believe Dr. Kass is dead wrong once again. Given his way thirty years ago, we never would have discovered the glories of IVF; countless families wouldn't even exist. If Kass, Brownback, and the president succeed in making therapeutic cloning a criminal act, American scientists not only won't discover the first round of cures for spinal-cord damage, diabetes, Alzheimer's, Parkinson's, and heart disease, we'll never know how many other cures we missed out on. The tragedy will become exponential.

In the meantime, a thunderclap. On February 13, scientists in Seoul, South Korea, announced they had succeeded in cloning human embryos and extracting stem cells from them. The team was led by Drs. Woo Suk Hwang and Shin Yong Moon, both of Seoul National University. Dr. Hwang emphasized that the research was subject to rigorous oversight by an ethics committee. It took place in test tubes and petri dishes; no embryo was, or could have been, implanted in a uterus. None of the sixteen volunteers who provided 242 unfertilized ova were paid. The project was funded by the government of South Korea, where reproductive cloning is illegal. The team's goal, Dr. Hwang stated forcefully, was not to clone human beings but to advance understanding of the causes and treatment of human disease.

Scientists and patients around the world hailed the results.

A Chicago embryologist spoke for a lot of us by saying, "My reaction is, basically, wow." Dr. Kass's reaction came even before the Koreans' paper was published in *Science*. Speaking for the President's Council, he said, "The age of human cloning has apparently arrived: Today, cloned blastocysts for research; tomorrow, cloned blastocysts for baby-making. In my opinion, and that of the majority of the council, the only way to prevent this from happening here is for Congress to enact a comprehensive ban or moratorium on all human cloning." In much the same spirit, Carrie Gordon Earll of Focus on the Family branded the South Koreans' research "nothing short of cannibalism."

But I'm here to tell you that *my* family—and, I assume, millions of others—was thrilled. Said Bridget, "*Finally!*"

The overarching fact that our president and the majority of his council seem unable to get their minds around is that human nature *evolves*. "Normal human" used to describe a four-foot-nine-inch club-wielding cretin draped in gore-spattered fur. It used to be "natural" for Tarzan, after impregnating Jane, to lope off in search of a new sperm receptacle, clubbing other men to death as he went, until—*blam!* And for his witch doctor to smear this wound with dung while grunting a few incantations. From the perspective of these early humans, we are what a Cro-Magnon Charles Krauthammer would fearfully denounce as "a class of superhumans," or the Addie Clark Harding caveman would hastily label "posthuman."

Glorious though it may be, evolution is also, as James Watson put it, "damn cruel," mainly because genetic mutations have introduced about fifteen hundred diseases into human DNA. What could we do about it? Not much until doctors like Rudolf Virchow (1821–1902) came along. Virchow was the German physician who finally convinced the medical establishment that the basic units of life were self-replicating cells. Building on François Raspail's axiom *Omnis cellula e cellula*—every cell, diseased or otherwise, originates from another cell—Virchow overturned the conventional wisdom that it was the entire body, or one of its "vapours," that became sick. Yet Virchow's most radiant brainchild may be that "medicine is a social science, and politics is nothing but medicine on a large scale." We still fall woefully short of this ideal, but as beneficent M.D.'s like Hwang, Moon, William Mayo, Jonas Salk, and Paul Farmer have shown, fighting back against disease is the most humane thing we can do. The most human.

Whatever epoch we live in, we all have to face getting caught at the worst possible point on the curve of medical progress: My cowgirl's campfire is visible on the horizon, yet I am accorded the honor of being the very last hombre to succumb to Syndrome X. "Remember when people had heart attacks?" some lucky duck in 2050 may guffaw, clutching her chest in mock agony. "I mean, can you *imagine*?" This fortunate woman would be exactly as human as any victim of plague or polio, and a lot more human, in my view, than the cretin with the club. However long it may seem to us now, her life span will still seem to *her* the way Nabokov and Beckett imagined it in the middle of the twentieth century: as a brief crack of light between two infinities of darkness.

•   •   •

Speaking of infinities of darkness, adolescence is the first pro-longed test for people suffering with Type I diabetes. Physical routines readily followed by obedient ten-year-olds suddenly be-come a series of temptations to rebellion—against parents and authority in general, against the unrelenting regimens them-selves. The flood of new hormones disrupting skin tone, aca-demic performance, and household peace also wreak havoc on a diabetic's cardiovascular system. Psychological anxiety goes ther-monuclear, which sets off more fuming rebellion. My doctors and parents say I can never smoke cigarettes? I'll retreble my efforts to buy them at 7-Eleven. And what harm can come from skipping my shot on homecoming night? When Bridget's doctor revealed that her sugar control wasn't nearly as tight as it should be, she started skipping blood tests as well. Her mantra became "Why should I struggle to take care of myself if I'm gonna die young anyway?"

In the meantime, I stepped up my visits to researchers, who by the early 1990s were working on ways to keep the islet cells of cows and pigs from being rejected by humans. I studied reports, wrote letters to congressmen, talked to more doctors. I imagined myself going blind; I found myself volunteering to "God" to deal with this fate instead of Bridget. My firstborn child, my talented and beautiful daughter, was being ravaged from the inside out by a rapist who was taking his time, and there was nothing I could do about it.

I began a novel about riding a bicycle from Chicago to Alaska. Narrated in the voice of a young woman with diabetes, it was my attempt to empathize as vividly as I could with the disease-ridden angst my daughter faced every day. *Going to the Sun* turned into a road trip connecting two love stories, and the character of Penny Culligan is an amalgam of myself, my sister Ellen, and Bridget. But Penny's diabetes is the plutonium rod—potent, relentless, explosive—fueling each strand of the narrative. The ending is designed to evoke both the hope and desperation the young woman feels as she makes her way into adulthood.

The longer you have this disease, the more severe its complications become. It's a hassle from day one, to be sure, but after fifteen or twenty years your kidneys begin to break down and your retinopathy becomes more severe. Bridget's had diabetes for twenty-five years now. She's frightened, exhausted, and angry. She's also determined to overcome her long actuarial odds and live something resembling a normal life. But your self-esteem takes big hits when you have a chronic disease. Your skin becomes sallow and spongy from all the punctures; you also get to worry about whether you can get pregnant, carry a baby to term, then survive long enough to see your child enter kindergarten. "Why should I have to listen to the history of your cold," Bridget sometimes wants to know, "or how tough your meeting was? At least your freakin' pancreas works!"

If a cure isn't developed in the next few years or so, Bridget will become more and more susceptible to a heart attack or stroke, however diligently she takes care of herself. She may still go blind, and her kidneys might fail. As her circulatory system gets ravaged further, the dainty feet she used to lace into white size 5½ softball spikes may need to be amputated.

·   ·   ·

What scares me the most, of course, is the possibility that Bridget's disease will take its course just before the cure comes online. Which is why I so heartily agree with the council's minority. American society, it writes in *Human Cloning and Human Dignity*, has "an obligation to heal the sick and relieve their suffering." The minority accords "no special moral status to the early-stage cloned embryo," because it has no capacity for consciousness in any form. Even more to the point, "the *potential* to become something (or someone) is hardly the same as *being* something (or someone)."

As to whether somatic cell nuclear transfer would lead to cloned children or human-animal hybrids—the slippery-slope argument—Harvard's Michael Sandel proposes that the research should proceed "subject to regulations that embody the moral restraint appropriate to the mystery of the first stirrings of human life." Specifically: strict licensing criteria for labs, laws against commodifying ova or sperm, and measures to keep private firms from monopolizing access to cell lines. The minority concludes that it's "perfectly possible to treat a blastocyst as a clump of cells usable for lifesaving research, while prohibiting any such use of a later-stage embryo or fetus." We shouldn't outlaw all cloning, in other words, just because its therapeutic applications *could* be misused. Even Michael Jackson's face doesn't get plastic surgeons arrested.

Finally, because of advances in SCNT, *any* human cell could theoretically become a person if it were doctored aggressively enough in a lab. "If mere potentiality to develop into a human being is enough to make something morally human," the minority continues, "then every human cell has a special or inviolable moral status, a view that is patently absurd."

In addition to Sandel, the enlightened minority includes Janet Rowley, the Blum-Riese Distinguished Service Professor at the Pritzker School of Medicine at the University of Chicago. Dr. Rowley is blunt in her opposition: "Our ignorance is profound; the potential for important medical advances is very great. Congress should lift the ban and establish a broadly constituted regulatory board, *now*."

A few hours after my chat with the chairman, I sit down with Dr. Rowley. "Dr. Kass makes the case that the council hasn't done anything to inhibit embryonic-cell research," I begin. "He claims Bush has *opened* the spigot."

"Well, I would disagree," says Dr. Rowley, an elegant, hazel-eyed woman with undyed silver-brown hair. "For many people in the majority, a fertilized ovum is a human being, and therefore taking that single cell and doing anything with it is murder. Others of us believe that while a fertilized ovum has the potential to become a human being, if this potential human being could in fact lead us to something that could save the lives of many human beings, then we think it's a matter of competing goods. Helping many, many individuals is justification for taking a single cell or an early multiple-cell organism and using it to benefit more individuals."

Before I can hug her or put my fist in the air, she continues: "Now, to a purist, of course, that's immaterial. It's 'man in his hubris intervening,' not nature or God or whatever entity you want to invoke."

"Yet God is never mentioned explicitly. . . ."

"No," Rowley says. "They would generally cite moral and philosophical reasons. But in our early conversations, it was brought up that in Jewish and Islamic law, a developing embryo didn't become human for forty days—well within the limits of the time frame in which embryos would be used for therapeutic research."

Think back to that human-development continuum in your high school biology textbook. Sperm meets ovum on the left, full-term fetus to the right. No reasonable person would let researchers destroy anything recognizably human, just as no one objects to putting blood under an electron microscope. The points of contention fall somewhere between a blastocyst and the forty-day-old embryo of religious tradition. Exactly where we draw the line, and whether we make a distinction between what happens in a petri dish and what *could* happen in a uterus *but doesn't*, is determined by either spiritual/faith-based beliefs or rational/scientific principles.

In a democratic society, then, who gets to draw it? Why not George W. Bush, for example, with the backing of his eminent council? Well, one reason is that the person officially charged with helping Dr. Kass push the majority's agenda through Congress is executive director Dean Clancy, who spent eight years on the staff of Dick Armey. Not only is Clancy opposed to embryonic-stem-cell research, he virulently opposes public schools and federal taxes, which makes him what most folks would call a fanatic. Such appointments extend the Bush-Cheney pattern of loading any dice that get tossed down the policy table. In December 2002, for example, Bush appointed Dr. W. David Hager to an FDA committee on reproductive drugs. Hager is not only ferociously opposed to therapeutic cloning but has been accused of refusing to prescribe contraceptives to unmarried women; to women suffering from premenstrual syndrome, he counsels prayer and Bible reading. (You heard me.) In February, a group of sixty scientists—including twenty Nobel laureates—issued a statement that this administration repeatedly censors reports written by its own scientists, stacks its advisory councils, and disbands those offering unwanted advice. "Other administrations have, on occasion, engaged in such practices," the scientists wrote, "but not so systematically nor on so wide a front." Bush's response to such criticism? In late February, he and Dr. Kass replaced two members of the minority—Elizabeth Blackburn and William F. May—with three new members who all oppose therapeutic cloning. Dr. Kass's fair, diverse council is now tilted thirteen to five.

The majority of a different president's council—John Kerry's, for example, or the one Al Gore would have appointed—could make an equally strong case in favor of therapeutic cloning. At least as many alternate chairmen with bring-us-to-our-knees credentials—Janet Rowley, for example, or Douglas Melton, codirector of the Harvard Stem Cell Institute—stand ready to argue that position. Most of our scrutiny, then, should focus on the person who makes the appointments.

In January 2002, the president greeted members of his council in the Roosevelt Room of the White House, asking them to be mindful of "the notion that life is—you know, that there is a Creator." It's precisely this willful confusion of realms, this thumbing of his nose at the sworn constitutional duty to keep church and state separate, that keeps folks like me from stomaching the president but makes millions of others just crazy about the guy.

Isn't it inevitable, then, that sectarian dogma will tip the balance on every tough issue? Not really. Plenty of conservative Republicans, such as Trent Lott, Orrin Hatch, and Nancy Reagan, support embryonic-stem-cell research. Senator Hatch has said, "I just cannot equate a child living in a womb, with moving toes and fingers and a beating heart, with an embryo about to be taken from the freezer and which will be lawfully discarded if we don't use it."

Sooner or later, of course, a Bush will need cell-replacement therapy, and he or she may have to fly to California, New Jersey, or maybe even Seoul. Much worse, the necessary treatment may not be ready yet *anywhere*. But here's another thing I have faith in: Once the cures are available, those who opposed therapeutic cloning in 2004 will damn well find a way to get themselves and their families treated. It's not even hard to imagine them elbowing their way to the front of the line at the clinic. "Oh, yeah?" says my daughter. "Over my dead body."

·   ·   ·

American medicine has long been guided by men and women of serious learning, not religiously correct politicians. We seem to understand that when science gets trumped by sectarianism, more bad things happen than good. The framers of our Constitution deliberately omitted God from its language, assigning supreme power to "We the People." They wanted to insulate us from holy wars, crusades, and oxymorons like "creation science."

Jimmy Carter, our first born-again president, faithfully kept religion and policy separate, and the intelligence of his heart gets more and more plain every year. In the early 1960s, moderate Democrat John Kennedy went out of his way to avoid giving even the slightest impression that his Catholicism might override his duties as chief executive. John Kerry, another Yankee Catholic, gives every indication he would do the same thing.

Back in July 2001, Kerry wrote a letter urging Bush to fully fund embryonic-stem-cell research. As Kerry said later, "Compassionate conservatism could have meant lifesaving treatments for those suffering from Parkinson's and Alzheimer's disease; instead it appears to be using words of compassion to mask efforts to keep a campaign promise to conservatives. . . . If, as he says, the president believes that stem-cell research may have lifesaving potential for millions, he should give scientists the tools to explore it rather than have the government impose burdensome restrictions." Kerry then cosponsored (with Republican Arlen Specter) a Senate bill to support embryonic-stem-cell research. The bill stalled in committee, but now, on the campaign trail, Kerry pounds away on this issue: "The medical discoveries that will come from stem-cell research are crucial next steps in humanity's uphill climb. . . . If we pursue the limitless potential of our science—and trust that we can use it wisely—we will save millions of lives and earn the gratitude of future generations."

In the meantime, here's how a wartime Republican balanced civic and spiritual responsibilities back in 1862, while thinking about the Emancipation Proclamation: "I am approached with the most opposite opinions and advice, and that by religious men who are equally certain that they represent the divine will. . . . I hope it will not be irreverent for me to say that if it is probable that God would reveal his will to others, on a point so connected with my duty, it might be supposed that he would reveal it directly to me. . . . These are not, however, the days of miracles, and I suppose it will be granted that I am not to expect a direct revelation. I must study the plain physical facts of the case, ascertain what is possible, and learn what appears to be wise and right." And he did.

San Francisco Magazine

"Innocence Lost" doesn't simply make a convincing case that California may have sentenced as many as 1,500 people to life in prison for crimes they didn't commit. This exhaustively reported, well-packaged investigation also explains how this happens so routinely—and why innocent lifers face such daunting obstacles that they might actually be better off on death row.

Nina Martin

Innocence Lost

The strangest thing happened to John Stoll this past spring. After twenty years in jail for an infamous crime he did not commit, a judge said it had all been a mistake, and he was set free. "You win some, you lose some," the prosecutor shrugged, refusing to offer any admission of error or hint of an apology for all that her office had put Stoll through. None of his family was in the courtroom; they were all dead or far away and not terribly interested in what happened to him anymore. He was released from custody on his sixty-first birthday; after treating him to filet mignon and chocolate cake, his lawyers took him to buy socks and underwear, and then they took him to live with them in San Jose, because he had nowhere else to go and barely a penny to his name.

John Stoll met only one other man in prison he is certain is innocent, though he is sure the California penal system is full of them—he just never asked. For one thing, the places where he was incarcerated—San Quentin, Avenal, Tehachapi, Mule Creek—were teeming with meth freaks, white supremacists, desperadoes, guys he had nothing in common with and did not especially want to get to know. Nor did he want to talk about his own ordeal; it would be asking for a knife in his back. Back in 1984, when he was a carpenter and foreman at a gas plant in Bakersfield, he had been accused of leading a child-sex-abuse ring whose supposed victims included his own five-year-old son. It was a weird, weird time in Kern County, with dozens of men and women accused of ritual sexual abuse by the same whacked-out group of cops, social workers, and prosecutors, but judges and jurors bought into the hysteria, and Stoll was lucky that his sentence for seventeen counts of child molestation was only forty years. (Some people got 400 years.) Over the next decade, most of those convictions were overturned after the child witnesses recanted or courts found that their testimony had been coerced; in one of the stranger twists, the man who had prosecuted Stoll was stabbed to death by a police investigator who suspected he was having an affair with the cop's son. Two of Stoll's codefendants won their state appeal fifteen years ago; his own appeal was denied in part because of a mistake his lawyer had made during the trial—failing to introduce a psychologist's finding that Stoll showed none of the telltale traits of a pedophile. In twenty years, Stoll told only six other inmates this story. "I did not need people thinking I was a child molester," he says. At one prison, he went to the library and razored all traces of his case from a law book so no one would discover his secret.

Every few years, Stoll would try to interest someone on the outside—a famous lawyer, a pro bono legal group—in helping him pursue another round of appeals. "I wrote to the ACLU. I wrote to everybody like that. The ACLU told me they weren't working on that particular type of case at that time. Then I saw that they were suing some city because of a manger scene in a park. And I'm thinking—what the hell! Here I am sitting in prison and you're worried about how Christmas is run." Eventually he lost heart. "It gets to be like picking open a scab, telling that story twenty times," Stoll says. "You've got to put it away." So when the lawyer who had won his codefendants' appeal found someone to help him, Stoll wasn't sure he wanted to cooperate. "Because after eighteen years, you know, it's pretty much: Do I want to do this again?"

It took another two years for lawyers at Santa Clara University School of Law's Innocence Project, part of a national pro bono movement dedicated to exonerating innocent inmates, to track down witnesses, put together a habeas petition, and persuade a state judge to free him. The hardest part of the process was seeing his son, Jed, for the first time since his 1985 trial. Of the six kids who had testified against Stoll then, five—now grown—recanted at a hearing last winter. Only Jed, not even in kindergarten at the time of the arrest, continued to insist that his father had molested him, though under questioning he could give no details. The boy Stoll remembers—happy, trusting, bewildered to have his father ripped from his life—had become a wary and troubled young man, himself the father of a child Stoll expects never to meet. Stoll was unrecognizable, too—still handsome, with penetrating blue eyes, but balding and gray. "He didn't have any idea who I was," Stoll recalls sadly. "The only reason he knew I was probably his father was because I was sitting in the defendant's chair. Oh my God . . . that was worse than the conviction—having him there and thinking I did something to him. Because I really love that little guy, you know? And I didn't do nothing to him. But if he . . . if he is going to believe it, I can't help it. There's nothing I can do."

Stoll says he talked to a child psychologist, who told him that Jed faced a heartbreaking dilemma: either his father had molested him, or he had been wrongfully imprisoned and Jed was to blame. "And to protect your sanity, you're going to say your dad did something," Stoll says. "The damn shame is—it's not his fault. He was a five-year-old child when this started, for God's sake. I had people say, 'Aren't you angry at your son?' How in the hell could I be mad at a five-year-old child that I loved to death?" There are tears in his eyes.

Stoll looks around the sun-filled cottage behind his lawyers' house, his home for a year while he gets back on his feet—the big, inviting bed; the new computer he is teaching himself to use; the calla lilies lounging by the door—and it's clear: none of this makes any more sense than anything else that's happened to him in the past twenty years. You wish you could tell him that it had all been a dream, that in the garden just outside, a lost little boy waits for his father to come out and play. But the afternoon is hot and still and the garden is empty.

·   ·   ·

John Tennison used to see Rick Walker and Albert Johnson all the time in the yard at Mule Creek State Prison, in the dusty town of Ione, thirty miles southeast of Sacramento. All three were African American men from the Bay Area doing very long sentences—Tennison and Walker for murder, Johnson for rape. "But we never knew much about each other's stories," Tennison says, a handsome thirty-three-year-old with a proud, wary face. "I didn't speak about my case to other inmates. I didn't pry about theirs."

Keeping quiet was something inmates learned early. Prisons are full of desperate people willing to snitch on each other for favors, better living conditions, a sentence reduction. "There's no telling what someone might get out of the conversation and use against you," he says. Not that anyone would have believed him if he had told his story. Tennison was innocent of the murder—a San Francisco gang killing in the late 1980s—for which he was serving a life term, with little possibility of early release. "You hear a lot of people say they're innocent. I would take it with a grain of salt."

Yet it turned out the other two men were innocent, too. Johnson was the first to be exonerated; he was serving thirty-nine years for two 1992 rapes in the Richmond area when DNA testing cleared him in October 2002. The following summer, Walker was set free after the Santa Clara County prosecutor's office finally conceded that he did not suffocate and mutilate a former girlfriend during a 1991 robbery-murder; he had been framed by his codefendant, one of the real killers, and convicted by a prosecutor who made secret deals with witnesses who turned out to be liars. Tennison was the last to get out, in August 2003, when a federal magistrate ruled that San Francisco police and prosecutors had violated his right to a fair trial by withholding evidence that pointed to someone else as the shooter; his codefendant, Antoine Goff, was exonerated as well. Now Tennison checks in with the others regularly, though he wouldn't call them close. "These guys are people who have walked in my shoes," he says. "We're trying to fit back into society the best way we can. It's like we were just dropped off on another planet."

Extraordinary as it may seem, yet another Bay Area man who'd been scheduled to spend the rest of his life in prison was freed last year, for a total of five exonerations in an eleven-month period—hardly the kind of record you'd expect in a place as liberal as this. Glen "Buddy" Nickerson Jr. was convicted of killing two San Jose men during a 1984 robbery. Within a few years, the evidence that had seemed clear-cut to prosecutors and jurors started to crumble as police investigators came under scrutiny and the real killers insisted he had nothing to do with the crime. Still, it took until March 2003 to persuade a federal judge to set Nickerson free. He had spent almost nineteen years behind bars.

In a recent essay, this is how Innocence Project founders Barry Scheck and Peter Neufeld characterized the wave of exonerations that has swept across the country in the last few years, shattering faith in the criminal justice system's ability to protect the innocent: "Nothing comparable has ever happened in the history of American jurisprudence; indeed, nothing like it has happened to any judicial system anywhere." Of the hundreds of wrongful convictions that have come to light, revelations about innocent people on death row have caused the greatest loss of confidence—116 capital convicts exonerated around the country, forensic lab chaos in the Texas county that sentences more people to death than anywhere else, an Illinois system so riddled with error that a Republican governor commuted 167 death sentences in one stroke. In California, juries are handing out fewer death sentences and the state Supreme Court is scrutinizing them more carefully than at any time since the late 1980s. Last February, squeamishness about the state's capital system came to this: convicted quadruple-murderer Kevin Cooper was within three hours and forty-five minutes of being executed by lethal injection at San Quentin when a federal appeals court ruled that his lawyers could do state-of-the-art DNA testing on incriminating hair and bloodstains, based on the *theoretical* possibility that traces of a preservative chemical found in earlier tests might have indicated evidence tampering.

Yet as circumspect as California has become about meting out the death penalty, it's been almost cavalier when it comes to locking people up for a very long time—"death by incarceration," some call it. By the end of June 2004, an astounding 30,492 state inmates—twice as many as in the entire European Union, which has a population over twelve times bigger—carried life sentences; of these, 7,500 are serving twenty-five-to-life terms under the three-strikes initiative (over half of them people whose third strike was not a violent or serious crime). Some 17 percent of California inmates are lifers, compared with 9 percent of prisoners in the United States as a whole.

All this despite the fact that the same kinds of problems that lead to wrongful convictions in death penalty cases also result in sending innocent people like Stoll, Tennison, and Goff to prison for the rest of their lives. Few criminal justice experts doubt that California, whose penal system is thought to be the third largest *in the world*, has put more innocent people behind bars than any other state. In the past fifteen years, with surprisingly little fanfare, at least 200 Californians have been freed after courts found they were unjustly convicted—nearly twice the number of known exonerations as in Illinois and Texas combined. Just a handful were death row inmates, versus dozens of men and women sentenced to very long terms. California's innocence problem, it turns out, is primarily a matter of life, not death.

Implicit in the state's lock-'em-up stance is a fundamental assumption: that the criminal justice system is just, and that in the rare cases when innocent people are sent to jail, the system corrects the error. This impression—aided and abetted by *Law & Order* reruns, eleventh-hour death penalty appeals, even the brief blast of publicity that attends each new exoneration—turns out to be wrong. As California has put the screws on the guilty, it's also gotten much tougher on the innocent.

San Francisco has spent the last year reviewing California's largely unexamined record on wrongful convictions, going back to 1989, the year of the country's first DNA exoneration. We've spoken to dozens of lawyers, prosecutors, judges, and criminal justice experts. We've read through thousands of pages of court documents in thirty cases. What we've learned about how the system treats innocent people facing life or very long terms should dismay anyone, liberal or conservative, who values decency, fairness, and the rule of law. California's legal system has its own inexorable momentum, which pushes for conviction even when the evidence should give serious pause. Once an innocent person lands in jail, the mistake becomes almost impossible to undo. For those convicted of the worst crimes, even parole is unlikely.

At every stage, the safeguards in place to protect the innocent seem small, considering the severity of a long or life sentence. Defendants facing the death penalty get two court-appointed trial lawyers plus funds for investigators and expert witnesses. If they are convicted, the state pays for multiple appeals in the California Supreme Court, then the federal courts. Lifers, on the other hand, are entitled to a single lawyer at trial and then another one for a state court appeal, with almost no chance of review by the state Supreme Court; after that, they're on their own. The state pays to reinvestigate cases that result in death sentences, but not botched cases that result in life. Capital cases get a decade or more of appellate scrutiny; lifer cases, just a year or two. As the U.S. Supreme Court sees it, "actual innocence" is reason in and of itself to reverse a conviction only if someone is on death row—not if the sentence is life.

In short, an innocent Californian convicted of murder is almost better off being sentenced to death than to life in prison—at least the case will get a long, hard look. Lawyers find death cases more glamorous, too. When he was the lawyer for John Tennison, Jeff Adachi, now San Francisco's public defender, tried to line up pro bono legal assistance to free his client. Several big law firms initially expressed interest. Then they learned Tennison was only a lifer. They declined to get involved.

How many innocent people are sitting in California prisons, unable to get anyone's attention or too beaten down even to try? How many millions of dollars does the state waste incarcerating people who've done nothing wrong? How many violent criminals continue to prey on an unsuspecting public because someone else is doing their time? The answers are mostly hidden, and expensive and time-consuming to uncover, so no one knows—and, it sometimes seems, not many people want to know. Around the state, a handful of small Innocence Projects exist to investigate these cases, and they have been overwhelmed, with an estimated 1,000 requests for help each year. The advent of DNA testing has revealed a higher error rate than most anyone suspected: in one eye-opening FBI study, out of 18,000 sexual assault cases in which biological evidence was available, pretrial testing cleared over 25 percent of the government's prime suspects, often after they'd already been arrested and arraigned. Among academics, the most conservative estimates put the wrongful conviction rate across the country at no less than 1 in 200 and probably 1 in 100; most experts believe a truer rate is between 1 in 50 and 1 in 20. By these estimates, the judicial system catches the right person 95 to 99.5 percent of the time—not a bad record, unless you happen to be one of the mistakes.

Judges, D.A.s, police, lawmakers—even many defense attorneys—defend California's legal system as among the nation's most careful and sophisticated and deny that lifelong incarcerations of innocent people are a major problem. Yet if the experts are correct, in a state with 163,500 inmates, up to 8,000 are not guilty of the crimes for which they were imprisoned. Meanwhile, the number of those innocent lifers who can expect to die in prison eventually—of disease, despair, violence, old age—is at least 150 and, if you believe the most dire estimates, as high as 1,500.

There's a temptation to look at the ones like John Tennison and John Stoll who do get out as proof that the system works. They're flukes. There's a temptation to see the confluence of events that put them in prison and kept them there as freak accidents. But so many accidents in such run-of-the-mill cases involving such a wide range of ordinary people mean something has gone seriously wrong. Some might look at these cases and conclude that California's criminal justice system is filled with reckless men and women who don't care when they do harm. But most of them—police, prosecutors, lawyers, judges—were just trying to do their job the best way they knew how. It's the system itself that has become the problem—enormous, impersonal, legalistic, myopic, and fueled by fear and wrath. Unable to admit its failures, unwilling to hold itself accountable, it is destined to perpetuate its injustices and repeat its mistakes. This is the system we created. But is it really what we had in mind?

The Conviction

All I wanted was somebody to answer one simple question—who seen the 430-pound fat guy?   **—Buddy Nickerson**

Buddy Nickerson spent the most important night of his life sleeping off a hangover. Earlier in the evening of September 14, 1984, he'd attended a party at a friend's house. Instead of going home, he'd dozed off in his pick-up in the friend's driveway. As usual, he made a vivid impression: his bare feet—big, like everything else about him—were hanging out the window, and his boots, which were in the house, stank. It wasn't till the next day that he heard about the murder of an acquaintance named John Evans on the rough edges of San Jose. Evans was the kind of guy whose high school class might have voted him "most likely to die in a blaze of gunfire." When he wasn't manufacturing and selling meth, he was a car painter of the naked-babe-on-the-hood variety, known for his ugly temper and the wads of cash he kept stashed around his house. According to his close friend Mike Osorio, three armed robbers—white guys of average build, wearing ski masks—had broken into the house where Osorio had fallen asleep watching TV with Evans's half brother. The assailants pistol-whipped the two men, then lay in wait for Evans, who returned home after midnight, sensed something was wrong, and started shooting. Evans and his half brother died at the scene; Osorio survived a point-blank bullet to the head. Neighbors reported seeing three normal-sized men fleeing in different directions, including one who—though wounded and bleeding—escaped over a fence.

Santa Clara County sheriff's investigators immediately pegged Nickerson, then twenty-nine, as one of the killers. Barely a month before, Evans had beaten up one of Nickerson's brothers so badly that he had been permanently paralyzed. Nickerson had a minor record, a reputation as a hothead, and an impressive collection of racist tattoos. But he wasn't too worried, even after he was arrested. Besides his alibi, there was the matter of his size: he weighed 430 pounds, twice as big as any of the men fleeing from the scene. There wasn't a hair or thread, not a fingerprint or drop of blood, tying him to the killings. Even if he had been able to exert himself in the way the cops claimed, surely someone his size would have left a trace. Nickerson was so sure the system would see the error of its ways that, with the death penalty on the table, he turned down an amazingly sweet deal: twelve years for a guilty plea. Why should he admit to something he didn't do?

The real murderers had left behind plenty of evidence of their involvement. Over the next few months, police picked up three more suspects, including a guy Nickerson knew named Murray Lodge, who had planned the robbery and shot the victims. Lodge thought it was hilarious that Nickerson had been arrested, since the two men hated each other's guts. Still, he told his own defense lawyer that Nickerson was innocent.

With no physical evidence tying Nickerson to the crime, the detectives had to find witnesses who could make their case for them. In the end, they came up with two credible enough to convince a jury. After initially telling the deputies that he had no idea who his attackers were, Osorio, the sole survivor—still dazed from the beating, the shooting, and the surgery to remove the bullet—changed his story and said Nickerson had been one of them. Osorio's new version was bolstered by a young man named Brian Tripp, who lived nearby. He had originally described the man he'd seen running from the scene as 200 pounds and apparently wounded, with a mustache. But after repeated discussions with investigators, he, too, identified Nickerson—hugely obese, uninjured, with a full, shaggy beard.

The story of how Buddy Nickerson came to be convicted of first-degree murder illustrates the most common problem leading to wrongful convictions in California: eyewitness error. In our analysis of thirty such cases, 60 percent involved at least one key witness who identified the wrong person. (When intentional perjury is included, the figure is 87 percent.) The reasons are familiar to anyone who's ever watched a TV crime show: everything from poor visibility and stress (Osorio's brain trauma definitely counts) to the surprising difficulty humans have distinguishing faces, especially those of another race. Witnesses don't just get it wrong when the suspect is a stranger and the crime occurred some distance away. A Los Angeles janitor named Jason Kindle was sentenced to seventy years to life for an armed robbery at the Office Depot where he mopped floors after five of his coworkers incorrectly identified him as the heavily disguised man who'd forced them to the floor and fled with $22,000. In all six California rape convictions later overturned by DNA testing, the victim's mistaken ID was the most important factor in sending an innocent person to prison for a very long time. The most striking error involved Kevin Green, a marine living in Orange County who was mistaken *by his own wife* for the attacker who raped and beat her, putting her in a coma, shattering her memory, and killing their unborn child. The real assailant, identified by a DNA hit sixteen years later, turned out to be the "Bedroom Basher," responsible for at least five other murders in the area. Even after the real attacker confessed, Green's ex-wife insisted Green did it.

Yet to call it "eyewitness error" is a mistake in itself; police lineups and other investigative techniques often help steer the witness toward a suspect who later proves blameless. Kindle's colleagues, for example, continued working around him for seven weeks after the robbery without pointing the finger at him; only after police detained him at the store, letting everyone know he was a suspect, did they pick him out of a photographic lineup. Herman Atkins spent twelve years in prison for rape in part because the victim saw his face on a wanted poster for another crime just before viewing him in a lineup. Even a clearheaded guy like Brian Tripp is vulnerable. Several years after Nickerson's trial, Tripp— by then a deputy sheriff in Colusa County—recanted and insisted Nickerson was not the suspect he'd seen after all. Tripp's explanation for his retraction: his law enforcement experience made him realize that the sheriff's investigators had subtly cajoled him to shape his story to fit their theory. "I began to feel that they had a suspect in mind that I was close to, um, helping them convict. I remember questions such as, 'Couldn't he have been larger?' or 'Are you sure he wasn't a heavier-set man?' and I think I began to doubt myself."

Another key factor in Nickerson's conviction, a federal court later concluded, was questionable police work—sloppy at best, misconduct at worst. Indeed, police errors and ethical lapses seem to be a particular problem in California, occurring in 63 percent of false convictions in our analysis, versus 38 percent in a nationwide study by the Innocence Project. (The figure zooms when you include the scores of exonerations in the Kern County sex-abuse cases and the LAPD's Ramparts scandal, in which a band of rogue cops did everything from plant drugs and guns on innocent people to beat up witnesses.) On TV, police investigators are dispassionate sleuths who examine the evidence and adjust their theories to fit it. In real life, cops often get invested in theories that, for various reasons—sympathy for the victim, pressure to wrap up a case, a gut feeling that the suspect is a bad person who should be off the streets—they are unwilling to abandon. "Where improprieties tend to happen most is when they really think the suspect is the culprit but they have a weak case, so they think they're justified if they stretch," says Janice Brickley, an attorney with the Innocence Project at Golden Gate University. In Nickerson's case, the friends he'd been partying with on the night of the murders said the sheriff's investigators threatened them in an attempt to shake his alibi (it didn't work); the detectives had also been caught hiding evidence. Later, in the death penalty trial of Nickerson's codefendant Murray Lodge, the same cops were discovered to have lied on the witness stand (they claimed they hadn't taped a confession; then the tape was found), leading the judge to declare they'd committed perjury.

In fact, police have been accused of improprieties in 83 percent of the Bay Area wrongful conviction cases in our analysis. But Los Angeles County's record of police mistakes and misconduct trumps all, often going hand in hand with the use of informants. For years a virtual snitch industry has existed in L.A. jails, with inmates routinely making up incriminating stories about their cell mates in exchange for favorable treatment. The Long Beach murder case against Thomas Lee Goldstein hints at how it worked. Police had little evidence against the ex-marine until they found a heroin-addicted informant with the unlikely name of Edward F. Fink who claimed Goldstein had confessed to him; Fink made the same claim about ten other cell mates. Prosecutors also hid a leniency deal that might have helped discredit Fink. Goldstein served twenty-four years in prison until a series of courts ordered him freed this year.

Prosecutors can fall prey to the same emotions that lure a cop over the line. They sometimes get cynical and wrapped up in cases in ways that make it difficult to see new evidence and information in an objective light. They genuinely believe the suspect is guilty; they want to help victims find closure with a conviction. They succumb to the adversarial mind-set and the competitive pressure to win. Indeed, misconduct or serious errors in judgment by prosecutors have been an issue in 47 percent of the false convictions in our analysis (nationally, the average is 34 percent)—most commonly, concealing deals with snitches and co-defendants, turning a blind eye when witnesses lie and cops cross the line, and making improper arguments to the jury.

Contributing to official misconduct is the unlikeliness of punishment. A *Los Angeles Times* investigation in 2000 found that the Los Angeles D.A.'s office declined to prosecute even when an officer had been caught in the act on tape or had confessed, or when the officer's lie had led to an innocent person's arrest. One L.A. cop involved in a wrongful conviction case was allowed to retire with a full pension after he'd been caught using police computers to spy on celebrities. The sheriff's investigators in Nickerson's case—whose misconduct led to two mistrials that cost Santa Clara County millions of dollars and convicted an innocent man—suffered no setbacks to their careers as a result of their actions; one went on to oversee all the department's investigations, including homicides. Meanwhile, none of the D.A.s accused of improprieties in any of the false convictions in this analysis has been disciplined by the state bar, the agency that acts as a watchdog over the 195,100 lawyers licensed to practice here.

Bad defense lawyering is another big problem. Around the state, innocent people have been sent away for long prison terms at least in part because their attorneys were inexperienced, lazy, incompetent, or just plain conflicted about representing someone they believed to be guilty. Court-appointed lawyers, particularly public defenders, tend to be overworked and underfunded and hence are more likely to cut corners. One East Bay lawyer failed to order DNA testing that might have cleared her client of two rapes. Another, whose client was eventually convicted of attempted murder, didn't get a translation of a taped confession by another man. Sometimes the lawyer's biggest error is a naive belief that a jury will not convict because the evidence is so weak. In fact, many jurors expect defendants to *prove* they are innocent, not just poke holes in the prosecution's case. Even in a liberal place like the Bay Area, plenty of jurors assume that defendants wouldn't be on trial if they hadn't done *something* bad.

The simple truth: even the most dedicated lawyer may not be good enough to save an innocent person from prison when the rest of the system is intent on conviction. That's what happened in the late 1980s, when San Francisco was convulsed by a murderous gang war hauntingly similar to the one it faces today. Then, as now, many of the victims were young African American men; the police, like the police today, had little help from the community in bringing killers to justice. Antoine "Soda Pop" Goff, a twenty-year-old vocational student "running with the wrong folks" at the time, sees his 1990 wrongful conviction for the murder of a young man named Roderick Shannon as part of the city's rush to crack down on the violence: "My opinion is that [police] had it out for me. I had a friend that was shot when I was in the car. They came around in their investigation and I never wanted to talk to them. So when they had an opportunity to link me to a case, they did."

The Shannon murder was one of the rare times when witnesses did come forward and a conviction seemed possible—

which may be why police worked so hard to protect their case when it started falling apart. The two young girls who named Goff also fingered John Tennison, a seventeen-year-old from a close-knit family who knew Goff slightly. The girls' stories contradicted each other, the physical evidence, and other people who had seen the crime go down, but that didn't deter the investigating officers, Napoleon Hendrix and future police chief Earl Sanders. When one of the girls recanted, saying she didn't witness any murder, Hendrix and Sanders pressured her to go back to her original version of events, the girl later said in a sworn statement. When another witness came forward to say that Goff and Tennison hadn't been at the crime scene—and named the gangbanger who was the real killer—the cops didn't turn over her name or information to the defense. When the young man she implicated, Lovinsky Ricard, volunteered in a taped confession to other police officers after the trial that he was, indeed, the shooter, police still didn't turn the tape over to the defense for another several months. By then, it was too late.

"I know I'll never make up for that time," says Goff, who got twenty-seven years to life. "I lost the best years of my life."

Tennison lost more than that. "My father passed away, my grandfather passed away, my two uncles passed away, my brother was murdered. I didn't get to see my dad before he died. I wasn't released for any of the funerals." His only contact with any of these events was when one of his relatives called or visited. "It was always good to see one another," he says. "But when it was time to leave, the tears would not stop. It was terrible, really."

The Appeal

They don't even read your case, man. They're just like, "Denied, denied, denied." —Rick Walker

Not many people get sent to prison to practice their chosen profession. Gloria Killian used to joke that she was one of the "lucky" ones. Convincing herself that she'd been dispatched to Frontera prison, aka the California Institution for Women, on a divine mission—to use her legal training to fight for the rights of forgotten and neglected women—made what happened to her easier to bear. Not that she actually *understood* what had happened to her. "It was like being wrapped in fog," she says, still sounding dumbfounded twenty-plus years later. "I couldn't get my hands around it. I kept pulling at it and pulling at it, but I couldn't figure it out. I literally did not know how I had gotten there."

What she did know had all the hallmarks of a paranoid delusion. Once upon a time, Killian had been the kind of feisty, confident woman who would just pick up and move to Alaska for the adventure of it, or talk her way into law school even though she had only one semester of college under her belt. But as she was approaching her mid-thirties, her life came unglued. She got mixed up with a guy she describes as bad news, quit McGeorge School of Law in Sacramento, and supported herself with a variety of jobs, including doing freelance detective work for her landlord, the co-owner of a coin shop.

The real nightmare started in 1981. One day, an elderly coin collector was robbed, hog-tied, and shot to death in his home; his seventy-six-year-old wife was gravely wounded. Someone called the Sacramento police and accused a law student named Gloria of being involved, so they picked her up. Killian couldn't believe it, and a judge didn't either; the charges against her were soon dropped. "But I had a really terrible, terrible feeling," Killian says. "I should have left town, but I didn't." Her premonitions came true a year later, when a repeat felon named Gary Masse was convicted of the shootings and sentenced to life without parole. Before going off to prison, he offered to help prosecutors nail his two accomplices. One, he said, was his cousin, a guy named Stephen DeSantis. The other, he claimed, was Gloria Killian—allegedly the brains behind the scheme. Masse had met Killian, though they weren't friends. She and her lawyers figured that he was trying to deflect police attention from his wife, who had helped him in a robbery attempt a few months before and was a potential suspect in this case. This time, the accusation stuck. In 1986, Killian was convicted of conspiracy and murder and sentenced to thirty-two years to life. "All I could think was, this is insane, this is insane, this is insane."

In prison, Killian's main goal was to keep from going crazy herself. Her salvation turned out to be a job at the law library. Sometimes she helped fifty women a day—with appeals, child custody and medical issues, parole board hearings; over her entire prison career, her "clientele" numbered in the thousands. She took a special interest in battered women who had killed their abusive spouses, then been convicted of felony murder, writing law review articles and thousands of letters to raise awareness about their plight. She even helped win clemency for one such battered woman—a California first. Yet when it came to her own case, Killian did almost nothing. Her court-appointed trial lawyer had been followed by a court-appointed appellate lawyer. After the state appeals court upheld her conviction, she didn't have enough grounds—no new evidence, no convincing proof that her constitutional rights had been violated—to begin another round of appeals. Nearly a decade after her conviction, she hardly even talked about her case. "Who would care?" she says.

Killian—fifty-eight now, with a warm, disarmingly direct manner that belies her sad eyes—is not a particularly religious woman. But in the early nineties, a series of things happened that might convince the most cynical person that God exists. First she was befriended by an elderly Pasadena prison volunteer named Joyce Ride (the mother of Sally Ride, America's first female astronaut). Next, Killian got a call from appellate lawyers representing her codefendant, DeSantis. Because he had been sentenced to death for his part in the robbery-murder, the lawyers had state funds and other resources that a lifer like Killian could only dream about. In the course of discovery, they had forced Sacramento prosecutors to turn over piles of documents, including several that pertained to her case. One was a secret letter, written by Masse to the prose-cutor, in which he emphasized that he had "lied [his] ass off on the stand" to help convict Killian; another was a letter from prosecu-tors supporting a sentence reduction for Masse because of his co-operation on the case. It was what Killian had been waiting for all these years—not just an explanation of what had happened to her, but rock-solid grounds for appeal. After paying a private detective to dig around in the case, Ride dipped into her savings again to hire a Santa Monica appellate specialist named William Genego to get Killian out of prison. Nearly $100,000 later, Ride had run out of money, but Genego kept going.

It took the former USC law professor more than six years of bat-tling with state and federal courts before he could convince one to throw out her conviction. Genego says he has run into the same set of difficulties in every other case he's handled on behalf of inno-cent clients sent to prison for very long terms—not just mistakes and misdeeds that can take years to uncover, but a profound un-willingness on the part of appeals courts to correct miscarriages of justice that do come to light. "The institutional mind-set [of the appeals courts] is that they are going to secure a conviction that they already got," Genego says. "Instead of admitting its mistakes, the system throws up roadblocks that make them harder to cor-rect." UC Irvine criminologist Ron Huff calls this phenomenon—which he, too, has seen repeatedly in twenty years of research into wrongful convictions—"ratification of error." "The further a case progresses in the system," he says, "the less chance there is that an error will be discovered and corrected."

On the face of it, California's legal system should be well equipped to right its occasional wrongs. Not only are there two layers of appeals courts—state and federal—but there are two kinds of review: a "direct" appeal of the verdict itself, and a habeas corpus petition to raise issues that come up after the trial. Cali-fornia's appeals court system is thought to work pretty well com-pared with that of some other states: it's reasonably efficient, well funded and staffed, and (in general) intellectually respected. At the federal level, the Ninth Circuit, which governs California and nine other western states, is still the most liberal in the nation.

Yet this system of safeguards is swamped by all the factors that work against an innocent defendant. The most basic problem: judges in a direct appeal can consider only the record of a trial. But the things that are mostly likely to lead to a reversal—like the secret letters in Killian's case, or the taped confession by another man in the Tennison and Goff case, or the psychologist's report in John Stoll's case—aren't in the record. Appellate courts cannot retry cases or second-guess juries; they're only supposed to make sure that the trial was legally fair (free of procedural or constitutional errors big enough to have affected the jury's decision) and that the verdict was "reasonable" based on the evidence (a verdict doesn't have to be correct to be "reasonable"). Given the narrow scope, the chances of getting a conviction overturned on direct appeal are very low. In the thirty cases in our analysis, it happened just twice.

The inherent conservatism of the appeals process has been magnified by the political transformation of the state's courts since the 1980s. The California Supreme Court, once considered the most liberal and activist high court in the country, has swung to the opposite extreme on law-and-order issues. The state's six Courts of Appeal have followed suit, even in the Bay Area, largely reflecting the politics of recent governors. The appeals court based in San Jose has the highest proportion of Republican appointees in the state (71 percent); the San Francisco-based court is 65 percent GOP. Twenty years ago, the Court of Appeal threw out 9 percent of convictions; last year, the reversal rate was 5 percent.

The decrease in reversals reflects another big change over the past two decades—the courts' growing tolerance of constitutional and legal errors in criminal cases, everything from coerced confessions to squelched evidence. These kinds of problems used to get convictions automatically overturned; now they are apt to be dismissed as "harmless" if—in the view of the appeals court—

the other evidence of guilt is overwhelming. Many appeals judges used to be prosecutors, which makes them even more inclined to see defendants as guilty and errors as harmless, says Dennis Riordan, a respected San Francisco appellate lawyer. Riordan takes the provocative position that the current crop of appellate judges is actually toughest on defendants who might be innocent. "It is often in the cases where the error is most blatant and the evidence is weakest that judges work the hardest to avoid reversal," he says, "because those cases are the most embarrassing to our judicial system and the ones in which it's going to be most difficult to ever get a conviction again."

The Habeas

If you don't have the best and the brightest fighting for you, with lots of money and support, you're not going to make it out. And if you'd had that kind of money, you probably wouldn't be in prison in the first place. **—Gloria Killian**

Defendants whose direct appeals have been denied do have another recourse. Known as the "Great Writ of Liberty," habeas corpus allows inmates like Killian to challenge their convictions by raising new evidence of innocence or showing a violation of their constitutional rights. But once again, innocent prisoners face enormous hardships.

The biggest is lack of money. At this stage, only people on death row are entitled to court-appointed lawyers. While state appeals courts may OK some funds for habeas lawyers and investigators in noncapital cases, the amounts are a pittance compared to the true costs—often in the hundreds of thousands of dollars—of digging up new evidence and putting together a writ strong enough to convince a skeptical court inundated with such claims.

And California courts—where habeas petitions are first filed—can be skeptical indeed. Take the case of Harold Coleman Hall, who spent nineteen years in prison for the 1985 murder of a Los Angeles woman named Nola Duncan. Hall, who had been picked up for another crime, had admitted killing Duncan, but he recanted, saying police had badgered him during a seventeen-hour interrogation. (Indeed, many of the facts of the murder flatly contradicted the confession.) But prosecutors had another damning piece of evidence: two pages of notes, in Hall's own writing, in which he had seemed to answer another inmate's questions about the case, in the process admitting his guilt. After Hall was sentenced to life without parole, his lawyers made a startling discovery: the written "confession" was a forgery. The snitch who had provided the notes to police admitted he had tricked Hall into answering innocuous questions, then erased them and substituted incriminating ones. The prosecution's own expert found signs of tampering; the exasperated trial judge said he had "no legal or moral choice" but to give Hall a new trial. But the Court of Appeal reversed that habeas ruling and upheld Hall's conviction, saying the judge hadn't expressly called the faked confession "false."

Luckily for people like Hall (and Killian, and Tennison, whose habeas writs were also rejected by state courts), they have the right to pursue their claims in federal court. But here again, there's no money for lawyers or investigators, unless an inmate can convince a court that his claims have merit (talk about a Catch-22). By the time Killian reached this stage, she had Genego working for her pro bono—a very rare situation indeed. Hall, on the other hand, found himself in the same boat as the vast majority of California prisoners. His attorneys had to drop out, leaving him to fend for himself for the next ten years.

Inmates who attempt do-it-yourself ("pro se") habeas writs are hampered by all the disadvantages you would expect, plus a few more. Hall had to overcome both his lack of education (he was a tenth-grade dropout) and constant lockdowns at the gang-infested Lancaster State Prison in the Mojave Desert, which sometimes shut down the law library for months at a time.

"You're constantly threatened with missing deadlines in your case," says Hall, who taught himself about the appeals process by reading legal newspapers and books. "I would have to type my papers three or four times because I couldn't xerox them in the library." Even when there wasn't a lockdown, Lancaster inmates were entitled to just two hours in the law library per week. The only way to get around these barriers, Hall eventually concluded, was to get a job in the law library. "That way, if I saw a lockdown coming, I could make sure I had copies of everything I needed in my cell." In prison, he adds, "they're always trying to defeat your purpose. If you're not strong enough to endure it, and figure out how to help yourself, eventually you give up."

The lack of legal help has become even more of a problem since a sweeping law, enacted in 1996, made it much more difficult get a habeas claim into federal court, period. Habeas "reform," a longtime goal of conservatives who complained that death row inmates were delaying their executions with frivolous appeals, was passed as part of an antiterrorism bill in the wake of the Oklahoma City bombing. Like so many statutes that try to speed up the execution process, it actually had a far greater impact on non–death penalty cases, with new deadlines, a higher burden of proof, and other daunting procedural hurdles. The law also requires federal courts to almost always defer to the state courts' previous ruling. Says Justice Alex Kozinski of the Ninth Circuit, "This essentially gives state courts the final say in most criminal habeas cases."

The 1996 law slams the door shut on all but a very few innocent prisoners. Killian's case shows how it can go in federal court even when you have a great lawyer and a strong case. After spending a couple of years jumping through procedural hoops, she and Genego scored a key victory: an evidentiary hearing before a federal magistrate. Besides the secret letters to and from the prosecutor, they had DeSantis's testimony that he had never heard of Killian—they even got Masse to admit on the stand that Killian *hadn't* planned the crime. The magistrate still ruled against them. Only after Genego appealed to the Ninth Circuit did Killian win her freedom—two years later.

Indeed, the Ninth Circuit is the last, and sometimes best, hope of innocent prisoners in California. "It's like I used to tell the other inmates—'When you get to the Ninth Circuit, you'll get someone to pay attention,'" Hall says. That faith was borne out in his own case—after lower federal courts ignored him, the Ninth Circuit took a hard look, decided his claims had merit, and appointed Genego to take over the appeal. "It is absolutely amazing that Harold was able to keep his case alive that far," Genego says. But he still needed one last stroke of luck—a panel of judges who would be receptive to his claims. Despite its liberal reputation, the Ninth Circuit has been transformed by the same revolution that's hit the state courts. While it continues to be relatively progressive, it's far more conservative than it used to be, not only in its politics but in how it views the role of judges. In the end, the court ruled two to one to overturn Hall's conviction. But the dissenting judge argued that he and his colleagues were bound to respect the state court's decision. "If one more judge who thought like that had been assigned to Harold's case," says Genego, "he spends the rest of his life in prison."

Parole

They mask it by calling it twenty-five years to life, but they're not letting those people out of prison. Those are death sentences.
—Rick Walker

It used to be that innocent inmates in California who had exhausted all their appeals had one small comfort: even if they were never exonerated, they might well be paroled. That was one of the few rays of hope for Rick Walker and his family after he was wrongfully convicted for the 1991 murder of his drug-addicted ex-girlfriend. Given the horror of the crime—the killers suffocated the victim by wrapping her head in duct tape like a mummy—he could easily have been sentenced to death or life without parole. Instead, he got twenty-five to life. In theory, this made him eligible for parole at the end of 2009. But once he was in prison, it didn't take long for the more experienced guys to set him straight. "There were guys that had seven years to life and they were still in there after thirty-two years. In reality, I was doing life without."

Walker is forty-eight years old now, a big bear of a man with the charisma of a natural-born preacher and a voice both commanding and gentle. His story echoes those of many innocent people accused of heinous crimes: bad choices magnified by worse luck. One of four sons, he came from a solid family—his mother was an East Palo Alto school trustee and later mayor, his father a powerful, strong-willed truck driver with a passion for old cars. He grew up in San Francisco, moved to the Peninsula with his family after graduating from high school, and found steady work as a car mechanic. But in his early thirties, he got caught up in the drug-and-violence epidemic that earned East Palo Alto the title of murder capital of the United States.

Another casualty was his ex-girlfriend, a Princeton grad turned junkie who owed money to a lot of people, including a drug dealer. One evening, the dealer and another man accompanied the woman to a Cupertino condo and killed her. Confronted with the evidence against him—his fingerprints were all over the duct tape—the dealer eventually claimed he had been put up to it by Walker, whose tempestuous relationship with the victim was well known. Unfortunately, Walker had a terrible alibi: he'd been shacked up in a motel for three or four days, smoking crack with a married lover who was afraid her husband would find out. Doubly unfortunate, his lawyer failed to do the obvious, like use room service records at the motel to confirm his story. The prosecutor, meanwhile, cut a testimony deal with Walker's codefendant that he hid from the judge and Walker's attorney, the codefendant's lawyer later admitted. The prosecutor also made a leniency agreement with another of Walker's ex-girlfriends, who testified—falsely—that Walker was a violent man (he kept this deal secret, too).

Other guys would have burned with rage at the injustice of it all. Walker's parents certainly did as they worked to free him, only to have every state and federal court reject his appeals. Walker was shocked when his father came to visit him, fifty pounds lighter and no longer the man he knew. "My mother told me that he would just lay there in his bed and cry," he says. "In essence, this killed my father. His son was in prison and he couldn't get him out." Shipped off to San Quentin and three other prisons, Walker was determined to use his conviction as an opportunity to turn his life around. He kicked his drug problem and became a lay preacher and counselor. He struggled to forgive. "There is nothing positive that can come out of me holding on to a grudge against a prosecutor or a judge," he says. "Anger just hurts me."

In other words, Walker was a model inmate—the ideal candidate for parole. The first step was a documentation hearing, at which a prisoner's activities and conduct are evaluated for possible credit for time served. But when he went to the hearing, he found that the warnings he'd heard were true. One parole commissioner put it bluntly: "It's unlikely that a person convicted of a capital crime like yours will ever get out of prison."

California's parole system started its hard right turn in the early 1980s, when a series of notorious criminals were released after serving stunningly short sentences for truly horrific crimes. First Governor George Deukmejian remade the Board of Prison Terms, replacing its bleeding heart with a skeptical core; the board—which reviews indeterminate sentences that carry a maximum of life—has recommended parole in just 2.5 percent of the cases that have come before it in the past six years. Then, in 1988, Deukmejian pushed through Proposition 89, giving the governor veto power over parole recommendations in homicide cases. By handing the ultimate authority to an elected official, voters ensured that very few convicted murderers would ever be freed. Again, an ax aimed at the worst criminals has fallen hardest on innocent prisoners. Says Cliff Gardner, a San Francisco appellate lawyer, "Whereas a wrongful conviction in a murder case used to be a ten-year or twelve-year mistake, now it's a thirty- or forty-year mistake."

Parole vetoes peaked during Gray Davis's five-year term; he rejected 97 percent of his board's recommendations. Likewise, Arnold Schwarzenegger, who vowed to accept most of his board's decisions, has so far overruled 61 percent of them. One inmate Schwarzenegger agreed to parole was Adam Riojas, an Oceanside man who had served thirteen years of a fifteen-to-life sentence for a 1989 drug slaying. After numerous witnesses came forward to say that Riojas's father had admitted shortly before his death that he was the actual killer, prosecutors told the parole board they believed Riojas might have been wrongfully convicted, and the board voted unanimously to release him. A year earlier, Davis—with exactly the same facts before him and the same recommendation for parole—had refused to set Riojas free.

In representing Riojas, Innocence Project lawyers from California Western School of Law in San Diego had to grapple with a dilemma so obvious and perverse that it was almost laughable. The board, by its nature, will always require inmates to take responsibility for their crimes and profess remorse. "They expect you to say what they want you to say, exactly the way they want to hear it, whether it happened that way or not," says Gloria Killian, who helped hundreds of women prepare for their hearings. "I was never going to say I was guilty, so they were never going to let me go."

A spokesman for the Board of Prison Terms denies this is the policy. But Walker heard the same thing. "One parole commissioner looked me in the face—I'll never forget this—and said, 'If

you don't admit that you did this crime, you'll never get out.'"
Walker felt the same way Killian did. He would never tell such a
lie to win his freedom. He would have to find another way out.

Exoneration

I believe God intervened in my case.   **—Rick Walker**

In the end, the only thing that could get Walker out of prison—
the only thing that ever frees an innocent prisoner locked up for
life—was the efforts of some amazing people and a freakish align-
ment of the stars. Walker was more fortunate than most.

For one thing, he had a mother who never lost faith in him.
Soon after his trial, Myrtle Walker asked a school board colleague
of hers to ask her daughter—a law student named Alison Tucher,
who was at the top of her class at Stanford—to take a look at the
case, including new evidence she and her husband had dug up.
Tucher quickly concluded Walker was innocent. After a stint
clerking at the U.S. Supreme Court, she returned to the Bay Area,
taking a job at—of all places—the Santa Clara County D.A.'s office, the same office that had prosecuted Walker. (She tried to
prod her colleagues to reexamine the case: "I didn't get very far.")
She moved to Morrison & Foerster and became Walker's pro
bono lawyer in 1999, tracking down new witnesses while breast-
feeding two babies, litigating complex commercial cases, and
making partner in record time.

In early 2003, Tucher wrangled an appointment with Karyn Sinunu, then chief of the D.A.'s homicide unit. Tucher's PowerPoint
presentation raised red flags for Sinunu; during her years as a
prosecutor she had run into many of the characters in the Walker
case and knew in her gut that something was amiss. Her office
spent the next four months doing its own investigation, eventually discovering that DNA on cigarette butts left at the crime
scene belonged to someone Tucher had identified as the second

killer. But in some ways, the clincher came when Sinunu's investigators actually met Walker and discovered what so many people already knew. "My vision of someone who's been wrongly convicted is a very bitter, angry person," Sinunu says. "But Rick took probably the worst possible thing that can happen to a person, and he turned it positive. He just doesn't have that blind, bitter rage. Once you meet him, you can see what a nonviolent person he is. He was not a killer."

The outcome for Walker—tears from the D.A., a concession of innocence, quick compensation by the state—is society's warm-and-fuzzy fantasy of how the system ought to respond to a miscarriage of justice. Two other Bay Area cases are more typical of the way things usually happen.

One of these involves Buddy Nickerson, the 430-pound biker mistaken for a 200-pound killer who was also prosecuted by Sinunu's office. Sentenced to life without parole, Nickerson was no more the model prisoner than he had been the model citizen. For the most part, he refused to work. "My job was making sure the TV antenna worked so that I could watch my TV programs." He figures he wasted a good sixteen years on prison moonshine, brewed in a plastic bucket out of catsup, Kool-Aid, sugar, and rotten fruit. He got sick and nearly died, and shed 100 pounds. He made no effort to file a habeas writ—there didn't seem to be any point. "My case was shut down. Basically, I was going to live my life in there. I took the outside world and put it up on a shelf, in a box."

If it seems that most exonerated prisoners are resilient, remarkable people, it's also probably true that the ones who will never be freed are more like Buddy Nickerson: beaten down and hopeless, the opposite of saintly, so angry and distrustful that they make it easy—for potential defense lawyers as well as prosecutors—not to care. Attorney M. Gerald Schwartzbach, who looks and sounds like Woody Allen channeling Perry Mason, was more empathetic than most, but even he was taken aback by Nickerson's surliness when he showed up in Tehachapi one day in 1992 and offered—free of charge—to try to prove his innocence. Schwartzbach had an ulterior motive: he was representing Nickerson's old nemesis Murray Lodge, who was facing the death penalty for the shootings. Schwartzbach figured that if he could cast doubt on the reliability of the sole survivor, Mike Osario (who had named Lodge as the gunman), jurors might let his client live. What better way to do this than to prove Osario's ID of Nickerson had been wrong? Nickerson had no idea how lucky he was—Schwartzbach was famous, with a string of landmark cases on his résumé, and he had state money to spend, since Lodge's was a capital trial. Nor did he much care. Nickerson had a swastika tattooed on his arm; Schwartzbach was Jewish. "Buddy told me he didn't want to talk to me," Schwartzbach recalls. "So I told him that if I left, his last chance of ever getting out of there other than in a box was going with me. And then he started to think—'Well, you know, maybe these Jews aren't so bad!'"

Over the next decade, Schwartzbach and his team scored some notable victories (including keeping Lodge off death row). But getting Nickerson out of prison proved much tougher. In 2002, after considerable back and forth, a federal judge gave them their best shot: a hearing on Nickerson's habeas claim. Schwartzbach and his team were feeling hopeful; in addition to the retraction of a key eyewitness and proof that the cops in his case were liars, they had Lodge's testimony and exonerating statements from all his accomplices. They even had a statement from a respected Santa Clara D.A. who, before joining that office, had been Lodge's first lawyer, saying that *he* was sure Nickerson was innocent. Then came a bombshell: an informant had come forward, claiming that Nickerson had confessed to him back in 1984, while the two were in county jail.

No one could fault prosecutors for fighting to keep Nickerson in prison. It's their job to vigorously defend a verdict. "We believed [the informant] was credible," says Gregory Ott, of the attorney general's office, which takes over for the local D.A. after a trial, handling most state and federal appeals. "What he was telling us was consistent with what we knew. He knew things he could not have made up."

But like so many informants prosecutors have relied on in wrongful convictions in California, this one had a shady pedigree and a motive to lie, the defense soon discovered. In addition to being a convicted murderer who had tried to pin his crimes on his own sister, he was a member of the violent Nuestra Familia inmate gang with a drug habit, an abysmal prison record, and so many enemies (for ratting out his fellow gang members) that he needed to be moved frequently—something prosecutors could help arrange. He had already helped convict another Santa Clara County murder defendant in a mostly circumstantial case. (That guy insists he's innocent, too.) The judge didn't believe a word the snitch said and ordered the state to set Nickerson free. Prosecutors had the option of retrying him but decided enough was enough. Schwartzbach is still furious about the last-ditch effort to nail his client. "What the D.A.'s office and the A.G.'s office did to keep Buddy in jail was outrageous," he says. "They should be ashamed of themselves." But noting that Osorio still says Nickerson was involved and that Lodge and the others may have lied to free their accomplice, Sinunu is adamant: "The district attorney is not conceding innocence."

That's the way it often goes in California exoneration fights. In the thirty cases we looked at, local and state prosecutors have fought exoneration the great majority of times, refusing to give in even after an appeals court has looked at new evidence of innocence and ruled the conviction was wrong. Prosecutors have kept innocent prisoners in jail well after the release date ordered by judges, threatened to retry them after every scrap of major evidence has been discredited, fought DNA testing that might strengthen appeals—even forced them to agree not to file suit before letting them go.

Then there's what's happened in the third Bay Area case, which some fear signals a new chapter in the state's battle with exonerees. Tennison and Goff finally won their release last year, thanks to the pro bono efforts of Keker & Van Nest, one of the finest law firms in the country. (Tennison's brother used to work in the San Francisco lot where many of the firm's lawyers park their cars.) Those efforts didn't stop when a federal magistrate issued her ruling letting them go; the lawyers also put together declarations of factual innocence, which Terence Hallinan, then San Francisco's district attorney, went along with. The declarations—quickly OKed by a judge—were a critical step in winning compensation under a state law that allows $100 for every day an innocent person is wrongfully imprisoned. This was the process Rick Walker went through to win speedy payment of $421,000 last year. Together, Tennison and Goff were owed at least $800,000.

State compensation exists in part because it's so difficult to get any money from the cities and counties whose actions led to wrongful conviction. "Our legal system has developed so many immunities and protections for law enforcement and prosecutors that there is no one held accountable for these great tragedies," says San Diego attorney Dwight Ritter, who sued local authorities on behalf of an innocent man named Frederick Daye who spent ten years in prison before a DNA test cleared him of rape. The court ruled that Daye was only entitled to damages for three days in jail; the jury gave him nothing, while the state awarded him almost $400,000.

But if, after everything else that had happened to Tennison and Goff, they expected the resolution of their story to be happy, they were sorely disappointed. Since the Legislature raised the compensation rate three years ago (before, California exonerees were entitled to a flat $10,000 no matter how long they'd been jailed), twenty-five people have filed claims, and only six have been approved, mainly in cases with DNA evidence. The state is grappling with a budget crisis; just as important, it's grappling with the elusive and often unprovable concept of innocence itself. In language unchanged for sixty years, the law requires not only that a claimant be innocent, but that "he did not, by any act or omission on his part, either intentionally or negligently contribute to the arrest or conviction." "It's a very tough standard," says Nathan Barankin, a spokesman for the A.G.'s office—which, despite its role fighting exonerations on appeal, acts as legal advisor to the board that decides exonerees' compensation, a relationship frustrated defense lawyers call a conflict of interest.

The A.G.'s office showed Tennison and Goff just how tough that standard may be. Deputy Attorney General Michael Farrell learned that the judge had spent approximately "a minute" glancing through the two men's documents before declaring them innocent. Hallinan's concession didn't carry much weight, either. Besides being a liberal, he had recently indicted Police Chief Earl Sanders, a cop in the case, in the Fajitagate scandal. Mainly, though, Farrell concluded that Tennison and Goff had failed to meet their burden of proof. The prosecution's key witness had never wavered in her claim that Tennison and Goff were the killers—never mind that the argument that had freed the two men was that this witness was a liar.

Farrell recommended that the claim be denied outright; instead, the board referred the case to an administrative law judge for a hearing. Late this summer, lawyers for Tennison and Goff faced off in Sacramento against Farrell—essentially a weeklong retrial of the murder case. The process was maddening and painful. "On the drive back, I would have tears in my eyes," Goff says. "It made me think about all the things we've been through and all the suffering we still have to go through."

Yet the hearing did give Goff a chance to do something he had never done, something many murder defendants are prevented by their lawyers from ever doing—tell his story in court.

"I couldn't wait to give my side," says Goff. "I've been waiting thirteen and a half years just to be able to give my side."

A decision is expected any day.

Buddy Nickerson, meanwhile, is like most exonerees; he's getting nothing. Without a finding of factual innocence, he has little chance of persuading the state to pay him for nineteen lost years. His lawyers are considering suing Santa Clara County, but they would face another fight against overwhelming odds. He could use the money. Unlike parolees, exonerees receive no state services—no mental health counseling, no job training, no help finding work or a place to live. Parolees get 200 bucks on their way out of jail; exonerees aren't in the parole system, so they may not get even that paltry sum. Even the simple process of claiming disability benefits or obtaining a driver's license is enormously difficult: How do you explain where you've been all this time? Why should you have to?

The first few nights Nickerson spent at home, he found his bed too soft and his room too big for comfort, so he slept on the floor of his father's garage, between two cars. He's spent the last eighteen months trying to get adjusted to life on the outside—staying sober, reconnecting with his family, riding the motorcycle his brother gave him, figuring out how to live on almost no money. In and out of hospitals for a variety of health conditions that went more or less untreated in prison, he's lost another hundred-plus pounds and is now less than half the size he was when he was arrested.

He has struggled to control his rage, not just at what Santa Clara County did to him, but at the inability of most people to understand what he went through in prison and what he's going through now. His previous girlfriend was a little afraid of him. "She'd say, 'You're not in the prison yard any more. You don't need that look.' My buddy calls it the survival look—you're letting people know not to piss with you." Perhaps his greatest source of comfort is other ex-cons. "They are there for me. I can call them anytime, night or day." The woman he's currently dating is one, too. "She understands where my head is."

Two things Nickerson has been very clear about. The first is staying out of trouble. Life is precious now. He wants to experience as much of it as he can. He also doesn't want to give any police officer a pretext for arresting him. "I've had cops tell me— 'Hey, Buddy, you'd be a big feather in somebody's cap if they busted you.'" This fear has made him a little paranoid sometimes: "If my car is out of my sight, OK, I search it. I put little markings on it that if somebody gets in my car, I know it."

His other primary mission is something a lot of people—the sheriffs who busted him, the prosecutors and jurors who convicted him, maybe even the man he used to be—wouldn't believe he was capable of achieving. He wants to be a good person.

One of his first priorities after his release was having that swastika erased from his arm, out of respect for Schwartzbach, a man he never would have believed he could have trusted, much less called a friend. The other racist tattoos are gone, too. He's not that guy anymore.

Some people might hear his story and think those nineteen years weren't lost after all, if this is what he's learned and the person he's become. But that's just another delusion, something we tell ourselves to ease our guilt and make sense of a terrible injustice.

Here's the truth. It wasn't prison that changed Buddy Nickerson. It was getting out.

Vanity Fair

FINALIST—PROFILE WRITING

This is a richly reported, riveting profile about Timothy Treadwell, a misfit who finds redemption in the wild, living among grizzly bears. Ned Zeman paints a carefully nuanced picture of this naturalist-adventurer, empathizing with his mission and at the same time explaining how his unchecked passion ultimately led to his death and that of his girlfriend.

Ned Zeman

The Man Who Loved Grizzlies

H e lived way out here, where it was just him and Alaska and to hell with everyone else. Here he was alone but never lonely, didn't even know what loneliness was. Soon everyone would be gone for the year, even the grizzlies. Days earlier, the place had crawled with bears, splashing through the streams, flipping boulders like dice. Then the creeks slowed, the salmon run thinned, and they were gone.

As they did every October, the bears were heading deeper inland, toward their dark mountain lairs, where they would sleep through the long winter. Only the stragglers remained here in Kaflia Bay, scrapping for what little food remained, hoping against hope that there was still a salmon or two in the creeks, or a few unpicked elderberries to be had somewhere between here and the mountains, among them a forbidding peak known as the Devil's Desk.

It was raining now and foggy. Slate-gray storm clouds hung low over the bay. Normally the water was so clear he could see straight to the rocky riverbed. But with the gloom and the rain swirling in sheets, the water was gray, churning. His hair was icy, almost crystalline, and his coat was soaked. He had a toothache, and he was tired. Even by his spotty hygienic standards—years in the Alaskan wilderness do that to you—he was filthy.

He was twenty-eight but looked older. Anyone who says nature is the fountain of youth hasn't lived in the wilds of southwestern

Alaska, where winters test even those genetically adapted to endure them—from the indigenous peoples, the Alutiiq, to the caribou and the killer whales, the moose and the wolves, the seals and the sea lions.

But especially the bears. For centuries, this corner of the subarctic has been known as Grizzly Country. Of the estimated 32,000 grizzlies left in the United States, around 31,000 live in Alaska, where they are, in more ways than one, larger than life. Known as Kodiaks, the bears on Kodiak Island are easily the world's largest, standing upwards of eleven feet tall and weighing as much as 1,500 pounds—the size of three Bengal tigers, five mountain gorillas, or eight men.

Even those who shoot them agree that grizzlies are wonders to behold, possessed of uncommon beauty and human-like qualities that border on the mystical. For centuries, local tribes saw them as gods or shamans. It was a worship born of fear, since grizzlies are the world's largest terrestrial predators, dominating the food chain with their power and size, speed and cunning. Capable of dragging a moose up a mountain and devouring it entirely, a grizzly eats whatever he wants, whenever he wants—including, at times, other grizzlies.

He knew this better than most, having seen it happen year after year to victims bigger and tougher than he was. As the sun disappeared, he moved slowly through the rain, shambling in that ungainly way of his. That's when he saw them, lurking low and quiet in the alders. There were two with strikingly similar features: both adults, both weather-beaten, both golden. He'd seen them before, especially the male, who until recently had traveled alone—had been a "rogue."

Now, it seemed, the male had taken a mate, a small, pretty female. Together they nested in a dense thicket of alders, near some of the age-old bear trails that crisscross Kaflia. He approached them cautiously. Inside their carefully constructed habitat, the golden pair stirred. He stood upright, inhaling the cold air, eyes straining to see. At this point, instinct took over and everything became a blur. It was October in Alaska, and he was a bear.

•　　　•　　　•

The golden couple, Timothy Treadwell and Amie Huguenard, lived by bears and died by bears. He was forty-six, she thirty-seven. They looked younger than their ages, and increasingly they looked alike: lean, fit, beach-blond. Neither was Alaskan, except in their minds, which had become tuned to that strange frequency that pulls a rare few into the deep wilderness, and ever closer to the line separating humans and animals.

After the couple's ghastly deaths—the first fatal maulings in the history of Katmai National Park—criticism was aimed squarely at Treadwell, a charismatic bear enthusiast who for years had been the Kodiaks' defender and goodwill ambassador, albeit a self-appointed one. With his good looks and goofy, surfer-dude demeanor—he lived in Malibu and had Hollywood benefactors—Treadwell had incessantly tempted death and fought bogeymen, both real and imagined.

Treadwell's also became the latest cautionary tale in a world gone animal-mad. Roy Horn (of Siegfried and Roy) getting mauled by one of his white tigers. "The Crocodile Hunter," Steve Irwin, feeding the man-eaters while holding his baby. Photographers Barbara Tyack (mauled in Kenya by a baboon), Bruno Zehnder (frozen to death in Antarctica among penguins), Michio Hoshino (killed in Siberia by a grizzly), and Peter Beard (trampled by an elephant in 1996). Primatologist Dian Fossey, likely killed by gorilla poachers.

Treadwell also battled poachers, if largely those of his imagination. He wasn't a scientist and had no formal training. He was a naturalist, an activist, a writer, and a photographer—not to mention a recovering addict, a Peter Pan, and a fabulist. A few weeks before his death, Treadwell wrote to a friend, "My photographs and stories are looking to the deep and secret world of bears that I do not believe any person has ever witnessed. One day I'll show this work to the public. Until then, I'll keep living it."

Even those who had long predicted Treadwell's death granted him this: he was a believer, who walked the walk. And he was in love.

•   •   •

Love. Inevitably for people who love animals, that's the million-dollar word. Having failed to find love or sanity or God, these bereft souls drift outward and inward, essentially becoming exaggerated versions of the old shut-in down the street, with her twenty cats.

In his 1997 memoir, *Among Grizzlies,* Treadwell obliquely referred to a "haunted" and "miserable" youth, in which he was a "handful" for his parents, whom he neither named nor described (other than to say they "loved me and did the best they could"). His dreams were escapist, typically involving interspecies transference in which he bore claws, fangs, or wings that transported him far from Ronkonkoma, on Long Island, where he was the third of five siblings (also unnamed), and where he coveted a teddy bear named Mr. Goodbear. "In my mind, I became a grizzly," he wrote. In his chest beat "the heart of a wild animal."

Intentionally or not, Treadwell was forging his own narrative, a classic quest in which the solitary hero puts the past behind him, slays dragons at every turn, and heads into the great unknown to find the holy grail. To wit: after two years at Bradley University in Illinois, Treadwell walked away from everything—his identity, his family, even his surname: Dexter. At Bradley, Tim Dexter had set three-meter diving records; in *Among Grizzlies,* there was no diving, no college, no Dexter.

Tim Dexter died in Long Beach, California, amid a cloud of drugs, guns, and brawling. He was arrested twice (for assault and for illegally firing a gun). He lived with cokeheads and dealers, slept with a loaded M16, and nearly overdosed on a "speedball" of cocaine and heroin. One night, tripping on LSD, he nose-dived off a third-floor balcony and landed facedown in the mud (which rendered a perfect imprint of his face, including his sunglasses). "I need to be somewhere really remote, far away from people," Dexter told a friend. "This might seem crazy, but when I was young I used to pretend I was a grizzly."

Every adventurer has his epiphany, and Treadwell's occurred in the biggest state, whose dangerous frontier beauty had always lured adventurers and escapists, among them Chris McCandless, the doomed young soul who died trying to live off the wilderness (and who was immortalized in Jon Krakauer's *Into the Wild*). Everything is bigger in Alaska, except the population, which is roughly on a par with Vermont's; the forty-ninth state is bigger than Texas, California, and Florida combined; it has seventeen of the country's twenty highest peaks and a glacier the size of Switzerland.

And then there are the bears. During Treadwell's first visit to Alaska, in 1989, a grizzly surged out of the bush, flashing razor teeth and fixing its gaze on Treadwell. Man and beast locked eyes. "The encounter was like looking into a mirror," Treadwell recounted. "I gazed into the face of a kindred soul, a being that was potentially lethal, but in reality was just as frightened as I was."

The grizzly fled. Where others would have seen a bear being a bear—if confronted, grizzlies will sometimes "bluff-charge" humans, and almost always flee—Treadwell saw something deeper, a "mutual recognition" that transcended conventional assumptions about interspecies communication. Given Treadwell's issues, one could chalk up his Big Moment as a classic case of Freudian projection: *Bereft White Male, 32, seeks salvation, love, family. Humans need not apply.* That said, virtually no one disputes that Treadwell had been, in one way or another, saved by the experience. "A revelation," he called it, and he never touched drugs again.

. . .

Kodiak Island looks like the love child of Ireland and Hawaii, especially in summertime, when sunshine makes the greens greener—green mountains, green fjords—and the North Pacific bluer. The island lies at the heart of a 177-mile-long archipelago off the coast of southwestern Alaska. In June, when Treadwell would typically arrive, the sky stays blue until midnight.

Heading into the town of Kodiak, Treadwell passed the aging canneries and commercial-fishing boats along the Gulf of Alaska, whose waters teemed with halibut, shrimp, and crab, not to mention sea lions and spouting killer whales. Essentially a fishing village—one stoplight, a few dozen businesses, a big blue Russian Orthodox church—Kodiak looks either glorious or gray, depending on the weather, which is surprisingly mild (similar to Vancouver's) but profoundly foggy, windy, and wet (like Glasgow's).

Each year 30,000 tourists pour into Kodiak, and most desire either to see bears or to shoot bears. In town, most businesses honor both the animals and the hunters who "take" them—a phenomenon Treadwell grasped the moment he checked into the Kodiak Inn, a rustic little hotel whose lobby features a giant stuffed grizzly.

"Goofy." That was Wanetta Ayers's first impression of Treadwell the day he materialized in front of her desk at the Kodiak visitors' bureau. Actually, that was everyone's first impression, followed by "childlike." Alaskans can spot forty-eighters a mile away, usually via their new Cabela's boots, and Treadwell was screamingly obvious: Prince Valiant haircut, black baseball cap (worn backward), black sunglasses, black coat.

Displaying more testosterone than experience, Treadwell confounded Alaskans, who tended to view grizzlies as "thousand-pound Rottweilers," in the words of Dan Eubanks, who tends bar at the Kodiak Inn. Treadwell was always spoiling for a confrontation, particularly with hunters. In his goofy way, he'd smile and say, "How would you like it if I was talking about murdering one of *your* relatives?" Alaskans didn't know whether to laugh or kick his ass.

Ayers and another local, Kathleen Parker, became Treadwell's protectors and interpreters, calmly explaining that many Alaskan families, including Ayers's, grew up eating wild game, often out of necessity. Treadwell had that effect on people. They always wanted to protect him, even those who disagreed with everything he believed in. Bill Sims, a renowned hunting guide and pilot, first encountered Treadwell in the Katmai National Park and Preserve, located on the long peninsula about thirty miles west of Kodiak Island.

·   ·   ·

Specifically, Treadwell was by Hallo Bay, in a savanna-like meadow he called "the Big Green." Blessed with Alaska's highest concentration of bears, the Big Green was steeped in grizzlies, who clammed on the flats, lazed in the grass, and tended their cubs. Because bear hunters were prohibited and bear viewers welcome, most of the grizzlies, having been habituated to civilization, treated humans with equanimity, even curiosity. Huffing and splashing and digging the scene, thousand-pound "killers" strolled the beach right alongside people.

And there was Treadwell, crouched in the grass, talking to bears in his soft singsong voice: "Hey there, little bear." He gave them cute names—Cupcake, Mr. Chocolate, Ms. Goodbear—and spent much of his time with Booble, a female whose golden fur matched her disposition. Treadwell shot endless video of Booble, who certainly seemed to like the attention. She would lie a few feet from Treadwell, napping and gurgling and playing with her toes.

Treadwell went everywhere Booble did, including the rivers where grizzlies spent late August, feasting on the salmon runs. Squatting like fat old men, the grizzlies just waited for red sockeyes to bounce off their chests and rocket into their mouths. Holding salmon like hot dogs, they ate only the fatty parts, discarded the remains, and then grabbed more fish. Fatter by the day, they entered a state of loginess known as "walking hibernation."

When he was in the woods, Sims preferred watching the most amusing creature of them all, Treadwell, endlessly popping in and out of the trees. Finally, loping up to Sims in that surfer-dude way of his, Treadwell introduced himself. Sims found him interesting, in a loopy sort of way. Next thing Sims knew, Treadwell was giving ad hoc grizzly seminars to some of Sims's clients.

"Welcome to the world of grizzly bears, which some people call 'brown bears,'" he would basically say, sometimes employing an Aussie accent, which he typically dialed up for women and children. "Grizzlies live further inland than browns, but they're basically the same bears. They can run thirty-five miles an hour, jump eleven feet in the air, and smell carrion from miles away. They're highly intelligent—after monkeys and us, the world's smartest animals. Smarter than dogs."

Inevitably, visitors inquired about the grizzly's darker tendencies, such as infanticide, cannibalism, and the occasional human mauling. "Grizzlies are misunderstood," Treadwell would say. "They can kill you with one swat. But, really, they're very shy around people. They see you, they think, Hunter! When they attack, which they hardly ever do, it's because you surprised them or fed them—fear or food."

He wasn't telling lies. Alaska averaged about five maulings a year, mostly "defensive attacks." Over the last hundred years, the "killer bears" had killed only forty-five people; in the last decade alone, dogs killed twenty-one.

·   ·   ·

Sims began packing lunches for Treadwell, who normally subsisted on power bars, peanut butter, and Coke; his wildlife skills were, in the early going, rudimentary. His homely little campsite was out in the middle of everything, utterly exposed. One bear entered his supply tent, opened a "bearproof" container, and stole fifty power bars. When grizzlies weren't bumping into his tents, storms were knocking them over; sometimes he stayed up all night, out in the wind and rain, holding on to his tent. "I should have been doing this a long time ago," Treadwell said after moving into an alder patch. "That was just lack of experience."

Still, unlike almost everyone who lived and worked among grizzlies, Treadwell neither carried pepper spray nor put an electric "bear fence" around his camp. "Doesn't seem fair to the bears," he'd say. "Why should they suffer for me?"

"These bears just tolerate us," Sims argued. "They've only got one thing in mind, and that's to get as much food in their bellies during summer because they've got a long winter ahead. They're not here to be our friends."

Treadwell fell silent, preferring Sims's company and food, which he devoured immediately, partly out of hunger, partly because he didn't want the bears smelling it and getting any ideas. Sims offered him fresh halibut to cook at his camp. "If you don't mind, I'll eat it here," Treadwell said, and did just that, eating it exactly as a bear would.

"Timothy," Sims frequently said, "your love for these bears is going to get you in some serious trouble."

"If it happens, it happens," Treadwell replied. "God forbid, if a bear takes me, let him go."

Every year, before heading out to the bears, Treadwell told his friend Kathleen Parker he loved her and said, "This is going to be my best summer yet! If I don't come back"—he'd grin—"this is what I love doing."

·   ·   ·

Men have always told bear stories. The earliest prehistoric cave drawings portrayed dancing bears and devil bears, god bears and man bears. The confusion was only natural, since the distinction between *Homo sapiens* and *Ursus arctos* wasn't entirely clear, and sometimes seemed only a matter of posture. Actually, the difference was perfectly clear to bears; it was the slow-witted *Homo sapiens* who took centuries to fathom and mimic the bears' simplest skills: hunting, fishing, foraging, spelunking.

By one theory, man and bear arrived in Alaska together, more or less, crossing a massive land bridge that once connected Asia and North America. That was 40,000 years ago, before the Bering Sea covered the bridge, and brown bears the continent. Some, it is believed, were trapped on an Arctic ice sheet and evolved into polar bears.

The rest became gods. "The grizzly is half human," thought the Tlingit tribesmen. Other tribes called bears "grandfather," "cousin," or "four-legged humans," according to *Giving Voice to Bear*, a 1991 book by David Rockwell. Sioux healers performed "grizzly dances," whereas the Ojibwa saw bears as shape-shifters—sometimes bear, sometimes shaman. And Dakota boys spent days crawling, snorting, and ritualistically "making a bear." Many tribal rites required initiates to acknowledge, summon, or "be" bears.

And with good reason, since grizzlies out-ranked them in the food chain. The members of some tribes wouldn't look a bear in the eyes; others wouldn't even say "bear." And most agreed that the one thing more dangerous than a pissed-off bear was a pissed-off bear that smelled blood, specifically menstrual, specifically a girl's first. Ojibwa girls were quarantined in huts during their first period cycles, and a menstruating girl was called *mukowe*: "she is a bear."

White explorers and settlers, including Lewis and Clark, were no less respectful. "The Indians give a very formidable account of the strength and ferocity of this anamal [*sic*], which they never dare to attack but in parties of six eight or ten persons," Lewis wrote in 1805, when up to 100,000 grizzlies roamed the North American wilderness. Calling them "furious and formidable,"

Lewis added, "It is astonishing to see the wounds they will bear before they can be put to death."

White hunters used nature's great leveler. "If you get crippled for life, you carry about you a patent of courage which may be useful in case you go into politics," explained one hunter about the mystique of his avocation. "Besides, it has its effect upon the ladies." And so began a century-long shooting spree that chased grizzlies out of every state except Alaska and those bordering Yellowstone or Great Smoky Mountains National Park.

Today, were it not for federal protection, grizzlies would exist only in Russia, in Canada, and in zoos, possibly under their Latin designation, *Ursus horribilis.*

·   ·   ·

Like all bear stories, Treadwell's got better with each telling. Sometimes he claimed membership in an old Aussie clan, the Treadwells; other times he claimed to have grown up as a poor English orphan. But that's pretty much all he said. He just didn't discuss his background.

By then Treadwell lived north of Malibu, near Zuma Beach, where his tiny apartment housed what few possessions he had. Working a series of bartending jobs in and around Santa Monica, he would scrape together just enough money to finance his Alaskan summers. Because he disliked cars—too claustrophobic—he rode a motorcycle, a Honda Magna he called "the Big Red Machine."

His bear-centricity was obsessive but not monomaniacal. He was a movie buff, an N.F.L. fan, and a closet MTV fan. And he especially loved women, who frequently loved him back. Conversations with his best guy friend, Warren Queeney, went like this: Girls, girls, girls, bears, girls, girls, bears. The whole grizzly-guy thing was catnip to women. "It's not me," Treadwell said. "It's my bear work they're attracted to. I never got laid like this until I started talking about bears."

But it never seemed to work out. Every spring, girlfriends asked the same questions: "What's going on? Where do we stand?" Actually, they stood on the phone in Los Angeles while Treadwell stood in Alaska. His most enduring friendship had been with Jewel Palovak, whom he'd met while working at Gulliver's, a medieval-themed restaurant in Marina del Rey. One night, she found Treadwell grilling a thick ahi tuna. "Oh, this is for the dog," he said. "We're having burgers."

In 1994, after *People* magazine published a short profile of Treadwell, HarperCollins offered a book deal. Treadwell certainly had material: piles of tapes, notes, letters, and musings of the sort that could be written only during endless hours in the wilderness, when his only non-ursine entertainments were reading, listening to music, and playing with Timmy, a scrappy red fox who endlessly fetched a tennis ball.

Working as Treadwell's co-author, Palovak helped focus his boundless enthusiasm, and, in 1997, *Among Grizzlies* was published to modest sales and reviews. The book proved a welcome antidote to a burgeoning publishing subgenre: bear-attack books, which popularized and fetishized ursine horror: *Killer Bears*, *Attack of the Killer Grizzly*, *Bear Attacks: The Deadly Truth*.

By then Treadwell was familiar to the quarrelsome agglomeration of scientists, naturalists, and lay enthusiasts known collectively as Bear People. Bear People didn't know what to make of Treadwell, and weren't to be confused with Grizzly People. The latter was Treadwell's new fund-raising apparatus, a decidedly grassroots operation headquartered in Palovak's kitchen; it published Treadwell's work and financed his "expeditions," as he now called them.

Having established what he was for, Treadwell now emphasized what he was against: poachers and park rangers. For decades, poachers had run freely through the wilderness, zipping in and out aboard undetectable boats and bush planes. Some were trophy hunters, others profiteers who carved out the bears' gallbladders and smuggled them to Asia, where they were peddled as aphrodisiacs.

Treadwell warned of gun-toting hooligans skulking in the murky Katmai nights. Sometimes he chased them off, he reported; one time, he said, they menaced him with guns. It was just their dumb luck that he never seemed to have a camera during these encounters. Also, there was the small matter of those pesky rangers and jealous Bear People, who claimed that poaching was no longer a problem in Katmai.

Meanwhile, the Park Service was enforcing a "seven-day rule," which required campers to relocate every week. Its rationale— something about allowing others access to prime campsites—did not sit well with Treadwell, whose faith in rangers had been shaken in 1998, when they fined him $150 for storing a food item in an Igloo cooler instead of a bearproof container. ("I am outraged and hurt," he protested.) To foil the rangers, Treadwell code-named his "secret locations" when referring to them in letters, calling Hallo Bay "Aubrey," after Bill Sims's granddaughter.

Treadwell commiserated with three of the world's top Bear Persons: Charlie Russell, Doug Peacock, and Barrie Gilbert. Russell and Peacock had spent decades living with and defending grizzlies, and all three recommended tough love: use bear fences. Although Gilbert hadn't lived the grizzly life—he was a professor at Utah State University—his was rare expertise. In 1977 a grizzly attacked him in Yellowstone, tearing off most of his face.

·   ·   ·

Before Amie Huguenard loved bears, she loved Treadwell. They met in 1996, in Boulder, Colorado, where Huguenard worked as a physician's assistant. Though raised in Indiana, Huguenard felt at home in Boulder, spending endless hours hiking and biking the Rockies, even in winter. She was lean, fit, and windswept, as if born in Levi's and fleece. She had attended college there, at the

University of Colorado, then returned after getting a master's degree from the University of Alabama.

Sometimes her appearance fooled people. She was tiny—five feet zero, one hundred pounds—and seemed shy. When she and Treadwell were around other people, he did the talking. But in private, among friends, she wasn't shy at all, revealing a high-pitched laugh and huge stamina; after a fifteen-hour workday, she'd run for miles. One of the osteopaths she worked with, Dr. Phillip Stahl, knew he could always get a rise out of her by joking about protected lands or baby seals. "They're very important," she would reply.

After attending one of Treadwell's lectures, Huguenard couldn't get him out of her head. In January 2000 she wrote him a letter. "Dear Mr. Treadwell," she began. "I had the pleasure of attending one of your presentations. . . ."

It began as friendship. "Great person," Treadwell scribbled beside Huguenard's phone number. "Good heart." Treadwell, being Treadwell, kept things light and loose. He wasn't thinking about the future, except as it pertained to bears.

He was working hard to sell his footage and expertise to television and movie studios. He filmed a segment of Paramount Television's *Wild Things* series, and was "technical adviser" on *Brother Bear*, an animated Disney movie. He took meetings with talent agents at CAA. Most notably, he produced and starred in a Discovery Channel special, *The Grizzly Diaries*. The show, which premiered in 1999, was mesmerizing: "Watch, amazed, as he comes face-to-face with an 850-pound bear."

And it was all true, more or less. Even the biggest males brushed against Treadwell, sniffing his camera. "Hey, sweetie," he'd say, and the giants would shamble away. Or not. Before Booble went off to gather food—the only time a mother will leave cubs—she nudged her little moppets toward Treadwell. In fact, several mothers availed themselves of the new day-care service, parking the kids at Treadwell's feet, heading off to run errands, then returning.

That bears were comfortable around Treadwell was indisputable. One of the few people who spent extensive bear time with him, Joel Bennett, thought the interaction ran deeper. A longtime bear activist and photographer, he saw that look in the bears' eyes. They looked at Treadwell the way dogs and cats looked at their keepers, as if trying to communicate something. What, exactly, he couldn't say.

·　　·　　·

Kaflia Bay was surrounded by a mountainous jungleland devoid of flat, open spaces. Landing there required Willy Fulton, a forty-two-year-old ex-cowboy with a thick mustache, a taste for Pink Floyd, and 6,000 flights under his belt. Fulton was a bush pilot, one of those souls who, using neither co-pilots nor landing strips, routinely negotiated the fiercest elements and meanest terrain. Bush pilots land on mountains and glaciers, in rivers and seas.

Fulton always landed in style, in a 1958 de Havilland Beaver with four seats, floats, and an orange-yellow exterior. When making its daily buzzes over Kodiak Island, the plane looked like a flying jack-o'-lantern. Hence its nickname, the Pumpkin. By 1999, Fulton was Treadwell's main pilot and confederate. (Bill Sims was busy running a lodge up north.) Three or four times a year, he shuttled Treadwell between Kodiak and Kaflia, which was roughly fifteen miles northeast of the Big Green.

Everything about Kaflia was rough, including its only regular visitors, grizzlies, who had not been habituated to humans. And the only way humans got through Kaflia was via the byzantine trails and tunnels forged and frequented by grizzlies. Otherwise, Kaflia was an impenetrable alder thicket. Code name: "the Grizzly Maze."

Kaflia bears often got ornery, snorting and growling and bluff-charging. The last sounds more benign than it is, for the simple reason that the chargee never thinks, Oh, he's just bluffing. But

Treadwell knew how to read bears. One day in 1998, while he was camping with Bennett, the alders shook wildly, followed by what Bennett could describe only as "a King Kong–like situation" charging down the hill. "Jesus!" Treadwell cried, leading Bennett out. "Let's go! Now!"

In his memoir, Treadwell briefly acknowledged what Bear People call the "twenty-fifth Grizzly": "one that tolerates no man or bear, one that will kill without bias." But he rarely gave voice to such unpleasant realities. When Bill Sims reminded him that bears kill bears, Treadwell said, "I really don't want to hear that." And whenever Wanetta Ayers inquired about bears who had obviously been killed by other bears, Treadwell shrugged. "Nature," he said. "The cycle of nature is continuing."

Occasionally, Treadwell crawled and grunted like a bear. I am grizzly, he sometimes told himself, when summoning courage. I am grizzly.

•   •   •

Treadwell became semi-famous in 2001, thanks to David Letterman. There he was, in the greenroom with Samuel L. Jackson, then he bounded onstage like a big, shaggy puppy. "The thing that I do is live as much like an animal as I can," Treadwell said, half joking. Later, while defending the grizzlies' unfair reputations, he blurted, "They're kinda party animals out there." It just popped out—the way things did when he got excited.

Letterman displayed some of Treadwell's photographs, including one of a big, nasty male, and later asked, "Is it going to happen that one day we read a news article about you being eaten by one of these bears?" The crowd roared. "This is dangerous work," Treadwell replied, making such a good impression that within a year Letterman called him back for an encore.

Before going on, Treadwell phoned his friend Warren Queeney, whom he called "Twenty-five" (after the number on Queeney's softball uniform). Queeney called Treadwell "Sixty-six," reasoning that he was one digit shy of satanic. "Twenty-five, it's Sixty-six," Treadwell said. "I'm on the forty-fourth floor of this great hotel. Too bad you're not here. We could've took a shit out the window."

Hollywood returned the love. Leonardo DiCaprio reportedly contributed nearly $25,000 to Grizzly People, which attracted several famous fans, including Pierce Brosnan, Gisele Bündchen, and screenwriter Robert Towne. Corporate sponsors—Patagonia, Konica Minolta—also chipped in. "Behind me is a beautiful wild brown grizzly bear here in Alaska," Treadwell said in a 2001 anti-poaching video. "Thanks to a grant from Leonardo DiCaprio and Leonardo DiCaprio's foundation to Grizzly People, I'm able to protect these animals. . . . People might be coming for these animals, try to hurt them."

Alaskans took a dimmer view, and tensions escalated. Grizzly People published a photo of a bear poacher "in action." But the man was actually a bear-viewing guide, and Treadwell had to apologize. He ignored Bear People Barrie Gilbert and Charlie Russell after they suggested he was sending mixed messages—preaching caution while displaying little. "At best he's misguided," said former Katmai National Park superintendent Deb Liggett. "At worst he's dangerous." In private, she implored Treadwell to "be safe," according to the *Anchorage Daily News*, adding, "My staff will never forgive you if they have to kill a bear because of you."

•　　　•　　　•

Treadwell gave grizzly lectures far and wide, and his target audience wasn't old enough to write checks. Although he had erased his own childhood, he never quite outgrew it. (When not in Alaska, his daily breakfast consisted of raw vegetables, bread, candy corn, and Coke.) The silly names and the singsong voice were meant for bears and kids:

"We stay how far from bears?"

"A hundred yards!"

"If a bear approaches, we . . . ?"

"Don't run!"

"And we don't feed them, because a fed bear is a . . ."

"A fed bear is a dead bear!"

The kid thing, like the bear thing, had an effect on the ladies, including Huguenard, who was now in her mid-thirties. She wanted a relationship and let Treadwell know that. "I think you're amazing," he replied. "But I'm really not the settling-down type. It's just the way I am, and I won't change."

That it was a line didn't make it untrue. The more Treadwell's peers began settling down, the faster he headed in the opposite direction. "I don't want any little ones running around," he told Kathleen Parker. He'd hurt enough women, and some had hurt him. Either way, he always ended up pissed off and heading back to bears, who never disappointed, never judged, never tried to change him.

Officially, he and Huguenard were just friends, not lovers; unofficially, they fell somewhere in between. Treadwell dithered, pulling away, then crept back closer, then away again; in romance, as in life, he ran hot and cold, with a tendency toward the dramatic. (His journal entries consistently indicated "the best day ever" or "the worst day ever.")

Huguenard refused to whine. "Tim's not [a family] guy," she told a friend. "He is who he is."

Her faith paid off in the strangest ways. In Kaflia, Treadwell contracted giardiasis, an intestinal parasite often called "beaver fever," owing to one of its sources—water contaminated by beaver fecal matter. Running a 104-degree temperature and hallucinating wildly, Treadwell phoned Huguenard and Palovak, neither of whom was in Alaska. "Why did you leave today?" he said to Palovak. "I saw you just walking today."

Treadwell refused to leave, so Huguenard Express Mailed drugs to Bill Sims, who air-dropped them over Kaflia. Later, in Kodiak,

Treadwell looked gaunt, having lost thirty pounds. "I'll talk to Amie," he told Wanetta Ayers. "She'll advise me what to do."

· · ·

Huguenard's first visits, in 2001 and 2002, both deepened and complicated the "friendship," as Treadwell called it. Though practically half his size, Huguenard hauled as much gear as he did; she hiked farther, faster, and higher. The quiet suited her, and so did the bears.

"Like heaven," she later told friends. "You haven't lived until you've bathed in a river with bears."

At first, in the Big Green, the grizzlies were a little nervous-making. But Treadwell proved a perfect guide, calmly repeating the safety rules. He never approached the bears, but sometimes they approached him. Treadwell would stand perfectly still, whispering instructions to Huguenard and salutations to bears. Grizzlies brushed right past—close enough for them to feel their breath, and sometimes their fur.

Naturally, he continued to give them names, among them Baby Letterman. His favorite was Downey, a fluffy young female who was to the Maze as Booble was to the Big Green. Downey was the poster bear, endlessly rolling on her back and popping out of the water.

But a few large males showed no love at all, among them a nasty old bear whose photo had been shown by Letterman. "The Big Red Machine," Treadwell named him (after one of his motor-cycles).

The Machine ruled Kaflia absolutely and neither man nor beast dared get near him; at one point, Treadwell had to hide in the farthest corner of the Maze. "I would love to be his friend, but he's not that type of bear," Treadwell concluded. "The Red Machine is from the old days, the old days of when bears came here and the sight, the smell of a person meant poacher, meant death. . . . How can I communicate to him that I am friend and all the rest are foe?"

Now Treadwell watched as an even fiercer bear forcibly deposed the Machine. Although smaller than the other males, the new alpha bear fought off all comers and earned his name, Demon. At various times, both the Machine and Demon had qualified as the dreaded Twenty-fifth Grizzly, Treadwell felt. He made sure Huguenard gave the males wide berths, which usually wasn't difficult, since neither bear wanted anything to do with them. Except once—when an aggressive male bear growled, backed them off, and disappeared.

"A short sunny streak is still on the horizon," Treadwell wrote in his journal on July 25, 2003, having just returned to the Maze, alone. "Wow! Wow! Wow! One of the most exciting days in my life at the Mazes—Back Creek. Popping over the Secret Trail . . . I could see several bears. Freckles still ruling—holding up the main area of the Back Creek—then a bear that looked like Downey, two that looked like Emmy and Baby Letterman." He followed them down a narrow bear trail shrouded by alders. "100% Downey! Arguably the closest bear for me in my entire life."

In late August, when the salmon run was slowing to a trickle, Demon reigned. A female dared to fish near him in order to feed her undernourished cubs. "Although I do not officially recognize the mother bear," Treadwell noted, "she seemed to know me." Then: "Demon exploded onto her. She fought him, appearing about one third his immense size. She successfully held him off— Or more likely Demon just let her be. Good Demon."

Just after dawn on August 21, Treadwell awakened to the sound of bears. "Much danger for me," he wrote. "I felt a great deal of paranoia, and rightfully so." Some 500 yards away, the creek "was loaded with bears and trouble. The chemistry between the bears was explosive—three killer bears . . . I felt the tension growing."

After a grizzly fight involving several bears, including the Machine, Treadwell found comfort in Downey, and vice versa. Emerging from the creek, banjo-eyed, Downey slopped right up to Treadwell, like a spooked dog that had found its master. Visibly relaxing, Downey sniffed the video camera and romped around Treadwell, who stood near the water's edge, looking as he always did after months in the wild: sunburned, not an ounce of fat to spare, hair bleached nearly white.

"Downey is seven years old, and I've known her since she was a spring pup," he said into the camera. "Like she was my own sister. And we've been here together." He looked at Downey. "You are the most beautiful thing," he said, and turned back to the camera. "And I will care for her. I will live for her. I will die for her." He was in tears.

Something about Treadwell seemed different, softer. He picked fewer fights with people, and at least tried to make peace with the Park Service, having at one point offered his services as Katmai's "official bear keeper."

"Amie's coming in today," Treadwell noted on September 14. "She's my girlfriend. She's wonderful."

•   •   •

In the Maze, Huguenard felt fear only when she was out there alone. "You're not alone," Treadwell said.

"I know," she replied.

"And you know what to do."

If a grizzly attacked, the plan was simple. "You have a second or two to get through it," Treadwell often said. "All by making an instant choice. Pull up, back away, or do nothing. Just feel as if there's ice in your veins and be fearless. He'll hate that."

She suffered everything, even the weasels. They had bedeviled Treadwell's campsite for weeks, usually under cover of darkness—squirming between the tarps, clawing at the tent, attacking in waves. "Get out! Get out!" Treadwell screamed, frantically shaking the tent. He later wrote, "These literally three-pound wormy animals were kicking my ass." He burst out into the Alaskan night, chasing weasels with a stick.

Late September brought crueler weather, which therefore lured more weasels and spiders to Kaflia's only dry place: the campsite. Huguenard had a large issue with small spiders, which skittered all over the Maze: wolf spiders, crab spiders, orb-web spiders. That none were harmful was beside the point, since arachnophobes tend to fear what spiders represent—i.e., death, disease, darkness—more than what they do (although they fear that too). The usual remedy, insecticide, wasn't an option. Tread-well wouldn't harm a fly.

.   .   .

Huguenard toughed it out, though sometimes on tiptoe or swad-dled in mosquito netting. Treadwell never ventured far from her, always keeping a watchful eye—but rarely filming her. He tried, but she was shy about that. "It's about the bears," she'd say, re-treating into her fleece. But one time, when she wasn't looking, Treadwell taped her anyway. She was out near the rocky shoreline, watching the bears. Slowly, she looked back at Treadwell with an expression that read, We're O.K., right?

Her nervous excitement was fitting, since the grizzlies were in the final stretch of their summer cycle, competing for the last fish. While the Machine lived in exile, Demon hovered in the creek, foaming at the mouth. "It is said that giant male bears do not allow much any animal near their food source," Treadwell re-ported, filming near the water's edge. "I am being let in very close to Demon and his food source. And, in a further sign that he trusts me, he has actually turned his back to me."

On September 26, Treadwell and Huguenard left Kaflia with mixed emotions. Treadwell hadn't seen Downey before they left, and Huguenard hadn't seen reason to leave. Actually, he wanted to leave more than she did.

At the airport, Treadwell discovered that their tickets cost more than expected. Plus, he didn't like the ticket lady's attitude. He turned to Huguenard. "I can't believe we're leaving," he said.

"What do you want to do?" she asked.

"What do *you* want to do?"

"I wanna do whatever you wanna do."

Treadwell contemplated the Downey situation and the forecast, which called for heavy rain, which meant fuller creeks, which meant he needed to call Palovak to reschedule their departure. "You're gonna think I'm crazy," he told her. "But there's a fish run and we're going to go back . . . and we want to make sure Downey's O.K. What do you think? Do you think I'm crazy?"

"I think you're gonna do whatever you're gonna do," Palovak replied. "Be safe. Good luck. And call me."

·   ·   ·

It rained and rained. In Kodiak, they passed three days waiting for the sky to clear. With another client, Fulton probably wouldn't have flown. But this was Tim, and he and Amie were practically vibrating. "We haven't said good-bye to them properly," they explained. On September 29, they were back in the Pumpkin, heading out for one last week in the Maze.

The weather had turned colder. The sky was gray; the landscape, ghostly. The alders were grizzly brown, making it even harder to see the bears. In fact, as the Pumpkin touched down in the water, there wasn't a single grizzly on the coast. They were on the move, heading inward and upward in search of what little food remained. Most of the salmon were gone, as were most berries, and bears who weren't fattened up needed to address the issue before the Big Sleep, which lasted roughly from November to April. Those who didn't eat enough were doomed to starvation or even predation—sometimes by other grizzlies.

Grizzlies outside the park face even greater peril. In October, hunters pour into the Kodiak archipelago, loaded for bear. (The main island is not protected, and so neither are Kodiak bears.) Because grizzlies seem to have some sort of sixth sense—"bear sense," as it's called—they tend to be on high alert in October; in fact, several years ago two bear attacks occurred this time of year. Both victims were hunters whose bleeding quarry had been smelled, claimed, and defended by hungry grizzlies.

One of the hunters bled to death; the other survived after stabbing the bear twenty times, then crawling for miles. As usual, though, the bears hadn't viewed humans as food, only as threats to their food. That's why most mauling victims live to tell the tale; once subdued, they're presumably as unappetizing as they are unthreatening. The most infamous time grizzlies preyed on humans was August 13, 1967, in Montana's Glacier National Park—the "Night of the Grizzlies," when, in separate incidents, bears killed two young women. The victims had three other things in common: spooked bears, unsealed food, and menstrual blood.

As the Pumpkin headed back to Kodiak, Treadwell and Huguenard excitedly splashed onto the rocky shore, bushwhacked over a small hill, and set up camp in their thicket, about 500 yards from the water. Two blue tents—one for them, one for supplies.

They heard bears before they saw them, crunching along the trails and tunnels, huffing and thumping through the brush. "Tracking through the jungle paths, many areas you can not see more than a few feet ahead," Treadwell had written to Bill Sims. "It's not *if* you will come across the bears in these paths. It's how often. Some bears are fine with it, some shy. And a few, like some of the big boys, can come after you hard."

On October 4, the Maze was golden with sunlight and grizzlies. And there was Downey, fishing and flopping and camera hogging. Euphoric, Treadwell called Fulton by satellite phone. "I'm hoping you can come out because you know where we are," he said. "The weather was a little dicey. But, let me just tell you, just between Amie, myself, and you, every fish ran, every bear was here. We made the best friggin' choice of our lives. . . . Once the [rain] settled down, boy, it was amazing out here. Thank you so much for risking everything and coming out and helping us that day. I know it seemed kinda weird, but thank you."

The next day, Treadwell phoned Palovak and had her call the airline. Pretending she was Huguenard, she made sure their seats were together. "Do you still want your low-fat meal?" the ticket lady asked, and confirmed their seats for two days later, on October 7. Both reservations were to Los Angeles. Before meeting Treadwell in Alaska, Huguenard had quit her job, landed a new one at Cedars-Sinai Medical Center, and set up their new place in Malibu.

·   ·   ·

During their last day in the Maze, Treadwell and Huguenard sat in their tent, packing their gear and listening to the rain. The only other sounds came from the occasional bear huffing or grunting or thumping along one of the trails just outside the tent. Bears had dug "daybeds" all over the place, and scat was everywhere.

Outside the tent, one of the bears wouldn't knock it off. He bumped the tent and shook the alders, and he was right there. After a while, Treadwell had had enough. He unzipped the tent and stepped out into the twilight. He didn't bother putting on his sneakers, which sat outside the tent, next to Huguenard's. Crackling underfoot, the ground was weedy and cold, not far above freezing. The alders obscured what little light there was, and he couldn't see more than twenty feet ahead. He moved slowly.

That's when he saw the bear, or when the bear saw him. Hearts racing, eyes straining in the dusk—humans and bears have roughly the same eyesight—the two males stood no more than five feet apart. Both were hungry and weather-beaten, especially the bear. He looked like he might be the area's oldest grizzly. His coat was mangy, and his rib cage protruded. Decades of battle had scarred his body and disfigured his face; his jaw drooped low, revealing gnarled teeth. He weighed 1,000 pounds.

Treadwell did what he always did in these situations. He waved his arms, shook the alders, and made himself bigger.

Inside the tent, Huguenard heard the commotion, which lasted longer than it typically did. Treadwell was saying something, presumably to the bear, but his voice was too faint to decipher. "Is it still out there?!" Huguenard shouted. At which point the alders shook harder and Treadwell's voice became a shriek. "Get out here!" he shouted. "I'm getting killed!"

Unzipping the tent, screaming as loudly as Treadwell, Huguenard confronted a massive blur of limbs, fur, and violence. The bear was all over Treadwell, dwarfing him. Following protocol, Huguenard yelled, "Play dead!" Treadwell went limp, or tried to. Shortly thereafter the bear came at him again, tearing into him with one-and-a-half-inch teeth and four-inch claws, and battering him with skillet-size paws.

Shouting and crying, but keeping her wits, Huguenard tried Plan B. "Fight back!" she yelled.

The harder Treadwell fought, the louder the bear raged, taking dead aim at Treadwell's head (as attacking grizzlies typically do). Treadwell weighed his dwindling options, yelling, "Hit him with a pan!"

Moments later, in all likelihood, Huguenard watched helplessly as Treadwell lay pinned on his back, staring up at the Big Red Machine.

·　　·　　·

At noon the next day, the weather remained grim. So Fulton took off while he still could, disappearing into the thick storm clouds that shrouded his fifty-minute flight to the Maze. As usual, he landed in the water, then idled toward the craggy beach. The fog hovered low; the afternoon was raw and wet, in the low forties. Normally, Treadwell's gear was already on shore, like luggage outside a hotel. Now there was nothing there, and no one. Not a bear in sight.

Finally, fifteen feet ahead, he detected signs of life. The alders shook rhythmically, the way they usually did when Treadwell dried out his tarp, and Fulton glimpsed a figure there. Having tied the Pumpkin to a rock, Fulton headed up into the alders, which were about eye-high. "Tim!" Fulton shouted, and shouted again. No reply.

He got a bad feeling and wanted the trusty twelve-gauge shotgun he usually kept in the Pumpkin. Moving fast, he turned and headed back. As he untied the plane, Fulton glanced over his left shoulder. Behind him, creeping swiftly through the alders, came the Machine. The bear hadn't made a sound, and now he moved toward him, huffing and thumping and closing fast as Fulton scrambled into the cockpit and slammed the door.

The Machine wouldn't quit, thundering right up to the plane. As Fulton's throat tightened and his limbs went numb, the bear moved away, along a coastal trail, eyes locked on the Pumpkin, as if daring Fulton to come out. Which Fulton couldn't. That firearms were prohibited here was beside the point, because his shotgun was back in Kodiak.

Fulton pulled the throttle and ascended over the Maze, watching as the bear returned to the campsite, or what was left of it. The tents had been flattened. Circling low over the campsite—fifteen times, twenty times—Fulton couldn't scare off the bear and couldn't locate the couple. He radioed a dispatcher, who contacted a nearby ranger station, about ninety miles away in tiny King Salmon. At 3:20 P.M., carrying three armed rangers, a white-and-yellow Cessna 206 float plane headed into swirling rain, dense fog, and fading daylight. Landing at the Maze would be a nightmare, so Fulton talked the pilot through it, advising him to fly as low as possible, until he spotted the Pumpkin.

By the time the Cessna arrived, at 4:26, Fulton had spent nearly three hours in and above the Maze, periodically glimpsing the bear. It was difficult to see, so Fulton had to return to the plane to flash his lights. Inside the Cessna, one of the rangers glimpsed the bear atop a hill. Then the bear disappeared.

Two of the rangers, Allen Gilliland and Derek Dalrymple, carried twelve-gauge shotguns; the third, Joel Ellis, a .40-caliber handgun. Crouched in "low ready" positions, they climbed the hill. Though still unarmed, Fulton guided them up through the alders, where Treadwell had been ripped to pieces. His remains were scattered along one of the bear trails, and the grizzly had been eating them. "Anyone here?!" they yelled over and over. The noise was intentional, since the last thing they wanted was a surprised bear.

Or bears. They didn't know how many they were dealing with. Nor were they sure whether Huguenard was dead or alive. "Hey, bear!" they shouted, then paused in the alders for a couple minutes, awaiting backup from Alaska state troopers due to arrive any minute. Scanning the hillside, they saw nothing and heard nothing.

"Bear!" Gilliland yelled, pointing to his right, where the grizzly had appeared out of nowhere, five yards from Ellis. The men shouted and shouted. Undaunted, the bear stepped toward them. Ellis fired first, then Gilliland and Dalrymple, hitting the bear's neck, shoulder, and left eye. Slowing, the bear absorbed eight rounds, then twelve, then fifteen. He dropped five yards from Fulton, struggling and groaning. Ten seconds later, having taken twenty-one rounds, the bear died.

.   .   .

Almost immediately, Fulton said, "I wanna look that bear in the eyes." After confirming that this was the same grizzly he'd seen earlier, Fulton and the others headed up to the campsite. There they found one of the flattened tents unzipped and facing a five-foot-by-four-foot pile of dirt, grass, leaves, and sticks. After kills, grizzlies commonly conceal their food in a "cache" like this one, and evidently the bear had been defending his. The cache was littered with human remains.

Two state troopers arrived, and some of the group conducted a perimeter search. At that point, Gilliland spotted a second bear moving up the trail they'd just walked. "Bear!" he yelled. The bear hesitated for a couple of seconds, then retreated. Moments later, Gilliland yelled again: "I found something!" He thought he'd heard the telltale popping of bear jaws, but saw no bears; instead, he saw a war zone, which would confirm their worst suspicions. Treadwell and Huguenard had been killed the way grizzlies usually dispatched prey—by going for their heads.

Rain and dusk fell faster. While the troopers photographed and videotaped the scene, Fulton and the rangers took deep breaths, gathered the remains, carried them down to the planes, and headed back up for more. Shortly thereafter, trooper Chris Hill shouted, "Bear!"

That's when they glimpsed a third grizzly in the brush. Though smaller than the first bear, the young "subadult" was far swifter, and was silently creeping thirty feet behind the men. Gilliland fired a warning shot. The bear slipped through the alders, appearing and disappearing. "Take a shot if you have one!" Ellis yelled.

"I don't have a good shot!" Gilliland replied.

The bear reappeared, paused briefly, stalking them in a "quartering" position—a posture they assume when faced with a threat. When the bear moved on them, Ellis and Hill opened fire. The bear fell and struggled to get up—until Gilliland shot it in the back of the head.

·   ·   ·

In the days and weeks following the Man-eater Attacks (as they were sometimes called), rumors flew: poachers had murdered Treadwell and Huguenard and left them to the bears; the couple had offered themselves up as grizzly martyrs; the killer bear was still out there, hunting humans; Huguenard had been pregnant, or menstruating, and her blood had attracted grizzlies from miles around. There was even a kind of second-gunman theory, which held that the larger bear had been a patsy, taking the fall for the smaller assassin in the grassy knoll.

If the facts indicated otherwise—and they did—answers remained elusive. Forty-two hours after the shootings, the weather cleared enough for investigators to land in Kaflia and slice open the Machine, whose belly revealed human remains, and whose markings revealed his past: he'd been tagged after the 1989 *Exxon Valdez* oil spill. Aside from basic wear and tear, though, the necropsy revealed no major malfunctions. The Machine was just another old grizzly.

Except he wasn't. When the investigators arrived, the smaller bear had already been torn apart and cached by other grizzlies. While it remained possible that the smaller bear (or a third bear) had initiated the attack, only to have his prey stolen by a bigger bear, logic and circumstance suggested differently. The Machine lay exactly where he had died, untouched by bears.

Three weeks later, by order of the Park Service, the Maze remained closed to outsiders. The only sign of life began: DANGER—BEAR-CAUSED FATALITY. By then, the grizzlies were long gone, having left behind only one pile of small bear bones and a second pile of bigger bones.

"A person could *not* have designed a more dangerous location to set up a camp," concluded bear biologist Larry Van Daele, who later said, "Who knows what goes on inside a bear? Bears don't 'think' the same as people do. What we do know is that Mr. Treadwell was not acting like most people do around bears, and consequently wasn't treated like most people."

Even Treadwell would have agreed with that; one of his favorite quotations came from a state official who predicted that Treadwell would "end up on some bear's breakfast plate." Ultimately, though, Treadwell's legacy hinges less on what one thinks about him than on what one thinks about "intelligent" animals. Those who believe men are men and beasts are beasts will always view the recent attacks as a cautionary tale whose quixotic antihero caused four violent deaths.

Those who detect a deeper interspecies connection—those who ask a Chihuahua how his day was, or who counsel their calicoes—tend to view the deaths as bittersweet tragedy. After all, just about every wild kingdom worth exploring was assayed by obsessive "lunatics" who laughed at danger: Dian Fossey, Thor Heyerdahl, Ernest Shackleton. Treadwell amassed more than twelve years' worth of field research, and some of the same scientists who ridiculed him have jockeyed for his research. At one point, Treadwell called his friend Louisa Willcox, Wild Bears Project director for the Natural Resources Defense Council, and pleaded, "Will you get these scientists off my back?"

· · ·

Anyone who questions Treadwell's motives hasn't seen his tapes, in which the mere sight of bears makes a grown man spin in circles, dancing by himself. And although Treadwell's poacher claims were exaggerated, often wildly so, his camera never lied. Last year he happened upon a man-made wooden structure resembling a football goalpost. In February, the Park Service acknowledged that the structure had indeed been a "skinning post" constructed by poachers.

But the most disquieting recording is the one nobody will see. For some reason, Treadwell's video camera taped the first six minutes of his attack (on audio only, since the camera was packed in a bag, with its lens cap on). The recording is a horror, documenting an onslaught so ghastly that it gave one of the troopers nightmares. That said, one can't help but hear the obvious: by the end, the sounds of man, woman, and bear were one and the same.

The New Yorker

In the hands of Adam Gopnik, critical writing achieves lift-off. With his intellect and wit, he carries his reader to deep new worlds. Best of all, he bends his talents in the service of his subject, never losing touch with his commitment to transmit the wonder of what he has discovered.

Adam Gopnik

Times Regained

This year marks the hundredth anniversary of the decision to take an hourglass-shaped traffic funnel between Forty-second Street and Forty-seventh Street on Broadway, which had been called Longacre Square, and rename it after the *New York Times*, which had just built its office there. This was less an honor than a consolation prize. The other, then bigger and brighter newspaper, the *New York Herald*, had claimed the other, then brighter and better square, eight blocks south, which still bears its ghostly name. Nine years later, in 1913, the *Times* scurried off to a prim side street and a Gothic Revival bishop's palace, where it has been lifting its skirts and shyly peeking around the corner at its old home ever since.

No other part of New York has had such a melodramatic, mood-ring sensitivity to the changes in the city's history, with an image for every decade. There was the turn-of-the-century Times Square, with its roof gardens and showgirls; the raffish twenties Times Square of Ziegfeld and Youmans tunes; the thirties Times Square of *42nd Street*, all chorus lines and moxie; the forties, V-J "On the Town" Times Square, full of sailors kissing girls; the wizened black-and-white fifties Times Square of *Sweet Smell of Success*, steaming hot dogs, and grungy beats; and then the sixties and the seventies Times Square of *Midnight Cowboy* and *Taxi Driver*, where everything fell apart and Hell wafted up through the manhole covers. No other place in town has been quite so high and quite so low. Within a single half decade, it had Harpo Marx in the Marx Brothers' valedictory movie, *Love Happy*, leaping ec-statically from sign to sign and riding away on the flying Mobil-gas Pegasus, and, down below, the unforgettable image of James Dean, hunched in his black overcoat, bearing the weight of a gen-eration on his shoulders.

Now, of course, we have the new Times Square, as fresh as a neon daisy, with a giant Gap and a Niketown and an Applebee's and an ESPN Zone and television announcers visible through tinted windows, all family retailing and national brands. In some ways, the Square has never looked better, with the diagonal slop-ing lines of the Reuters Building, the curving Deco zipper, even the giant mock dinosaur in the Toys R Us. There are, of course, people who miss the old Times Square, its picturesque squalor and violence and misery and exploitation. Those who pointed at the old Times Square as an instance of everything that capitalism can do wrong now point to the new Times Square as an instance of everything that capitalism can do worse. Where once Times Square was hot, it is now cold, where once varied, now uniform, where once alive, now dead. Which just proves, as with the old maxim about belief, that people who refuse to be sentimental about the normal things don't end up being sentimental about nothing; they end up being sentimental about anything, shedding tears about muggings and the shards of crack vials glittering like diamonds in the gutter.

And yet, whatever has been gained, something really is missing in the new Times Square. The forces that created it, and the mixed emotions that most of us have in its presence, are the subject of James Traub's *The Devil's Playground* (Random House), which is both an engaged civics lesson and a work of social history. The book begins with an ironic moment—Traub takes his eleven-year-old son to the new Forty-second Street to see the old *42nd Street*—and then spirals back into history, moving decade by decade over the past century.

Traub, a writer for the *Times*, hates city myth but loves city history: on every page you learn something about how the city really happened, and how it really happens now. He is particularly good at wrestling complicated history into a few tight pages. He gives the best account we have of the original sin of New York: the birth, in 1811, of the iron street grid almost before there were any streets. The decision to lay a crisscross of numbers over the city without any breaks for public squares, plazas, or parks—a deliberately brutal nod to the governing principle of commerce—is why we still, sadly, call any awkward and accidental space created by the diagonal of Broadway intersecting an avenue a "square."

Traub also has a gift for filtering social history through a previously invisible individual agent. As always, the vast forces of mass culture turn out to be the idiosyncratic choices of a few key, mostly hidden players. The character of the signs in Times Square, for instance, was mostly the invention of O. J. Gude, the Sign King of Times Square. Gude, a true aesthete with a significant art collection, was the first to sense that the peculiar shape of Times Square—a triangle with sign-friendly "flats" at the base and the apex—made it the perfect place for big electric national-brand signs, or "spectaculars," as they were called, even before the First World War. In 1917, when Gude put up a two-hundred-foot-long spectacular, on the west side of Broadway between Forty-third and Forty-fourth, featuring twelve gleaming "spearmen" who went through spasmodic calisthenics, it was as big an event in American pop culture, in its way, as the opening of *The Jazz Singer*, ten years later. Gude also had the bright idea of joining the Municipal Art Society, the leading opponent of big signs, and later helped shape the zoning ordinances that essentially eliminated big electric signs anywhere in midtown *except* in Times Square.

Times Square is famous for what used to be called its "denizens"—Damon Runyon, George S. Kaufman, Clifford Odets, A. J. Liebling—and Traub writes brief lives of a lot of them. But the history of the place isn't really a history of its illuminati; it's a history of its illuminations. Though social forces and neon signs flow out of individuals, they don't flow back into individuals so transparently. George S. Kaufman, to take one instance, was exclusively a creature of the theatre; if, like the galleries in SoHo in the nineteen-nineties, the Broadway theatre had in the thirties picked up and moved to Chelsea, Kaufman would have followed it blindly and would never have been seen on Forty-second Street again. Even Runyon has about as much to do with the history of Times Square as P. G. Wodehouse does with the history of Mayfair: his subject is language, not place, and in all of Runyon's stories it would be hard to find a single set-piece description of Times Square, a single bulb on a single sign. Individual artists help make cities, but cities don't make their artists in quite so neatly reciprocal a way. Dr. Johnson's "London" is a poem; "The London of Dr. Johnson" is a tour-bus ride.

·   ·   ·

Traub gives no false gloss to the decay of Times Square; it was really bad. The neighborhood declined to a point where, by the mid-seventies, the Times Square precincts placed first and second in New York in total felonies. (Harlem had a third as many.) These were crimes of violence, too: a rape or an armed robbery or a murder took place nearly every day and every night. Stevie Wonder's great 1973 song "Living for the City" has a spoken-word interlude in which the poor black kid from the South arrives on West Forty-second Street and in about five minutes is lured into the drug business. This was a song, but it was not a lie.

Traub's account of the area's transformation is lit from behind by another, still longer and larger one—Lynne B. Sagalyn's masterly *Times Square Roulette: Remaking the City Icon*, just issued in paperback (M.I.T.). Sagalyn teaches real estate at the University of Pennsylvania, and her book, the fruit of more than a decade of scholarly labor, is as mind-bendingly detailed an account of the relations of property and culture as one can find outside Galsworthy or Trollope. It's full of eye-opening material, if one can keep one's eyes open long enough to find it. Sagalyn's book is written, perhaps of necessity, in a prose so dense with city acronyms and cross-referential footnotes that it can defeat even the most earnest attention. Nonetheless, its material is the material of the city's existence. Reading it is like reading an advanced-biology textbook and then discovering that its sole subject is your own body.

Traub and Sagalyn agree in dispelling a myth and moving toward a history, and the myth irritates them both—Traub's usual tone of intelligent skepticism sometimes boils over here into exasperation. The myth they want to dispel is that the cleanup of Times Square in the nineties was an expression of Mayor Giuliani's campaign against crime and vice, and of his companion tendency to accept a sterilized environment if they could be removed, and that his key corporate partner in this was the mighty Disney, which led the remaking of West Forty-second Street as a theme park instead of an authentic urban street. As Traub and Sagalyn show, this is nearly the reverse of the truth. It was Mayor Koch who shaped the new Times Square, if anyone did, while the important private profit-makers and players were almost all purely local: the Old Oligarchs, the handful of rich, and mostly Jewish, real-estate families—the Rudins, Dursts, Roses, Resnicks, Fishers, Speyers, and Tishmans, as Sagalyn crisply enumerates them. Mayor Giuliani, basically, was there to cut the ribbon, and Disney to briefly lend its name.

The story follows, on a larger scale than usual, the familiar form of New York development, whose stages are as predictable as those of a professional wrestling match: first, the Sacrificial Plan; next, the Semi-Ridiculous Rhetorical Statement; then the Staged Intervention of the Professionals; and, at last, the Sorry Thing Itself. The Sacrificial Plan is the architectural plan or model put forward upon the announcement of the project, usually featuring some staggeringly obvious and controversial device—a jagged roof or a startling pediment—which even the architect knows will never be built, and whose purpose is not to attract investors so much as to get people used to the general idea that something is going to be built there. (Sometimes the Sacrificial Plan is known by all to be sacrificial, and sometimes, as in "The Lottery," known to everyone but the sacrifice.) The Semi-Ridiculous Rhetorical Statement usually accompanies, though it can precede, the Sacrificial Plan, and is intended to show that the plan is not as brutal and cynical as it looks but has been designed in accordance with the architectural mode of the moment. ("The three brass lambs that stand on the spires of Sheep's Meadow Tower reflect the historical context of the site . . ." was the way it was done a decade ago; now it's more likely to be "In its hybrid façade, half mirror, half wool, Sheep's Meadow Tower captures the contradictions and deconstructs the flow of. . . .") The Staged Intervention marks the moment when common sense and common purpose, in the form of the Old Oligarchs and their architects—who were going to be in charge in the first place—return to rescue the project from itself. The Sorry Thing Itself you've seen. (At Ground Zero, Daniel Libeskind supplied the sacrificial plan, and now he is pursuing all of the semi-ridiculous rhetoric, in the forlorn hope that, when the professionals stage their intervention, he will be the professional called on.)

The only difference in the Times Square project was that, because of its size, it all happened twice. (Actually, there were two dimensions to the remaking of Times Square—the West Forty-second Street projects, and the reclaiming of the Square itself—but each depended on the other, and, though administratively distinct, they were practically joined.) The first Sacrificial Plan appeared in the late seventies, and was called "the City at Forty-second Street." Presented by the developer Fred Papert, with the support of the Ford Foundation and with proposed backing from Paul Reichmann, of Olympia & York, it envisioned a climate-controlled indoor-mall Forty-second Street, with a 500,000-square-foot "educational, entertainment, and exhibit center," and a 2.1-million-square-foot merchandise mart for the garment trade, all strung together with aerial walkways and, lovely period touch, equipped with a monorail. Mayor Koch wasn't happy about the plan; "We've got to make sure that they have seltzer"—that it's echt New York—"instead of orange juice," he said. But mostly he worried because someone else would be squeezing the oranges.

Still, the plan did what such plans are meant to do: establish the principle, civic-minded rather than commercial, that something had to be done here, and the larger principle that whatever was done should be done on a large scale—the old, outdoor theatre-and-arcade Forty-second Street could be turned into "a consumer-oriented exposition center with people moving across 42nd Street by means of pedestrian bridges," as one early draft of the rhetoric put it. As the initiative passed from the developers to the Koch administration, a further principle was established. The transformation could be made only by large-scale condemnation of what was already there, and the city and state together proposed a new way to link up private and public: the developers would get the right to build on condition that they paid directly for public improvements. The price of your tower on top was a cleaner subway station below.

Still more significant, and what should have been seen as a portent in the first Sacrificial Plan, was the felt need to pull away from the street completely. This was not simply snobbery but self-preservation; Forty-second Street wasn't dying but raving. The porno shops on West Forty-second Street weren't there because the middle class had fled. They were there because the middle class was there. The people who bought from the porn industry were the office workers who walked by the stores on the way to and from work, and the tourists who wanted to take back a little something not for the kids. The XXX video rooms and bookstores and grind-house theatres were going concerns, paying an average of thirty-two thousand dollars a year in rent; peep shows could gross five million a year. Though the retailers were obviously entangled with the Mafia, the buildings were owned by respectable real-estate families—for the most part, the same families who had owned the theatres since the thirties, the Brandts and the Shuberts. Times Square was Brechtville: a perfect demonstration of the principle that the market, left to itself, will produce an economy of crime as happily as an economy of virtue.

This—the crucial underlying reality in the Forty-second Street redevelopment—meant that the city, if it was to get the legal right to claim and condemn property in order to pass it over, had to be pointing toward some enormous, unquestioned commercial goal, larger or at least more concrete than the real goal, which was essentially ethical and "cultural." For once, the usual New York formula had to be turned right around: a question of virtue had to be disguised as a necessity of commerce. On Forty-second Street, a group of perfectly successful private businessmen in the movie-theatre business were being pushed aside in favor of a set of private businessmen in the tall-building business, and the legal argument for favoring the businessmen in the tall-building business was that they had promised that if you let them build a really tall building they would fix up the subway station.

This produced the Second Sacrificial Plan, of 1983: Philip Johnson and John Burgee's immense four towers straddling either side of Times Square on Forty-second, each with a slightly different pedimented top. The Semi-Ridiculous Rhetorical Statement invoked for this plan was that the pedimented tops "contextualized" the big buildings because they recalled the roofline of the old Astor Hotel, a victim of development twenty years before. They were by far the biggest and bulkiest buildings that had ever been proposed for midtown; Sagalyn gasps at the sheer zoning outrage of it. They had to be that big to establish their right to be at all. The Brandt family, which owned many of the theatres, sued and lost. "The Durst family interests put their name on five lawsuits," Sagalyn reports, "but the rumors of their financial backing of many more are legion." (The Dursts owned various individual lots along the street, which they intended to put together for their own giant building.) After ten years, they lost, too. Forty-seven suits were launched, and the plan withstood them all. The Johnson models, fortresses designed to withstand a siege of litigation, had triumphed. But nobody really wanted to build the buildings.

•   •   •

In the interim between the First Sacrificial Plan and the Second, however, something had changed in the ideology of architecture. A new orthodoxy had come into power, with an unapologetic emphasis on formal "delirium" and the chaotic surface of the city. In Rem Koolhaas's epoch-marking manifesto *Delirious New York* (1978), the buzz, confusion, danger, and weirdness of New York were no longer things to worry about. In fact, they were pretty much all we had to boast of. To an increasing bias in favor of small-scale streetscapes and "organic" growth was added a neon zip of pop glamour. The new ideology was Jane Jacobs dressed in latex and leather.

By what turned out to be a happy accident, this previously academic, pop-perverse set of ideas had influenced minds at the Municipal Art Society—the very group that had fought against the idea of signs and signage in Times Square at the turn of the century. In 1985, after the appearance of the Johnson plan, the Municipal Art Society, under the impeccable direction of the white-shoed Hugh Hardy, took on as its cause the preservation of the "bowl of light" in Times Square and "the glitz of its commercial billboards and electronic signs." After being digested in various acronymic gullets, this campaign produced not only new zoning text (sections ZR81–832 and ZR81–85, as Sagalyn duly notes) but, as an enforcement mechanism, an entirely new unit of measurement: the LUTS, or "Light Unit Times Square." (Each sign had to produce a minimum LUTS reading; the lighting designer Paul Marantz gave it its name.)

And so the Municipal Art Society became the major apostle of a continuing chaotic commercial environment in Times Square, while the big developers had to make the old Beaux-Arts case for classical order, lucidity, and space—for "trees and clean streets . . . museums and sidewalk cafés," in the plaintive words of the developer David Solomon. Eventually, in the early-nineties decline, Prudential, which had been holding on to the development on West Forty-second Street, was forced to sell its rights at a discount—to the Durst family, which had been leading the litigation against the plan all along but which, as everyone could have predicted, was there at the finale to develop and build, including 4 Times Square, the big building in which these words are being written.

None of this, however, could have created the new Times Square had it not been for other, unforeseeable changes. The first, and most important, was the still poorly explained decline in violent crime. (Traub tours the Eighth Avenue end of Forty-second with one of the district's privately financed security officers, who points out that there is still plenty of prostitution and drug-trafficking but very few muggings or assaults; even chain-snatching and petty theft are now rare.) This decline allowed for the emergence of the real hyperdrive of the new Square, the arrival of what every parent knows is the engine of American commerce: branded, television-based merchandise directed at "families" (that is, directed at getting children to torture their parents until they buy it). The critical demographic fact, as a few have pointed out, is the late onset of childbearing, delayed here until the habit of New York is set and the disposable income to spend on children is larger. When Damon Runyon was writing, the presence of Little Miss Marker in the Square was the material for a story. Now Little Miss Marker runs the place.

Of all the ironies of the Times Square redevelopment, the biggest is this: that the political right is, on the whole, happy with what has happened, and points to Times Square as an instance of how private enterprise can cure things that social engineering had previously destroyed, while the left points to Times Square as an instance of how market forces sterilize and drive out social forces of community and authenticity. But surely the ghosts of the old progressives in Union Square should be proudest of what has happened. It was, after all, the free market that produced the old Times Square: the porno stores were there because they made money, as part of a thriving market system. Times Square, and Forty-second Street, was saved by government decisions, made largely on civic grounds. Nothing would have caused more merriment on the conservative talk shows than the LUTS regulations—imagine some bureaucrat telling you how bright your sign should be—but it is those lights which light the desks of the guys at the offices of Clear Channel on Forty-second Street, and bring the crowds that make them safe. Civic-mindedness, once again, saved capitalism from itself.

·   ·   ·

And yet you don't have to have nostalgia for squalor and cruelty to feel that some vital chunk of New York experience has been replaced by something different, and less. Traub ends with the deconstructionist Mark Taylor, who trots out various depressions about the Society of Spectacle to explain the transformation, all of which are marvelously unilluminating. Times Square may be spectacular—that is what its signmakers have called their own signs for a century—but in the theoretical sense it's not a spectacle at all. It's not filled by media images that supplant the experience of real things. It's a tangible, physical, fully realized public square in which real people stare at things made by other people. The absence of spectacle, in that sense—the escape from the domination of isolated television viewing—is what still draws people on New Year's Eve, in the face of their own government's attempts to scare them away. (Dick Clark, of course, is a simulacrum, but he was born that way.)

Traub toys with the idea that the real problem lies in the replacement of an authentic "popular" culture, of arcades and Runyonesque song-pluggers, with a "mass" culture, of national brands and eager shoppers. But it's hard to see any principled way in which the twenty-foot-tall animatronic dinosaur at the new Toys R Us howls at the orders of mass culture, while O. J. Gude's dancing spearmen were purely Pop. The distinction between popular culture and mass culture is to our time what the distinction between true folk art and false folk art was to the age of Ruskin and Morris; we want passionately to define the difference because we know in our hearts that it doesn't exist. Even fairy tales turn out to be half manufactured by a commercial enterprise, half risen from the folkish ground. The idea that there is a good folkish culture that comes up from the streets and revivifies the arts and a bad mass culture imposed from above is an illusion, and anyone who has studied any piece of the history knows it.

All the same, there is something spooky about the contemporary Times Square. It wanders through you; you don't wander through it. One of the things that make for vitality in any city, and above all in New York, is the trinity of big buildings, bright lights, and weird stores. The big buildings and bright lights are there in the new Times Square, but the weird stores are not. By weird stores one means not simply small stores, mom-and-pop operations, but stores in which a peculiar and even obsessive entrepreneur caters to a peculiar and even an obsessive taste. (Art galleries and modestly ambitious restaurants are weird stores by definition. It's why they still feel very New York.) If the big buildings and the bright signs reflect the city's vitality and density, weird stores refract it; they imply that the city is so varied that someone can make a mundane living from one tiny obsessive thing. Poolrooms and boxing clubs were visible instances of weird stores in the old Times Square; another, slightly less visible, was the thriving world of the independent film business, negative cutters, and camera-rental firms.

There is hardly a single weird store left on Broadway from Forty-second Street to Forty-sixth Street—hardly a single place in which a peculiar passion seems to have committed itself to a peculiar product. You have now, one more irony, to bend east, toward respectable Fifth Avenue, toward the diamond merchants and the Brazilian restaurants and the kosher cafeterias that still fill the side streets, to re-create something that feels a little like the old Times Square. (Wonderful Forty-fifth Street! With the Judaica candlesticks and the Japanese-film rental and the two-story shops selling cheap clothes and stereos, lit up bright.) Social historians like to talk about the Tragedy of the Commons, meaning the way that everybody loses when everybody overgrazes the village green, though it is in no individual's interest to stop. In New York, we suffer from a Tragedy of the Uncommons: weird things make the city worth living in, but though each individual wants them, no one individual wants to pay to keep them going. Times Square, as so often in the past, is responding, in typically heightened form, to the general state of the city: the loss of retail variety troubles us everywhere, as a new trinity of monotony—Starbucks, Duane Reade, and the Washington Mutual Bank—appears to dominate every block. We just feel it more on Broadway.

Do we overdraw Times Square history, make it more epic than it ought to be? Piccadilly and Soho, in London, and Place de Clichy, in Paris, are similar places, have known similar kinds of decline and similar kinds of pickup—but without gathering quite the same emotion. We make Times Square do more work than it ought to. Other great cities have public spaces and pleasure spaces, clearly marked, and with less confusion between them. When Diana died, it was Kensington Palace, not Piccadilly, that got the flowers, and in Paris it is the Champs-Élysées, not Place de Clichy, that gets the military parade on the fourteenth of July. Which returns us, with a certain sense of awe, to the spell still cast by the original sin of the 1811 grid plan. We make our accidental pleasure plazas do the work of the public squares we don't have. This is asking a lot of a sign, or even a bunch of bright ones lighting up the night.

National Journal

WINNER—
COLUMNS AND
COMMENTARY

Jonathan Rauch's columns

exemplify the best in political

analysis and commentary.

Reasoned, heartfelt, and

persuasive even at their most

contrarian, they bring

Washington's policy debates

to life.

Jonathan Rauch

Good Plan, Republicans. But It Didn't Work in Britain.

The idea of an "ownership society" is not new. In August of 1949, twenty-three-year-old Margaret Roberts, out of Oxford and standing for office for the first time, addressed (according to a British newspaper) a "garden meeting of Young Conservatives at the home of Mr. J. E. Brittenden" in Orpington, Kent. "We Conservatives," said Margaret Thatcher, as she would later be known, "want power more widely diffused through private ownership, so that you never get more power in the hands of the government than you get in the hands of the people."

Years later, she and her party acted upon her vision, and the economic results were good. But politically, things worked out badly. Very badly. The story has more than a little relevance for America's Republicans today.

In this space a few weeks ago, I argued that the Republican Party's win, 51 percent to 48 percent, in the 2004 presidential election leaves it far from majority status. (See *NJ*, 11/13/2004, p. 3450.) "You must be nuts," would be an accurate summary of the e-mail I received from Republicans. One reader was kind enough to attach a red-versus-blue map of U.S. counties—a map that shows a sea of Republican red, because the Democratic vote is concentrated in cities. Lest I miss the point, the map was captioned, "My country!" Many Republicans, and some Democrats, look at the Republican sweep in 2004 and conclude that the GOP rules, and the Democrats are cast into outer darkness.

Actually, the situation is a little more complicated and a lot more interesting. Obviously, the Republicans enjoy a parliamentary majority. That is, they control both the executive and legislative branches of the national government, much as the winning party would do in a parliamentary system. What they do not have is a popular majority: a partisan base large enough to win national elections. They are closer to a popular majority than are the Democrats. They have the opportunity, which the Democrats do not, to fashion their parliamentary majority into a popular majority. They have a plan to do so, and it is a credible one. Democrats should be worried.

But so should Republicans.

For the last couple of decades, America has had, in effect, two minority parties. Both parties are dominated by ideological activists who are more extreme than the electorate. The Democrats are to the left of the average voter; the Republicans, to the right. Neither party can govern except in coalition with a large body of nonideological centrists, who feel (and often are) neglected by both parties. In 2004, both parties held their bases, but the Republicans improved their performance in the center. That won them the election, but it gives them little cause to relax. The center remains in neither party's camp; in the 2004 presidential race, independents split their vote evenly.

Whichever party finds and dominates the center will command a popular majority, possibly for years to come. Which party will that be? Domination requires three ingredients: a will to move to the center, a program that appeals to centrists without alienating the base, and a compelling leader with the same kind of broad appeal. Democrats have the will, but they do not have a program, or a leader. Their position is similar to that of the British Labor Party in the 1980s, when Labor had the will to capture the center but not the way.

In contrast, the Republicans have no shortage of leaders-in-waiting. President Bush may be too polarizing a figure to convert independents into Republican loyalists, but waiting behind him are Sen. John McCain, R-Ariz., former New York City Mayor Rudolph Giuliani, California Gov. Arnold Schwarzenegger, outgoing Secretary of State Colin Powell, and perhaps Sen. Chuck Hagel, R-Neb. All, except possibly Hagel, are figures with star power, and all could have a centrist appeal.

The Republicans also have a plan. I've called it demand-side conservatism; Republicans are calling it the ownership society. (See *NJ*, 7/26/2003, p. 2404.) Reducing the supply of government by cutting spending has been a political loser, so the new idea is to reduce the demand for government by giving people more control over their pensions, health insurance, schools, and so on. Give people partial ownership of Social Security, for example, and they should shift their loyalty from the party of government (the Democrats) to the party of empowerment (the Republicans). Writing last month in *The Weekly Standard*, Fred Barnes quotes Bush campaign manager Ken Mehlman as saying that the ownership-society agenda will lock in millions of voters by "changing the incentives of politics."

The Republicans' plan, then, is to use their parliamentary majority to drive an ownership agenda that will create a popular majority. That was also the British Conservatives' plan.

In 1976, soon after Thatcher attained the Conservative leadership, the party published a manifesto titled *The Right Approach*. It called for giving the people "more power as citizens, as owners, and as consumers," by "lowering taxes when we can, by encouraging homeownership, by taking the first steps toward making this country a nation of worker-owners, by giving parents a greater say in the better education of their children." That should sound familiar. When it came to power in 1979, the Thatcher government made good on its word by selling off 1.7 million public-housing units, privatizing public industries, and creating tax and insurance incentives to encourage people to switch to "portable personal pensions."

The economy responded. Entrepreneurial energy began to pulse through Britain's sclerotic veins. Meanwhile, the Labor Party was reeling. It detested the Thatcher agenda but lacked new ideas and the will to break with its left-wing union base; it staggered from one weak leader to the next. The Labor Party appeared to be in terminal decline.

What the Tories then discovered is what ruling parties all too easily forget: There is no position more treacherous than having a parliamentary majority without a popular majority. With undivided power goes undivided credit, but also undivided blame. Worse, the possession of a parliamentary majority may embolden the party's extremists and lull the party away from the center, thus blocking, rather than advancing, progress toward a popular majority.

In Britain, the public liked the results of Thatcher's policies but never really bought into her ideology of self-reliance. Most people saw no need to choose between independence and government support. "Whatever works," was their view.

Moreover, while economic modernizers steered the Thatcher government, cultural conservatives dominated the Conservative Party and busied themselves with such matters as a "no promo homo" law (against "promoting" homosexuality). Tory opponents of British integration into the European Union, whatever their case's merits, appeared backward-looking and anti-modern. After Thatcher's ouster as leader in 1990, the party's divisions spilled into plain view.

Labor—make that New Labor—was meanwhile rushing to the center under an appealing and very shrewd young leader. The party "must reconnect with the mainstream majority," Tony Blair said. He was not afraid to knock partisan heads together and usurp Conservative economic policies. In the 1997 election, he promised not to raise income-tax rates and proclaimed that Labor would spend no more than the Conservatives had budgeted. He promised to be tough on crime and tough on the causes

263

Good Plan, Republicans. But It Didn't Work in Britain.

of crime. He adopted the Conservatives' economic program but welded it to cultural modernism ("cool Britannia"). In startlingly short order, the center belonged to Labor, and, with it, a popular majority. The Conservative Party, once seemingly indomitable, lay nearly in ruins.

Britain, of course, is not the United States, and in one respect, Bush's agenda differs markedly from Thatcher's (and Ronald Reagan's): Thatcher wanted to reduce both the demand for and the supply of government. Bush seems to think he can spend his way to smaller government, reducing the demand for government while, at least in terms of spending, *increasing* the supply. His approach, while arguably more cynical than Thatcher's, may prove more politically successful. Perhaps more important, no Democratic Blair has appeared. Yet.

Still, Democrats have a peculiar strength. They know they are in trouble. They know what will become of them if they do not capture the center. The Republicans now control the whole federal government. Most of their leaders are to the right of the party, and the party is to the right of the public. Their House speaker seems intent on governing from the party's center, not the country's. As it did on intelligence reform, the congressional party is likely to resist Bush when he pulls toward the center. Republicans have the program and the personnel to build a center-right majority. But so did Britain's Conservatives.

Vanity Fair

FINALIST—
FEATURE WRITING

In recounting the musical bond with Def Jam Records' founder Rick Rubin that led to Johnny Cash's stirring final decade of artistry, David Kamp fashions an exquisite and unlikely buddy story of two remarkable men from two generations. The tale is fierce, steeped in incongruities, and accompanied by a deeply spiritual soundtrack.

David Kamp

American Communion

The last song that Johnny Cash ever wrote is called "Like the 309." Like the first single he ever recorded, "Hey Porter," from 1955, it's a train song. Cash loved trains—he made two concept albums about them in the early 1960s, *Ride This Train* and *All Aboard the Blue Train,* dangled his legs from atop a boxcar on the cover of his '65 album, *Orange Blossom Special,* and, in the liner notes to his 1996 album, *Unchained,* listed "railroads" second in his litany of favorite song subjects, right after "horses" and just before "land, judgment day, family, hard times, whiskey, courtship, marriage, adultery, separation, murder, war, prison, rambling, damnation, home, salvation, death, pride, humor, piety, rebellion, patriotism, larceny, determination, tragedy, rowdiness, heartbreak, and love. And Mother. And God."

Trains resonated with Cash, and no wonder. He spent his first years in a house hard by the railroad tracks in Kingsland, Arkansas. He counted among his earliest memories the image of his father, Ray, a Depression-era cotton farmer who rode the freights in search of work when there wasn't cotton to pick, jumping out of a moving boxcar and rolling down into a ditch, coming to stillness only as he lay before the family's front door. Trains were in Cash's veins, insinuating their *boom-chicka-boom* rhythms into his early records for Sam Phillips's Sun label (in fact, he later recorded a nostalgic album harking back to his Sun years called *Boom Chicka*

Boom) and serving him lyrically as metaphors for adventure, progress, danger, strength, lust, and American Manifest Destiny.

But "Like the 309" is less lofty than all that. "See everybody, I'm doin' fine / Load my box on the 309," he sings. "Put me in my box on the 309 . . . Asthma comin' down like the 309." Yielding to a fiddle solo, Cash stops singing and starts . . . *wheezing*—tubercularly, hammily, on purpose; he's conflating the groaning, hacking sounds of his dying body with those of an old locomotive. It's "Hey Porter" turned on its ear, the boxcar interment of the brazen, respiratorily robust young buck who sang in the earlier song, "Tell that engineer I said thanks a lot, and I didn't mind the fare / I'm gonna set my feet on Southern soil and breathe that Southern air." And Cash is playing it for laughs.

Every time Cash does one of his comic wheezes, the fellow to the left of me on the couch chuckles but keeps his eyes closed. He listens to the playback intently, legs folded in the lotus position, arms relaxed, feet unshod, his body rocking back and forth in time to the music, lending him the air of a shaman communing with the other world—or, given his untrimmed beard, a Lubavitcher *rebbe* in the throes of Sabbath davening. When the song ends, the bearded fellow snaps to and says, "Let me play you another one." The next recording, also from the final weeks of Cash's life, is of a folk song called "The Oak and the Willow," which begins, "He once was as strong as a giant oak tree / Now he bends in the wind like a willow. . . ." Another song about death, but this time dead serious, and beautiful. Sung from the point of view of a dying man's son, the lyrics conclude, "A part of my heart will forever be lost when the oak and the willow are gone." As the song ends, the bearded fellow, Rick Rubin, still has his eyes closed, but that doesn't keep the tears from running down his face.

•   •   •

In the decade they knew each other, from their first meeting in 1993 to Cash's death on September 12 of last year, Rubin pro-

duced five studio albums for Cash. From the moment their collaboration was announced, it caused a stir—at first, just for the
odd-couple novelty of their pairing: the Man in Black, confirmed
citizen of Nashville, and the inscrutable ZZ Top–lookin' dude
who founded the hip-hop label Def Jam records in his New York
University dorm room with Russell Simmons and later made a
name for himself as a producer of hard-rock acts such as AC/DC,
Slayer, and Danzig.

But no one was less fazed by the seeming incongruity of the new
alliance than Cash—"I'd dealt with the long-haired element before and it didn't bother me at all," he commented, drolly adding
that he found "great beauty in men with perfectly trained
beards"—and it didn't take long for people to look past the Bard-
Beard angle and get stirred up by the music itself. The first fruit of
their collaboration, *American Recordings*, released in 1994, recon-
nected Cash with his fundamental Johnny Cash–ness, featuring
just him and his guitar, playing the rootsy, heartfelt material that
he longed to play but that achy-breaky 1980s Nashville had wanted
no part of. The subsequent albums of the American series—so
named because all the sequels except *Unchained* have "American"
in their title (*American III: Solitary Man; American IV: The Man
Comes Around*) and because Rubin's label also happens to be called
American Recordings—were even better, mixing the rootsier material with Rubin-suggested, idiomatically unlikely songs that,
once Cashified, came to be celebrated in the rock world: Soundgarden's high-grunge yowler "Rusty Cage" re-done as a bluegrass
shuffle; Depeche Mode's aloof synth-pop song "Personal Jesus" as
a swamp blues; and, most celebratedly, Nine Inch Nails' drug-
addict confessional "Hurt" as an old man's devastating appraisal
of his life, with the most stunning climax in a pop song since the
orchestral *glissando* in the Beatles' "A Day in the Life." As for "Like
the 309" and "The Oak and the Willow," they'll appear on the as-
yet-unsubtitled *American V*, most of which was recorded last year
in the four-month span between the May 15 death of Cash's wife,
June Carter Cash, and his own passing—a raw, grief-stricken pe-

riod during which Cash kept his loneliness at bay by writing and recording at a furious pace, as often as his strength would allow. *American V* comes out this fall.

Seldom in the annals of modern music, where snuffed promise and blown opportunities are a requisite part of the *Behind the Music* drama, has something turned out as *right* as the Cash-Rubin partnership. Everybody won: Cash, re-energized and alight with inspiration, was afforded a happy ending to the recording career he'd effectively given up on, and the world was presented with a late-period chunk of Johnny Cash music that, on its own merits— divorced from sentimentality and the wishful thinking that typi- cally surrounds comeback efforts by older artists—stands with the best work he ever did. "It's like Matisse doing the jazz dancers when he was in his eighties, you know?" says Rosanne Cash, the eldest of Cash's children and a fine singer-songwriter herself. "Like a whole new level of art and depth and mastery and confidence. Rick came at just the right time, and Dad was just the right age that that could be unlocked in him. He got all his old confidence back. Only it was kind of a mature confidence—it wasn't that kind of punky, rebellious confidence of his early years."

For Rubin, the personal experience of getting to know Cash was even more edifying than the satisfaction he took in reconnecting the old-timer with his muse. The two men wound up enveloped in something more intense than a friendship, a deep kindredness that greatly moved Cash's family and friends, and, frankly, kind of freaked them out. "You could see that their connection went back into the mists of time somewhere," says Rosanne. "Like these guys didn't just meet eleven years ago."

As Rubin progressed from his thirties to forties, and Cash from his sixties to seventies, the two became confidants and sounding boards on matters spiritual as well as musical—a sort of *Tuesdays with Morrie* scenario without the slush and hokum, and with a more reciprocal exchange of wisdom between the dying man and the younger man. Plus really cool tunes.

Rubin is not what you think he is. The long hair, the Hell's Angels beard, and the wraparound shades he wears in public suggest a standoffish, substance-abusing ogre who speaks, if he speaks at all, in noncommittal grunts—a grouch savant fluent only in the visceral language of *rawk*. In fact, he's chatty and thoughtful, with the dulcet speaking voice and gentle mien of a divinity student. He adheres to a vegan diet and seldom wears shoes. He claims never to have taken drugs, and to have been drunk only once in his life, when he took a mixology class while attending a Harvard summer program in his teens, "and for the final, we had to mix, like, thirty different drinks and taste them all, and I got really drunk and I hated it." The shelves of Rubin's library, in his home just above the Sunset Strip in Hollywood, are crammed with religious texts and path-to-enlightenment guides: the Old and New Testaments, the Koran, *The Great Code* (Northrop Frye's definitive lit-crit companion to the Bible), how-tos on both raja and hatha yoga, *Listening to Prozac, Mind over Back Pain*, something called *The Knee of Listening*, by someone called Adi Da.

Just off the library, in the south end of the living room, stands a tableau that, at first blush, seems comic—an enormous stone Buddha statue, flanked by two nearly-as-enormous stereo speakers. But this is pretty much Rubin in a nutshell: an earnest spiritual quester who finds deliverance in both meditation and loud music. "I used to be a magician, from the time I was nine years old till I was seventeen years old," he says. "When you're that age, you can't really tell the difference between magic and spirituality and the occult. They were all kind of part of this same other world. And I honestly find the same thing in music. It's this other magic world, and it takes me away."

·   ·   ·

Cash, though a devout Christian, didn't dismiss Rubin's patchwork spirituality as hooey. A fellow bibliophile and comparative-religion junkie, the antithesis of the stereotypical southern rustic with a suspicion of fancy book learnin', he delighted in his producer's pan-theological curiosity. Out of their frequent discussions of religion developed an odd custom, certainly unprecedented in producer-artist relations: for the last few months of Cash's life, he and Rubin took Holy Communion together every day, even if they weren't physically in the same place, and even though Rubin, who was born Jewish and doesn't profess allegiance to any one faith, is not technically eligible to receive the sacrament. At an appointed time, Rubin would call Cash and Cash would "officiate," instructing Rubin to visualize the wafer and wine.

"I'd close my eyes," Rubin says, closing his eyes, "and he would say [*Long pause, intake of breath*], 'And they retired to a large upper room for the Passover feast, and Jesus picked up the bread, took a piece of the bread, and passed the bread around. And he held up the bread and he said, "This is my body, which is broken for you. Eat, and do this in remembrance of me."' [*Eyes open.*] Then Johnny would say, 'Visualize the eating, swallow. *Feel* it. Wait a minute.' And then he would say [*Eyes closed again*], '. . . and then he picked up the jug of wine. He poured the wine, and he said, "This is my blood, which is shed for the remission of your sins. Drink, and do this in remembrance of me." And they all did drink.'"

"Even after he passed away," Rubin says, "I continued doing this with him. I would say that, for between probably four and five months, it felt exactly the same, his presence was much more available—I could get quiet and I could hear him say it. After that, for some reason, it started changing a little bit. I don't know enough about the afterlife to know why that would be, but something changed. As time has gone on, it's a little harder to do. But I still do it."

It's strange to reconcile this tender admission with the demo CDs by Slipknot and Audioslave that are strewn about the floor—

and stranger still to think that this is the same man who wore a hellion's black leather jacket and took a pie to the face in the goofily raucous 1986 video for the Beastie Boys' "Fight for Your Right (To Party)"—but there's no doubting Rubin's sincerity, or the solace he finds in Cash's flickering, fading presence. In darkness, having spent several hours in Rubin's incense-scented library, I return to my hotel, down the road, and turn on MTV. Wouldn't you know it, there's Rubin in another hip-hop video, a new one, by another of his production clients, Jay-Z. Decked out in those wraparound shades and a skullcap, Rubin rides shotgun in Jay-Z's car, bobbing expressionlessly to the beat while Jay raps, "I got ninety-nine problems but a bitch ain't one."

.　　　.　　　.

In the early 1980s, Johnny Cash was trapped in a kind of pre-iconic limbo, having not died young enough for his legend to be burnished by the romance of early flameout, having not grown old enough to bask in the warmth and reconsideration of a sentimental public. Though he remained a decent live draw, his record sales were in the tank, and his longtime label, Columbia, couldn't be bothered with him, focusing its energies on younger country acts. Sensing his label's lack of interest, Cash became uninterested himself, going through the motions on his new albums because he suspected they wouldn't get played or promoted anyway—a chicken-and-egg cycle of indifference for which, he admitted, he bore some blame. The chicken metaphor is apt, because in 1984, in a frustrated act of self-sabotage, he recorded an "intentionally atrocious" single, in his words, called "Chicken in Black." Though he didn't write the song himself, "Chicken in Black" parodied his Man in Black image by inventing a scenario in which an ailing Cash undergoes a brain transplant, receiving the brain of a bank robber called the Manhattan Flash, while Cash's original brain is implanted in a chicken, who goes on to wow them at the Grand

Ole Opry, and . . . well, it's really not worth going into any more detail. Columbia took the bait; in 1986, after twenty-eight years, he was dropped from the label.

"It was a sad reflection on where country music had come," says Kris Kristofferson, one of Cash's closest friends. "When I was growing up, the big stars of country, Roy Acuff, Ernest Tubb—once they made it, they were there forever. It wasn't like pop music: Here today, gone tomorrow. But when country music got so much bigger, largely through Cash, who was a bridge to Bob Dylan and Neil Young and people like that, it became more like pop music. And Columbia—which he *built*—did something awfully cold."

Cash found a deal in 1987 with Mercury-Polygram, but no further commercial success. The only thing that sustained his public profile in any meaningful way was his participation in the Highwaymen, a part-time supergroup of crinkly country outlaws whose other members were Waylon Jennings, Willie Nelson, and Kristofferson. By 1991, Cash wrote in his 1997 autobiography, *Cash*, "I'd given up. I'd already started thinking that I didn't want to deal with record companies anymore. Saying goodbye to that game and just working the road, playing with my friends and family for people who really wanted to hear us, seemed very much like the thing to do. I began looking forward to it." Which was fine—Cash was financially well-off, with homes in Tennessee, Virginia, and Jamaica, and didn't need hit records to put food on the table.

But still, it was an ignominious end to a recording career that had caught fire at Sun in 1956 with "I Walk the Line" and "Folsom Prison Blues," and reached its apex in the late sixties with two electrifying jailhouse-concert albums for Columbia, *At Folsom Prison* (1968) and *At San Quentin* (1969). The prison albums had been especially validating to Cash, in that their success won him the respect of the counterculture and sealed the deal on his first comeback. Just a few years earlier, he'd been hooked on barbiturates and amphetamines, had detonated his first marriage, to Vi-

vian Liberto (the mother of Rosanne and his three other girls), and acquired an image as Nashville's most temperamental star, notorious for having kicked out the footlights of the Opry stage in a fit of pique. By '68, though, he had gotten religion, gotten off pills, and married the woman who facilitated both processes, June Carter, his soul mate, stage-mate, and a scion of country's legendary Carter Family. Cash's 1970s were pretty good, too, particularly in the early going, when he had his own variety series on ABC, *The Johnny Cash Show*, and established his enduring persona on the title song of his album *Man in Black*: the oaken-voiced troubadour who "wear[s] the black for the poor and the beaten down / Livin' in the hopeless, hungry side of town." But by the 1980s, alas, as country coifs crept mullet-ward and Nashville became enamored of line dancing, it was Cash who was feeling beaten down.

●   ●   ●

Rick Rubin, by contrast, had had a very good 1980s—so good, in fact, that by 1985, when he was only twenty-two, he was already starring as himself in a barely fictionalized movie account of the rise of Def Jam records, *Krush Groove*. A year earlier, while he was still an undergraduate studying film at N.Y.U., he and Russell Simmons, a Queens-born promoter and manager of the rappers Run-D.M.C. (and the older brother of Run, a.k.a. Joey Simmons), had started up the label, and that same year Def Jam scored its first big hit, "I Need a Beat," by the sixteen-year-old LL Cool J. Two years later, Rubin produced the first rap album ever to go to No. 1 on the Billboard Hot 100, the Beastie Boys' *Licensed to Ill*, and engineered hip-hop's signal moment of crossover into the white-rock world, pairing Run-D.M.C. with Aerosmith on a remake of the latter's "Walk This Way."

By the early nineties, Rubin had amicably parted ways with Simmons, moved to Los Angeles, and started his own label, the more rock-oriented Def American, while also moonlighting as one of rock's busiest producers-for-hire, working with the Red Hot Chili Peppers, Tom Petty and the Heartbreakers, and Mick Jagger. In 1993, having decided that the word "def" had become passé, he dropped it from the name of his label. With that change came a desire in Rubin to sign a different kind of act to his roster. "At my current label, I had only ever worked with new bands," he says. "But as a producer, I had gotten to work with grown-up artists. And I just thought it'd be nice to find the right grown-up artist who, maybe, is in the wrong place, who I could really do something great with. And the first person who came to mind was John. He already had legendary status, and maybe had been in a place where he hadn't been doing his best work for a while."

· · ·

The late eighties and early nineties saw a lot of veteran artists pulled from the shelf and dusted off—it was popular music's era of re-reckoning, a time when CD reissues and the advent of the "classic rock" radio format inspired music fans to halt their relentless pursuit of the new and reconsider the old-timers they'd consigned to the nostalgia circuit. A consensus suddenly arose that, wait a minute, Tony Bennett and Burt Bacharach aren't elevator-music practitioners but *elegant masters of songcraft*, and that such dormant architects of sixties pop as the Beach Boys' Brian Wilson and the Byrds' Roger McGuinn might have something new to offer. Then there were scrappers such as Bob Dylan and Neil Young, who never disappeared or fell off the A-list but went through serious creative funks, and who managed to will themselves back to fighting form without anyone's help.

Cash had made a few stabs at artistic resurrection in the 1980s, covering two Bruce Springsteen songs on his 1983 album, *Johnny 99*, and an Elvis Costello tune on his first Mercury album, *Johnny Cash Is Coming to Town*, but he floundered when it came to sustaining any kind of compelling vision for the length of an entire album. "I knew he was looking around for some fresh inspiration and enthusiasm," says Rosanne Cash. "But he's the kind of guy who needs somebody to provide the keyhole. And he didn't have that."

As it happened, Rubin was not the only person with Cash revivalism on the brain. U2 had already enlisted Cash to sing lead on "The Wanderer," the final song of the band's 1993 album, *Zooropa*, and, around the same time, Cash was getting feelers from the organizers of Lollapalooza, the alternative-music festival, about joining their ragtag road show of pierced, tattooed youthquakers. But Rosanne, protective of her father, feared that he would be turned into some kind of cute artifact-mascot for the Lollapalooza kids. "I just said, 'Dad, please don't do it,'" she says. "I didn't want him to put himself in a situation where he wouldn't get the kind of respect he deserved."

Rosanne was equally dubious when her father announced to her in the summer of '93 that he was signing up with Rick Rubin and American Recordings. "I thought, This is odd. I wonder how this is gonna work," she says. "Just knowing the acts Rick had worked with, it did cross my mind: Is he gonna try to make some kind of parody out of Dad?"

Acting quickly after his brainstorm to sign Cash, Rubin had gotten in touch with Lou Robin, Cash's manager since the early seventies, to arrange a meeting. Robin wasn't all that clued-up on Rubin's oeuvre—his bookings for Cash were strictly for "forty-five and up" audiences, he says—but he decided there was no harm in having Rubin come visit backstage the next time Cash was performing in the Los Angeles area. And so it came to pass that, one night early in 1993, Rubin drove south to Santa Ana, in Orange County, to see Cash play a show with his backup band and his wife, plus June's two sisters, Helen and Anita, at a dinner theater.

"Other than the fact that it was packed and the audience was going crazy, it would have been depressing," says Rubin of the show's setting. "But it was, in fact, a great show—more of a revue than a concert, a family show. A lot going on. June's sisters came out and they sang Carter Family songs. As soon as I saw it, I was thinking, Wow—I imagine that him playing in theaters would be a much better experience. And my goal was to make that transition happen as quickly as possible."

Backstage after the show, Cash rose from his seat to shake the hand of his unusually comported visitor, who was dressed, the singer later recalled, in "clothes that would have done a wino proud." They exchanged hellos . . . and then stared at each other, silently, for a solid two minutes.

"I'm thinking, What do I say? How do I break the ice here?" says Lou Robin. "They were just kind of sizing each other up."

Eventually, both men overcame their intrinsic shyness and got to talking. "I said, 'What're you gonna do with me that nobody else has done to sell records for me?'" Cash recalled in a 1997 interview with Terry Gross of National Public Radio. "He said, 'Well, I don't know that we *will* sell records. I would like you to go with me and sit in my living room with a guitar and two microphones and just sing to your heart's content, everything you ever wanted to record.' I said, 'That sounds good to me.'"

And thus began Johnny Cash's revival.

· · ·

For several weeks that autumn, Rubin sat in his living room like the musicologist Alan Lomax on a Mississippi porch, listening and recording intently while a gnarled, authentic article of Americana banged away at his repertoire. From about two o'clock in the afternoon to eight each night, Cash, with just an old Martin acoustic for accompaniment, did spirituals, love songs, hillbilly songs, old originals, favorites by Jimmie Rodgers and Kris Kristofferson—dozens of songs, all of which Rubin got on tape.

"A lot of the material on the first album, and on the first disc of the box set that we put out [*Unearthed*, a collection of outtakes released last year], is material recorded during those first meetings, of just getting to know each other, and him playing me songs," Rubin says. "You know, 'This is a song that I remember, when I was picking cotton, that we used to sing.' Or 'This is one that my mom used to sing to me.' Or 'This is one that I used to hear on the radio.' Or 'This is one that I recorded in 1957 and no one really ever heard it, but it always meant a lot to me.'"

"It gave me a profound sense of déjà vu," Cash told the journalist Sylvie Simmons in an interview shortly before his death (published in the book that accompanies *Unearthed*). "It very much reminded me of the early days at Sun Records. Sam Phillips put me in front of that microphone at Sun Records in 1955 for the first time and said, 'Let's hear what you've got. Sing your heart out,' and I'd sing one or two and he'd say, 'Sing another one, let's hear one more. . . .'"

For Rubin, it was as much an education as a get-to-know-you exercise, because, truth be told, he hadn't been a studious Cash fan before signing him. Like any American kid growing up in the non-South, outside the sphere of Opry influence—in Rubin's case, in Long Beach, New York, an upper-middle-class suburb in the Buttafuoco belt of Long Island—he absorbed Johnny Cash by osmosis, simply because Cash was one of those figures who were ubiquitous in the formative years of people born in the sixties, forever on TV variety shows and in the collective cultural consciousness. "I thought of the image of the Man in Black," says Rubin. "The Man in Black was a big part of who he was in real life, as well as a mythical image associated with him. I would always try to find songs that were suited for that."

·   ·   ·

Of the songs that emerged from the living-room sessions, there was none more black than "Delia's Gone," an old traditional that Cash had performed years before but forgotten the words to, forcing him to come up with some of his own. A twisted psycho-ballad about a remorseful jailbird who done killed his woman

("Delia, oh Delia / Delia all my life / If I hadn't shot poor Delia / I'd have had her for my wife"), "Delia's Gone" set the tone for what became *American Recordings*, a solo acoustic set of mostly dark songs, worlds away from "Chicken in Black."

Rubin had originally imagined that these songs would be fleshed out with a band, and brought in various musicians, including Mike Campbell and Benmont Tench from the Heartbreakers and Chad Smith and Flea from the Red Hot Chili Peppers, to back Cash on the new material. "But after going through that process, after trying a lot of things, the acoustic demos were the most exciting to me," says Rubin. "Once we decided that that's what the album was going to be, I suggested, 'How would you feel about getting up in a little club and doing some of these songs acoustically? Just to see what it's like playing them in front of an audience, by yourself?' And he said he was open to it, but he was clearly nervous about it."

Remarkably, Cash had never performed solo in his long career. Even at the very beginning, in the *boom-chicka-boom* days of "Hey Porter" and "I Walk the Line" at Sun, it was not Johnny Cash, but Johnny Cash and the Tennessee Two, his buddies Luther Perkins on lead guitar and Marshall Grant on bass. But on a Monday late in 1993, Rubin called the Viper Room, Johnny Depp's tiny Sunset Strip club, just down the hill from Rubin's house, to see when it next had an open night for a simple solo set. That Thursday, before an invited audience, Depp stepped onstage and said, "You know, I never thought I'd get to say this, but here's Johnny Cash!" Cash, by himself, took the microphone and went right into "Delia's Gone." "He was really nervous about it, never having relied on his own guitar, and I was nervous watching him," says Tom Petty, a good friend of both Cash and Rubin. But Cash held the audience rapt, and with each eruption of applause after a song, he gained confidence in himself and in Rubin's plan.

American Recordings was released in the spring of 1994, its cover a stark, sepia-tone photograph by Andrew Earl of Cash in a preacherman's black frock coat (which really was the coat that he wore regularly) standing in a wheat field, flanked by a black dog and a white dog. There was no title on the cover, just the word CASH in enormous block letters above his head—a conscious attempt to reinforce Cash's mythic status; it might as well have said GOD. Martyn Atkins, who was American Recordings' creative director at the time and designed the cover, says, "I told Rick, 'Let's make a statement, let's make it as bold as possible.' Johnny had been a bit Vegas-y, a bit Branson, for a while, and we needed to take people back to what he truly was, to the character of the early days."

The produced–by–Rick Rubin angle won *American Recordings* the most attention a new Johnny Cash album had received in more than two decades, and the praise was unanimous; *Rolling Stone* gave it five stars, and the LP went on to win a Grammy for best contemporary folk-song album. MTV even gave some airplay to the video for "Delia's Gone," the album's opener and first single, which featured Kate Moss as Delia, lying motionless as the bloodstains from Cash's bullets spread across her sundress. Johnny Cash was officially hippified.

·   ·   ·

"Out on the road it started feeling like 1955 again," Cash wrote in his autobiography. "I began playing young people's places like the Fillmore [and] discovered all over again how it felt to play for a crowd of people with no chairs or tables, standing on their feet, jammed together, energizing each other."

Still, Cash had dates to fulfill at the oldster venues, too, putting him in a situation tantamount to that of the '66 Beatles, whose touring obligations had them playing their old mop-top hits to screaming-girl audiences even as they already had the progressive, psychedelic music of *Revolver* in the can. "He was kind of living in two worlds musically at that point," says Tom Petty. Indeed, the Nashville *machers* and programming directors of country radio didn't know quite what to make of *American Recordings*. "It just wasn't their flavor of what country was," says Lou Robin. "They weren't gonna play 'Delia's Gone.' But pretty soon Americana radio picked up on it, and they liked it very much."

Even Cash's buddies in Nashville were perplexed, if accommodating. "That first record caught us off guard," says David Ferguson, Cash's longtime recording engineer. "We never imagined John singin' just *naked*, with no reverb or echo. We didn't know what to think. But we found out Rick was good for John. Here's this new young rich guy that's into his music and wants to turn him into even more of a superstar than he is!"

Unchained, the 1996 follow-up to *American Recordings*, was even more outré by country standards, in that it contained songs by Beck and Soundgarden. The first album had some songs on it by non-country songwriters, such as Tom Waits's "Down There by the Train," Leonard Cohen's "Bird on a Wire," and, most eyebrow-raising, the heavy-metalist Glenn Danzig's "Thirteen," but all these songs, even in their original form, fit comfortably into Rubin's Man in Black schematic. However, there was absolutely nothing about Soundgarden's "Rusty Cage," with its swirling, air-raid-siren electric guitars and screamy vocals by Chris Cornell, that suggested it was a natural for Johnny Cash. Except to Rubin. "When I played Johnny the Soundgarden version, he was horrified. He thought I was insane," Rubin says. "He just looked at me like 'What are you thinking? Have you really gone off the deep end? I don't think I can sing that.'" Unwilling to give up, Rubin recorded a demo version of what he heard in his head, with him singing and the guitarist Dave Navarro on backup.

"Rusty Cage," needless to say, sounded just like a Johnny Cash song when it was finished, with Cash singing the climactic line "Gonna break my rusty caaaage . . ." about twelve octaves lower than Cornell had (or so it seemed), and then intoning, rather than singing, the kicker, ". . . and *run!*" As he gained Cash's trust, Rubin began burning rock-pop compilation CDs and overnighting them to Cash's home in Hendersonville, Tennessee, allowing Cash to pick and choose which songs he wanted to have a go at. Sometimes, Cash would politely leave certain songs uncommented upon; the same compilation that had Nine Inch Nails' "Hurt" on it, for example, also included two untried songs by the Cure, "Lovesong" and "Never Enough." But at other times, as in the case of Depeche Mode's "Personal Jesus," Cash was so impressed as to say, "I wish I'd written that song myself."

Picking non-country songs for Cash was a fraught business, for there was a fine line between the bold reach and the humiliating exercise in kitsch. During the *Unchained* sessions, Cash and the Heartbreakers tried out Robert Palmer's "Addicted to Love," a what-the-hell juxtaposition that Rubin was initially convinced could work. "We recorded a basic track of it, and it was hard to stop from laughing," says Mike Campbell, the Heartbreakers' guitarist. "But the thing is, *Johnny* wasn't laughing. He was totally caught up in it, trying to learn it and find a way into it. [*Imitating Cash's grave basso*] 'Might as well face it, you're addicted to love. . . .'"

·   ·   ·

More often than not, though, Cash demonstrated a gift for making any song his own. *American III: Solitary Man*, released in 2000, opened with a cover of Petty's "I Won't Back Down," a song that, in its author's original, 1989 version, was a casual, poppy affair, its defiant lyrics more of a premise than a statement. But when Cash sang, "You can stand me up at the gates of hell but I won't back down," it took on a whole new resonance, evoking an image of the singer robed, sandaled, and stoic, clutching a staff in a Cecil B. DeMille movie. "When I heard his version, it was like I'd never done it," says Petty. "It dropped my jaw—something about the authority his voice carried. When the army and C.I.A. people called me and asked me to use it in their training programs, they wanted to use the Johnny Cash version. I guess it sounded more American."

Unchained is the most "up" of the American albums, its full-band sound a reaction to the sparseness of *American Recordings.* After it won the 1997 Grammy for best country album, Cash and Rubin took out a full-page ad in *Billboard* that reprinted the famous 1970 photograph of Cash jovially flipping the bird to the camera during a concert at San Quentin State Prison, with the accompanying text, "American Recordings and Johnny Cash would like to acknowledge the Nashville music establishment and country radio for your support."

•   •   •

Something went horribly wrong with Cash's health between the making of *Unchained* and *American III.* He had never looked young, even in youth, but he started to age unnaturally fast, like Keir Dullea in the final weird-out sequence of *2001: A Space Odyssey*—his hair falling out, his forehead veins bulging, his body stooped, his hands trembling.

In truth, Cash had been a physical wreck from the get-go of his collaboration with Rubin, "in a tremendous amount of pain since the day I met him," the producer says, most noticeably from a medical procedure on his jaw in the eighties in which some facial nerves were severed, leaving him with a pronounced droop on the left side of his mouth. He'd also had bypass surgery in 1988, was a diabetic, was prone to bouts of pneumonia, and had ravaged his digestive system with booze and painkillers. (A relapse had landed him in the Betty Ford Center in the early eighties.) "He was very stoic," says Rosanne Cash. "He was from the old school, where you suffered, and it was, you know, like an *art.* You just did it—you didn't talk about it."

But around '96, he started demonstrating Parkinson's-like symptoms—shakes, disorientation, dizziness, a general weakness

—that couldn't be ignored. "It was like he was holding a team of wild horses at bay, for as long as he could, and then he just didn't have the strength to hold it at bay anymore," says Rosanne.

Late in '97, Cash nearly died, his doctors unable to rouse him from a medically induced coma. As Rosanne explains it, "He had pneumonia, and his lungs were so weakened that they had to put him on a ventilator. And because they put him on a ventilator, he couldn't be conscious the whole time. So they put him under with medication, to keep him sedated and give his lungs a chance to heal. And they tried to bring him out, but he wouldn't come out."

June, a devoted "prayer warrior," in her husband's words, turned to the johnnycash.com Web site to exhort all his fans to pray for Cash on a specific Tuesday night, twelve days into his coma. Rubin, for his part, hired a "professional pray-er, a woman in New York who was a Christian who had some kind of powerful ability," to join in the vigil. That night, the Cash family gathered around his hospital bed and clasped hands, "and within a matter of hours," June later recalled, "he just started squeezin' my hand."

    •   •   •

Eventually, Cash was assigned the vague diagnosis of diabetic autonomic neuropathy, which is not a disease but a collection of symptoms caused by nerve damage. Essentially, his nerves were so shot that involuntary functions like blood pressure, respiration, and vision were badly affected. Cash was forced to give up touring, which left him with just the recording studio as a creative outlet. Whereas *Unchained* was recorded mostly in Los Angeles, *American III* and *American IV* were recorded largely at Cash's studio in Tennessee, a little cabin on his compound in Hendersonville, north of Nashville. When his strength permitted, Cash made brief trips to L.A. to finish the tracks.

It's a measure of Rubin's respect for Cash that he was willing to record in Tennessee, because, truth be told, the place put the normally beatific producer in a state of unease. Cash paid no mind to Rubin's eccentricities and appearance, and the effervescent, compulsively hospitable June adored him, relishing the challenge of preparing him vegan meals and dragging him along on her frequent antiquing trips in the countryside. But in the larger context of the Nashville recording community, "I felt alien," Rubin says. "You know, ordering a pizza with no cheese and getting laughed at." In one instance, the Cashes decamped from their main home in Hendersonville for a weekend getaway to their place in Virginia, completely forgetting that Rubin, who was due back in L.A. that day, was still asleep in their guest room. Rubin awoke to find himself locked in and unable to get out. When he finally was able to yank a door open, he set off the alarm system, which prompted the police to arrive and discover what they took to be an unkempt vagrant who had broken into the Cash home. Rubin protested, "No, I'm really Johnny's producer, I'm supposed to be here," but was held on suspicion, missing his flight. It was only after he found a copy of John L. Smith's *The Johnny Cash Discography* in Cash's library and demonstrated to the cops that he had indeed produced Johnny Cash albums, holding out his driver's license for corroboration, that they let him go.

Perhaps because the specter of death loomed, Cash and Rubin's discussions of their shared enthusiasm, religion, intensified in the later years. Until they got to know each other, neither man had ever found anyone else in the music industry as curious as he was about matters spiritual—though they couldn't have come about this curiosity in more different ways. Cash's story, as one would expect, is biblically dramatic: One day in 1967, strung out on drugs and in a nihilistic funk, he wandered into a Tennessee cavern called Nickajack Cave and crawled as far as he could, for two or three hours, until his flashlight batteries wore out and he lay down, presumably to die. But then, lying there in pitch-darkness, he had an epiphany that God, rather than he, controlled his destiny and would choose his time to die. Cash resumed crawling, blindly, until he felt a breeze, followed it, and writhed his way out of the cave's mouth—where he found his mother and June waiting with a basket of food, having discovered his Jeep at the entrance. Rubin, on the other hand, never had any particular epiphany. Though he got no kick from the rote, ritualistic Judaism practiced by his family and was expelled from Hebrew school for goofing off, he says he always felt some sort of "yearning" and a sense that, somehow, his life was a continuation of a previous one. Whereas his fellow Def Jam veterans went through knucklehead phases before maturing into fine spiritual men—Adam Yauch of the Beastie Boys is now a practicing Buddhist, Joey Simmons is now an ordained minister known as Reverend Run—Rubin found his laid-back, Zen demeanor early, meditating and lighting incense even as he went through his punk-rock phase. (The hard-ass appearances in the Beastie Boys and Jay-Z videos are mere comedy, he says, "theater of the absurd, like pro wrestling.")

The ritual of taking Communion together arose out of a theological discussion Cash and Rubin were having one night in April of 2003. Rubin was staying with the Cashes in Hendersonville, having planned to accompany them to the Country Music Television channel's big night of the year, the Flameworthy Awards, at which Cash was to receive a special-achievement award. But Cash was too ill to go, so June agreed to accept the award in his stead while he and Rubin stayed home and watched the ceremony on TV.

Some months earlier, in a previous theological discussion, Rubin had told Cash of his fascination with Dr. Gene Scott, a white-bearded, cigar-smoking televangelist who broadcasts out of a cathedral in Los Angeles. "He's this old, eccentric, really smart, crazy person," says Rubin. "He's often belligerent to his audience. But at the same time, when he actually teaches, the teaching is unbelievable—just scholarly, brilliant, more like a university class than like a typical sermon. He did all these shows about Communion, and it really moved me. I was brought up Jewish and had never done a Communion. I made a copy of the tapes and sent them to Johnny. At first he was wary, because the guy's really bonkers. But at the end of it, he was crying, and said, 'I've heard fifty sermons on this topic, and that was, by far, the best teaching of that that I've ever heard.'"

Somehow, as they were sitting there watching the Flameworthy Awards, the topic of Communion came up again. "And I said, 'You know, I would love to try it sometime,'" says Rubin. "And he said, 'Let's do it together, right now.' He called and had someone on his staff get his Communion kit, and we did Communion for the first time." With the TV still blaring in the background, Cash performed the priest's role, speaking the words and presenting the offering of wafer and wine—"crackers and grape juice," Rubin says, "because that's what happened to be in the house. After that, I suggested that we start doing it together every day. We continued on doing it right up until the end."

•　　•　　•

Cash was in and out of the hospital regularly in his final years, yet he kept on recording when his health permitted, mostly in his cabin in the woods, and, when he wasn't up to even that, while sitting on the bed in what used to be his son John Carter Cash's room in the main house. His voice on *American III* and *American IV* is noticeably more quavery and unsteady, a circumstance of which he was conscious and, at times, embarrassed, but it lent the songs a poignancy and drama that even he couldn't have pulled off in his physical prime. Never was this clearer than in tracks one and two of *American IV*, "The Man Comes Around" and "Hurt"—a wham-bam mortality diptych that represented the summit of the American series. "The Man Comes Around" was a brand-new Cash original, inspired by a bizarre dream he had in which he walked into Buckingham Palace and found Queen Elizabeth sitting on the floor. Taking notice of Cash, Her Majesty pronounced, "Johnny Cash, you're like a thorn tree in a whirlwind!" "It kept haunting me, this dream," Cash told Larry King in November 2002, around the time of *American IV*'s release. "I kept thinking about it, how vivid it was, and then I thought, Maybe it's biblical." Sure enough, Cash found the thorn-tree reference in Job and spun the dream into a song based on the book of Revelation. "My song of the apocalypse," he called it. With its spoken introduction—"And I heard, as it were, the noise of thunder . . ."—"The Man Comes Around" sounds as ancient and scary as any of the old rural ballads collected by Harry Smith on *The Anthology of American Folk Music*, and was praised as Cash's best new song in years.

•   •   •

"Hurt" was another of Cash's Rubin-provoked radical departures, a song by Trent Reznor, who, in his guise as the band Nine Inch Nails, traffics in spookerama atmospherics and songs about alienation and despair. (Reznor recorded his version of "Hurt" in the Los Angeles house where the Manson family murdered Sharon Tate.) Cash's youngest child and only son, John Carter, a burly, bearded, metal-loving guy who was in his twenties when his father started working with Rubin and often acted as a sounding board for his dad on Rubin's heavier suggestions, said even he was taken aback by the concept of his father doing "Hurt." "I was a little wary about it, because I sort of cut my teeth on Nine Inch Nails, so to speak," he says. "The aggression and the hopelessness of it seemed almost like a little bit too much."

Unlike Soundgarden's "Rusty Cage," Nine Inch Nails' "Hurt" wasn't blaringly loud or electrified. The issue was the words. "It's a strange song," says Rubin. "I mean, the opening line is 'I hurt myself today.' It's such a strange thing to say. And then the next line is 'To see if I still feel. . . .' So it's self-inflicted. It's such a strange thought to open a song with." In Reznor's hands, the song was sung by a junkie clear-eyed enough to recognize the ruin he'd made of his life: "What have I become / My sweetest friend / Everyone I know goes away in the end." In Cash's version, with his pitch wobbling uncertainly over the words "What have I become," the singer became an old man lamenting his mortality and frailty, feeling he's outlived his usefulness.

The song's power made it an obvious candidate for a single and, therefore, a video. Rubin enlisted his friend Mark Romanek, the virtuoso visualist behind the best videos of Nine Inch Nails, Lenny Kravitz, and Madonna, to direct the clip. "The initial conception was to do a somewhat stylized piece—in Los Angeles, at a soundstage—and it was going to be based very loosely on imagery from Samuel Beckett plays," says Romanek. "We were going to have some cameos of people like Beck and Johnny Depp." But logistics sent that highfalutin plan out the window. At the time, autumn of 2002, Cash wasn't willing to travel to Los Angeles, and he was headed in a matter of days to his home in Jamaica, where he always went when the Tennessee weather turned colder and tempted pneumonia.

Romanek and his crew had no choice but to go to Tennessee and come up with something on the fly. Rubin suggested that maybe they could film in the House of Cash, a roadside building in Hendersonville where Cash kept his offices, and where his mother, who died in 1991, used to run a small museum of his memorabilia. "The museum was in a state of some disrepair, because there had been some flood damage, and it had been closed for, I think, a good fifteen years," Romanek says. "When I saw the state it was in I went, 'Wow, this is great, this is really interesting.' And the idea of showing the museum without prettifying it or fixing it back up kind of led me to the idea that, well, you know, let's just show Johnny in the state that he's in."

The resulting video was shocking in the exact opposite way from how videos are usually shocking—not because it featured explicit images of sexuality and gunplay, but because it featured explicit images of mortality and infirmity. Romanek discovered a trove of archival films at the House of Cash—home movies, TV appearances, promo films, all of Cash in his pompadoured, virile prime—and intercut them with new scenes of the messy, uncatalogued jumble of stuff in the House of Cash and of the feeble, tremoring Cash himself, seated in his dark living room, surrounded by his collection of bronze Remington sculptures. At one moment during the filming, June descended the stairs above the living room to watch the proceedings. "I glanced over and I saw June on the stairs," says Romanek, "looking down at her husband with this incredibly complex look on her face—filled with love and earnestness and pride, and a certain amount of sadness." With her permission, Romanek included a couple of shots of June as she looked on, and these shots, of her stricken, loving gaze at her dying man, are the most devastating part of the whole film.

●　　　●　　　●

The "Hurt" video was a sensation upon its release in early 2003, a "Have you seen it?" word-of-mouth phenomenon that elicited both praise and concern that Johnny and June had gone too far, revealed too much of their pain and frailty. The Cash children burned up the phone lines discussing it, wondering if it was such a good idea. "I cried like a baby when I saw it, I was sobbing," says Rosanne. "June was just sitting there, just watching it, patting me. See, they had a kind of an unflinching eye. They weren't sentimental in that way. It's like, they're artists—they use their life for their work."

Romanek's film of "Hurt" would go on to be nominated for video of the year and best male video at MTV's 2003 Video Music Awards (and would lose in the latter category to "Cry Me a River," by Justin Timberlake, who rightly labeled his victory "a travesty"). Cash was reveling in all the attention the video was getting when, in early May of last year, June was admitted to the hospital for what was expected to be routine gallbladder surgery. But her doctors unexpectedly discovered a severe problem with a heart valve, and her health quickly deteriorated. She predeceased her husband, dying on May 15. "It was so shocking to think—you know, all of our anxiety had been focused on Dad for ten years, and the whole time she was slipping away," says Rosanne.

"I think my mother knew very well that she was a lot sicker than everybody else thought she was," says John Carter, Cash's sole child with June. "I think she knew. And I think I had a perception that she believed that she was not long for this world." Rosanne remembered, in retrospect, a time in the summer of 2001 when the family had gathered at her father's place in Virginia for a *Vanity Fair* photo shoot by Annie Leibovitz. At one moment, June took Rosanne aside and said, furtively, "I just want you to know that your daddy and I have had a wonderful life together. We've had so many adventures. We've been so happy together, and we've just loved every minute of it."

"I was just so taken aback," says Rosanne. "It was unlike her, 'cause she was usually very light and very chattery. I said, 'It's not over, June.' And then I forgot about it, because, you know, she was a little crazy. I thought, 'Oh, she just had a cuckoo moment.'" But June was usually "fun crazy," says Rosanne, and this time, she realized after the fact, June had been serious and on the level—she knew she was dying but kept mum for the sake of her ailing husband.

•   •   •

"I spoke to Johnny maybe a half-hour or an hour after she passed away," says Rubin, "and he sounded, by far, the worst I'd ever heard him. He sounded terrible. He said that he'd experienced so much pain in his life and that nothing came anywhere near to how he was feeling at that moment. Normally, it was easy to be optimistic and make him feel better. But on this call I just didn't know what to say. I just listened, and tried to send loving energy and support to him, and really take it all in and try to share what he was going through. At some point I asked him, 'Do you think you could look inside, somewhere, and find some faith?' And when I said that, it was like he became a different person. He went from this meek, shaky voice to a strong, powerful voice, and he said, 'MY FAITH IS UNSHAKABLE!'"

Cash wasted little time in getting back to work on music. "It actually got more intense after June died," says Rubin. "Because before, we always worked kind of casually, either whenever we had a song or whenever he felt like recording. Now he said to me, 'I want to work every day, and I need you to have something for me to do every day. Because if I don't have something to focus on, I'm gonna die.'"

Rubin cues up a recording that Cash made and sent to him shortly after June's death. It's a gospel song by Larry Gatlin called "Help Me." Elvis Presley did a version in the early seventies, but, like lots of Elvis's seventies work, the song was gunked up with excessive, *700 Club*-style orchestration and choir vocals, the soul and emotion schmaltzed right out of it. Cash's version of "Help Me" is pure, naked grief, almost too private to listen to. "I never thought I needed help before," Cash sings to God; "I thought that I could do things by myself." And then—this is the chorus, the part where Elvis unfurled the words in an unctuous croon—Cash stops the guitar, and all you hear is playback hiss and his cracked, worn voice, pleading rather than singing: "With a humble heart, on bended knee, I'm beggin' you—please—*help me.*"

"He was just dismantled with grief," says Rosanne. "And so he was just working as much as he could. But it was heartbreaking." The Cash children were resigned to the idea that their father didn't have long, that, as John Carter puts it, "he yearned so much to be with my mother that he wanted to just go with her." But Rubin wasn't having any of this. Since he'd only ever known Cash to be an unwell man, miraculously rebounding from one severe health crisis after another, he thought this, too, was surmountable.

In his endless hunger for books about health and enlightenment, Rubin had come across the works of a doctor named Phil Maffetone, a performance expert and kinesiologist who specialized in devising comprehensive nutrition and exercise programs for extreme athletes, people who compete in triathlons, ironman competitions, and ultra-marathons. "I've never been one for exercise in my life, but I read his book, and it got me inspired," says Rubin. Via e-mail, he got in touch with Maffetone, who promptly informed Rubin that he had given up his practice and wasn't seeing patients anymore. But Rubin persuaded Maffetone, who turned out to be a music enthusiast, to treat Cash.

Cash, at that point, was wheelchair-bound and barely able to see because of diabetes-related glaucoma. But within a short time Maffetone had Cash walking unaided again—"no walker, no cane, nothing," Rubin says—and improving in general. He called Rubin one day and announced, "I'm gonna come out to L.A. for a month, and we're gonna work, and we're gonna continue doing all the stuff on my program. And when I get back home, I'm gonna have a party on the lawn of my house, invite all of my friends over, and I'm gonna push my wheelchair into the river!"

Rubin flew to Nashville for the last time in the summer of 2003 to work with Cash on *American V*. "I was supposed to be there for two or three days," says Rubin, "but we were really doing good and making progress, kind of on a roll. So I extended my stay. And then, the next morning, when I woke up, I got the call that he was back in the hospital."

Nevertheless, Cash rallied with Maffetone's help, and was intent on attending MTV's Video Music Awards on August 28, since "Hurt" was nominated in six categories (it won in one, best cinematography). However, his doctors—his regular ones, not Maffetone—pronounced him insufficiently healthy to make the trip from Tennessee to New York, and by early September he was hospitalized again.

This time it was pancreatitis, yet another complication of the diabetes. Cash spoke to Rubin once more on the phone, promising that he would be out to L.A. soon to work on the album. But he didn't pull through, passing away on September 12, at the age of seventy-one. "Rick seemed to be more shocked about it than we were," says Rosanne. The Cash children had endured their father's struggles long enough to see the writing on the wall, but Rubin, who had gotten just ten years of Cash's companionship, had a hard time accepting the finality. "The way I saw it," he says, "we were going to go on for at least another ten years."

.   .   .

There's still lots more from the American sessions in the vaults, and therefore the potential for Rubin to issue posthumous Cash albums in near perpetuity, à la Tupac Shakur. But Rubin insists that *American V* will be the final word, "'cause there's something that doesn't feel good about the Tupac-ing."

Cash's presence is down to embers now, making the Communion ritual a different experience for Rubin, a solitary one. But he keeps at it, and stays in touch with the Cash clan. A few months ago, he received an unexpected package from John Carter. Inside it was a little leather case holding a flask, a cup, a snippet of Scripture (John 6:35), and some instructional notes written in Johnny Cash's hand ("Open the bread. Give thanks. Eat. Pour wine")—it was Cash's personal Communion kit. Included was a note:

Rick:

One of my father's greatest joys in life was spreading his faith, and I never saw him more joyous than when he shared it with you. He cherished, as I know you did, the daily Communion with you. It seems only fitting that you should have this. You were many things to my father in the last decade of his life—mentor, defining inspirator, producer—but, most of all, a friend. My father learned to believe in your vision, and, in doing so, reawakened his own. His vision lives on, as does the faith he instilled in so many. May your heart grow in faith and peace.

Blessings,
John Carter

The New Republic

FINALIST—
REVIEWS AND CRITICISM

Contrarian, uncompromising, and often openly contemptuous, Jed Perl has a gift for tossing grenades at "the cracked values of an art world where most of the people in charge no longer know what gives a work of art life." Pity the fool who fails to meet his exacting standards. This passionate and erudite critic is capable of reforming public opinion with a single broadside.

Jed Perl

Modern Immaturity

I.

The re-opening of the Museum of Modern Art is exhilarating and dismaying in almost equal proportions. The timing is certainly perfect, for we are in the midst of one of those stretches of pellucid autumn weather when Manhattan is the apple of the whole world's eye and a visit to the museum's talismanic Midtown location can give you an old-fashioned Gotham City lift. The museum, which has spent more than $400 million on a renovation and expansion so vast that it amounts to a whole new building, has surely found the right man for the job. Yoshio Taniguchi, MoMA's architect, brings an opulent delicacy to this daunting project. His mingling of stone and metal and glass is a new version of the classic MoMA experience—an experience of moving through spaces that are quietly, transparently luxurious, in their own way as intoxicating as the glass of champagne or the dry martini that you drink later, after leaving the museum, in one of the neighborhood's watering holes. The good news at MoMA— the building and the relatively straightforward installations of selections from the museum's collections—is so encouraging that when the bad news hits you may find yourself reeling. Far from accepting the hard fact that the time has come to embrace a solid maturity, a maturity grounded in an assessment of its glorious past that is at once forthright and modest, the Modern has insisted on remaining the aging hipster who long ago had one too many of those martinis and fled midtown Manhattan in search of the next snort of art-world cocaine.

For the moment the Modern's triumphs and the Modern's fiascoes are suspended, contradictions without a resolution, amid the refinements of Taniguchi's architecture. The sad truth, though, is that as you go through the museum, you are probably going to find it difficult to keep the triumphs and the fiascoes apart for very long, because the aging hipster has forced the museum's great collections into a dismayingly frozen form, while those priceless holdings in early twentieth-century art are being used further to inflate the prestige of a sicko contemporary art market. MoMA, while it has sometimes purveyed an ivory-tower vision of art, has never been far from the hurly-burly of the art world, and the unspoken crisis at the heart of the museum today is that the director and many of the trustees and the curators are at least as conscious of the market as they are of the classics that they hold as a public trust. As for the state of the art market, all you have to do is look at the news that came out of the auction rooms on the very November day that the Museum of Modern Art celebrated its seventy-fifth anniversary. Forty blocks south, at Phillips, de Pury & Co., a vinyl serigraph by Barbara Kruger, a photograph of a hand holding a sign that reads, "I shop therefore I am," sold for more than $600,000, leading a prominent dealer to remark, "People want quality, and this was quality."

I have never wanted to like a museum renovation as much as I wanted to like this one. And my reasons have everything to do with quality, though not the Barbara Kruger kind. The artists and the museumgoers whom I know want this renovation to work—they want MoMA to shimmer—precisely because so many of them grew up in the Museum of Modern Art and there discovered what excellence was, and now they know how desperate is the need for a place where a new generation can go and grapple with questions of quality. John Elderfield, the chief curator of

Painting and Sculpture, and his distinguished colleagues will argue that they are merely following the modern tradition wherever it leads. They are also glad to remind us that the immense contemporary galleries—where they have parked some work by Matthew Barney and Andy Warhol and Chris Ofili (whose *Prince Amongst Thieves* is a mixed-media painting including glitter and elephant dung)—offer nothing more than a working definition of the state of quality now. But the issue is not Barney or Warhol or Ofili, all of whom will continue to be bought and sold and praised whether the curators at the Modern exhibit them or not. The issue is that for more than forty years, since MoMA began to ratify contemporary taste with its presentations of Jasper Johns, Frank Stella, and Jean Tinguely, the museum has been using Picasso, Matisse, Mondrian, and Brancusi as negotiating positions in an art-world futures game. Forty years ago the critic Thomas B. Hess, a brilliant thinker virtually all of whose work is now out of print, wrote that "the Museum of Modern Art is a useful indicator of the fluctuations in official, big-money taste (which it leads)," and that remains true today, except that official taste has become more official and the money has become bigger.

I was first taken to the Modern by my parents in the 1950s. As an adolescent in the 1960s I haunted the place during family visits to New York. And in the 1970s I was always there with painter friends, learning from what was on the walls. Even back then I could see that the museum gave off some weird vibes, which had a lot to do with the futures game that was going on in the back rooms and the temporary exhibitions and the final galleries of the permanent collection, where the curators made predictions as to what was going to last. If the museum has always had a way of appearing sleekly confident one moment and peevish the next, it is because its great collections have never exactly given its wildly ambitious staff the commanding presence in the contemporary art world that many of them craved. The disjunction between the museum's classic collections and the business that it does in contemporary art is now more pronounced than ever before. While there are still many artists who believe that the past is a guide to the future, they are not generally the ones whose work is selling for hundreds of thousands of dollars, which puts the museum in the position of shilling for a bunch of artists who at best, as in the case of Brice Marden, have a rigidly academic understanding of the classics, or more generally do not understand them at all.

Ironically, for a museum that has always wanted to embrace the cutting edge, the Modern has never figured out how to present the kind of art that came of age in the renovated industrial spaces of downtown New York. Even the work of an original such as Robert Gober, that master of disquietude, can look glib in the what's-hot-now barn of a space where contemporary art is presented on the second floor. As for the core of the permanent collection, the masterworks imposingly arrayed on the fifth floor are given a more icily routinized presentation than ever before. The installation of art since 1945 feels curiously unconfident. And the long list of artists who are sidelined or overlooked in the galleries devoted to painting and sculpture and prints and drawings tells us exactly how little the museum cares for the views of the honorable opposition—an honorable opposition that has been a force to be reckoned with in New York since well before Hess registered his protest some forty years ago.

II.

When Glenn D. Lowry, MoMA's director, refers to this as the *new* Museum of Modern Art, he may not know how right he is. There is a sense in which the Museum of Modern Art no longer exists, if we mean by that the museum where Alfred H. Barr Jr. was the guiding force from the beginning, in 1929, well into the 1960s. That museum was a unique institution, a one-time event in history, where not only was all of modern visual culture exhibited, but where the scholarly study of modern art was also to a large degree defined, and where the audience for modern art as we know it can be said to have been invented. In place of that unique institution we now have a museum that is in some sense like all other museums, with a permanent collection that is its capital—its raison d'être—and a staff that should be devoted to that collection and to the kind of scholarly pursuits and temporary exhibitions that build on its essential meanings.

The old Modern was to a large degree an act of self-invention. Barr and his colleagues put certain facts on the ground; they created a certain reality. The new Museum of Modern Art must preserve that reality and see that it lives on. It ought not to surprise us that the museum has maintained, at least for the moment, a fairly straightforward presentation of art from Cézanne through the Surrealists, except for all the wild speculation about its future form that the museum has engaged in over the past eight or ten years. To go through *Imagining the Future of the Museum of Modern Art*, a volume published in 1998 that featured the offerings of the ten architects who were invited the previous year to help reshape the museum, is to confront speculations about the nature of the museum and the city that are often recklessly abstruse and self-absorbed. And before temporarily closing its doors on West Fifty-third Street and moving out to Queens for several years, the museum went through a yearlong upheaval known as "MoMA2000," which involved anti- or non-chronological hangings and a series of tiny theme shows offered like glittery boutiques at a shopping mall.

For years now there has been a desire, on the part of people both inside and outside the museum, to escape from the fairly straightforward presentation of the collections that had been evolving for sixty years and had come to be called, as if it were some Stalinist plot, "the story." I have to say that I am tired of this whole line of thinking—of being told that MoMA's permanent collection galleries used to be a one-way street, a conveyor belt with the Great Tradition arrayed in neat rows. The Modern was never the wearisomely oppressive experience that it is now often said to have been. There was an intensity about that unfolding succession of galleries; they conveyed the authentic fever of belief. It was inspiring, even if it was also sometimes infuriating. And you were free to look at the paintings one by one, you were free to walk back from one room to another, you were free to overlook certain things and to love some more than others, you were free to decide that you preferred certain works that were not in the collection to the ones that were.

Barr and William S. Rubin—who was for all intents and purposes Barr's successor in the late 1960s until his retirement in the 1980s—promoted and presented some of the very ideas and values that their detractors accuse them of overlooking. To say that their Modern had no use for metaphor and narrative is simply untrue; Barr and Rubin showed Klee in great depth, they explicated the complex psychological and mythological dimensions in Picasso. And the aspects of the twentieth century that the Modern from time to time de-emphasized made others curious about the lacunae; it was the power of their vision that, practically since the beginnings of the museum, spurred a variety of countervisions. Some people now assume that any form of authority is a form of oppression, but authority is also a spur to creativity, to original thinking, to independence, and that was how the old Painting and Sculpture collection affected several generations.

•   •   •

I expect that many people are going to cling to the new fifth-floor installation as if it were an oasis in a desert. I did, at least when I first visited the new museum. After the shambles that the Modern made of the work of its two favorite artists little more than a year ago with "Matisse Picasso," a misbegotten exercise in the principle that opposites attract, it is a huge pleasure to see Matisse and Picasso left more or less to their own devices. Visitors are going to be so damn glad to see some of MoMA's paintings and sculptures—as well as the wonderful prints and drawings and the Atgets in the photography galleries. And the Modern made an inspired move when it acquired Ellsworth Kelly's immense *Sculpture for a Large Wall*, the work designed in the 1950s for the Transportation Building in Philadelphia that now does itself proud in one of the immense sixth-floor galleries.

But the more I looked, the more I became aware of what was not on display. There is an argument for not making too much of specific inclusions and exclusions, since the museum has a vast collection and had to make hard choices about what to show, and is surely committed to rotating the permanent collection, at least to some degree. I can forgive them for removing Vuillard from the opening galleries, and I can live with the museum's traditional lack of enthusiasm for Gris. But the more I reflected on what I was seeing, the more the selections seemed to suggest the freezing of the permanent collection into what amounts to an exaggerated caricature of its old self—an exercise in iron-clad formalism with little cake-decoration spritzes of Dadaism thrown in.

And by the time I had been in the permanent collection for a couple of hours, the weird vibes were coming straight out of the galleries full of modern masters. Most disturbing, especially considering that Elderfield is an internationally acknowledged expert on Matisse, is MoMA's continuing refusal to look at Matisse's achievement in the 1920s and 1930s. For years, the contention was that the museum did not have the right works from this period, when Matisse lived in Nice and made his most searching inquiries into the human figure as a three-dimensional volume. More than a decade ago, when William S. Paley left his collection to the Modern, it contained two great Nice-period Matisses, which William Rubin wrote were "acknowledged masterpieces" that would "help redress the imbalance" in the collection. And yet this side of Matisse's art—these paintings of the female figure that rival the work of Giorgione and Titian—remains in storage.

I am also depressed by the museum's insistent downplaying of Braque. This continues in spite of one of the wisest acquisitions of recent years, Braque's stupendous *Studio V* (1949–1950), which has been sandwiched between dreary works by Dubuffet and Bacon. Years ago, at the time that Rubin mounted the great show "Picasso and Braque: Pioneering Cubism," Clement Greenberg observed that the title ought to have been alphabetical—that Braque deserved his due; but here is Braque, for some people a greater painter than Picasso, placed in the same shadowy—and maybe even shadowier—relationship with Picasso.

Some of the choices in the permanent collection—I refer to the showcasing of a group of middling South American artists—suggest a rather obvious and perhaps excessively close connection with a particular trustee, Patricia Phelps de Cisneros, who has given these works to the museum. While artists such as Jesús Rafael Soto and Hélio Oiticica may deserve a hearing, these choices, which the curators surely want us to believe show that they are thinking outside the box, cannot mask the fact that when it comes to art that fails to walk the old Ab-Ex-to-Pop-to-Minimal-to-Conceptual line, the museum remains indifferent. Such extraordinary American geometric painters as Ilya Bolotowsky and Burgoyne Diller—whose work would complicate and enrich the current view of the 1960s—are still disregarded. And while the Museum of Modern Art has not been willing to accept Balthus as a central figure in the art of the second half of the twentieth century, it at least used to be scrupulous about saluting his achievements in the 1930s—until now, when I look in vain, even as such return-to-realism incompetents as Elizabeth Peyton and Luc Tuymans and Peter Doig are given a warm welcome. And although a good deal of fuss is made about the continuing relevance of intaglio techniques in the print galleries, it is Damien Hirst who gets the nod, while Morandi, whether as a printmaker, a draftsman, or a painter, is invisible. Also absent from this graphics offering is Bill Jensen, the most formidable intaglio printmaker of the moment, although Deborah Wye, the current curator of Prints and Illustrated Books, once devoted a small MoMA show to his work.

The Masterpiece Theater presentation of early twentieth-century art probably accelerates an inevitable process by which the MoMA collections, although they are unparalleled in their depth and strength, are losing the totemic power that they once had. The sight of *Les Demoiselles d'Avignon* or *Broadway Boogie Woogie* will still bring a rush of excitement, but there is so much extraordinary modern art on display in the world today—elsewhere in New York, in Washington, in London, in Paris—that one is now emboldened to do comparisons that, while not bringing the Modern up short, place it in more of a dialogue with other collections of modern art. Barr's sense of the grandeur of modern art as an incremental leap within the Great Tradition has become generally accepted. And his populist ambitions, which inspired him to give the museum the quality of a social club and even an ongoing carnival, have not only educated America but have led in some instances to the worst excesses of the funhouse museums of our own time. The Modern now exists in an element that Barr and his colleagues created. The treasures of the Modern are no longer, if you will, the definitive modern masterpieces, but masterpieces pure and simple. They are no longer connected to the intensity, the feverishness that a generation ago ran through the museum like an electric current.

Older museumgoers, those who began going in the 1940s or 1950s or 1960s, will feel the difference. There was something that gripped you when you walked into the Modern: a sense of alarm, almost of panic, at how much was at stake. The old Modern had a vision not only of what you ought to see but also of what you ought to feel, and how you ought to live your life. And the insouciance, the high spirits, the New York chic that were all a part of the museum's mystique were related to that electric current, and that was an entirely different thing from the fast-track act that the museum has more and more purveyed in the past quarter-century. This fall the old electricity is gone, and there is not enough of the dignity that needs to grow up in its place—a dignity that honors what was, and acknowledges what now can and cannot be.

III.

Yoshio Taniguchi, the Japanese architect who won the competition for the rebuilding of the Modern in 1997 after an international talent search, is very much the hero of the moment. His work in New York—the culmination of years spent designing museums in Japan, which are the subject of the one major temporary show at MoMA right now—reflects a steadiness of purpose and an innovative traditionalism that points the Modern in the right direction. Taniguchi is the first architect in recent times to produce a large, multi-purpose museum that really works. He has finessed the problem of working with an already existing structure that gave I. M. Pei such trouble at the National Gallery and the Louvre, and that capsized Herzog and de Meuron at Tate Modern. Taniguchi has created the kind of overarching unity that eluded Richard Meier at the Getty. (MoMA in some respects resembles that institution, with its varied functions as a center for scholarship, education, and art.) Working with the patchwork of spaces that the Modern has acquired on the block bordered by Fifth and Sixth Avenues and West Fifty-third and West Fifty-fourth Streets, Taniguchi has given a new shine to the best of the old Modern—the Sculpture Garden, the façade of the 1939 International Style building on West Fifty-third Street—while creating whole that is entirely his own.

Architecture is always a matter of relating the parts to the whole, and it is imperative that the elements that we experience close up be linked, in some essential way, to the sense of the building as an enveloping experience. The big museums by Pei, Meier, and Herzog and de Meuron can leave you feeling like an ant in a maze. Taniguchi's Modern has its towering spaces and its long vistas, but they do not leave you feeling puny or irrelevant. This architect knows how to humanize the chill that is often associated with modern buildings; his sensitivity recalls the work that Gordon Bunshaft did at Lever House in the 1950s. The secret at MoMA, I think, is that Taniguchi makes us feel that the space originates with us. He does this through the aptness and the refinement of the details that we experience up close, and unlike Meier, who at the Getty was unable to give those bits of exquisite architectural tailoring some larger dimension, Taniguchi uses them as leitmotifs that expand into grand themes.

Taniguchi's Modern is crisp, cool, sleek—but also quirky and soothing and inviting. The feeling for space—the overhanging rooflines and smaller boxlike structures tucked in larger boxlike structures—suggests invitations piled upon invitations. And all this high modern fanfare is no tease, for the Modern has the kind of collections that give Taniguchi's purist drama its strong internal engine. Visitors can now enter the museum not only from West Fifty-third Street but also from West Fifty-fourth Street, and the long corridor that links the two streets and functions as public space has a relatively low ceiling, one that echoes the proportions of street-level shops, and makes our first steps inside the museum an extension of the life of the city, which is altogether appropriate for this museum that has always been knit so deeply into the urban fabric. Turning to go into the museum—this is where you give your ticket—the space heightens and suddenly we see before us the Sculpture Garden, that island in the city, and to our right an elegant staircase that is altogether new but that echoes and indeed invokes the legendary staircase that was sidelined in the building program of a quarter-century ago.

·　　·　　·

Taniguchi's work never upstages the art. Indeed, in your first moments in the museum what may mostly strike you are your glimpses of the collection: an Ellsworth Kelly painting over the information counter, Miró's *Mural* opposite the stairs, Rodin's *Balzac* set against the Sculpture Garden rather than in it as it had been in the past. Going up the stairs, you are in the five-story-high atrium, a space that is grand but somehow not overwhelming, and that is the perfect frame for Barnett Newman's *Broken Obelisk*, a sculpture that has never looked this good before. Beyond the Newman hangs the three-panel Monet *Water Lilies*. And, looking up, you can glimpse, through a window looking into the Painting and Sculpture galleries, Matisse's *Dance*. Taniguchi has a feeling for modern luxe, in the attenuated steel elements that define floors and frame windows. His rhythmic sense is superb, whether in the bit of open space that separates the panels of a glass parapet, or in the articulation of the walls that face the garden. In the galleries, Taniguchi has kept his interventions to a minimum. He has wisely preserved the old MoMA tradition of including a few windows that frame New York City streetscapes and skyscapes. And he has lined the doorways between the galleries in sleek metal that gives just the right touch of glamour—it's an architectural exclamation point. A resplendent staircase linking the fourth- and fifth-floor galleries floats in the air, a geometric fantasy come to life. Taniguchi brings a spare athleticism to the Museum of Modern Art.

Given the seeming effortlessness of Taniguchi's achievement, we need to remind ourselves of how daunting his assignment was. The museum has been acquiring real estate on West Fifty-third Street for most of its history, and there was never a master plan, at least not for very long. The museum's first major construction project, the building designed by Philip L. Goodwin and Edward Durell Stone that opened in 1939, was one of the earlier International Style structures in the city, and its façade, complete with curved canopy, has been exquisitely restored. Philip Johnson's additions, with dark metal framing sheets of glass, are less admired now than they ought to be, and some of Johnson's work, too, has been preserved. The museum's last major renovation, designed by

Cesar Pelli and completed twenty years ago, involved construction of an apartment tower, which is an important source of income for the museum, and Taniguchi has had to work around that tower as he moved the museum's center of gravity westward, toward the site of the Dorset Hotel on Fifty-fourth Street, the purchase and demolition of which essentially made this project possible. Taniguchi's canniness rests in his decision at once to accept the sense of discrete volumes and voids that was bequeathed to him and to unite them through his strong constructivist feeling, a feeling for form that he underscores through the graphic articulation of two-dimensional surfaces. Instead of masking the Pelli tower—the bottom floors of which are in fact part of the museum—Taniguchi has made us aware of this tower as a volume that originates in the Sculpture Garden and that the museum wraps around. On Fifty-third Street, where the old façades have been preserved, we have a glimpse of the museum's history. From Fifty-fourth Street, every surface is Taniguchi's, except that the Sculpture Garden was designed by Philip Johnson, so again there is a balancing, a negotiation.

The incorporation of disjunctive elements is by now a cliché of architectural renovations, and of the postmodern spirit in general, but for Taniguchi, who is at heart a classicist, there must be a resolution. He obviously has a taste for variety, and it seems to grow out of a liberal sense of the play of possibilities rather than a hunger for the eccentric gesture. Perhaps the secret is that he does not regard the various layers of the building as historical artifacts. The Sculpture Garden, designed in the early 1950s, is not an example of retro-chic that he offers with a wink, but a triumph of urban planning that he feels as pressure on the work that he is doing here. Taniguchi thinks dialectically, rather than confrontationally. He works his way into the givens of the situation and acts through them, and the effect is a kind of architecture that exerts a gentle pressure. You may not notice how much he has done. That is his triumph.

IV.

The decision to put the design of the museum in the hands of Yoshio Taniguchi is at once the most conservative choice and the most radical choice that the Museum of Modern Art has made in recent years. When I walk through the museum, I am quite sure that Taniguchi's articulation of space and sense of color and feeling for detail are very close to those of the terrific architects who preceded him, Goodwin and Stone and Johnson; and although this is to some degree an illusion, it is the illusion that the museum quite rightly wants to create. This architect who has never before worked outside of Japan has understood the Museum of Modern Art better than the hometown team.

It is in everything except the new architecture—in the selection of works on display and in the hanging of the collections—that I feel a disquietude about the pressures of the past, a disquietude that expresses itself through a mixture of begrudging conventionality and dutiful contemporaneity that seems mostly designed to throw sops to the various constituencies that the museum wants to keep happy. There may be a tendency to blame the museum's opportunistic tendencies on Glenn Lowry, who in the nearly ten years that he has been director has transformed MoMA from museum where the curator was king to a more conventionally structured institution. But the uniquely close relationships that some of MoMA's curatorial visionaries once had with some of the trustees may have died a natural death, a victim of a more general regularization of giving in the arts.

Reading the movements of an institution as large, as complex, and as byzantine as the Modern is not an easy task. And students of the history of the Museum of Modern Art—New York is full of them—will want to remind us that the Modern's sense of self was always changing, and was often quite mercurial. Although the museum acquired works of art from the very beginning, the intention in the early decades was to have a shifting collection and to deaccession works when they reached a certain age. It was only in 1953, when the museum realized what a priceless hoard it had, that the permanent collection as an enduring fact was enshrined. And if the very idea of a permanent collection was one that has had a fluid career at the Modern, the Modern's relation to the achievements of the present—to contemporary painting and sculpture, not to mention to new architecture and design and photography and film—has also been extraordinarily vexed. There has not been a time when New York's artists didn't believe that the Modern underrated their importance, or overlooked them entirely, or when one group of artists didn't believe that the Modern was paying too much attention to another group of artists. And Barr, in several eloquent statements, was candid about the museum's limitations as a predictor of trends, although that never stopped him from trying to play that most dangerous game.

When Barr is invoked at MoMA today, it is often as the hyperenergetic director of the earliest decades, as the prophet of experimentation, of the new. Barr had first envisioned his museum as laboratory devoted to aesthetic investigations, with departments dedicated to everything from industrial design to photography and film, and he had wanted it to be dynamic, energetic, provisional. By the 1960s, however, Barr saw that his work had helped to jump-start an entire art world, and he seems to have begun to feel that what the Modern could do best was supply solidity, continuity—with its peerless collections as an anchor and a beacon. The aspect of Barr's legacy that the Modern would be wisest to study now is the legacy of his later years, when without ever turning his back on the whirl of the present he came to feel that his most essential work would be on the permanent collection, which he lovingly catalogued, and which he then left in the hands of William Rubin, who immeasurably enriched its holdings (while also going off on some fairly dubious contemporary tangents).

There are many reasons why the powers that be at the Modern are reluctant to accept the proposition that the museum's most useful role is now a custodial role, but there really aren't any good ones. The fact is that nobody any longer looks to the Modern for guidance on contemporary art. The art world presents nearly endless opportunities to see the latest thing—in galleries and at the increasingly influential art fairs and the biennials and the other international exhibitions that mean so much to dealers, to collectors, and to the curators who watch the money trail. Robert Storr, the curator who left the Modern a few years ago, has been making news in some of those flash-point locales, organizing "Disparities and Deformations," which is currently at SITE Sante Fe, and taking on the directorship at the Venice Biennale, where he will be in charge in 2007.

On its seventy-fifth anniversary, the Museum of Modern Art needs to begin to grapple with the challenges that come with maturity. MoMA needs to face the fact that the only experiment that's still worth pursuing involves figuring out how to properly honor the treasure house that the permanent collection has become. The brightest events at the Modern in recent years have been shows that reaffirmed the museum's traditional interests, such as the display of Russian avant-garde books in 2002 and the fine exhibition "Tall Buildings" at MoMA Queens over the summer, which reminded us of the voice that the museum used to have in urban matters. I am heartened to learn that among the museum's upcoming events are exhibitions focusing on the relationship between Pissarro and Cézanne, Redon's works on paper, and Seurat's drawings. These are exhibitions that promise to take us back to the chronological beginnings of the museum, even as they illuminate the beginnings of modern art.

The hardest beginning that lies before the Modern involves beginning to accept the fact that a museum that was once a laboratory is now a monument. With his subtle re-imagining of the Museum of Modern Art, Yoshio Taniguchi has shown us what the monument can look like, but his makeover has also given a new lease on life to the museum's by-now-inveterate status as an aging hipster with some life left in it yet. Of course, New Yorkers love nothing more than an adorable aging hipster—especially when the hipster has just pulled off makeover as fabulous as this one. But how many more makeovers can there be? And how many more snorts of art-world cocaine before the trips to rehab in Queens do not work anymore? There comes a time when you have to accept reality and finally grow up, and in this regard the Museum of Modern Art still has a long way to go.

National Geographic

WINNER—ESSAYS

Much of the American public still fails to accept the truth of the theory of evolution. Nevertheless, National Geographic's courageous cover story dared readers to shake off their prejudices. Firmly but tactfully, David Quammen marshals genetic data, antibiotic-resistant germs, and the anklebone of a fossil whale to build the case for Charles Darwin's great insight, concluding that "the evidence for evolution is overwhelming."

David Quammen

Was Darwin Wrong?

E volution by natural selection, the central concept of the life's work of Charles Darwin, is a theory. It's a theory about the origin of adaptation, complexity, and diversity among Earth's living creatures. If you are skeptical by nature, unfamiliar with the terminology of science, and unaware of the overwhelming evidence, you might even be tempted to say that it's "just" a theory. In the same sense, relativity as described by Albert Einstein is "just" a theory. The notion that Earth orbits around the sun rather than vice versa, offered by Copernicus in 1543, is a theory. Continental drift is a theory. The existence, structure, and dynamics of atoms? Atomic theory. Even electricity is a theoretical construct, involving electrons, which are tiny units of charged mass that no one has ever seen. Each of these theories is an explanation that has been confirmed to such a degree, by observation and experiment, that knowledgeable experts accept it as fact. That's what scientists mean when they talk about a theory: not a dreamy and unreliable speculation, but an explanatory statement that fits the evidence. They embrace such an explanation confidently but provisionally—taking it as their best available view of reality, at least until some severely conflicting data or some better explanation might come along.

The rest of us generally agree. We plug our televisions into little wall sockets, measure a year by the length of Earth's orbit, and in many other ways live our lives based on the trusted reality of those theories.

Evolutionary theory, though, is a bit different. It's such a dangerously wonderful and far-reaching view of life that some people find it unacceptable, despite the vast body of supporting evidence. As applied to our own species, *Homo sapiens*, it can seem more threatening still. Many fundamentalist Christians and ultra-orthodox Jews take alarm at the thought that human descent from earlier primates contradicts a strict reading of the Book of Genesis. Their discomfort is paralleled by Islamic creationists such as Harun Yahya, author of a recent volume titled *The Evolution Deceit*, who points to the six-day creation story in the Koran as literal truth and calls the theory of evolution "nothing but a deception imposed on us by the dominators of the world system." The late Srila Prabhupada, of the Hare Krishna movement, explained that God created "the 8,400,000 species of life from the very beginning," in order to establish multiple tiers of reincarnation for rising souls. Although souls ascend, the species themselves don't change, he insisted, dismissing "Darwin's nonsensical theory."

Other people too, not just scriptural literalists, remain unpersuaded about evolution. According to a Gallup poll drawn from more than a thousand telephone interviews conducted in February 2001, no less than 45 percent of responding U.S. adults agreed that "God created human beings pretty much in their present form at one time within the last 10,000 years or so." Evolution, by their lights, played no role in shaping us.

Only 37 percent of the polled Americans were satisfied with allowing room for both God and Darwin—that is, divine initiative to get things started, evolution as the creative means. (This view, according to more than one papal pronouncement, is compatible with Roman Catholic dogma.) Still fewer Americans, only 12 percent, believed that humans evolved from other life-forms without any involvement of a god.

The most startling thing about these poll numbers is not that so many Americans reject evolution, but that the statistical breakdown hasn't changed much in two decades. Gallup interviewers posed exactly the same choices in 1982, 1993, 1997, and 1999. The creationist conviction—that God alone, and not evolution, produced humans—has never drawn less than 44 percent. In other words, nearly half the American populace prefers to believe that Charles Darwin was wrong where it mattered most.

Why are there so many antievolutionists? Scriptural literalism can only be part of the answer. The American public certainly includes a large segment of scriptural literalists—but not *that* large, not 44 percent. Creationist proselytizers and political activists, working hard to interfere with the teaching of evolutionary biology in public schools, are another part. Honest confusion and ignorance, among millions of adult Americans, must be still another. Many people have never taken a biology course that dealt with evolution nor read a book in which the theory was lucidly explained. Sure, we've all heard of Charles Darwin, and of a vague, somber notion about struggle and survival that sometimes goes by the catchall label "Darwinism." But the main sources of information from which most Americans have drawn their awareness of this subject, it seems, are haphazard ones at best: cultural osmosis, newspaper and magazine references, half-baked nature documentaries on the tube, and hearsay.

Evolution is both a beautiful concept and an important one, more crucial nowadays to human welfare, to medical science, and to our understanding of the world than ever before. It's also deeply persuasive—a theory you can take to the bank. The essential points are slightly more complicated than most people assume, but not so complicated that they can't be comprehended by any attentive person. Furthermore, the supporting evidence is abundant, various, ever increasing, solidly interconnected, and easily available in museums, popular books, textbooks, and a mountainous accumulation of peer-reviewed scientific studies.

No one needs to, and no one should, accept evolution merely as a matter of faith.

.   .   .

Two big ideas, not just one, are at issue: the evolution of all species, as a historical phenomenon, and natural selection, as the main mechanism causing that phenomenon. The first is a question of what happened. The second is a question of how. The idea that all species are descended from common ancestors had been suggested by other thinkers, including Jean-Baptiste Lamarck, long before Darwin published *The Origin of Species* in 1859. What made Darwin's book so remarkable when it appeared, and so influential in the long run, was that it offered a rational explanation of how evolution must occur. The same insight came independently to Alfred Russel Wallace, a young naturalist doing fieldwork in the Malay Archipelago during the late 1850s. In historical annals, if not in the popular awareness, Wallace and Darwin share the kudos for having discovered natural selection. The gist of the concept is that small, random, heritable differences among individuals result in different chances of survival and reproduction—success for some, death without offspring for others—and that this natural culling leads to significant changes in shape, size, strength, armament, color, biochemistry, and behavior among the descendants. Excess population growth drives the competitive struggle. Because less successful competitors produce fewer surviving offspring, the useless or negative variations tend to disappear, whereas the useful variations tend to be perpetuated and gradually magnified throughout a population.

So much for one part of the evolutionary process, known as anagenesis, during which a single species is transformed. But there's also a second part, known as speciation. Genetic changes sometimes accumulate within an isolated segment of a species, but not throughout the whole, as that isolated population adapts to its local conditions. Gradually it goes its own way, seizing a new ecological niche. At a certain point it becomes irreversibly distinct—that is, so different that its members can't interbreed with the rest. Two species now exist where formerly there was one. Darwin called that splitting-and-specializing phenomenon the "principle of divergence." It was an important part of his theory, explaining the overall diversity of life as well as the adaptation of individual species.

This thrilling and radical assemblage of concepts came from an unlikely source. Charles Darwin was shy and meticulous, a wealthy landowner with close friends among the Anglican clergy. He had a gentle, unassuming manner, a strong need for privacy, and an extraordinary commitment to intellectual honesty. As an undergraduate at Cambridge, he had studied halfheartedly toward becoming a clergyman himself, before he discovered his real vocation as a scientist. Later, having established a good but conventional reputation in natural history, he spent twenty-two years secretly gathering evidence and pondering arguments—both for and against his theory—because he didn't want to flame out in a burst of unpersuasive notoriety. He may have delayed, too, because of his anxiety about announcing a theory that seemed to challenge conventional religious beliefs—in particular, the Christian beliefs of his wife, Emma. Darwin himself quietly renounced Christianity during his middle age, and later described himself as an agnostic. He continued to believe in a distant, impersonal deity of some sort, a greater entity that had set the universe and its laws into motion, but not in a personal God who had chosen humanity as a specially favored species. Darwin avoided flaunting his lack of religious faith, at least partly in deference to Emma. And she prayed for his soul.

In 1859 he finally delivered his revolutionary book. Although it was hefty and substantive at 490 pages, he considered *The Origin of Species* just a quick-and-dirty "abstract" of the huge volume he had been working on until interrupted by an alarming event.

(In fact, he'd wanted to title it *An Abstract of an Essay on the Origin of Species and Varieties Through Natural Selection,* but his publisher found that insufficiently catchy.) The alarming event was his receiving a letter and an enclosed manuscript from Alfred Wallace, whom he knew only as a distant pen pal. Wallace's manuscript sketched out the same great idea—evolution by natural selection—that Darwin considered his own. Wallace had scribbled this paper and (unaware of Darwin's own evolutionary thinking, which so far had been kept private) mailed it to him from the Malay Archipelago, along with a request for reaction and help. Darwin was horrified. After two decades of painstaking effort, now he'd be scooped. Or maybe not quite. He forwarded Wallace's paper toward publication, though managing also to assert his own prior claim by releasing two excerpts from his unpublished work. Then he dashed off *The Origin,* his "abstract" on the subject. Unlike Wallace, who was younger and less meticulous, Darwin recognized the importance of providing an edifice of supporting evidence and logic.

The evidence, as he presented it, mostly fell within four categories: biogeography, paleontology, embryology, and morphology. Biogeography is the study of the geographical distribution of living creatures—that is, which species inhabit which parts of the planet and why. Paleontology investigates extinct life-forms, as revealed in the fossil record. Embryology examines the revealing stages of development (echoing earlier stages of evolutionary history) that embryos pass through before birth or hatching; at a stretch, embryology also concerns the immature forms of animals that metamorphose, such as the larvae of insects. Morphology is the science of anatomical shape and design. Darwin devoted sizable sections of *The Origin of Species* to these categories.

Biogeography, for instance, offered a great pageant of peculiar facts and patterns. Anyone who considers the biogeographical data, Darwin wrote, must be struck by the mysterious clustering pattern among what he called "closely allied" species—that is, similar creatures sharing roughly the same body plan. Such closely allied species tend to be found on the same continent (several species of zebras in Africa) or within the same group of oceanic islands (dozens of species of honeycreepers in Hawaii, thirteen species of Galápagos finch), despite their species-by-species preferences for different habitats, food sources, or conditions of climate. Adjacent areas of South America, Darwin noted, are occupied by two similar species of large, flightless birds (the rheas, *Rhea americana* and *Pterocnemia pennata*), not by ostriches as in Africa or emus as in Australia. South America also has agoutis and viscachas (small rodents) in terrestrial habitats, plus coypus and capybaras in the wetlands, not—as Darwin wrote—hares and rabbits in terrestrial habitats or beavers and muskrats in the wetlands. During his own youthful visit to the Galápagos, aboard the survey ship *Beagle*, Darwin himself had discovered three very similar forms of mockingbird, each on a different island.

Why should "closely allied" species inhabit neighboring patches of habitat? And why should similar habitat on different continents be occupied by species that aren't so closely allied? "We see in these facts some deep organic bond, prevailing throughout space and time," Darwin wrote. "This bond, on my theory, is simply inheritance." Similar species occur nearby in space because they have descended from common ancestors.

Paleontology reveals a similar clustering pattern in the dimension of time. The vertical column of geologic strata, laid down by sedimentary processes over the eons, lightly peppered with fossils, represents a tangible record showing which species lived when. Less ancient layers of rock lie atop more ancient ones (except where geologic forces have tipped or shuffled them), and likewise with the animal and plant fossils that the strata contain. What Darwin noticed about this record is that closely allied species tend to be found adjacent to one another in successive strata. One species endures for millions of years and then makes its last appearance in, say, the middle Eocene epoch; just above, a similar but not identical species replaces it. In North America, for example, a vaguely horselike creature known as *Hyracotherium* was succeeded by *Orohippus*, then *Epihippus*, then *Mesohippus*, which in turn were succeeded by a variety of horsey American critters. Some of them even galloped across the Bering land bridge into Asia, then onward to Europe and Africa. By five million years ago they had nearly all disappeared, leaving behind *Dinohippus*, which was succeeded by *Equus*, the modern genus of horse. Not all these fossil links had been unearthed in Darwin's day, but he captured the essence of the matter anyway. Again, were such sequences just coincidental? No, Darwin argued. Closely allied species succeed one another in time, as well as living nearby in space, because they're related through evolutionary descent.

Embryology too involved patterns that couldn't be explained by coincidence. Why does the embryo of a mammal pass through stages resembling stages of the embryo of a reptile? Why is one of the larval forms of a barnacle, before metamorphosis, so similar to the larval form of a shrimp? Why do the larvae of moths, flies, and beetles resemble one another more than any of them resemble their respective adults? Because, Darwin wrote, "the embryo is the animal in its less modified state" and that state "reveals the structure of its progenitor."

. . .

Morphology, his fourth category of evidence, was the "very soul" of natural history, according to Darwin. Even today it's on display in the layout and organization of any zoo. Here are the monkeys, there are the big cats, and in that building are the alligators and crocodiles. Birds in the aviary, fish in the aquarium. Living creatures can be easily sorted into a hierarchy of categories—not just species but genera, families, orders, whole kingdoms—based on which anatomical characters they share and which they don't.

All vertebrate animals have backbones. Among vertebrates, birds have feathers, whereas reptiles have scales. Mammals have fur and mammary glands, not feathers or scales. Among mammals, some have pouches in which they nurse their tiny young. Among these species, the marsupials, some have huge rear legs and strong tails by which they go hopping across miles of arid outback; we call them kangaroos. Bring in modern microscopic and molecular evidence, and you can trace the similarities still further back. All plants and fungi, as well as animals, have nuclei within their cells. All living organisms contain DNA and RNA (except some viruses with RNA only), two related forms of information-coding molecules.

Such a pattern of tiered resemblances—groups of similar species nested within broader groupings, and all descending from a single source—isn't naturally present among other collections of items. You won't find anything equivalent if you try to categorize rocks, or musical instruments, or jewelry. Why not? Because rock types and styles of jewelry don't reflect unbroken descent from common ancestors. Biological diversity does. The number of shared characteristics between any one species and another indicates how recently those two species have diverged from a shared lineage.

That insight gave new meaning to the task of taxonomic classification, which had been founded in its modern form back in 1735 by the Swedish naturalist Carolus Linnaeus. Linnaeus showed how species could be systematically classified, according to their shared similarities, but he worked from creationist assumptions that offered no material explanation for the nested pattern he found. In the early and middle nineteenth century, morphologists such as Georges Cuvier and Étienne Geoffroy Saint-Hilaire in France and Richard Owen in England improved classification with their meticulous studies of internal as well as external anatomies, and tried to make sense of what the ultimate source of these patterned similarities could be. Not even Owen, a contemporary and onetime friend of Darwin's (later in life they had a bitter falling out), took the full step to an evolutionary vision before *The Origin of Species* was published. Owen made a major contribution, though, by advancing the concept of homologues—that is, superficially different but fundamentally similar versions of a single organ or trait, shared by dissimilar species.

For instance, the five-digit skeletal structure of the vertebrate hand appears not just in humans and apes and raccoons and bears but also, variously modified, in cats and bats and porpoises and lizards and turtles. The paired bones of our lower leg, the tibia and the fibula, are also represented by homologous bones in other mammals and in reptiles, and even in the long-extinct bird-reptile *Archaeopteryx*. What's the reason behind such varied recurrence of a few basic designs? Darwin, with a nod to Owen's "most interesting work," supplied the answer: common descent, as shaped by natural selection, modifying the inherited basics for different circumstances.

Vestigial characteristics are still another form of morphological evidence, illuminating to contemplate because they show that the living world is full of small, tolerable imperfections. Why do male mammals (including human males) have nipples? Why do some snakes (notably boa constrictors) carry the rudiments of a pelvis and tiny legs buried inside their sleek profiles? Why do certain species of flightless beetle have wings, sealed beneath wing covers that never open? Darwin raised all these questions, and answered them, in *The Origin of Species*. Vestigial structures stand as remnants of the evolutionary history of a lineage.

Today the same four branches of biological science from which Darwin drew—biogeography, paleontology, embryology, morphology—embrace an ever growing body of supporting data. In addition to those categories we now have others: population genetics, biochemistry, molecular biology, and, most recently, the whiz-bang field of machine-driven genetic sequencing known as genomics. These new forms of knowledge overlap one another seamlessly and intersect with the older forms, strengthening the whole edifice, contributing further to the certainty that Darwin was right.

He was right about evolution, that is. He wasn't right about *everything*. Being a restless explainer, Darwin floated a number of theoretical notions during his long working life, some of which were mistaken and illusory. He was wrong about what causes variation within a species. He was wrong about a famous geologic mystery, the parallel shelves along a Scottish valley called Glen Roy. Most notably, his theory of inheritance—which he labeled pangenesis and cherished despite its poor reception among his biologist colleagues—turned out to be dead wrong. Fortunately for Darwin, the correctness of his most famous good idea stood independent of that particular bad idea. Evolution by natural selection represented Darwin at his best—which is to say, scientific observation and careful thinking at its best.

·　　·　　·

Douglas Futuyma is a highly respected evolutionary biologist, author of textbooks as well as influential research papers. His office, at the University of Michigan, is a long narrow room in the natural sciences building, well stocked with journals and books, including volumes about the conflict between creationism and evolution. I arrived carrying a well-thumbed copy of his own book on that subject, *Science on Trial: The Case for Evolution.* Killing time in the corridor before our appointment, I noticed a blue flyer on a departmental bulletin board, seeming oddly placed there amid the announcements of career opportunities for graduate students. "CREATION VS. EVOLUTION," it said. "A series of messages challenging popular thought with Biblical truth and scientific evidences." A traveling lecturer from something called the Origins Research Association would deliver these messages at a local Baptist church. Beside the lecturer's photo was a drawing of a dinosaur. "Free pizza following the evening service," said a small line at the bottom. Dinosaurs, biblical truth, and pizza: something for everybody.

In response to my questions about evidence, Dr. Futuyma moved quickly through the traditional categories—paleontology, biogeography—and talked mostly about modern genetics. He pulled out his heavily marked copy of the journal *Nature* for February 15, 2001, a historic issue, fat with articles reporting and analyzing the results of the Human Genome Project. Beside it he slapped down a more recent issue of *Nature*, this one devoted to the sequenced genome of the house mouse, *Mus musculus*. The headline of the lead editorial announced: "HUMAN BIOLOGY BY PROXY." The mouse genome effort, according to *Nature*'s editors, had revealed "about 30,000 genes, with 99% having direct counterparts in humans."

The resemblance between our 30,000 human genes and those 30,000 mousy counterparts, Futuyma explained, represents another form of homology, like the resemblance between a five-fingered hand and a five-toed paw. Such genetic homology is what gives meaning to biomedical research using mice and other animals, including chimpanzees, which (to their sad misfortune) are our closest living relatives.

No aspect of biomedical research seems more urgent today than the study of microbial diseases. And the dynamics of those microbes within human bodies, within human populations, can only be understood in terms of evolution.

Nightmarish illnesses caused by microbes include both the infectious sort (AIDS, Ebola, SARS) that spread directly from person to person and the sort (malaria, West Nile fever) delivered to us by biting insects or other intermediaries. The capacity for quick change among disease-causing microbes is what makes them so dangerous to large numbers of people and so difficult and expensive to treat. They leap from wildlife or domestic animals into humans, adapting to new circumstances as they go. Their inherent variability allows them to find new ways of evading and defeating human immune systems. By natural selection they acquire resistance to drugs that should kill them. They evolve. There's no better or more immediate evidence supporting the Darwinian theory than this process of forced transformation among our inimical germs.

Take the common bacterium *Staphylococcus aureus*, which lurks in hospitals and causes serious infections, especially among surgery patients. Penicillin, becoming available in 1943, proved almost miraculously effective in fighting staphylococcus infections. Its deployment marked a new phase in the old war between humans and disease microbes, a phase in which humans invent new killer drugs and microbes find new ways to be unkillable. The supreme potency of penicillin didn't last long. The first resistant strains of *Staphylococcus aureus* were reported in 1947. A newer staph-killing drug, methicillin, came into use during the 1960s, but methicillin-resistant strains appeared soon, and by the 1980s those strains were widespread. Vancomycin became the next great weapon against staph, and the first vancomycin-resistant strain emerged in 2002. These antibiotic-resistant strains represent an evolutionary series, not much different in principle from the fossil series tracing horse evolution from *Hyracotherium* to *Equus*. They make evolution a very practical problem by adding expense, as well as misery and danger, to the challenge of coping with staph.

The biologist Stephen Palumbi has calculated the cost of treating penicillin-resistant and methicillin-resistant staph infections, just in the United States, at 30 billion dollars a year. "Antibiotics exert a powerful evolutionary force," he wrote last year, "driving infectious bacteria to evolve powerful defenses against all but the most recently invented drugs." As reflected in their DNA, which uses the same genetic code found in humans and horses and hagfish and honeysuckle, bacteria are part of the continuum of life, all shaped and diversified by evolutionary forces.

Even viruses belong to that continuum. Some viruses evolve quickly, some slowly. Among the fastest is HIV, because its method of replicating itself involves a high rate of mutation, and those mutations allow the virus to assume new forms. After just a few years of infection and drug treatment, each HIV patient carries a unique version of the virus. Isolation within one infected person, plus differing conditions and the struggle to survive, forces each version of HIV to evolve independently. It's nothing but a speeded up and microscopic case of what Darwin saw in the Galápagos—except that each human body is an island, and the newly evolved forms aren't so charming as finches or mockingbirds.

Understanding how quickly HIV acquires resistance to antiviral drugs, such as AZT, has been crucial to improving treatment by way of multiple-drug cocktails. "This approach has reduced deaths due to HIV by severalfold since 1996," according to Palumbi, "and it has greatly slowed the evolution of this disease within patients."

Insects and weeds acquire resistance to our insecticides and herbicides through the same process. As we humans try to poison them, evolution by natural selection transforms the population of a mosquito or thistle into a new sort of creature, less vulnerable to that particular poison. So we invent another poison, then another. It's a futile effort. Even DDT, with its ferocious and long-lasting effects throughout ecosystems, produced resistant house flies within a decade of its discovery in 1939. By 1990 more than 500 species (including 114 kinds of mosquitoes) had acquired resistance to at least one pesticide. Based on these undesired results, Stephen Palumbi has commented glumly, "humans may be the world's dominant evolutionary force."

Among most forms of living creatures, evolution proceeds slowly—too slowly to be observed by a single scientist within a research lifetime. But science functions by inference, not just by direct observation, and the inferential sorts of evidence such as paleontology and biogeography are no less cogent simply because they're indirect. Still, skeptics of evolutionary theory ask: Can we see evolution in action? Can it be observed in the wild? Can it be measured in the laboratory?

The answer is yes. Peter and Rosemary Grant, two British-born researchers who have spent decades where Charles Darwin spent weeks, have captured a glimpse of evolution with their long-term studies of beak size among Galápagos finches. William R. Rice and George W. Salt achieved something similar in their lab, through an experiment involving thirty-five generations of the fruit fly *Drosophila melanogaster.* Richard E. Lenski and his colleagues at Michigan State University have done it too, tracking 20,000 generations of evolution in the bacterium *Escherichia coli.* Such field studies and lab experiments document anagenesis—that is, slow evolutionary change within a single, unsplit lineage. With patience it can be seen, like the movement of a minute hand on a clock.

Speciation, when a lineage splits into two species, is the other major phase of evolutionary change, making possible the divergence between lineages about which Darwin wrote. It's rarer and more elusive even than anagenesis. Many individual mutations must accumulate (in most cases, anyway, with certain exceptions among plants) before two populations become irrevocably separated. The process is spread across thousands of generations, yet it may finish abruptly—like a door going *slam!*—when the last critical changes occur. Therefore it's much harder to witness. Despite the difficulties, Rice and Salt seem to have recorded a speciation event, or very nearly so, in their extended experiment on fruit flies. From a small stock of mated females they eventually produced two distinct fly populations adapted to different habitat conditions, which the researchers judged "incipient species."

•　　　•　　　•

After my visit with Douglas Futuyma in Ann Arbor, I spent two hours at the university museum there with Philip D. Gingerich, a paleontologist well-known for his work on the ancestry of whales. As we talked, Gingerich guided me through an exhibit of ancient cetaceans on the museum's second floor. Amid weird skeletal shapes that seemed almost chimerical (some hanging overhead, some in glass cases) he pointed out significant features and described the progress of thinking about whale evolution. A burly man with a broad open face and the gentle manner of a scoutmaster, Gingerich combines intellectual passion and solid expertise with one other trait that's valuable in a scientist: a willingness to admit when he's wrong.

Since the late 1970s Gingerich has collected fossil specimens of early whales from remote digs in Egypt and Pakistan. Working with Pakistani colleagues, he discovered *Pakicetus*, a terrestrial mammal dating from 50 million years ago, whose ear bones reflect its membership in the whale lineage but whose skull looks almost doglike. A former student of Gingerich's, Hans Thewissen, found a slightly more recent form with webbed feet, legs suitable for either walking or swimming, and a long toothy snout. Thewissen called it *Ambulocetus natans*, or the "walking-and-swimming whale." Gingerich and his team turned up several more, including *Rodhocetus balochistanensis*, which was fully a sea creature, its legs more like flippers, its nostrils shifted backward on the snout, halfway to the blowhole position on a modern whale. The sequence of known forms was becoming more and more complete. And all along, Gingerich told me, he leaned toward believing that whales had descended from a group of carnivorous Eocene mammals known as mesonychids, with cheek teeth useful for chewing meat and bone. Just a bit more evidence, he thought, would confirm that relationship. By the end of the 1990s most paleontologists agreed.

Meanwhile, molecular biologists had explored the same question and arrived at a different answer. No, the match to those Eocene carnivores might be close, but not close enough. DNA hybridization and other tests suggested that whales had descended from artiodactyls (that is, even-toed herbivores, such as antelopes and hippos), not from meateating mesonychids.

In the year 2000 Gingerich chose a new field site in Pakistan, where one of his students found a single piece of fossil that changed the prevailing view in paleontology. It was half of a pulley-shaped anklebone, known as an astragalus, belonging to another new species of whale. A Pakistani colleague found the fragment's other half. When Gingerich fitted the two pieces together, he had a moment of humbling recognition: The molecular biologists were right. Here was an anklebone, from a four-legged whale dating back 47 million years, that closely resembled the homologous anklebone in an artiodactyl. Suddenly he realized how closely whales are related to antelopes.

This is how science is supposed to work. Ideas come and go, but the fittest survive. Downstairs in his office Phil Gingerich opened a specimen drawer, showing me some of the actual fossils from which the display skeletons upstairs were modeled. He put a small lump of petrified bone, no larger than a lug nut, into my hand. It was the famous astragalus, from the species he had eventually named *Artiocetus clavis*. It felt solid and heavy as truth.

Seeing me to the door, Gingerich volunteered something personal: "I grew up in a conservative church in the Midwest and was not taught anything about evolution. The subject was clearly skirted. That helps me understand the people who are skeptical about it. Because I come from that tradition myself." He shares the same skeptical instinct. Tell him that there's an ancestral connection between land animals and whales, and his reaction is: Fine, maybe, but show me the intermediate stages. Like Charles Darwin, the onetime divinity student, who joined that round-the-world voyage aboard the *Beagle* instead of becoming a country parson, and whose grand view of life on Earth was shaped by close attention to small facts, Phil Gingerich is a reverent empiricist. He's not satisfied until he sees solid data. That's what excites him so much about pulling whale fossils out of the ground. In thirty years he has seen enough to be satisfied. For him, Gingerich said, it's "a spiritual experience."

"The evidence is there," he added. "It's buried in the rocks of ages."

Vanity Fair

FINALIST—
REVIEWS AND CRITICISM

Media critic James Wolcott is by turns acidic, insightful, and marvelously on the money. In this essay, he persuasively argues that blogging is heir to journalism's great traditions. Wolcott uses his pen like a howitzer, blasting media pooh-bahs and laying waste to their shibboleths.

James Wolcott

The Laptop Brigade

Are we in danger of drowning in blogorrhea? Of being swamped like Bob Hope and Jackie Gleason at the end of *How to Commit Marriage* in chin-high sludge? Only a few years ago blogs—short for Web logs, frequently updated journals that source other blogs and Web sites—were tiny blips on the computer screen, aquarium bubbles. Back then the buzz generators were nicely bankrolled online magazines such as *Salon, Slate, Nerve* (moody erotics for horny neurotics), and the now defunct *Inside*—many of whose contributors exuded cachet—and bare-bones rap sheets for news junkies such as Romenesko and the Drudge Report. Although a few "real writers"—such as Andrew Sullivan, the former editor of *The New Republic*, Mickey Kaus, also formerly of *The New Republic*, and Virginia Postrel, author of *The Future and Its Enemies*—opened blog hangouts, bloggers tended to be lumped in the amateur division and relegated to the drafty basement. Most were considered harmless hobbyists, like ham-radio operators and model-train enthusiasts, or personal diarists doodling on the laptop, hoping someday to get laid.

In a January 2004 edition of *Meet the Press*, journalist Roger Simon, a panelist on Tim Russert's political roundtable, voiced this attitude when he defined blogs for the Rip van Winkles in the audience. "Look, a true blog is 'I woke up this morning, I decided to skip chem class, now I want to write about the last episode of

Friends.' That's what blogs are. You know, it's people talking to each other." Yapping, he made it sound like, which of course it often is. Nevertheless, Simon tripped over his mustache with his chem-class crack. His notion of a blog is as outdated as a Jack Carter comedy routine about kids today and their wiggy gyrations. Far from being a refuge for nose-picking narcissists, blogs have speedily matured into the most vivifying, talent-swapping, socializing breakthrough in popular journalism since the burst of coffeehouse periodicals and political pamphleteering in the eighteenth century, when *The Spectator, The Tatler,* and sundry other sheets liberated writing from literary patronage. If Addison and Steele, the editors of *The Spectator* and *The Tatler,* were alive and holding court at Starbucks, they'd be Wi-Fi-ing into a joint blog. If Tom Paine were alive and paroled, he'd be blog-jamming against the Patriot Act, whose very name he'd find obscene.

•   •   •

Papers like The Tatler *and* The Spectator *were written to be talked about. The essays enter a cultural debate that was highly oral and social rather than textual and academic, and coffeehouses were the chief sites of this debate. . . . Coffeehouses were crucial arenas for the formation and expression of public opinion about plays and poetry, politics and finance, dress and manners.*
    —From Erin Mackie's introduction to
        The Commerce of Everyday Life:
      ***Selections from* The Tatler *and* The Spectator**

Blogs aren't written to be talked about, they're written to be written about. Conversation takes place on the screen, poppy fields of densely packed words issuing as far as the eye can scroll. Every variety and flavor of interest, enthusiasm, furtive itch, and crazed addiction breeds a squalling litter of blogs: nature blogs, fiction blogs, poetry blogs, fashion blogs, media blogs, music blogs, tech blogs, porn blogs, pet blogs, photography blogs, weather blogs, regional blogs, blogs that blog other blogs (such as Sully-Watch, which applies a magnifying glass to Andrew Sullivan's performing-flea antics). Off-line magazines have their own online blogs, such as *The American Prospect*'s Tapped (Matthew Yglesias's pithy summaries of weekend op-eds—"*George Will*. It's almost as if the president isn't very smart or something"—are a must-read), *The New Republic*'s &c. column, and Gregg Easterbrook's Easterblogg, which nearly blew itself up in the cockpit when Easterbrook lambasted Miramax's Harvey Weinstein and Disney's Michael Eisner for behaving like money-hungry Jews in foisting Quentin Tarantino's ultra-violent *Kill Bill* on the culture—Easterbrook had some splainin' to do for that little outburst.

The poet Philip Larkin envisioned death as a void state of disconnection—nothing to think with, nothing to link with—and in the blogosphere thinking and linking are also co-dependent verbs. No blog can be an island entire unto itself. Visitors vote with their mouse clicks, and the vitality of a blog site derives from the rising number of hits it receives—the return visits. The higher the hit count, the heavier the hit traffic; the heavier the hit traffic, the larger the popularity; the larger the popularity, the greater the love. This is why there is no graver act than to remove a site from one's blog roll, eliminating the link. It can be a haughty kiss-off or a sad rebuke; either way, it's public notice that you no longer wish to be associated with this louse. By thy links they shall know thee, and the fact that neo-liberal blogger Mickey Kaus (Kausfiles at *Slate*) links to both Lucianne Goldberg, the right-wing Broom-Hilda of Monica Lewinsky infamy, whose comments section teems like a cauldron with racist, homophobic hate speech, and Ann Coulter, the She-Wolf of Sigma Chi, is evidence to his foes not of the Mickster's catholicity but of his scaly lizardry.

Just as eighteenth-century periodicals were often organs of the Whig and Tory Parties, blog sites cluster according to political outlooks. Internet space may appear to be an expanding universe of uncharted dimensions with no fixed center or hitching post, but a brain scan of the blogosphere would reveal the same hemispheric divide between left and right that prevails in the flesh realm. Not that there isn't some friendly fraternization. The Talking Points Memo blog of Joshua Micah Marshall, a journalist for the *Washington Monthly* and *The Hill*, is respected on both sides of the junction. Tacitus, a moderate-conservative blogger (that is, sane), is blog-rolled on some liberal sites. Sharing an opposition to the Sousa march of the American Empire, libertarian bloggers such as Lew Rockwell link to articles by anti-imperialistic lefties at Alexander Cockburn's Counterpunch site. But mostly liberals and conservatives congregate at their own tables in the cafeteria and shoot straw wrappers at each other, dirty looks. Sit them at the same table and huffiness can ensue.

$$\bullet \qquad \bullet \qquad \bullet$$

On the January weekend before the New Hampshire primary, the Blogging of the President site—BOP, as it's more familiarly known—hosted a panel discussion about blogging, the Howard Dean phenomenon, and participatory democracy in the Internet Age that was broadcast on public-radio stations across the country. The BOP site is a group blog featuring one of the most cerebral, provocative, history-enriched ongoing symposia to be found on the Web. Its mainstays include Jay Rosen, Stirling Newberry, and Christopher Lydon, who are to political blogdom what Samuel Johnson and his fellow members of the Club were to London, only without the port and cold mutton. To bridge the hemispheric split, BOP invited a number of the leading bloggers from both left and right to join the jawfest, including Josh Marshall, Jeff Jarvis, Andrew Sullivan, and a mystery man who goes by the handle Atrios.

Bad blood simmered between the last two. Atrios once posted an open letter to *Salon* on his blog, Eschaton, deploring its hiring

337

The Laptop Brigade

of Andycakes to whack out a weekly column on liberal idiocy. "I have a hard time believing that people are really going to pay to read essentially the same drivel—'LIBERALS STUPID AND BAD AND TREASONOUS'—that they can read for free over in his own little sandbox." For more than an hour the BOP confab was cordial, civilized, and nonconfrontational; then Sullivan, whom I picture biding his time and biting his lip, struck. He accused Atrios of hiding behind anonymity to lob garbage. "You attack personally but can't be attacked because no one knows who you are!" Sullivan complained. Take off your *Phantom of the Opera* mask, fiend! "I just choose to keep my personal and professional life separate," Atrios replied.

It wasn't exactly a rematch of the Norman Mailer–versus–Gore Vidal clash of titans on *The Dick Cavett Show*, but the issue percolated, coming to a boil with an article on *Salon* a week later. The author, Christopher Farah, lit into the whole pirate crew of "anonybloggers"—Josh Freelantzovitzes who get their rude jollies pumping raw sewage into the Internet about professional byliners whose jobs they probably covet. These masked marauders "have made names for themselves by having no names at all and by using the safety and security of their secret identities to spread gossip, make accusations and levy the most vicious of insults with impunity," Farah wrote. He cited Media Whores Online, as a major environmental polluter, and a media-satire blog called the Minor Fall, the Major Lift. But public enemy No. 1 again was Atrios, whose graffiti slurs included calling Nicholas Kristof of *The New York Times* "human scum," and publishing an e-mail reputedly from a maid named Maria who claimed President Bush had taken cruel sexual advantage of her. Farah failed to register that the maid's woeful tale of seduction and betrayal was a parody of the *National Review Online*'s house blog, which had been running anonymous e-mails from readers accusing John Kerry of unsubstantiated assaults on human decency, such as *trying to cut into line*. (Punk'd, *Salon* quickly edited that goof from the text, sparing

Farah further embarrassment.) Feeling vindicated, Andrew Sullivan gave the article a hearty Cornfield County salute: "Anony-blogger Atrios recently called the New York Times' Nick Kristof 'human scum.' Welcome to the pond, Nick! Of course, Atrios is immune from personal attacks because he's anonymous."

•   •   •

The Farah article really got the frogs hopping in Bloggyville. Jonah Goldberg of *N.R.O.* sympathized with the anti-anonyblog-gers. He, too, had been taunted by strange kids on the play-ground. Pro-Atrios posters pointed out that Atrios isn't anony-mous, but pseudonymous, a crucial distinction. There are practical reasons to deploy the secret identity of a pseud. Bloggers risk losing their jobs by posting under their real names, even if the blog isn't work-related. Adopting a pseud can also open up unex-plored sides of a writer's persona, much as online role-playing does on game sites and in sex chat rooms. Online, reputation ac-crues much as it does in print. The blogger has blog cred to pre-serve and protect, and an inaccurate or bogus-arguing blogger faces backlash however faceless the blogger himself/herself may be. Most important, pseudonyms have a long, respectable history in pamphleteering, journalism, and fiction. The Federalist Papers were authored under the name Publius. Janet Flanner covered Paris for *The New Yorker* under the name Genêt. *The New Repub-lic*'s TRB column was written for decades by Richard L. Strout of *The Christian Science Monitor.* Philip Larkin wrote schoolgirl porn under the lesbian disguise of Brunette Coleman. (O.K., maybe not the best example.) And I would add, based on my own subjective impressions, the reason Andrew Sullivan attracts so many personal attacks isn't that he's recognizable and his attack-ers aren't, but that he makes it so easy and *fun.* He's like a bad tenor begging to be pelted with fresh produce.

On the surface the battle between Andy and Atrios is a minor spat between a drama queen and a shrinking violet, but it has deeper ripples. That Sullivan, a well-known byliner, television pundit, and former Gap model, felt impelled to pick a fight with a lesser-known blogger was a sign of insecurity—shaky status. It signifies the shift of influence and punch-power in the blogosphere from the right to the left. It is Atrios, not Andrew Sullivan, who is in ascendance in the blogosphere. Only a few years ago the energy and passion were largely the property of the right hemisphere, where Sullivan, Glenn "Instapundit" Reynolds, and *N.R.O.*'s Victor Davis Hanson fired up the neurons against the defeatism, anti-Americanism, and death's-head specter of Islamic terrorism billowing from the ruins of Ground Zero. Each morning, after subjecting myself to the depresso news in the daily papers and wishing I had a rabbit hole to dive into, I'd frequent these blogs for morale uplift, mentally applauding their jeers at matchstick figures on the left such as Susan Sontag, Noam Chomsky, and Edward Said (sentiments I'm ashamed of now), and saluting their bugle calls as the U.S. geared up to topple the Taliban. (Like millions of Americans, I lead a very active vicarious life—I get around a lot inside my head.) But I parted sympathies with the bugle boys when they repositioned their bombsights for Iraq. Honest, confused souls could disagree over the case for overthrowing Saddam Hussein. It was the ugly rhetoric, fathead hubris, and might-makes-right triumphalism that repulsed. Warbloggers hunkered into B-grade versions of the ideological buccaneers in the neoconservative camp. Punk-ass laptop Richard Perles, they excoriated dissenters as wimps, appeasers, and traitors, peddled every xenophobic stereotype (the French as "cheese-eating surrender monkeys," etc.), and brushed aside the plight of the Palestinians with brusque indifference or outright contempt. And the warbloggers behaved like they owned the legacy and sorrow of September 11, as if only they understood How Everything Changed and those who disagreed had goldfish bowls on their heads. "For the Clintonites, 9/11 didn't really happen," Sullivan preposterously claimed as recently as January 2004. When I stray into these sites now, it's like entering the visitors' center of a historical landmark. The rhododendrons need dusting, and the tour guide isn't listening to himself, having done his spiel endless times before.

.   .   .

Liberal blogs are now where the bonfires blaze. They set the tempo, push the debate, and crack the best jokes. TBogg, for example, with his continuing saga about America's Worst Mother and her four children, Leona, Hibiscus, Mandalay, and Grunion (the brats' names change with each installment). Atrios's Eschaton is a major stomping ground for anti-Bush information and anti-warblog humor. Josh Marshall's Talking Points Memo has always been essential, but over the last year he has surpassed himself with brilliant running analyses of the Valerie Plame scandal, lengthy Q&As with Wesley Clark and George Soros, and detective work on Bush's sketchy National Guard service (about which Kevin Drum at Calpundit has also done superb Sherlock Holmes sleuthing). Middle East scholar Juan Cole's blog has established itself as the go-to site for informed, incisive interpretations and info on what's unraveling in Iraq and the rest of the region. Economist Brad De-Long, when not defending Paul Krugman against his nitpickers, is the Harold Bloom of data crunching, finding secret harmonies hidden in the numbers. Bob Somerby blows his tiny ration of cool regularly at the Daily Howler, documenting the lies, flip exaggerations, and smarmy chumminess of the dominant media—their cackling incompetence. During the early Democratic primary contests, Al Giordano, who blogs out of South America for BOP and his own site, Big, Left, Outside, enjoyed the hottest streak of almost any handicapper, the first to hear John Kerry's hulking footsteps about to overtake Howard Dean.

Gracious in victory, Giordano gave a nod to Daily Kos, the blog site that had been a powerful transmitter of the Dean message. "My olive branch, and authentic praise, to a guy who dressed himself in glory," began Giordano's tribute to the namesake host of the Daily Kos. After Dean lost New Hampshire, Kos conceded that the Dean cause itself was probably lost. "I doubt that all my friends and readers here can understand how painful and hard that it was for Kos to admit. But, in the end, he chose truth over illusion. And I predict . . . that the Daily Kos will continue as the top blog on the Internet, as we pull on the Court Appointed President's arms and legs and quarter him in the months to come." Kos, the newly crowned king of Blogistan!

·   ·   ·

Who he?, as Harold Ross might ask. Kos is the army nickname of Markos Moulitsas Zúniga, who was born in Chicago in 1971 and raised in El Salvador, returning to the U.S. when his family fled that country's civil war. After high school, he enlisted in the army and was stationed in Germany, an artillery guy. After earning two bachelor's degrees, he moved to San Francisco and started Daily Kos in 2002. In those days of misty watercolor memories it took Daily Kos a month to get the number of hits that it now racks up in a day. The blog quickly differentiated itself from the gaggle. "I pounded my niche," he says, covering politics as an archipelago of anthills with his readers filing ant reports from the various colonies. It was political coverage from a bustling bottom-up perspective rather than a pundit's Olympian perch. Daily Kos's first spike in hitsville came during the summer of the 2002 midterm elections, when it provided exhaustive state-by-state breakdowns of each race. It was inside baseball with outsiders' enthusiasm—electoral sabermetrics. The second "huge spike," according to Kos, came during the buildup to the Iraq war, which Kos opposed. A military veteran, he couldn't be accused of being a weenie peacenik, and Daily Kos, along with antiwar.com and others, magnetized the Web opposition. The number of hits jumped from 20,000 a day to 100,000 plus. Kos and his partner, Jerome Armstrong, mapped out the online strategy of the Howard Dean campaign, which, whatever the spinout of Dean's candidacy, demonstrated blogging's efficacy as a fund-raising and enlistment tool. Kos's latest brainstorm is to use the blogosphere as a "farm system" to fund and groom the next wave of liberal writers and pundits, a counterforce to the conservative-think-tank infrastructure and its modeling academies, where juicy novices master the Ann Coulter Hair Toss and special tanning secrets.

From the outset Daily Kos was devised as a choral suite rather than a solitary squawk box. "Without the community, I wouldn't be anything," Kos says. He opened up the main column to some of the best posters from the comments section, and set up a diaries section for posters—blogs within his blog. Some of the most talented Daily Kossacks splintered off to start blogs of their own, listed on the Kos's blog roll under "Alumni." "The meritocracy of the blogosphere appeals to me," Kos says. Age, race, sexual persuasion, wardrobe choices—none of these signify online, where no one knows what you look like unless you post pictures of yourself with your cats. One Daily Kos grad is Steve Gilliard, a dynamo blogger whose posts about the insurgency in Iraq were more scarily prophetic than anything blathered by the military experts on cable news. It was Gilliard who threw down the dueling glove at the mainstream press which, he said, holds people accountable but freaks all over the car lot when accountability is expected of them. "I think it would be a really, really good idea to track reporters word for word, broadcast for broadcast, and print the results online," Gilliard proposed. "Keeping score of who's right and wrong, how many times they repeat cannards [*sic*] like Al Gore invented the internet and make obvious errors. Not accusations of ideology, but actual data and facts." It'll buggeth the journalists mightily, but it's also doing the press a favor. "If someone had actually checked Jayson Blair's work, the *Times* might have fired his ass years earlier." Gilliard's proposal has become more popularly known as the Adopt a Journalist program, debated and discussed on BOP, NPR's *On the Media*, and elsewhere.

Al Giordano sees it as a stealthy insurrection: "The Internet, like Kerry, sneaks up on the frontrunner, Commercial Media, without letting its footsteps be heard, while it gets written off and underestimated by the very forces that seem to be in charge."

·   ·   ·

What the Adopt a Journalist program symptomizes is how fed up so many smart, informed, impassioned Internet newshounds are, how unwilling they are to play bystander and watch the media make another monster mash of the presidential election, as they did in 2000, or help stampede us into another misguided war. "Why Oh Why Can't We Have a Better Press Corps?" wails Brad DeLong on a regular basis on his site, and it's a question that resonates across the blogosphere. Because the press seems incorrigible. Paul Krugman writes a *Times* column urging political reporters not to repeat the gauche frivolity of 2000, driveling on about earth tones and alpha males, and what's happened so far? Bright chatter about Wesley Clark's sweaters and long eyelashes (really!—Jacob Weisberg of *Slate* found them a fetching detail), maunderings about Howard Dean's wife by such happy homemakers as Sally Quinn and Maureen Dowd, and much speculation about Botox deposits in craggy visages. Patti Smith's war cry about rock 'n' roll was "We created it—let's take it over." Journalism can't and shouldn't be taken over by bloggers, but they can take away some of the toys, and pull down the thrones.

The New Yorker

"The Gift" is a respectful but candid portrait of a man, Zell Kravinsky, and his fixation—giving away his kidney to a virtual stranger. Ian Parker gives this profile a layered, intellectual context with thoughtful meditations on extreme, unhindered—and possibly misguided—charity. All the while Parker manages a tone that is judiciously neutral, leaving moral judgments to the readers.

Ian Parker

The Gift

Last summer, not long after Zell Kravinsky had given almost his entire forty-five-million-dollar real-estate fortune to charity, he called Barry Katz, an old friend in Connecticut, and asked for help with an alibi. Would Katz call Kravinsky's wife, Emily, in Philadelphia, and say that the two men were about to take a weeklong trip to Katz's ski condominium in Vermont? This untruth would help Kravinsky do something that did not have his wife's approval: he would be able to leave home, check into the Albert Einstein Medical Center, in Philadelphia, for a few days, and donate a kidney to a woman whose name he had only just learned.

Katz refused, and Kravinsky became agitated. He said that the intended recipient of his gift would die without the kidney, and that his wife's reluctance to support this "nondirected" donation—it would be only the hundred and thirty-fourth of its kind in the United States—would make her culpable in that death. "I can't allow her to take this person's life!" Kravinsky said. He was, at forty-eight, a former owner of shopping malls and distribution centers, and a man with a single thrift-store suit that had cost him twenty dollars.

"You think she'd be taking a life?" Katz asked.

"Absolutely," Kravinsky replied.

Katz then asked, warily, "Do you mean that anybody who is not donating a kidney is taking someone's life?"

"Yes," Kravinsky said.

"So, by your terms, I'm a murderer?"

"Yes," Kravinsky said, in as friendly a way as possible.

After a pause, Katz said, "I have to get off the phone—I can't talk about this anymore," and he hung up. A few weeks later, Kravinsky crept out of his house at six o'clock in the morning while his wife and children were still asleep. Emily Kravinsky learned that her husband had donated a kidney when she read about it in a local newspaper.

.　　　.　　　.

Kravinsky, whose unrestrained disbursement of his assets—first financial, then corporeal—has sometimes been unsettling for the people close to him, grew up in a row house in the working-class Philadelphia neighborhood of Oxford Circle, amid revolutionary rhetoric. "My father would say how great things were in the Soviet Union, and how shabby they were here," Kravinsky recalled recently. "He would rail against rich people and the ruling class."

Kravinsky's father, Irving, who is now eighty-nine, was born in Russia to a Jewish family, which immigrated to America when he was a boy. A tank commander in the Second World War, he was a socialist whose faith in the Soviet Union was extinguished only after that country no longer existed. He worked as a printer, Kravinsky told me, "thinking he'd be in the vanguard of the revolution by remaining in the proletariat"; and when Zell, who had two older sisters, began to excel in school his success seems to have been taken by his father as a sign of class disloyalty. After Zell graduated from elementary school with a prize as the best student, Irving told him, "Well, next year you'll be nothing."

James Kahn, a childhood friend of Kravinsky's, and a fellow-member of the chess team in high school, told me that Zell's father and mother—Reeda Kravinsky is a former teaching supervisor, now seventy-eight—"were steadfast in denying him any praise."

He added, "I think what he did later was almost in desperation—doing the most extreme thing possible, something that they couldn't deny was a good thing." Reeda told me, "I think we did praise him, but maybe he didn't get enough attention, for an outstanding child."

As a boy, Kravinsky could hope to gain his parents' attention either by conforming or by rebelling; he did both. "Zell was simultaneously more left-wing and more right-wing than I was," Kahn said. He had an active social conscience—he read books on Gandhi, and, at the age of twelve, he picketed City Hall in support of public housing. (He remembers this as the last time he did anything that met with his father's approval.) But, by the standards of the late sixties, Kravinsky was unfashionably curious about money. He first invested in the stock market when he was twelve, and told me that he was "pretty young when I understood money better than my father did."

In Kravinsky's eyes, his father had humiliated himself in his relationships with money. Citing his radical politics, Irving Kravinsky said he couldn't apply for union work. "He was terrifically exploited," Kravinsky recalled. "He was afraid to ask for a raise. My mother yelled at him, day and night, said he wasn't a man, and 'Zell's more of a man than you are.'"

In 1971, Kravinsky won a scholarship to Dartmouth. He majored in Asian studies, wrote poetry, took up meditation, and grew his hair long. Soon after graduation, Kravinsky returned to Philadelphia, where he got a job at an insurance company. He began a relationship with a co-worker there, and moved in with her; the match lasted less than a year, but it had the side effect of introducing Kravinsky to real estate. He bought a duplex in the working-class neighborhood of Logan for ten thousand dollars, and rented out half of it. When the couple split up, Kravinsky kept the apartment, then sold it for a two-thousand-dollar profit.

As Kravinsky acquired a taste for property, he looked for ways to satisfy his idealistic self—in which good intentions were mixed with habits of self-criticism and a preemptive resentment about being ridiculed or undervalued. In 1978, he began to work with socially and emotionally troubled students in Philadelphia's public schools. "I became a teacher in the ghetto," Kravinsky recalls. "Everyone I went to college with laughed at that. I was written off as a failure."

The job offered moral satisfaction, but it also depressed Kravinsky—his pride in self-sacrifice counterbalanced by the thought that he was being taken for a ride. (Once, after school, he took a promising student to the theatre and, as he walked the boy home, he was mugged in a way that made Kravinsky think he might have been set up.) He grew more involved in real estate: he bought a condo, then a house in Maine; his deals became grander, and he began to see profits of tens of thousands of dollars. "Nobody in my family had ever made that much money," he said. He spent very sparingly, preferring to reinvest; by 1982, he owned a three-story building near the University of Pennsylvania campus, but he lived in the smallest, gloomiest apartment, with no shower, kitchen, or windows.

Barry Katz, who met Kravinsky around this time, and who is now a developer of luxury homes in Connecticut, found him to be brilliant and articulate, "with the kind of intensity you don't encounter in many people. He also had a lost-puppy quality." Kravinsky had skipped a year in high school and one in college, and, according to Edward Miller, another old friend, who is now a lecturer in English literature, his intellectual and emotional maturity seemed out of step. "You could call it high-school-geek syndrome," Miller said.

In 1984, Kravinsky was devastated by the death of Adria, the elder of his two sisters, from lung cancer. She was thirty-three; Zell was thirty. "She was the only person in my family who liked me in any meaningful way," Kravinsky said, describing the guilt he still feels for not showing her enough affection, and for not persuading her to quit smoking. "We were close, but there were so many things that kept me from spending more time with her. I wish I could go back." Kravinsky entered a period of deep depression. He shared a house with Miller, who remembers that Kravinsky mostly stayed in his room, writing poetry on a typewriter. Kravinsky stopped teaching in 1986, and he gave two of his three properties to his surviving sister, Hilary, and sold the other.

It was a despairing time, but it jolted Kravinsky out of the life of the self-abnegating schoolteacher. He expanded his intellectual ambitions, completing a Ph.D. in composition theory at Penn's School of Education. (His unusual dissertation proposed a "table of rhetorical elements," which was inspired by the periodic table.) He also took courses at the New School, in New York, and at the School of Criticism and Theory, at Dartmouth; in 1990, he began a second Ph.D. at Penn, with a dissertation, "Paradise Glossed," that dissected the rhetoric of Milton with mathematical rigor. At Penn, he started teaching undergraduate courses in Renaissance literature, and met and married Emily Finkelstein, a doctor who is now a psychiatrist with an expertise in eating disorders. Kravinsky became a resident adviser, and the couple lived frugally in student housing. ("Free rent, free meals—the greatest deal in the world," Kravinsky recalled.) They had the first of four children in 1991.

Kravinsky's Milton dissertation was "an intense close reading and quite wonderful," according to Maureen Quilligan, then the graduate chairperson of Penn's English department and now a professor at Duke. "It's one of the best I've ever read. It sounded like deconstruction, although he'd got there without having to do any deconstruction theory." After it was finished, Kravinsky taught an undergraduate Milton course at Penn that Quilligan describes as "fantastically successful—the kids responded to it with the wildest enthusiasm, and they worked hard for him and had a sublime intellectual experience." At the end of each lecture, Kravinsky would stand at the door and shake hands with every student. "He said he was hunting for another Milton," Quilligan remembers.

Though he was admired by students—and had impeccable leftist credentials—he was galled to find that his intellectual interests were considered insufficiently avant-garde by academe. As Kravinsky saw it, "What they didn't like was that Milton was the great classical liberal. Classical liberalism, bourgeois liberalism— they felt the same way about it as my father." Quilligan says that he was handicapped by "the eccentricity of his intellectual and spiritual intensity, added to the fact that he had written about a single white male author." Kravinsky recalls going to job interviews carrying letters of recommendation from scholars as distinguished as Stanley Fish, "and at every one they said, 'You have a spectacular portfolio, both of your Ph.D.s are relevant, Fish said you "can do anything"—but we're looking for diversity.'" Only the University of Helsinki offered him a job.

By 1994, he had decided to give up on an academic career. Instead, he would make a living in real estate. Kravinsky said that his wife was skeptical. "She said I'd become a bum," he told me. But, thanks to his earlier real-estate record, and his evident mathematical brilliance, Kravinsky was able to persuade the United Valley Bank to lend him two million dollars, with which he bought two apartment buildings—around a 150,000 square feet in total—one near Penn, the other near St. Joseph's University. Kravinsky knew that in a recession people will go back to school, and that the ratio of rent to property prices will be highest where a university is in a run-down urban area. He was also fearless about being highly leveraged.

Kravinsky was improvising—"Nobody ever taught me how to succeed, or took me under their wing"—but his portfolio quickly grew, and within a year he had assets of six million dollars and debts of four million. Though he was now wealthy, he spent no more than he had before, with the exception of a 130,000-dollar house that he bought in Jenkintown, a Philadelphia suburb, in 1995. (His second child had just been born.) "There was little of the mogul apparent to the eye," Barry Katz said. Even to his close associates, Kravinsky's business seemed implausible. Edward Miller took a job with him as an apartment manager but was never convinced that the property empire was real. "I didn't fully believe it," he told me. "I thought that somehow it was a deck of cards." These mistaken thoughts were reinforced by seeing "the most disorganized, chaotic organization you can imagine—leases at the bottom of closets, under the toilets, soaking wet." Miller was also surprised to see how blithely neglectful Kravinsky could sometimes be of contractors and janitors, as if he were grateful for the chance to take a vacation from the patient, solicitous persona he showed to his friends.

Property management ultimately did not suit Kravinsky— " 'Tenants and toilets'; there's a phrase that suggests the agony," he said—and in 1998 he began selling most of his rental properties (now about four hundred apartments) and turning to commercial real estate, investing at a level where the building is a mere premise for an intricate dance of numbers. "Everything else can change, but numbers remain the same; numbers are your best friends," Kravinsky said. "I needed to leverage my intellect, return to math."

Kravinsky bought supermarkets and warehouses; that is, he looked for tenants with good credit ratings and with long leases, then paid for the buildings with loans bundled into bonds by Wall Street banks and sold to institutional investors. These loans have a singular advantage: if things go wrong, nobody comes for your stereo. In 1999, in a typical deal, Kravinsky bought a clothing-distribution center in Ohio for $16.8 million. He put up $1.1 million and borrowed $15.7 million. If the building decreased in value by 100 percent, he would lose $1.1 million; if it increased in value by 100 percent, he would make $16.8 million.

"Most people think the more you borrow the riskier it is," Kravinsky has said. "In my system, the more you borrow the safer it is." (On a single day in April, 1999, he borrowed 32 million dollars. He remembers Emily asking, "How much do we have to pay on that?" It was around 10,000 dollars a day. She said, dryly, "Well, if worst comes to worst, I can just treat a hundred people a day.") Kravinsky made full use of the tax advantages of commercial-real-estate investments: in the eyes of the I.R.S., a shopping mall depreciates in value, like an office chair, and one can set that depreciation against income tax, overlooking the fact that a mall, over time, is likely to increase in value.

Kravinsky knew how to make money, but he had no talent for spending it. His investments were an expression of his intellect— they were splendid rhetorical gestures, and to take money out for, say, a swimming pool would be to lose the debate. Even as he became rich, he was arguing at home against buying two minivans to replace a 1985 Toyota Camry. (He eventually gave in, and lost the Camry, which has since become an object of regret and longing.) The children did not get pocket money, and Emily had to fight to have the front porch repaired. ("Emily was certainly complicit in the family's frugality, but she became frustrated by Zell's refusal to spend money," a friend of the Kravinskys' told me.) Kravinsky worked from home. He recalled how one well-dressed man came to interview for an accountant's job and, seeing Kravinsky's modest home and casual dress, ran away. Kravinsky watched him disappear down the street and called out, "Where are you going?" The interviewee shouted, "I don't believe you," and kept running.

• • •

About three years ago, as Kravinsky's assets rose to nearly 45 million dollars—a million square feet of commercial real estate, along with lofts, houses, and condos—friends began to hear him talk of giving all his assets to charity. He had long entertained philanthropic thoughts, although, as Katz told me, "I don't think it ever occurred to Zell that the by-product of what he was doing would be wealth on this scale." In 1998, Kravinsky had tried to donate some properties and empty lots to the University of Pennsylvania. He says that the university was wary of him, and "didn't even take me out to lunch." As his portfolio grew, however, Kravinsky's charitable impulse became more urgent. Edward Miller remembers sitting at his dining table one night with Kravinsky and James Kahn, "and Zell began to talk of giving away his wealth. And we said, 'Don't do it.'" Kahn asked him why he didn't give away a third of his fortune, and use the rest to become richer, and ultimately give even more money away. As Miller recalled, "We berated him for three or four hours. We said, 'You're depressed.' He seemed like King Lear, dividing his kingdom so he could 'unburdened crawl toward death.'"

For the moment, Kravinsky's friends prevailed. "I think he wanted to be talked out of it," Miller said. But Kravinsky, the skilled rhetorician, seems to have discovered something unanswerable in his own rhetoric. "The reasons for giving a little are the reasons for giving a lot, and the reasons for giving a lot are the reasons for giving more," he recently said. Kravinsky feared that he might lose his assets, or his impulse to give, or that his wife would challenge the idea. Emily was philanthropically inclined, but, as Kravinsky recalled it, he needed to "walk her into the idea" of total divestment—gift by gift, keeping the emphasis on public health, which attracted her, and promising that quitting real estate would bring him closer to the family. "I said I'd have more time for the kids," he told me. "She thought it was crazy to give everything away, but she said, 'At least we'll be out of the business.'" The gifts were made with her blessing and in her name. "My impression was that she decided she didn't want to be made out to be a Scrooge," a friend of the Kravinskys told me.

In 2002, Zell and Emily gave an 87,000-square-foot apartment building to a school for the disabled in Philadelphia. The same year, they gave two gifts, worth $6.2 million, to the Centers for Disease Control Foundation. The gifts were partly in the form of a distribution center, four condominiums, three houses, and a parking lot; Kravinsky placed them in a fund named for his late sister, Adria. In March 2003, the Kravinskys created the Adria Kravinsky Foundation, to support a School of Public Health at Ohio State University; the gift included three warehouses, four department stores, and a shopping center in Indianapolis. Together, these were worth around 30 million dollars. Karen Holbrook, the president of O.S.U., called the gift "a magnificent commitment."

Kravinsky had put some money aside—he had established trust funds for his wife, his children, and the children of his surviving sister. But his personal assets were now reduced to a house (on which he had a large mortgage), two minivans, and about 80,000 dollars in stocks and cash. According to Katz, "He gave away the money because he had it and there were people who needed it. But it changed his way of looking at himself. He decided the purpose of his life was to give away things."

•   •   •

Jenkintown, Pennsylvania, is a mixed-income community of about four thousand people which tries to maintain a small-town character within the sprawl of housing developments and shopping malls just north of Philadelphia. I made my first visit to Kravinsky in November, parking in front of a wooden-shingled house with a broken photocopier on the front porch and a tangle of bicycles, tricycles, and wagons. A handwritten sign by the door, a marker of spousal frustration, read, "Put Your Keys Away Before You Forget."

Kravinsky came to the door several minutes after I rang the bell. He is slight, and looked both boyish and wan, with pale, almost translucent skin. He wore sneakers, a blue plaid shirt, and tan trousers with an elasticized waist. He seemed distracted, and I realized later that the timing of my visit was awkward: he knew that his wife would not want a reporter in the house, but she had gone out, and two of his four young children were home, so he could not immediately go out to lunch with me.

He invited me into a house crowded with stuff, including a treadmill in the middle of the living room. He cleared away enough books and toys for me to sit down on a sofa. His daughter, who is nine, came into the room to say hello, but when Emily Kravinsky came home, a moment later, she walked straight past us into the kitchen, taking the girl with her. Kravinsky followed. He came back after a few minutes and picked up his coat, and as we left the house he said, "She wants us out of here."

We drove to a restaurant in a nearby mini-mall. He ordered a mushroom sandwich and a cup of warm water that he didn't touch. "I used to feel that I had to be good, truly good in my heart and spirit, in order to do good," he said, in a soft voice. "But it's the other way around: if you do good, you become better. With each thing I've given away, I've been *more* certain of the need to give more away. And at the end of it maybe I will be good. But what are they going to say—that I'm depressed? I am, but this isn't suicidal. I'm depressed because I haven't done enough."

Within a few minutes, Kravinsky had talked of Aristotle, Nietzsche, and the Talmud, and, in less approving terms, of the actor Billy Crudup, who had just left his pregnant girlfriend for another woman. ("How do you like that!") Kravinsky's mostly elevated range of reference, along with a rhetorical formality and a confessional tone, sometimes gave the impression that he was reading from his collected letters. "What I aspire to is ethical ecstasy," he said. "*Ex stasis:* standing out of myself, where I'd lose my punishing ego. It's tremendously burdensome to me." Once achieved, "the significant locus would be in the sphere of others."

His cell phone rang, and a mental switch was flicked: "You have to do a ten-thirty-one and put fresh money in on terms that are just as leveraged . . . going 8 percent over debt. . . . I think we should do it. It's nice to start with a blue chip."

These contrasting discourses have one clear point of contact. In our conversations, Kravinsky showed an almost rhapsodic appreciation of ratios. In short, ratios are dependable and life is not. "No number is significant in itself: its only significance is in relation to other numbers," he said. "I try to rely on relationships between numbers, because those relationships are constant—unlike Billy Crudup and the woman he impregnated. Even if the other relationships in our lives are going to hell in a handbasket, numbers continue to cooperate with one another."

.   .   .

In the months following the first of Kravinsky's financial gifts, a new ratio began to preoccupy him: the one-in-four-thousand chance that a person has of dying in an operation to donate a kidney. In early 2003, he read an article in the *Wall Street Journal* that introduced him to the idea of nondirected kidney donations, in which an altruistic-minded person gives an organ to benefit a stranger—someone in the pool of 60,000 people on America's kidney-transplant waiting list. The demand for kidneys outstrips the supply; the buying and selling of organs is illegal, and although there are between fifteen and twenty thousand deaths in America each year that could yield organs, about half of families deny permission for the bodies of their relatives to be used in this way, often disregarding the dead person's donor card. Kravinsky was so struck by the article that he cut it out and kept it in a desk drawer.

The notion of nondirected organ donation is not new. Joseph E. Murray, who directed the first successful human kidney-transplant operation, in 1954, in Boston, recently recalled that, by that time, he had received three offers of kidneys—from a prisoner, a homeless man, and a nun. They could not be accepted; early transplants were generally between identical twins, for a precise biological match. But in the early sixties advances in immunosuppressant drugs allowed surgeons to begin transplanting from deceased donors to unrelated recipients and from living donors other than twins—typically, blood relatives. By 1963, there were no medical barriers to nondirected donation. But while kidney transplants became almost routine—last year, there were 6,500 living-donor and 8,700 deceased-donor transplants in America—nondirected donation did not.

On occasion, altruists engaged in a somewhat less radical practice, donating kidneys to people they had not met but whose plights had attracted their attention (say, through a newspaper article). But doctors were resistant even to this idea, and questioned the sanity of these donors; according to a paper published in *Seminars in Psychiatry* in 1971, the practice was viewed by most physicians as "impulsive, suspect, and repugnant." Doctors were also under the impression, now revised, that related donations were almost always better than unrelated ones. In addition, a kidney-removal operation was initially far more painful and invasive than it later became; until the mid-nineties, it was often necessary to break the donor's rib, and the donor was frequently left with a long scar.

In the late nineties, by coincidence, two donors independently approached two hospitals with a request to make a nondirected kidney donation, and neither hospital could think of a good reason for turning them away. Joyce Roush, a transplant nurse from Indiana, introduced herself to Lloyd Ratner, a leading transplant surgeon then at Johns Hopkins, in Baltimore. "I was quite skeptical," Ratner told me. "I said, 'Give me a call and we'll consider,' thinking she'd never call me. She called and called." And at the University of Minnesota a would-be donor with a long record of altruistic acts made the same request, saying, "I want to do this and go home and be happy." Following bioethical consultation, and psychiatric testing of the donors, the hospitals accepted the offers: in Minnesota, the anonymous donor's kidney was transplanted in August 1999; a few weeks later, at Johns Hopkins, Joyce Roush donated one to a thirteen-year-old boy. Now, several dozen nondirected donations are performed each year in the U.S.

Kravinsky considered the risks. Although Richard Herrick, who received the first kidney transplant, died eight years later,

Ronald Herrick, his donor and twin brother, is still alive. As Herrick's example suggests, and medical research confirms, there are no health disadvantages to living with one kidney. One is enough—it grows a little bigger—and the notion that a spare should be packed for emergencies is misconceived: nearly all kidney disease affects both.

The risks are in the operation. "I had a one-in-four-thousand chance of dying," Kravinsky told me. "But my recipient had a certain death facing her." To Kravinsky, this was straightforward: "I'd be valuing my life at four thousand times hers if I let consideration of mortality sway me."

He made one other calculation: there was a chance that one of his four children—then aged between three and eleven—might need a kidney that only he could supply. Kravinsky took into account the rarity of childhood kidney disease, the fact that he had only ten or so years left as a viable donor, and the fact that siblings tend to be the best kidney matches—his children were well provided with siblings. He decided that the risk was no greater than one in two hundred and fifty thousand, and that it was a risk he could accept. In fact, Kravinsky began to think of a donation as "a treat to myself. I really thought of it as something pleasurable."

·   ·   ·

In a now famous 1972 essay, "Famine, Affluence, and Morality," the Australian philosopher Peter Singer set up the ethical puzzle that has become known as the Shallow Pond and the Envelope. In the first case, a child has fallen into a shallow pond and is drowning; Singer considers saving the child, and reflects on the inconvenience of muddy clothes. In the second, he is asked by the Bengal Relief Fund to send a donation to save the lives of children overseas.

To ignore the child in the pond would be despicable, most people would agree; to ignore an envelope from a charity would not be. (And the law supports that view.) But Singer's contention was that the two derelictions are ethically alike. "If we can prevent something bad without sacrificing anything of comparable significance, we ought to do it," he has written. To allow harm is to do harm; it is wrong not to give money that you do not need for the most basic necessities.

Many philosophers disagree—and would argue, in one way or another, that we can have greater faith in our intuitive moral judgments. Colin McGinn, a philosopher at Rutgers, has called Singer's principle "positively bad, morally speaking," for "it encourages a way of life in which many important values are sacrificed to generalized altruism" and devalues "spending one's energies on things other than helping suffering people in distant lands. . . . Just think of how much the human race would have lost if Newton and Darwin and Leonardo and Socrates had spent their time on charitable acts!" Singer has his adherents: in 1996, Peter Unger, a philosopher at New York University, published "Living High and Letting Die," an extension of Singer's analysis whose aim was to show how we let ourselves off the ethical hook too easily. According to Unger, we placate our consciences with an "illusion of innocence."

By the spring of 2003, Zell Kravinsky had become a man with no such illusion. "It seems to me crystal clear that I should be giving all my money away and donating all of my time and energy," Kravinsky said, and he speculated that failure to be this generous was corrosive, in a way that most people don't recognize. "Maybe that's why we're fatigued all the time," he mused—from "the effort" of disregarding the greater need of others. "Maybe that's why we break down and suffer depressions: we have a sense that there's something we should be remembering and we're not. Maybe that's what we should be remembering—that other people are suffering."

He discussed the idea of kidney donation with his family and friends. "I thought, at first, that people would understand,"

Kravinsky told me. "But they don't understand math. That's an American pastime—grossly misunderstanding math. I've had to repeat it over and over. Some people eventually got it. But many people felt the way my wife did: she said, 'No matter how infinitesimal the risk to your family, we're your family, and the recipient doesn't count.'"

Arguments about philanthropic extremes tend to be arguments about families. In *Bleak House*, Dickens says of his character Mrs. Jellyby that she "could see nothing nearer than Africa": in a home full of trash, she is so busy helping the unfortunate abroad that she disregards her children, who are filthy and covered with bruises—the "notched memoranda of their accidents." As Esther Summerson, the novel's moral center, says of Mrs. Jellyby, "It is right to begin with the obligations of home. . . . While those are overlooked and neglected, no other duties can possibly be substituted for them." This is a reasonable case for philanthropic restraint, but it's also an excuse for philanthropic inaction: the narrator of Nick Hornby's novel *How to Be Good* wrestles with this argument, guiltily, after her husband makes a sudden conversion to virtue—giving away money and goods, and offering their spare room to a homeless teen-ager. "I'm a liberal's worst nightmare," her husband says, in response to the narrator's Esther-like fears for her children's comfort. "I think everything you think. But I'm going to walk it like I talk it."

Chuck Collins, a great-grandson of Oscar Mayer, is a rare nonfictional example of someone who gave away all his assets during his lifetime—a half-million-dollar inheritance, which he donated to charity nearly twenty years ago. He became used to hearing pleas in behalf of his (then only potential) offspring. "People would say, 'That's fine, you can be reckless in your own life, but you shouldn't do that to your children,'" Collins told me. "But I think parents make decisions for their kids all the time—that's what parenting is." He now has a daughter, who does not live like a Jellyby. "Of course, we have to respond to our immediate family, but, once they're O.K., we need to expand the circle. A larger sense of family is a radical idea, but we get into trouble as a society when we don't see that we're in the same boat."

Kravinsky's conversations with his family, and about his family, left him feeling like an alien. "The sacrosanct commitment to the family is the rationalization for all manner of greed and selfishness," he said. "Nobody says, 'I'm working for the tobacco company because I like the money.' They say, 'Well, you know, I hate to do it, but I'm saving up for the kids.' Everything is excused that way. To me, it's obscene."

During one of our conversations, I asked Kravinsky to calculate a ratio between his love for his children and his love for unknown children. Many people would refuse to engage in this kind of thought experiment, but Kravinsky paused for only a moment. "I don't know where I'd set it, but I would not let many children die so my kids could live," he said. "I don't think that two kids should die so that one of my kids has comfort, and I don't know that two children should die so that one of my kids lives."

Judith Jarvis Thomson, a philosopher at M.I.T. and the author of *The Realm of Rights*, later told me, "His children are presumably no more valuable to the universe than anybody else's children are, but the universe doesn't really care about *any* children— yours or mine or anybody else's. A father who says, 'I'm no more concerned about my children's lives than about anybody else's life' is just flatly a defective parent; he's deficient in views that parents ought to have, whether it maximizes utility or not."

Someone who knows both Kravinskys well told me, "If your spouse is doing something to himself, he is, to a certain extent, doing it to you also. Zell would be an exasperating person to be married to." Susan Katz, the wife of Kravinsky's friend Barry Katz, told me, "I thought he was crazy. I thought it was just weird. If you're a father, you can't put your life at risk." Kravinsky said that his wife's initial attitude echoed these sentiments—she was "adamantly opposed," on the ground of familial responsibility.

She eventually grew more accepting of the idea, at least in the abstract. During a recent telephone conversation in which her anger about Zell's actions was made clear, Emily disputed this description, saying that her opposition was constant, and derived from her opinion that Zell, who has digestive difficulties, was unsuited to an operation of this kind. "I have no objection to nondirected organ donations," she said. "I think they're a very good thing, if the donor is medically appropriate for elective surgery, and if the donation is carried out in a medical center that's prepared to provide good care."

The rest was math and poetry: Kravinsky has said that he was driven by "the mathematical calculus of utilitarianism," which gives primacy to the idea of the "greatest good." But he acknowledges, too, another impulse, which emanated from what he calls his romantic or neurotic self: to give a kidney was a self-sacrificing, self-dramatizing act. The utilitarian in Kravinsky might give up his coat to a stranger, if to have no coat would not disable him as a champion of the coatless; but the romantic in Kravinsky would give the coat unquestioningly, loudly renounce coat-wearing worldwide, and then give away his pants.

•   •   •

In April 2003, Kravinsky called the Albert Einstein Medical Center, an inner-city hospital where he could be fairly confident that a donated kidney would go to a low-income African American patient. Kravinsky told me that the transplant coordinator who spoke to him was "pretty leery of the whole thing, and kept telling me there was no payment." The hospital had never operated on a nondirected donor. But he went there to meet a surgeon, who believed Kravinsky's reports of two Ph.D.s and his philanthropy only after doing a Google search, and then a psychiatrist, who told him, "You're doing something you don't have to do." Kravinsky replied, "I *do* have to do it. You're missing the whole point. It's as much a necessity as food, water, and air."

Kravinsky acknowledged that he suffered from depression and that he did not have his wife's approval for the donation. He allowed the hospital to speak to his own psychiatrist, but said that he would not be able to bring Emily in for joint consultations. The hospital accepted this, after officials learned that family support of nondirected donors is often hesitant, at best. "The consensus was, if this is what he wants to do and he's a competent individual, you can't deny him because someone doesn't want him to do it," Radi Zaki, the director of the Center for Renal Disease at Albert Einstein, said. "But we made the process hard for him. We delayed, we put him off. The more impatient he got, the more delay I gave him. You want to make sure this is the real deal."

In June, Kravinsky was accepted for the operation. Donnell Reid, a twenty-nine-year-old single black woman studying for a degree in social work, whose hypertension had forced her to undergo dialysis for eight years, was informed that she was the possible recipient of a kidney from a nondirected donor. "It was so surreal," she recently told me. "You're going about your life, and then you get this phone call." She went in for tests, then waited. "I prayed. I left it in God's hands." She told none of her friends: "It was such an overwhelming thing, such an awesome thing, I wanted to meditate on it on my own." A week later, on July 7, she learned that she had been selected for the operation, and the next day, at Kravinsky's request, they met at the transplant center. They talked for two hours. She described her plans for the future, and thanked him for a generosity "beyond words."

On July 22, Kravinsky left home early—"I snuck out"—and drove to the hospital, where Zaki asked him again if he would like to reconsider his decision. "He was very calm," Zaki recalls. Kravinsky had not told his wife the details of his plan, but he had approached a reporter at the Philadelphia *Daily News,* a local tabloid, which ran a story that morning. In a three-hour operation that started at 8 A.M.—a laparoscopic removal, requiring minimal incisions—he gave up his right kidney to Reid, who was in the room next door.

The next morning, Kravinsky called his wife from his hospital bed. Because of his digestive complications, he had to be taken off opiate-based painkillers, and he says that he took nothing in their place. (Zaki, affectionately describing Kravinsky as a "dramatic" patient, disputed this memory of total abstinence.) Zell asked Emily for help: "She was furious. She didn't want me to die, but, on the other hand, she was beyond human rage." She said that she was willing to talk to the doctors about his treatment. She also threatened to divorce him.

At that moment, Kravinsky recalled, "I really thought I might have shot it with my family." His parents were also appalled. When Reeda Kravinsky visited her son in the hospital, she recalled, "I was so filled with anger that I didn't speak." Meanwhile, Kravinsky's mind was still turning on philanthropic questions. "I lay there in the hospital, and I thought about all my other organs. When I do something good, I feel that I can do more; I burn to do more. It's a heady feeling." He went home after four days, and by then he was wondering if he should give away his other kidney.

·   ·   ·

A few weeks ago, in a Barnes & Noble bookstore in Jenkintown, Kravinsky pulled out his shirt a couple of inches and showed me a tidy scar, no more than six inches long, on his right hip. "Once in a while, I remember I only have one kidney," he said, smiling— apparently struck anew by the thought that the donation had been a surgical act as well as a symbolic one. "It feels a little weird—'Oh, yeah, I only have one!'—but the other body parts are very happy, they have breathing room." It was an unusually upbeat thought, connected to a moment of moral clarity. "It was a good deed," he said. "However I screw up morally in the future, this is something nobody can take away."

Kravinsky's mood had improved since our first meeting, four months after the operation, when he had seemed vulnerable. He was always engaging, eccentric company—during lunch at a restaurant, he opened twenty packets of sugar and poured the contents into his mouth; he gave the impression that he would rather wait forever in a stationary elevator than be the one to press the button—but he was dispirited. He often spoke in fateful terms about his marriage, which had held together but was under constant stress. He worried about his relationship with his children—he showed me touching poems he had written about them—and their relationship with the world. (In the schoolyard, a child had approached one of his sons, saying, "Why don't you just donate me that cheese stick?") He said he had lost his sense of direction. "I feel unmoored," he told me.

Having redefined his life as a continuing donation, but having given away everything that came immediately to hand, Kravinsky was not sure how to proceed. His utilitarian and romantic selves were now in competition, and he did not trust his ability to distinguish between the two, or to distinguish between them and vanity. He saw a baffling choice between engagement and disengagement, between creating wealth and withdrawing into a life of poverty. When Kravinsky's thoughts migrated to rhetorical extremes, the choice seemed to be between life and death.

Several times, Kravinsky talked of giving away his other kidney and living on dialysis, and then he would upbraid himself for hesitating. "If I didn't have kids, and I saw a child who was dying for want of a kidney, I would offer mine," he said. He sometimes imagined a full-body donation. "My organs could save several people if I gave my whole body away," he told me. "But I don't think I can do that to my family. Or, at least, I can't endure the humiliation. I've thought about it: my kids would be under a cloud, everybody would pillory me as a showboat or a suicide. I know it's a thing I ought to do; other lives are equal to my own, and I could save at least three or four. I have fantasized about it. I've dreamed about it. But I don't have the nerve." He said that "before it happened I'd have to endure the screams and yells from my family.

Then I would be committed." He laughed. "My wife and my sister are psychiatrists."

Kravinsky could see one clear role for himself: as a promoter of a free market in kidneys, an idea with limited but growing intellectual support. Richard A. Epstein, a libertarian law professor at the University of Chicago, championed this argument in his 1999 book, *Mortal Peril: Our Inalienable Right to Health Care?*, urging a "frontal assault on the present legal regime" and its "moral philosophy of false comradeship." He wrote, "No one disputes the Beatles' proposition that 'money can't buy you love,' but the proposition does not require any form of *ban* on the payment of cash in certain human relations." Epstein recently told me, "When I talk about this now, nobody treats me as a complete kook. People are a little more respectful." In Kravinsky's opinion, an efficient market would quickly set a price for a kidney at 10,000 dollars or so. "College kids would do it. A college kid goes to a party, there's a greater risk of dying from drugs or alcohol or a car crash than one in four thousand." He said that any anxiety about exploitation was misplaced: "If the risk is lower than the other ways to make the money, where's the exploitation? How dare people be so condescending."

A few weeks after this discussion, Kravinsky called me. He had just been approached by a local woman in her forties who had spent years on dialysis, and who was running out of places on the body where a dialysis needle can enter a vein. She wanted to buy a kidney. Not long before, two young women had jointly written to Kravinsky; both were interested in selling a kidney. He told me that he had arranged to bring the women together at a café near his house. He would be an unpaid broker in a kidney sale. "I'll take the heat, which will probably mean getting arrested," he said. (The 1984 National Organ Transplantation Act prohibits the sale of kidneys.) "I feel very nervous, but I feel the decision's been made—because I'm not going to let that woman die, and who else in America would do this? I'm the only person who can save her life by setting this up. I'm not going to do anything that stands in the way of saving a life, whether it's my money, my reputation. It's a very big step, but there's no choice. The choice is, I say no and the rest of my life I know that someone died."

He called me when he got home, a few hours later. "Oh, brother, she's in bad shape," he said of the would-be recipient. He said that "everyone had liked each other" at the meeting, and an agreement had been reached. The recipient would take a kidney from whichever of the two women was a better match: both would present themselves to a hospital as friends offering a dona-tion. The sick woman had agreed to pay 50,000 dollars for the organ.

Kravinsky was energized—he foresaw a test case, a shift in public opinion. He was ready to embrace infamy. But when we spoke again he was worried about legal consequences. "Can you imagine *me* in prison for five years?" he asked.

Later, when I brought up the subject once more, he said that a lawyer had told him to "just leave it alone." He was taking every opportunity to promote kidney donation, but he had given up the role of broker. Today, the three women remain in touch, but they have not yet closed a deal.

•   •   •

According to Kravinsky, his family was living on about 60,000 dollars a year, from Emily's part-time medical practice and from interest derived from Zell's remaining capital. The children were in public schools; the minivans were paid for. "The real test of my vanity would be if I gave everything away," Kravinsky said. "Not just to the point of a working-class existence but to the point of poverty."

Yet even while Kravinsky aspired to a life spent "passing out pamphlets on the subway," as he put it, it pained him to think of giving up the language of finance, which he spoke so well. "To really achieve wealth, you have to have a love of money—you have to enjoy the play of numbers behind your eyelids," he said.

Indeed, near the end of last year, Kravinsky had begun talking to a local venture capitalist; together they planned a real-estate partnership that would invest on behalf of others in the kind of commercial property that Kravinsky had experience buying and selling. He would give his half of the shares to charity. Other charities could invest without paying fees. Kravinsky initially talked of this as a single stratum in a layered life of agitation, donation, and sacrifice, but this spring, as he began to talk to real-estate agents, the partnership began to emerge as a new full-time job. His mood lightened, and he seemed giddy whenever I overheard him using the jargon of amortization, appraisals, and conduit financing. "I do feel a kind of bonhomie—it's strange—in business," he admitted.

Not long ago, Kravinsky toured a Cingular wireless-call center in eastern Kentucky, a building being offered at thirteen million dollars. His guide, the office manager, was a young tanned woman who wore pin-striped trousers. Kravinsky, bouncy and a little flirtatious, looked like a graduate student in geology, and, as he walked among the thousand desks laid out in honeycomb arrangements under signs reading "I Am Proud to Be Part of the Perfectly Awesome Crew," everyone looked up. "It's just a glue-down carpet?" he asked the office manager. "Are these load-bearing walls? Is that eight inches of concrete?" At the end of the tour, he said, with feeling, "This is a beautiful center, I have to say."

He was no longer adrift, yet he had not discovered ethical ecstasy, either. Peter Singer has called him "a remarkable person who has taken very seriously questions of what are our moral obligations to assist people." He says, "I think it's very difficult for people to go as far as he has, and I don't think we should blame people who don't, but we should admire those who do."

Kravinsky himself held on to self-doubt. He did buy the Kentucky call center; soon afterward, he spent the night at the sunny, high-ceilinged home of Barry and Susan Katz, in Westport, Connecticut. He got up late, and, long after his friends had finished breakfast, he sat eating cereal at the head of a polished black table. He was unrested, and was troubled by the thought that a renewed career in real estate might block his path to virtue.

"But don't you think giving away 45 million dollars was a good first step?" Barry Katz asked him, taking up the challenge of having moral absolutism as a weekend house guest.

"No," Kravinsky replied. "That's not the hard part. The hard part is the last 10,000 dollars a year—when you have to live so cheaply you can't function in the business world." He added, "If I need a coat to visit an investment banker's office because I'll look bizarre if I don't have one, but then I see somebody shiver, I should give my coat to him."

"But what if you made enough money, after meeting with the investment banker, to fund research into AIDS prevention, something extremely good for the world?" Katz asked. "You're not going to get very far in an investment banker's office wearing sackcloth."

"I think suits are despicable. Suits and ties. I think I should go into the office naked." Kravinsky was smiling. "If I went into the office of a banker naked, I'd be. . . ."

"You'd be arrested," Katz said.

Katz remembered the time he had hung up on Kravinsky a few weeks before the kidney operation. "He almost broke off with you," Susan Katz told Kravinsky.

"Oh, Barry," Kravinsky said. "It isn't that I think people are evil. But it's a fact that our actions, in some sense our thoughts, let some people live and some people die."

Susan, sitting at the other end of the table, looked at Kravinsky with fond exasperation and asked, "This is how you think every day, really? That's got to be tough. It seems so sad. You seem so sad."

"Well, I am sad." Kravinsky had arranged everything within arm's reach—orange juice, mug, salt, sugar, cereal box—into a tight cluster on his placemat. His adventure in donation had been a rhetorical opportunity—a showcase for his underappreciated talent for argument. But for a moment the debate had slowed, and Kravinsky spoke less forcefully, in apparent recognition of the unequal ratio of sacrifice to sustenance, of good done to moral certainty felt.

"But shouldn't there be more joy in this?" Barry said.

"I don't think of it as something that's joyful. Why should I feel joy?"

"I just feel that if you really were on this path to enlightenment, whatever it is, you would feel joy."

"It's not enlightenment," Kravinsky said quietly. "It's the start of a moral life."

The Atlantic Monthly

WINNER—FICTION

Written with remarkable grace and confidence, Aryn Kyle's "Foaling Season" focuses on a young woman who tells the story of helping her father, a horse trainer, endure the compromises he must make to keep his business and family intact.

Aryn Kyle

Foaling Season

Six months before Polly Cain drowned in the canal, my sister, Nona, ran off and married a cowboy. My father said there was a time when he would have been able to stop her, and I wasn't sure if he meant a time in our lives when she would have listened to him, or a time in history when the Desert Valley Sheriff's Posse would have been allowed to chase after her with torches and drag her back to our house by her yellow hair. He had been a member of the sheriff's posse since before I was born, and he said that the group was pretty much the same as the Masons, except without the virgin sacrifices. They paid dues, rode their horses in parades, and directed traffic at the rodeo where my sister first laid eyes on her cowboy. Only once in a great while were they called upon for a task of real importance, like clearing a fallen tree from a hunting trail, or pulling a dead girl out of the canal.

Polly Cain disappeared on a Wednesday afternoon, and at first people were talking kidnapping. An eleven-year-old girl was too young to be a runaway, so they figured someone must have snatched her. But then they found her backpack on the dirt road that ran alongside the canal, and soon they called my father. For the two days the sheriff's posse dragged the canal, they traded in their white tuxedo shirts and black-felt Stetsons for rubber waders that came up to their armpits, and they walked shoulder to shoulder through the brown water. I passed them on my way home from school. It was only April, but already the mayflies were starting to hatch off the water, and I watched my father swat them away from his face. I waved and called to him from the side of the canal, but he clenched his jaw and didn't look at me.

"We found that girl today," he said when he came home the next afternoon. I was making Kool-Aid in a plastic pitcher, and he stuck his finger in and then licked it. "Tangled in one of the grates."

"Is she dead?" I asked, and he stared at me.

"You stay away from that canal when you're walking home, Alice," he said.

"Will there be a funeral?" I pictured myself like a woman in the movies, standing beside the grave in a black dress and thick sunglasses, too sad to cry.

"What do you care?"

"We were partners in shop class. We were making a lantern." The truth was that Polly had been making the lantern while I watched. She had been a good sport about the whole thing and let me hold it when our teacher, Mr. McClusky, walked by, so that he would think I was doing some of the work.

"I don't have time to take you to a funeral, Alice," my father said, and he put his hand on top of my head. "There's just too much work around here. I've already lost two days."

I nodded and stirred the Kool-Aid with a wooden spoon. There was always too much work. My father owned a stable. Between posse meetings he gave riding lessons and bred and raised horses, which he sold to people who fed them apple slices by hand and called them "baby." In the mornings my father and I fed the horses while it was still dark, and I would walk to school shaking hay from my hair and clothing, scratching at the pieces that had fallen down the front of my shirt. In the afternoons we cleaned the stalls and groomed and exercised the horses. It was foaling season, and Dad didn't like to leave the barn even for a minute, in

case one of our mares went into labor. It was just as well. I didn't
have a black dress.

"You've been a trooper, kid," he said. "When your sister comes
back, things will calm down."

He always did this—talked about how my sister would come
home and everything would be the way it was. For a while I'd
wondered if he might be right. It had all happened so fast. Nona
met Jerry on a Sunday, and on Thursday she packed four boxes
and a backpack and went off in his pickup truck. Jerry rode
broncs on the rodeo circuit and married my sister at a courthouse
in Kansas. My father said that Jerry would break his spine riding
broncs, and Nona would spend the rest of her life pushing him
around in a wheelchair and holding a cup for him to drool into.
She wasn't the marrying kind, my father said. She wouldn't be satisfied to spend her life on the outside of an arena, cheering for
someone else.

But the months had passed by, and Nona's letters were still
filled with smiley faces and exclamation points. Compared with
the horse-show circuit, she wrote, rodeos were a dream. She and
Jerry ate steak for dinner and slept in motels, which was a big step
up from horse shows, where we ate granola bars and drank soda
pop and slept in the stalls with the horses so that no one could
steal them during the night.

Her letters were always addressed to me. They opened with
"Baby Alice," and closed with "Give my love to Mom and Dad." I
would leave the letters on the counter for my father to read, which
he hardly ever did, and after a few days I would go up to my
mother's room and read the letters aloud to her.

My mother had spent nearly my whole life in her bedroom.
Nona said that before we came along, our mother had been a star
in horse shows, had won left and right, and even had her picture
in the paper. She said that one day, when I was still a baby, our
mother had handed me to her, said she was tired, and gone upstairs to rest. She never came back down. Dad moved into the

guest bedroom so as not to disrupt her, and we were careful to take our shoes off when we walked past her room. She didn't make much of a fuss. She didn't call for extra blankets or crushed ice or quiet. She just stayed in bed with the curtains drawn and watched television without the sound. It was easy to forget she was there.

I would sit on her bed and read Nona's letters to her by the blue light of the TV screen, and she would pat my leg and say, "Real nice. It sounds real nice, doesn't it, Alice?"

I would breathe through my mouth to filter the sour, damp scent of her yellow skin and oily hair. My mother made me say the name of the town each letter had come from, and what I thought it looked like. I pictured the rodeo towns as dry, dusty places with dirty motels and lines of fast-food restaurants, but I tried to be inventive: McCook, Nebraska, had chestnut trees lining every street; Marion, Illinois, had purple sunsets; and Sikeston, Missouri, had a park with a pond in the middle where people could feed ducks. When I couldn't think anymore, I would say that I had to go to the bathroom or that I had to help Dad in the barn, and I would creep out of her bedroom and shut the door behind me.

After Nona left, my father said, we were lucky to get Sheila Altman. She lived on the other side of Desert Valley and went to a new school with computers and air-conditioning. Sheila Altman had green eyes and a soft voice. She said "If I might" and "Would you mind," and never forgot to say "Please" and "Thank you." I wanted to rip her baby-fine hair out in tufts. When her mother drove her to our house, Sheila would rush into the stable to kiss the horses and feed them carrots she had brought from home. Mrs. Altman would get out of the car with her camera and checkbook and watch her daughter scramble into the barn. "Well, Mr. Winston," she would say, "you've got your work cut out for you today."

Mrs. Altman had told my father that for the past few years she had spent thousands of dollars to send Sheila to equestrian camp, where for one week she got to care for a horse as if it were her own, feeding it, grooming it, and cleaning its stall. My father had jokingly said that he would let Sheila clean his stalls for half that, but when Mrs. Altman gasped and said "Really?" he didn't falter.

"For *this* girl?" he said. "Absolutely." After that Mrs. Altman drove Sheila across the valley every day after school and paid my father to let her groom our horses and muck out our stalls. While Sheila was there, my father was chipper and lighthearted. He told her what a hard worker she was and said he didn't know how we had managed without her. After she was gone, he would rub my back and say, "You give that girl anything she wants, Alice. Talk nice to her. Sheila Altman is our meal ticket. And she doesn't have attitude, like your sister."

My father had always said that Nona had a wicked tongue and an ungrateful heart, but he usually smiled when he said it. She threw fits like nobody's business. When she was thirsty, she shrieked. When she was hot, she cried. And when she was mad at my father, her face would get so tight and rigid that it looked like it might split apart right between her eyes.

My father was being kind when he said I didn't have the temperament for showing, because what he meant was that I didn't have the talent. I couldn't remember to smile and keep my heels down and my toes in and my elbows tight and my back straight all at the same time. When I focused on smiling, I dropped my reins, and when I thought about sitting up straight, my feet slipped out of the stirrups. My father said that he needed me more outside the ring anyway, but I saw how it was. We had a reputation to maintain and a livelihood to earn. In the end, I wasn't good for business.

But Nona had been good enough for both of us. She smiled and laughed and winked at the judges. Outside the ring she would let little girls from the stands sit on her horse. While she showed them how to hold the reins and where to put their feet, she would aim her voice at their parents and say, "You're a natural!" Then she would flash her smile at the mother and say, "My daddy gives lessons. You all should come out sometime."

Yellow Cap was the last horse my father bought for her. He was a palomino—the flashiest, biggest, most beautiful animal in the ring. The first time I saw him, I thought he would kill my sister for sure, but Nona mounted him easily. She jiggled the reins and said, "There's my boy." Yellow Cap's neck arched, and his body tucked, and they rode around the arena like they were under a spotlight. My father watched from the sidelines with some prospective clients and said, "That horse would walk on water if she asked him to."

•   •   •

The day after Polly was pulled from the canal, we didn't have shop class. Instead the whole sixth grade was taken into the gymnasium and invited to pray if we wanted to. Then we were told to go home and talk with our parents about what we were feeling.

When I got to my house, Mrs. Altman and my father were gathered around Sheila, who was wearing my sister's show clothes.

"I don't know," Mrs. Altman was saying. "I'm not sure about the color."

"I was just thinking that," my father told her. "I was just thinking the same thing about the color."

"She looks better in red." Mrs. Altman made a circular motion with her finger, and Sheila gave me a shy smile as she turned around to let her mother see the back.

"We have a red shirt," my father said. "Alice, go up to Nona's room and get the red shirt." Sheila stared down at the pavement, and I dropped my backpack and went into the house.

I had to pick my way between piles of ribbons and trophies to get to the closet, and when I opened it, Nona's smell was gone from the clothes. I pushed my face into the different fabrics, trying to find a trace of her, the sweet, powdery scent of her deodorant, the fruity smell of her lotion, but there was nothing.

My mother's door was open a crack when I passed it, with the red shirt still on its hanger.

"Alice, is that you?"

I creaked the door open and braced myself against the wave of stale air. My mother was propped up on three pillows, and the TV light flickered across her face. I arranged my feet in the doorway, careful not to let them cross the line where the hallway carpet changed into the bedroom carpet.

"Be my good girl and close the window." She tossed her pale hand limply at the wrist and sighed heavily. "Those little white bugs are coming in. I'm afraid they'll bite me in my sleep."

"Mayflies don't bite, Mom," I said, but I crossed the room to close the window.

"I hate them," she said. "Filthy things. Off that horrible water."

In the blue glow of the TV the mayflies looked gray and sickly, and I tried to fan them out the window. I could feel my mother's stare on the back of my neck. "Would you like to stay and tell me what you learned in school today?" She patted the bed beside her.

I held up the red shirt. "I have to take this to Dad."

She blinked at me for a second and then looked back at the television. "Better hurry, then."

Sheila really did look much better in red, and my father sold Nona's shirt to Mrs. Altman for twice what he had paid for it.

·　　·　　·

In shop class I didn't know what to do with the half-finished lantern. I was afraid to weld, and I didn't think I could tape the pieces together. But the boys couldn't get enough of welding, and several of them bid for the chance to finish the lantern for me. In the end I accepted an offer of three dollars and a Pepsi, and then watched while they pieced my lantern together.

Mr. McClusky told me that it would be a nice gesture to give the lantern to Polly's mother, and after school I practiced what I might say when I rang Polly's doorbell. I had barely known Polly and had never met her mother, but such a heartfelt gesture would probably make her cry. Maybe she would ask me to stay and visit. She would make me tea and feed me gingersnaps while she ran her fingers through my hair. "Come back anytime," she would say. "Stay the night if you want."

But while I was practicing the right way to make my gesture, I noticed the places on the lantern where I had smudged the paint by touching it to see if it was dry. Polly's mother probably had rooms full of perfect things Polly had made over the years: neatly sewn beanbags from home ec, symmetrical clay pencil holders from art, the kinds of things that when I made them always came out crooked or lumpy. Giving her a crummy lantern would only confuse her. Instead of taking it to Polly's house I wrapped the lantern in notebook paper and put it in my backpack. I walked home along the canal, sipping my Pepsi and wishing I had let the boys paint my lantern too.

My father was sitting in front of the barn, polishing Nona's show saddle, when I got home. His face was red, and the skin around his lips looked tight and drawn. "Your mother's been crying all day," he said when he saw me. "Where have you been?"

"At school, like I always am."

"Don't you use that tone with me."

I stared at my feet.

"Now you go upstairs and be sweet to your mother. Tell her how much you love her. Make her feel special. Then come back and help me. There's a million things to do. I'm sick of doing all the work around here."

I looked at him. Nona wasn't coming back. Not ever. "Maybe Sheila Altman can do it when she gets here."

My father stood up then, and he seemed bigger than any human being had ever been. For a second I thought he might hit me, and I tried to gauge the distance to the house. I might be able to outrun him. But then he put his hands up to his face, and his shoulders sagged. "Please, Alice," he said through his fingers. "Please."

Upstairs, my mother's face was streaked, and strands of her hair clung to the damp patches on her cheeks.

"Why are you crying, Mom?" I asked from the doorway. I meant for it to sound sweet, but it came out tired. "Are you sick?"

She let out a cry when she saw me. "Come here to me." Every part of my body went stiff, but I thought of my father with his face in his hands, and I held my breath as I crossed the room to her. She pulled me into the bed with her and pressed my head against her shoulder.

"He sent you up here, didn't he? I've been a nuisance today."

"Dad's worried about you," I told her.

Her hair fell across my face, and I tried to lift my head to breathe. "I used to be able to make him smile," she whispered. "He used to look at me like I was a movie star. Do you believe that?" She sighed and straightened herself. Then she bit her lip and looked down at her hands. "She was smart," she said quietly. "Smart to leave when she did."

I didn't know what to say.

"She would have been used up here. She would be old fast, and used up. And now she gets to travel to new places and meet new people." She turned her head away from me.

Her nightgown was wrinkled, and in the light of the television her skin looked dull and heavy. "I made you something," I told her. "In school."

"You did?" Her mouth opened and she touched her hand to her chest. "Really truly?"

I rummaged in my backpack. "It's a lantern," I said. "See? You put a candle here and then you can hang it and it will light your room."

My mother gasped as I handed it to her. She touched her fingers along the welded edges and the paint-smeared center. "You made this? For me?"

"Uh huh."

"Oh, baby," she said, and hugged me. "You and I will take care of each other, won't we?"

I stood up and backed to the door. "I have to go help in the barn now. Dad said."

Outside, Mrs. Altman was writing a check to my father. When I came up beside him, he raised his eyebrows at me, and I nodded. "She's fine," I said, and he sighed.

"Who?" Mrs. Altman asked with a bright smile. "Mrs. Winston?" My father and I glanced at each other. "I'd love to meet her."

"My wife keeps to herself," my father said awkwardly, his eyes on the check.

"She's sick," I added, and they both looked at me.

"With what?" Mrs. Altman glanced at my father.

"She has an allergy to the sun," I said. "And to fresh air." My father opened his mouth slightly.

"How awful!" Mrs. Altman said. "What happens to her?"

"Her head gets big," I said. They both stared. "And she gets hives. And fevers. And sometimes she faints." My father nudged me.

Mrs. Altman clasped her hands. "That's dreadful," she said. "The poor thing!"

After she handed over the check and followed her daughter into the barn, my father gave me a searching look. "You're a wicked lying fiend, Alice Winston," he said. But he smiled when he said it.

Sheila Altman helped us clear the show horses out of the barn to make room for the broodmares, who got to live indoors when they birthed. While we brought the pregnant mares in from the pasture, Sheila squealed and clapped her hands.

"I can't wait for the babies!" she said to me.

Our broodmares had simple names like Misty, Lucy, Ginger, and Sally. They were slow and quiet, with long heads, matted manes, and misshapen stomachs. Sheila put her hands on the mares' barrel stomachs and said she could feel the foals moving inside.

"It kicked!" she told me. "I swear I felt it kick."

After she left, I took Cap from his pen and tried to brush the snarls from his mane and tail. My father watched, and as I pulled the loose hair from the brush and let it fall on the ground, he cleared his throat.

"Mrs. Altman wants to buy Cap for Sheila," he said.

I felt my fingertips go cold, and I pretended to clean more hair from the brush. "He's too much horse for her."

My father picked an invisible piece of lint off his shirt. "You want to show this year?"

I stared at him.

"Then keep your opinions to yourself."

•   •   •

Polly Cain's funeral was to begin at five o'clock on a Thursday afternoon, at the cemetery across from the water slide. When I got home from school, I practiced looking sad and remorseful in the mirror. Maybe my father would change his mind and take me, and then Polly's mother would pick me out of the crowd as someone who had been close to Polly. I would walk slowly up to her and let her pull me against her body. As I stared at myself in the mirror, I imagined the afternoons I would spend sitting with Polly's mother at her kitchen table, with photo albums spread before us. She would point out pictures of Polly in Halloween costumes and at piano recitals. "See?" she would say. "See how much you look like her?" I would lean my head against her shoulder, and her hair would smell like strawberries and lemons. I would tell her how much I missed Polly, how nothing would ever be the same now that she was gone, and she would kiss my eyelids and fingers and cry into the palms of my hands. "She was my best friend in the world," I would say. And maybe it wouldn't be a real lie. No one could prove she wasn't my best friend. She was dead, after all.

But before I could persuade my father to take me, our mare Lucy gave birth to the first foal of the year, and I knew that I would not be at the cemetery to pay my last respects. I helped my father wrap Lucy's tail with an Ace bandage, so that the foal wouldn't get tangled in it. We moved around the mare on our knees, clearing the sawdust away from her legs to keep it from clogging the foal's nostrils. The foal came out, thin and wet, breaking the fetal sac open with its weak white hooves.

"It's a colt," my father said, grinning. "Look at him." I pressed myself across the colt's body to keep him still while my father cut the umbilical cord, and then we watched him try to stand on his tiny, pointed feet.

My father cupped the back of my head in his hand. "You did good, Alice," he said. "You're a pro." We waited in the stall doorway until the colt was balanced on his trembling legs. For a second we felt as if we had made something happen.

When we heard the Altmans' minivan pull up in the driveway, my father closed his eyes and said, "Christ, I don't have the energy for this today."

Mrs. Altman got out of the car and began examining the grille. "There are tiny white insects all over the place," she told us. "Their little corpses are stuck all over my car."

My father shook his head at me and then walked over to look. "Mayflies," he announced. "They hatch off the canals. We found about a hundred of them stuck in that girl's hair when we pulled her out of the water."

Mrs. Altman had taken a towel from the back seat and was trying to wipe the front of her car. "Down the road it almost looks like it's snowing, there are so many of them." She looked at me and stopped. "My God, Alice. What's happened?"

I glanced down and saw that my T-shirt was stained with blood where I had leaned against the colt.

"We got our first foal this afternoon," my father said, gesturing at the barn.

"I can't believe we missed it," Sheila wailed. "You should have called us!"

My father turned to me and rolled his eyes. "We'll have plenty more," he said.

Sheila and her mother crowded around Lucy's stall and began clicking and cooing at the foal. Lucy bared her teeth and flattened her ears. My father nudged Sheila away. "Let's give them a while to adjust," he said. "The mothers are a little protective at first."

"I can't believe I forgot my camera today," Mrs. Altman said. "What a day to forget."

"We might get another tonight," I said. "They sometimes come right on top of each other."

"Mom, can I stay—please?" Sheila clasped her hands against her chest and rose up on her toes. "If you wouldn't mind, that is," she added, glancing at my father.

In my head I tried to will my father to say no, but he didn't look at me. "She can stay the night," he told Mrs. Altman. "Alice and I will be up all night checking on the mares anyway."

"Oh, please, Mom?" Sheila begged. "It will be like a slumber party."

Mrs. Altman adjusted the fold of her collar. "Tomorrow is a school day, but for something like this—this is a life lesson, and I think that's more important. You'll get to see the miracle of birth. It's the most beautiful thing in the world, isn't it, Alice?"

I wanted to tell her about the blood and the smell and the sound a mare made when her flesh began to rip around the opening for the foal. I wanted to tell her about our bay mare a few years back, whose uterus had come out when she birthed and hung behind her like a sack of jelly. I wanted to tell her that the bay had screamed a human scream but stood, trembling, to let the foal nurse. I wanted her to know that when the vet had come to put the mare down, Nona covered my eyes, but I could hear the bones crack when she hit the ground. The foal had cried out in its watery whinny for three whole days afterward. But I smiled and said, "Yes. Beautiful."

Mrs. Altman left us money to order pizza and said that she would pick Sheila up in the morning. As she got into her minivan, she asked me if Sheila could borrow clothes so that she wouldn't bloody up her nice ones. I thought about Polly's funeral, just starting across town. Her mother would have taken a seat already. People would be parking their cars and nodding to one another solemnly as they walked across the grass. I had never been to a funeral, but I imagined that everyone would come quietly, dignified and respectful in smart black dresses and stiff suits. They would sit rigid against the pain, but would yield to it as the funeral progressed. Their bodies would soften and then lean into one another, arms circling waists and shoulders, fingers interlacing, as she was lowered into the ground.

We ate our pizza on paper napkins and played gin rummy in the tack room. We took turns walking through the barn to check on the mares, and at two in the morning Sheila came back at a run. "Ginger's lying down!" she shrieked. "She's sweating really bad."

"Here we go," my father said, and we trooped behind him through the barn. My father tossed me an Ace bandage and pointed to Ginger's tail. I knelt behind her and saw that her tail was already wet with clots of blood and mucus. Her muscles rippled across her body, and her back legs pushed into the sawdust.

"You're gonna get kicked," Sheila whispered into her fingers.

"She can't kick if she's lying down, dummy," I told her. My father pinched the back of my arm. "I mean, it's okay." I pulled the wet strands of Ginger's tail into the bandage and closed it with a safety pin.

Sheila took a step back and whispered, "Hurry, Alice."

My father knelt beside Ginger's head with his hands on her neck. He stroked her mane and talked in a low voice. "That's my girl," he said. "Come on, sweetheart." Most of the time my father referred to the broodmares as bitches or nags, but while they were birthing he would click his tongue and whisper to them as if they were children. "That's it, love," he purred. "You're okay."

Sheila crept beside my father and began breathing loudly in short breaths, like women on television do when they are in labor.

"You talk to her," he told Sheila, and she leaned down to touch Ginger's muzzle. My father patted her shoulder and added, "Just be careful she doesn't throw her head and knock your teeth out."

I could hear the other horses pacing and pawing at the ground outside. The pens were rattling, and my father told me to go check them. Ginger began to moan, and Sheila backed out of the stall with her hands over her mouth. "I'll come with you," she whispered.

The show mares had gathered around the pasture fence. They were lying on the ground, their eyes rolled back and their bodies foamy with sweat. They lifted their heads and brought them down hard on the grass while they groaned and snorted.

"What's wrong with them?" Sheila said.

"They're trying to birth," I told her, and for a second I thought it could be true.

Her mouth trembled. "But they aren't pregnant."

"They get the smell," I said. "They get the smell of the new foals, and they try to birth." I glanced to see if she believed me. In less than a month the show mares would be back in the barn, clean and clipped and ready for the show season. By then Sheila could be bored with horses, could switch to piano or gymnastics or ice-skating. We could dress Sheila Altman in my sister's clothes and sell her my sister's horse, but what could she understand about the way things worked? Sheila Altman—what could she understand about wanting?

Sheila's face froze, and she covered her ears with her hands. I felt a wonderful nastiness rise inside myself. "Isn't it beautiful?"

Sheila shuddered and turned away. "I can't look at them," she said.

Along the driveway the geldings were stomping at the ground and ramming the gates of their pens with their chests. Their heads were wildly high, and the whites of their eyes caught the moonlight. Yellow Cap whinnied, and I ran to his pen while Sheila watched. "It's okay, Cap," I told him.

"He's freaking out," Sheila said nervously. "They're all freaking out."

"He's fine," I told her, and reached out to pet him, but he jumped and pulled away. "Come on, boy," I called, and unlatched the gate to go in with him.

As I slid the gate open, Cap reared up, and his shoulder hit me in the face, knocking me to the ground. I heard the metal gate clang against the pen, and the sound of Cap's hooves on the gravel as he ran toward the road.

"Stop him!" I called to Sheila, but she stared after him without moving. My hip and leg felt rubbery and weak when I stood up, and my hands were shaking as I steadied myself on the fence. "I have to go get him," I told her.

"Alice, your face is bleeding," she said. I could taste blood and dirt between my teeth, and I touched my hand to my mouth. I couldn't tell what was bleeding. My whole face felt numb.

"He could get hit by a car," I said.

"He went toward the canal. We should get your dad."

I pushed past her, and she grabbed my hand. "We could tell him that *I* let Cap out. He won't get mad at me, I don't think. Or we could get your mom." I looked at her. "It's night, so maybe she could come outside. Come on, Alice, you're bleeding bad. Let me come with you."

The only thing that could get me in more trouble than losing Cap was losing Sheila Altman. Her mouth puckered as if she was about to cry, and I shook my hand away from her. "I'll be right back, Sheila. Don't be a baby."

I ran until I thought my lungs were going to rise up into my mouth. I tripped twice along the side of the road. When I had to slow down, I called for Cap and clicked my tongue. My nose was running, and I walked to the sound of my breath heaving. I wiped my nose with the back of my hand and rubbed the raw sting in my elbow where I had scraped it when I tripped. The mayflies were floating in front of me, and I waved my arms to push them away. Up ahead I could just make out where the canal water should have been, but there was a glimmering fog over it: the bugs were rising off the canal by the millions, their snowflake bodies and paper wings a blizzard over the water. I started along the dirt road but had gone only several feet when I had to stop and shield my eyes from the storm of insects.

I could feel my heart beating in my throat and ears. I couldn't make out the water, but I could feel its coolness all around, and I pulled myself as far to the side of the road as I could. I waved my hand, but the bugs swelled like vapor. I pressed my lips together to keep them out of my mouth and shook my head as hard as I could. I felt my way along with the weeds at the side of the road, bending at the waist to grasp them with the tips of my fingers.

"Here, Cap! Here, boy!" My voice was high and raspy, and lost itself in the thick swarm of insects. I spun my arms in front of me, but the mayflies were catching in my nostrils and ears, and I had to stop to paw at my face. When I saw the outline of Cap's body through the frost of wings, I thought it might be a mirage, but I stumbled toward him with my arms stretched out.

I put my hands on his side, running them along his body until I came to his head. Yellow Cap was standing stock-still, his knees locked and his muscles twitching. His eyes were wide and his nostrils flared, snorting at the cloud of bugs. "There's my boy," I said, and he tossed his head, knocking me backwards. I hadn't thought to bring a halter or a rope, so I tugged at his mane and ears to get him to follow me. But Cap's eyes were frozen with fear, and his legs were rigid on the ground. I couldn't see where we were on the road, and all around us I sensed the water that had killed Polly Cain. Maybe she had just tripped and fallen in. Maybe she had dropped something. I thought of the time I had accidentally in-haled in a swimming pool—the way the water stabbed pain into the backs of my eyes, made my body retch and heave. No houses were close by. No one would have heard her scream.

I kicked at Cap's leg, and he bristled. "Come on!" I shouted. "Come on, you stupid horse. Move!" I pulled as hard as I could. I twisted his ear between my fingers and wrapped my arms around his neck to pull, but my body hung useless from his in the swarm of white. I would never get him back. He would bolt into the water. His hooves would catch in the grates. His legs would snap. His lungs would fill. And I wouldn't be able to stop it. I wouldn't even be able to see it happen—only to hear it. "Please!" I screamed. "You stupid, stupid horse. Please!" I tried to pick up his front foot and move it a step forward, but I couldn't tell which way was safe.

When I heard my father's voice through the hum of insect wings, I thought I was imagining. But then I heard it again. "Alice!"

"Dad, I'm here! I have him. We're here!"

"I can't see a goddamned thing!"

"Here!" I called again, choking back a wave of sobs.

His hand touched my shoulder. "Jesus Christ! What the hell are you doing?"

"Cap got out. I was afraid he'd get hit or lost or fall in the water." My fingers were wound through his mane, and I twisted to get them free.

My father pushed me hard and then caught me by the arm be-fore I fell. "I could kill you," he said. "I could kill you for being so stupid." I tried to pull away, but I stumbled in the white haze and grasped the pocket of my father's pants to steady myself.

He took off his shirt and wrapped it around Cap's neck. He had to pull hard, but Cap followed, and we tried to brush the in-sects away from his eyes as we led him back to the road. My father went ahead, holding my arm to guide me while I clicked my tongue to keep Cap moving. The mayflies swirled around us like a warm, dry snowstorm, and when I looked up, I could see them rising into the black sky.

When the insects thinned, and we found ourselves on pavement, we stopped, breathless. My arm ached where my father was holding me and when he saw me wince, he let go. I rubbed at my arm. "Sheila shouldn't have told you," I said. "I was fine."

"Like hell," my father said, but his voice was quiet, and he loosened his grip to let Cap nibble at the weeds. He looked back over the clouded water and shook his head.

I held up the palms of my hands and touched at the insects' delicate bodies, at their sheet-white wings, as they billowed up from the canal. The petals of their wings brushed against my palms and evaporated into the darkness. In the moonlight my father's bare chest was pale and smooth against the rough tan of his arms.

"What about the mares?" I asked. "Should you have left them?"

"Alice, horses birth all the time. If a person had to be there to help them, they would have died out centuries ago."

We walked back along the road with Yellow Cap between us, his head low like a dog's.

"Well, Sheila Altman got her money's worth tonight," my father said finally.

"I hate her," I said. I didn't care anymore.

"I know you do." He smiled and pulled at Cap.

"I hate you giving her Nona's horse."

My father was quiet for a second. "This horse is worth a hell of a lot of money, Alice. More than you could even understand." He sighed. "If I sell him, I can afford to hire someone to help me out here."

I stopped. "You have Sheila," I told him, and he laughed. I touched Cap's neck. "You have me."

My father started walking again, faster, and I had to run to keep up. A car passed us on the road, and once it was in front of us, I saw the trail of mayflies behind it, their bodies sprinkling dead onto the pavement.

When we reached the driveway, my father stared up at the house. "There's a light on in your mother's room." He pointed and I looked. It was small, yellow. A candle. A cloud of mayflies hovered at the light, touching the glass of the window.

"It's the lantern I made her."

"You made her a lantern?"

"Sort of." Polly Cain's nimble fingers lay still beneath feet of dry, dusty earth. I only painted the lantern.

"Why did you do that?"

I looked up at the window. "She wanted something. That was all I had."

He ran his thumb along my lip and then wiped the blood from my face with the heel of his hand. "Why don't you go in to bed now?" I turned my face into his touch and let my chin rest in the cup of his palm. He smelled like sweat and hay and leather. "You're no good to me if you're all worn out. Get some sleep." He started toward the pens, tugging at the shirt around Cap's neck.

"I'm not tired," I told him. "Really. Not at all. I'll stay up."

Before he came out of the pen, he rubbed the spot between Cap's ears and patted his neck. The gate clanged shut, and as my father passed me, he shook his head. "Any other girl would go up to bed." He put his hand around my upper arm and squeezed. "You must be tougher than the rest of them."

My arm was still tender from where he had seized me at the canal, but I flexed my muscle to make it hard. I waited for him to say something, but Sheila Altman came thumping out of the barn waving her arms above her head. "She did it," she cried, jumping up and down. "Oh, my God. It's perfect. Come see, come see!"

The foal was small and wet like all the others, and we huddled together to see over the stall door. Under the weak, yellow barn light it lay with its spindly limbs curled. The mare stood above it, eyes half closed as she lowered her head and paused to take in her foal's scent. Outside, the sky was turning tinsel-gray, and the air had a deeper chill. Pieces of hay and dust hazed the air around us, and we stood silent in the barn, smelling of blood and earth and night, and watched their heads draw together to touch for the first time.

Contributors

ANDREW CORSELLO joined *GQ* as a correspondent in 1995. His first feature for the magazine, about his near death experience by liver failure, was nominated for a National Magazine Award—as was his June 2003 essay, "The Vulgarian in the Choir Loft," which has also been anthologized in *The Best American Magazine Writing, 2004* (HarperCollins). His subjects have ranged from the wrestler-turned-movie star The Rock to Frédéric Chopin's Fourth Ballade in F Minor. Two of his pieces, "Metamorphosis" and "The Electric Boy Genius," are currently being developed into motion pictures. Before coming to *GQ*, Corsello was a staff writer for three years at *Philadelphia Magazine*. Earlier, Corsello worked at *The American Lawyer*.

ADAM GOPNIK has been a staff writer at *The New Yorker* since 1986 and is the author of the best-selling book *Paris to the Moon* (Random House, 2000). Gopnik served as *The New Yorker's* art critic and has also written fiction and humor pieces and more than one hundred stories for the magazine. Gopnik's essays received a National Magazine Award in 1997 and again in 2001. From 1983 until 1985 he was the fiction editor at *GQ*. Other published material includes an essay on the life and work of photographer Richard Avedon in "Richard Avedon: Evidence, 1944–1994" (Random House, 1994) and an article on the culture of the United States in the *Encyclopedia Britannica*.

SEYMOUR M. HERSH first wrote for *The New Yorker* in 1971 and has been a regular contributor to the magazine since 1993. He has been awarded the Pulitzer Prize, five George Polk Awards, the National Magazine Award, and more than a dozen other prizes for investigative reporting on My Lai, the CIA's bombing of

Cambodia, Henry Kissinger's wiretapping, and the CIA's efforts against Chile's Salvador Allende, among other topics. Hersh has published eight books, most recently *Chain of Command*, which was based on his reporting for *The New Yorker* on Abu Ghraib.

CHRIS JONES is a writer-at-large and the resident Canadian at *Esquire* magazine, where he has worked since 2002. Before that, he wrote about boxing and baseball for the *National Post* newspaper in Toronto. He is currently turning "Home" into a book, which will be published by Doubleday in 2006.

DAVID KAMP joined *Vanity Fair* in 1996. He has written numerous pieces for the magazine on topics ranging from the remaking of the Elizabeth Taylor version of Cleopatra to 1950s Las Vegas entertainers. He has also written cover profiles of Matt Damon and Chris Rock. Before joining *Vanity Fair*, Kamp was an editor and writer at *GQ* for four years. He started his career as a writer and editor for *Spy*, working under Graydon Carter.

PAUL KVINTA is a contributing editor for *National Geographic Adventure*. He has also written for *Men's Journal, Outside, GQ,* the *New York Times Magazine,* and *Scuba Diving,* and has read his essays for *Weekend All Things Considered* on National Public Radio. Kvinta earned degrees in journalism and anthropology at the University of Texas at Austin, and before becoming a magazine journalist, he worked as a janitor in a Montessori school and tutored the UT women's golf team.

ARYN KYLE's fiction has appeared in *The Atlantic Monthly, The Georgia Review, The Alaska Quarterly Review, StoryQuarterly, Best New American Voices, 2005,* and elsewhere. She received her MFA in fiction from the University of Montana and was a Tennessee Williams Scholar at the 2004 Sewanee Writer's Conference. Aryn lives in Colorado and is currently at work on a novel.

JAMES MCMANUS is the author of *Positively Fifth Street*, two books of poems, and four novels, most recently *Going to the Sun*. His work has appeared in *Best American Sports Writing, Best American Political Writing, The Good Parts: The Best Erotic Writing in Modern Fiction*, and twice in *Best American Poetry*. *Physical: An American Checkup*, a book-length account of his visit to the Mayo Clinic and the issues raised in "Please Stand By," will be published by FSG in January 2006

NINA MARTIN has been a writer and editor specializing in legal, health, and women's issues for over two decades. Her pieces have appeared in *San Francisco* (where she has served as executive editor), *Health* (where she was senior editor), *Elle, O, Real Simple*, and the *Washington Post*, among others. In 2003, Martin began her yearlong investigation in which she examined the records of dozens of wrongful convictions throughout California, compiling the most extensive database of such cases in existence. Her piece has been used as a basic teaching tool in law schools around the state as well as by lawmakers examining how to fix California's criminal justice system. Martin, now the editor of *BabyCenter* magazine, lives in Berkeley.

IAN PARKER has been a staff writer of *The New Yorker* since May 2000. Parker primarily writes profiles and has written about a range of cultural figures including the poet James Fenton, photographer Mario Testino, and Elton John. Parker came to *The New Yorker* from *Talk*, where he was a contributing writer. Before joining *Talk*, he was the television critic for the *London Observer*. He has also been a staff writer and a features editor for *The Independent* and has contributed articles to *Granta*, the *New York Times Magazine, The Modern Review*, and *The Sunday Telegraph*.

JED PERL has been covering the contemporary art scene for *The New Republic* since 1994. As a contributing editor for *Vogue*, Perl's art pieces appeared in the magazine six times a year. He covered the art world for *The New Criterion*, and his work has appeared in *The Yale Review*, *The New York Times Book Review*, and *Elle*, among others. He received an Ingram Merrill Foundation Award in 1994 and has taught art history at Pratt Institute, the Philadephia College of Art, and Parsons School of Design. Perl is author of *Eyewitness: Reports from an Art World in Crisis*; *Paris Without End: On French Art Since World War I*; *Gallery Going: Four Seasons in the Art World*; and *New Art City*.

SAMANTHA POWER is a lecturer in public policy. Her book, *A Problem from Hell: America and the Age of Genocide*, was awarded the 2003 Pulitzer Prize and the 2003 National Book Critics Circle Award for general nonfiction. Power was the founding executive director of the Carr Center for Human Rights Policy at Harvard (1998–2002). From 1993 to 1996, Power covered the wars in the former Yugoslavia as a reporter for *U.S. News and World Report*, the *Boston Globe*, and the *Economist*. She is the editor, with Graham Allison, of *Realizing Human Rights: Moving from Inspiration to Impact*. She has written a new introduction to Hannah Arendt's *Origins of Totalitarianism* and has begun work on a book on the causes and consequences of historical amnesia in American foreign policy.

DAVID QUAMMEN was educated at Yale and Oxford University and is a renowned science and nature writer. Quammen is a two-time National Magazine Award winner for his science essays and columns in *Outside* magazine. In addition to his columns in *Outside*, essays, nonfiction, and fiction, Quammen has also been published in *National Geographic Magazine*, *Harper's*, *Rolling Stone*, and *The New York Times Book Review*.

JONATHAN RAUCH, a senior writer and columnist for *National Journal* in Washington and a correspondent for *The Atlantic Monthly*, is the author of several books and many articles on public policy, culture, and economics. In 1989 he was named by *Washingtonian Magazine* as a "rising star of Washington journalism." His most recent book, *Gay Marriage: Why It Is Good for Gays, Good for Straights, and Good for America* (2004), was called by the *Economist* "a powerful book, clear, tolerant and persuasive . . . obligatory reading."

GARY SMITH, who joined *Sports Illustrated* in 1982, is considered one of the finest magazine writers in the country. Smith has written a number of in-depth profiles including pieces on Muhammad Ali, Jim Valvano, and Mia Hamm. Smith has been nominated for nine National Magazine Awards, winning three times for feature writing and once for profile writing. In January 2000, *Writer's Digest* named Smith one of the "Fifty Writers to Watch" in the coming decade. His previous experience includes working at the *Wilmington News-Journal, Philadelphia Daily News, New York Daily News*, and *Inside Sports*. He has also written for *Rolling Stone, Esquire*, and *Life*. A collection of his work, *Beyond the Game: The Collected Sportswriting of Gary Smith*, was published in 2001.

JAMES WOLCOTT returned to *Vanity Fair* as a contributing editor in 1997. His monthly column covers pop culture, media, and the literary scene. In 2003, Wolcott received a National Magazine Award for three articles in the Reviews and Criticism category. He began his career in the circulation department at *The Village Voice* in 1972. He first joined *Vanity Fair* in 1983 and wrote the "Mixed Media" column. Wolcott then worked as staff writer at *The New Yorker* for four years, before returning to *Vanity Fair*. His work has appeared in *Esquire, Harper's*, and *The Wall Street Journal*, to name a few. His first novel, *The Catsitters*, was published in 2001.

NED ZEMAN joined *Vanity Fair* as senior editor in May 1997 and became contributing editor three years later. He has written cover stories on such celebrities as Madonna and Julia Roberts, as well as profiles on the late photographer Bruno Zehnder and the late agent Jay Moloney. Prior to *Vanity Fair*, Zeman was executive editor of *Buzz* from 1996 to 1997 and a senior writer for *Sports Illustrated* in 1994. He spent six years as a staff writer at *Newsweek* from 1988 to 1994, during which time he also wrote for *Spy* under Graydon Carter. He resides in Los Angeles.

2005 National Magazine Award Finalists

NOTE: All nominated issues are dated 2004 unless otherwise specified. The editor whose name appears in connection with finalists for 2005 held that position, or was listed on the masthead, at the time the issue was published in 2004. In some cases, another editor is now in that position.

General Excellence

This category recognizes overall excellence in magazines. It honors the effectiveness with which writing, reporting, editing, and design all come together to command readers' attention and fulfill the magazine's unique editorial mission.

Under 100,000 Circulation

The American Scholar: Anne Fadiman, editor, for Winter, Spring, Summer issues.

The Believer: Heidi Julavits, Ed Park and Vendela Vida, co-editors; Andrew Leland, managing editor, for June, September, November issues.

Print: Joyce Rutter Kaye, editor-in-chief, for January/February, July/August, September/October issues.

ReadyMade: Shoshana Berger, editor-in-chief, for March/April, May/June, September/October issues.

The Virginia Quarterly Review: Ted Genoways, editor, for Winter, Spring, Fall issues.

100,000 to 250,000 Circulation

Baseline: Tom Steinert-Threlkeld, editor-in-chief, for March, April, December issues.

Dwell: Allison Arieff, editor-in-chief, for March, October/November, December issues.

Foreign Policy: Moisés Naím, editor and publisher, for May/June, July/August, September/October issues.

Los Angeles Magazine: Kit Rachlis, editor-in-chief, for June, September, October issues.

Teacher Magazine: Virginia B. Edwards, editor, for August/September, October, November/December issues.

250,000 to 500,000 Circulation

The Atlantic Monthly: Cullen Murphy, managing editor, for January/February, July/ August, November issues.

Cure: Dr. Vinay K. Jain, editor-in-chief; Melissa Weber, managing editor, for Summer, Fall, Winter issues.

Details: Daniel Peres, editor-in-chief, for March, August, September issues.

Martha Stewart Weddings: Darcy Miller, editorial director; Melissa Morgan, executive editor, for Winter, Summer, Fall issues.

New York Magazine: Adam Moss, editor-in-chief, for June 7, November 15, November 22 issues.

500,000 to 1,000,000 Circulation

Cook's Illustrated: Christopher Kimball, founder and editor, for August, October, December issues.

Esquire: David Granger, editor-in-chief, for March, September, November issues.

Gourmet: Ruth Reichl, editor-in-chief, for March, August, October issues.

Vibe: Mimi Valdés, editor-in-chief, for March, May, November issues.

Wired: Chris Anderson, editor-in-chief, for February, October, November issues.

1,000,000 to 2,000,000 Circulation

Fortune: Rik Kirkland, managing editor, for April 5, April 19, May 31 issues.

Men's Health: David Zinczenko, vice president and editor-in-chief, for March, October, November issues.

The New Yorker: David Remnick, editor, for February 16 and 23, May 10, August 30 issues.

Real Simple: Kristin van Ogtrop, managing editor, for May, October, December/ January issues.

Vanity Fair: Graydon Carter, editor, for March, October, December issues.

Over 2,000,000 Circulation

Glamour: Cynthia Leive, editor-in-chief, for October, November, December issues.

Good Housekeeping: Ellen Levine, editor-in-chief, for September, October, November issues.

National Geographic: William L. Allen, editor-in-chief, for June, November, December issues.

Newsweek: Richard M. Smith, Chairman and editor-in-chief; Mark Whitaker, editor, for May 31, November 15, December 27–January 3 issues.

Sports Illustrated: Terry McDonell, managing editor, for April 26, September 27, December 6 issues.

Personal Service

This category recognizes excellence in service journalism. The advice or instruction presented should help readers improve the quality of their personal lives.

BabyTalk: Susan Kane, editor-in-chief, for "You Can Breastfeed!" by Kristin O'Callaghan, August.

Budget Living: Sarah Gray Miller, editor-in-chief, for "Show Me the Way Home," by Dimity McDowell, April/May.

Money: Robert Safian, managing editor, for two packages compiled by the writers and editors of *Money*, "101 Things Every Investor Should Know!" March; "101 Things Every Consumer Should Know!" July.

Self: Lucy Danziger, editor-in-chief, for its breast cancer handbook, "Your Breasts, Healthy for Life," October.

U.S. News & World Report: Brian Duffy, editor, for "How to Be a Smart Patient," November 8.

Leisure Interests

This category recognizes excellent service journalism about leisure-time pursuits. The practical advice or instruction presented should help readers enjoy hobbies or other recreational interests.

Golf Digest: Jerry Tarde, chairman and editor-in-chief, for "The Ultimate Guide to the Ultimate Buddies Trip," December.

National Geographic Adventure: John Rasmus, editor-in-chief, for "Grail Trails," by Charles Graeber and Jim Gorman, June/July.

O, The Oprah Magazine: Oprah Winfrey, founder and editorial director; Amy Gross, editor-in-chief, for "Attention Shoppers!" September.

Runner's World: David Willey, editor-in-chief, for "Fall Shoe Guide," September, and "Winter Shoe Guide," December, by Warren Greene and Ray Fredericksen.

Sports Illustrated: Terry McDonell, managing editor, for its 2004 "Olympic Preview," August 2.

Reporting

This category recognizes excellence in reporting. It honors the enterprise, exclusive reporting, and intelligent analysis that a magazine exhibits in covering an event, a situation, or a problem of contemporary interest and significance.

5280 Magazine: Daniel Brogan, editor and publisher, for "Conduct Unbecoming," by Maximillian Potter, February/March.

The Chronicle of Higher Education: Philip W. Semas, editor-in-chief; William Horne, managing editor, for "Degrees of Suspicion: Inside the Multimillion-Dollar World of Diploma Mills," by Thomas Bartlett and Scott Smallwood, June 25.

The Chronicle of Higher Education: Philip W. Semas, editor-in-chief; William Horne, managing editor, for its special report on plagiarism by Thomas Bartlett, Scott Smallwood, David Glenn, and Scott McLemee, December 17.

National Geographic Adventure: John Rasmus, editor-in-chief, for "Stomping Grounds," by Paul Kvinta, August.

The New Yorker: David Remnick, editor, for "Dying in Darfur," by Samantha Power, August 30.

Public Interest

This category recognizes journalism that has the potential to affect national or local policy or lawmaking. It honors investigative reporting or ground-breaking analysis that sheds new light on an issue of public importance.

5280 Magazine: Daniel Brogan, editor and publisher, for "Private Stites Should Have Been Saved," by Maximillian Potter, June/July.

Fortune: Rik Kirkland, managing editor, for "Why We're Losing the War on Cancer (and How to Win It)", by Clifton Leaf, March 22.

Harper's Magazine: Lewis H. Lapham, editor, for "Gambling with Abortion: Why Both Sides Think They Have Everything to Lose," by Cynthia Gorney, November.

The New Yorker: David Remnick, editor, for the three articles by Seymour M. Hersh, "Torture at Abu Ghraib," May 10; "Chain of Command," May 17; "The Gray Zone," May 24.

San Francisco: Bruce Kelley, editor-in-chief, for "Innocence Lost," by Nina Martin, November.

Feature Writing

This category recognizes excellence in feature writing. It honors the stylish-ness and originality with which the author treats his or her subject.

The Atlantic Monthly: Cullen Murphy, managing editor, for "A Sea Story," by William Langewiesche, May.

Esquire: David Granger, editor-in-chief, for "Home," by Chris Jones, July.

GQ: Jim Nelson, editor-in-chief, for "The Wronged Man," by Andrew Corsello, November.

Texas Monthly: Evan Smith, editor, for "They Came. They Sawed," by John Bloom, November.

Vanity Fair: Graydon Carter, editor, for "American Communion," by David Kamp, October

Profile Writing

This category recognizes excellence in profile writing. It honors the vividness and perceptiveness with which the writer brings his or her subject to life.

The New Yorker: David Remnick, editor, for "The Gift," by Ian Parker, August 2.

Rolling Stone: Jann S. Wenner, editor and publisher, for "The Twilight of Bob Guccione," by John Colapinto, April 1.

Sports Illustrated: Terry McDonell, managing editor, for "Walking His Life Away," by Gary Smith, July 26.

Vanity Fair: Graydon Carter, editor, for "The Man Who Loved Grizzlies," by Ned Zeman, May.

Vanity Fair: Graydon Carter, editor, for "The Making of a Sniper," by Donovan Webster, September.

Essays

This category recognizes excellence in essay writing on topics ranging from the personal to the political. Whatever the subject, it honors the author's eloquence, perspective, fresh thinking, and unique voice.

The Atlantic Monthly: Cullen Murphy, managing editor, for "How Serfdom Saved the Women's Movement," by Caitlin Flanagan, March.

Esquire: David Granger, editor-in-chief, for "Please Stand By While the Age of Miracles Is Briefly Suspended," by James McManus, August.

Ms.: Elaine Lafferty, editor-in-chief, for "Between a Woman and Her Doctor," by Martha Mendoza, Summer.

National Geographic: William L. Allen, editor-in-chief, for "Was Darwin Wrong?" by David Quammen, November.

The New Yorker: David Remnick, editor, for "Last of the Metrozoids," by Adam Gopnik, May 10.

Columns and Commentary

This category recognizes excellence in short-form political, social, economic or humorous commentary. The award honors the eloquence, force of argument and succinctness with which the writer presents his or her views.

National Journal: Charles Green, editor, for three columns by Jonathan Rauch, "On Same-Sex Marriage, Bush Failed the Public and Himself," March 6; "Fix the Mc-Cain-Feingold Law. Oops—Can I Say That?" September 25; "Good Plan, Republicans. But It Didn't Work In Britain," December 18.

The New Yorker: David Remnick, editor, for three columns by George Packer, "Wars and Ideas," July 5; "The Political War," September 27; "Questions of Greatness," October 25.

SmartMoney: Fleming Meeks, editor, for three columns by Roger Lowenstein, "The Wrong Diagnosis," March; "How Greedy Was My Valley," April; "What Goes Up . . . ," December.

Vanity Fair: Graydon Carter, editor, for three columns by Christopher Hitchens, "A Prayer for Indonesia," January; "I Fought the Law," February; "The Gospel According to Mel," March.

Vanity Fair: Graydon Carter, editor, for three columns by James Wolcott, "The Bush Bunch," July; "Color Me Khaki," September; "Rummy on the Rocks," October.

Reviews and Criticism

This category recognizes excellence in criticism of art, books, movies, television, theater, music, dance, food, dining, fashion, products, and the like. It honors the knowledge, persuasiveness, and original voice that the critic brings to his or her reviews.

GQ: Jim Nelson, editor-in-chief, for three reviews by Alan Richman, "The Restaurant Commandments," July; "The Thing That Ate New York," November; "Stick a Fork in Jean-Georges," December.

The New Republic: Peter Beinart, editor, for three pieces by Jed Perl, "Beyond Belief," February 16; "Firings," April 5; "Modern Immaturity," November 29 & December 6.

The New Yorker: David Remnick, editor, for three reviews by Adam Gopnik, "Times Regained," March 22; "The Big One," August 23; "Will Power," September 13.

The New Yorker: David Remnick, editor, for three reviews by Louis Menand, "Bad Comma," June 28; "Nanook and Me," August 9 and 16; "The Unpolitical Animal," August 30.

Vanity Fair: Graydon Carter, editor, for three pieces by James Wolcott, "Makeover Madness," January; "The Laptop Brigade," April; "Bland Ambition," August.

Magazine Section

This category recognizes excellence of a regular department or editorial section of a magazine, either front- or back-of-book and composed of a variety of elements, both text and visual. Finalists were selected based on the section's voice, originality, design, and packaging.

AARP The Magazine: Steven Slon, editor, for its front-of-book section "Navigator," March/April, May/June, September/October.

ESPN The Magazine: Gary Hoenig, editor-in-chief, for its front-of-book section "The Jump," March 29, May 10, August 2.

New York Magazine: Adam Moss, editor-in-chief, for its "Strategist" section, October 18, October 25, November 22.

Popular Science: Scott Mowbray, editor-in-chief, for its section "How 2.0," April, May, June.

Runner's World: David Willey, editor-in-chief, for its front-of-book mega-section "Warmups," July, September, November.

Single-Topic Issue

This category recognizes magazines that have devoted an issue to an in-depth examination of one topic. It honors the ambition, comprehensiveness, and imagination with which a magazine treats its subject.

Discover: Stephen L. Petranek, editor-in-chief, for its special Einstein issue: "One Hundred Years of Genius Without Limits," September.

Fortune: Richard Kirkland, managing editor, for its fiftieth-anniversary issue on the Fortune 500, April 5.

Gourmet: Ruth Reichl, editor-in-chief, for its special issue on New York, March.

Newsweek: Richard M. Smith, chairman and editor-in-chief; Mark Whitaker, editor, for "How He Did It," a special issue on the presidential election, November 15.

Print: Joyce Rutter Kaye, editor-in-chief, for its sex issue, July/August.

Design

This category recognizes excellence in magazine design. It honors the effectiveness of overall design, artwork, graphics, and typography in enhancing a magazine's unique mission and personality.

Details: Daniel Peres, editor-in-chief; Rockwell Harwood, design director, for January/February, March, September issues.

Everyday Food: Margaret Roach, editor-in-chief; Melissa Morgan, executive editor; Scot Schy, design director, for March, November, December issues.

Kids: Fun Stuff To Do Together: Jodi Levine, editorial director; Melissa Morgan, executive editor; Deb Bishop, design director, for July/August, September/October, Winter issues.

Ski: Kendall Hamilton, editor-in-chief; Eleanor Williamson, art director; Tom Brown, consulting creative director, for October, November, December issues.

W: Patrick McCarthy, chairman and editorial director; Dennis Freedman, vice chairman and creative director; Edward Leida, executive vice president and group design director; Kirby Rodriguez, art director, for July, September, October issues.

Photography

This category recognizes excellence in magazine photography. It honors the effectiveness of photography, photojournalism, and photo illustration in enhancing a magazine's unique mission and personality.

Country Home: Carol Sheehan, editor-in-chief; Mary Emmerling, creative director; Susan L Uedelhofen, art director, for September, October, November issues.

Details: Daniel Peres, editor-in-chief; Rockwell Harwood, design director; Judith Puckett-Rinella, photography director, for March, September, November issues.

Gourmet: Ruth Reichl, editor-in-chief; Richard Ferretti, creative director; Erika Oliveira, art director; Amy Koblenzer, photo editor, for October, November, December issues.

Kids: Fun Stuff To Do Together: Jodi Levine, editor-in-chief; Melissa Morgan, executive editor; Deb Bishop, design director; Brooke Reynolds and Robin Rosenthal, senior art directors; Stacie McCormick, photo editor, for Winter, July/August, September/October issues.

New York Magazine: Adam Moss, editor-in-chief; Luke Hayman, design director; Jody Quon, photography director; Chris Dixon, art director; Cory Jacobs, photography editor, for August 16, August 23, November 22 issues.

Photo Portfolio/Photo Essay

This category recognizes a distinctive portfolio or photographic essay. It honors either photos that express an idea or a concept, or documentary photojournalism shot in real time.

Aperture: Melissa Harris, editor-in-chief; Yolanda Cuomo, art director, for "Loretta Lux's Changelings," by Loretta Lux, text by Diana C. Stoll, February.

Condé Nast Traveler: Thomas J. Wallace, editor-in-chief; Robert Best, design director; Kathleen Klech, photography director; Kerry Robertson, art director; Esin Ili Göknar, picture editor, for "Empire of Ice," by Len Jenshel and Diane Cook, July.

Departures: Richard David Story, editor-in-chief; Bernard Scharf, creative director; Jennifer L. Martin, director of photography; Trent Johnson, art director, for "To Catch a Thief," by Torkil Gudnason, November/December.

Los Angeles Magazine: Kit Rachlis, editor-in-chief; Joe Kimberling, art director; Kathleen Clark, photo editor, for "City of Ash," by Robert Polidori, April.

The New Yorker: David Remnick, editor; Elisabeth Biondi, director of photography, for "Democracy 2004," by Richard Avedon, November 1.

Time: James Kelly, managing editor; Arthur Hochstein, art director; Michele Stephenson, director of photography, for "The Tragedy of Sudan," by James Nachtwey, October 4.

Fiction

This category recognizes excellence in magazine fiction writing. It honors the quality of a publication's literary selections.

The Atlantic Monthly: Cullen Murphy, managing editor, for "An Incomplete Map of the Northern Polarity," by Nathan Roberts, January/February; "Foaling Season," by Aryn Kyle, May; "The One in White," by Robert Olen Butler, July/August.

Harper's Magazine: Lewis H. Lapham, editor, for "Natasha," by David Bezmozgis, May; "Commission," by Tim Winton, September; "Introduction to Speech," by Ron Carlson, December.

The New Yorker: David Remnick, editor, for "The Last Words on Earth," by Nicole Krauss, February 9; "Passion," by Alice Munro, March 22; "Old Boys, Old Girls," by Edward P. Jones, May 3.

The Paris Review: Brigid Hughes, executive editor, for "The Fifth Wall," by Malinda McCollum; "The Wamsutter Wolf," by Annie Proulx; "Everyone Else," by Antoine Wilson, Fall.

The Virginia Quarterly Review: Ted Genoways, editor, for "The Immortals," by John McNally, Spring; "Happy," by Dean Bakopoulos, Summer; "The Futurist," by James P. Othmer, Fall.

General Excellence Online

This category recognizes outstanding magazine Internet sites, as well as online-only magazines and Web logs, that have a significant amount of original content. It honors sites that reflect an outstanding level of interactivity, journalistic integrity, service, and innovative visual presentation.

The Atlantic Online (www.theatlantic.com): Sage Stossel, senior editor.

BusinessWeek Online (www.businessweek.com): Kathy Rebello, editor.

ConsumerReports.org (www.consumerreports.org): Laura R. Bona, editor.

Nerve.com (www.nerve.com): Michael Martin, editor-in-chief.

Style.com (http://www.style.com): Jamie Pallot, editorial director, CondéNet.

National Magazine Award Winners, 1966–2005

General Excellence

1973	*BusinessWeek*
1981	*ARTnews*
	Audubon
	BusinessWeek
	Glamour
1982	*Camera Arts*
	Newsweek
	Rocky Mountain Magazine
	Science81
1983	*Harper's Magazine*
	Life
	Louisiana Life
	Science82
1984	*The American Lawyer*
	House & Garden
	National Geographic
	Outside
1985	*American Health*
	American Heritage
	Manhattan, inc.
	Time
1986	*Discover*
	Money
	New England Monthly
	3-2-1- Contact
1987	*Common Cause*
	Elle
	New England Monthly
	People Weekly
1988	*Fortune*
	Hippocrates
	Parents
	The Sciences
1989	*American Heritage*
	Sports Illustrated
	The Sciences
	Vanity Fair
1990	*Metropolitan Home*
	7 Days
	Sports Illustrated
	Texas Monthly
1991	*Condé Nast Traveler*
	Glamour
	Interview
	The New Republic
1992	*Mirabella*
	National Geographic
	The New Republic
	Texas Monthly
1993	*American Photo*
	The Atlantic Monthly
	Lingua Franca
	Newsweek
1994	*BusinessWeek*
	Health
	Print
	Wired
1995	*Entertainment Weekly*
	I.D. Magazine
	Men's Journal
	The New Yorker
1996	*BusinessWeek*
	Civilization
	Outside
	The Sciences
1997	*I.D. Magazine*
	Outside
	Vanity Fair
	Wired

1998	*DoubleTake*
	Outside
	Preservation
	Rolling Stone
1999	*Condé Nast Traveler*
	Fast Company
	I.D. Magazine
	Vanity Fair
2000	*National Geographic*
	Nest
	The New Yorker
	Saveur
2001	*The American Scholar*
	Mother Jones
	The New Yorker
	Teen People
2002	*Entertainment Weekly*
	National Geographic Adventure
	Newsweek
	Print
	Vibe
2003	*Architectural Record*
	The Atlantic Monthly
	ESPN The Magazine
	Foreign Policy
	Parenting
	Texas Monthly
2004	*Aperture*
	Budget Living
	Chicago Magazine
	Gourmet
	Newsweek
	Popular Science
2005	*Dwell*
	Glamour
	Martha Stewart Weddings
	The New Yorker
	Print
	Wired

Personal Service

1986	*Farm Journal*
1987	*Consumer Reports*
1988	*Money*
1989	*Good Housekeeping*
1990	*Consumer Reports*
1991	*New York*
1992	*Creative Classroom*
1993	*Good Housekeeping*
1994	*Fortune*
1995	*SmartMoney*
1996	*SmartMoney*
1997	*Glamour*
1998	*Men's Journal*
1999	*Good Housekeeping*
2000	*PC Computing*
2001	*National Geographic Adventure*
2002	*National Geographic Adventure*
2003	*Outside*
2004	*Men's Health*
2005	*BabyTalk*

Leisure Interests

(formerly Special Interests)

2002	*Vogue*
2003	*National Geographic Adventure*
2004	*Consumer Reports*
2005	*Sports Illustrated*

Special Interests

1986	*Popular Mechanics*
1987	*Sports Afield*
1988	*Condé Nast Traveler*

1989	*Condé Nast Traveler*		1993	*IEEE Spectrum*
1990	*Art & Antiques*		1994	*The New Yorker*
1991	*New York*		1995	*The Atlantic Monthly*
1992	*Sports Afield*		1996	*The New Yorker*
1993	*Philadelphia*		1997	*Outside*
1994	*Outside*		1998	*Rolling Stone*
1995	*GQ*		1999	*Newsweek*
1996	*Saveur*		2000	*Vanity Fair*
1997	*Smithsonian*		2001	*Esquire*
1998	*Entertainment Weekly*		2002	*The Atlantic Monthly*
1999	*PC Computing*		2003	*The New Yorker*
2000	*I.D. Magazine*		2004	*Rolling Stone*
2001	*The New Yorker*		2005	*The New Yorker*

Reporting

1970	*The New Yorker*
1971	*The Atlantic Monthly*
1972	*The Atlantic Monthly*
1973	*New York*
1974	*The New Yorker*
1975	*The New Yorker*
1976	*Audubon*
1977	*Audubon*
1978	*The New Yorker*
1979	*Texas Monthly*
1980	*Mother Jones*
1981	*National Journal*
1982	*The Washingtonian*
1983	*Institutional Investor*
1984	*Vanity Fair*
1985	*Texas Monthly*
1986	*Rolling Stone*
1987	*Life*
1988	*The Washingtonian and Baltimore Magazine*
1989	*The New Yorker*
1990	*The New Yorker*
1991	*The New Yorker*
1992	*The New Republic*

Public Interest

1970	*Life*
1971	*The Nation*
1972	*Philadelphia*
1974	*Scientific American*
1975	*Consumer Reports*
1976	*BusinessWeek*
1977	*Philadelphia*
1978	*Mother Jones*
1979	*New West*
1980	*Texas Monthly*
1981	*Reader's Digest*
1982	*The Atlantic*
1983	*Foreign Affairs*
1984	*The New Yorker*
1985	*The Washingtonian*
1986	*Science85*
1987	*Money*
1988	*The Atlantic*
1989	*California*
1990	*Southern Exposure*
1991	*Family Circle*
1992	*Glamour*
1993	*The Family Therapy Networker*

414

National Magazine Award Winners, 1966–2005

1994	*Philadelphia*		2002	*The New Yorker*
1995	*The New Republic*		2003	*Sports Illustrated*
1996	*Texas Monthly*		2004	*Esquire*
1997	*Fortune*		2005	*The New Yorker*
1998	*The Atlantic Monthly*			
1999	*Time*			
2000	*The New Yorker*		**Essays**	
2001	*Time*		2000	*The Sciences*
2002	*The Atlantic Monthly*		2001	*The New Yorker*
2003	*The Atlantic Monthly*		2002	*The New Yorker*
2004	*The New Yorker*		2003	*The American Scholar*
2005	*The New Yorker*		2004	*The New Yorker*
			2005	*National Geographic*

Feature Writing

Columns and Commentary

1988	*The Atlantic*		2002	*New York*
1989	*Esquire*		2003	*The Nation*
1990	*The Washingtonian*		2004	*New York*
1991	*U.S. News & World Report*		2005	*National Journal*
1992	*Sports Illustrated*			
1993	*The New Yorker*			
1994	*Harper's Magazine*		**Reviews and Criticism**	
1995	*GQ*			
1996	*GQ*		2000	*Esquire*
1997	*Sports Illustrated*		2001	*The New Yorker*
1998	*Harper's Magazine*		2002	*Harper's Magazine*
1999	*The American Scholar*		2003	*Vanity Fair*
2000	*Sports Illustrated*		2004	*Esquire*
2001	*Rolling Stone*		2005	*The New Yorker*
2002	*The Atlantic Monthly*			
2003	*Harper's Magazine*			
2004	*The New Yorker*		**Single-Topic Issue**	
2005	*Esquire*		1979	*Progressive Architecture*
			1980	*Scientific American*
			1981	*BusinessWeek*
Profile Writing			1982	*Newsweek*
			1983	*IEEE Spectrum*
2000	*Sports Illustrated*		1984	*Esquire*
2001	*The New Yorker*			

1985	American Heritage	1992	Vanity Fair
1986	IEEE Spectrum	1993	Harper's Bazaar
1987	Bulletin of the Atomic	1994	Allure
	Scientists	1995	Martha Stewart Living
1988	Life	1996	Wired
1989	Hippocrates	1997	I.D.
1990	National Geographic	1998	Entertainment Weekly
1991	The American Lawyer	1999	ESPN The Magazine
1992	BusinessWeek	2000	Fast Company
1993	Newsweek	2001	Nest
1994	Health	2002	Details
1995	Discover	2003	Details
1996	Bon Appétit	2004	Esquire
1997	Scientific American	2005	Kids: Fun Stuff to Do
1998	The Sciences		Together
1999	The Oxford American		
2002	Time		
2003	Scientific American		
2004	The Oxford American		
2005	Newsweek		

Magazine Section

| 2005 | Popular Science |

Photography

1985	Life
1986	Vogue
1987	National Geographic
1988	Rolling Stone
1989	National Geographic
1990	Texas Monthly
1991	National Geographic
1992	National Geographic
1993	Harper's Bazaar
1994	Martha Stewart Living
1995	Rolling Stone
1996	Saveur
1997	National Geographic
1998	W
1999	Martha Stewart Living
2000	Vanity Fair
2001	National Geographic
2002	Vanity Fair
2003	Condé Nast Traveler
2004	City
2005	Gourmet

Design

1980	Geo
1981	Attenzione
1982	Nautical Quarterly
1983	New York
1984	House & Garden
1985	Forbes
1986	Time
1987	Elle
1988	Life
1989	Rolling Stone
1990	Esquire
1991	Condé Nast Traveler

Photo Portoflio/Photo Essay

2004	W
2005	Time

Fiction

1978	The New Yorker
1979	The Atlantic Monthly
1980	Antaeus
1981	The North American Review
1982	The New Yorker
1983	The North American Review
1984	Seventeen
1985	Playboy
1986	The Georgia Review
1987	Esquire
1988	The Atlantic
1989	The New Yorker
1990	The New Yorker
1991	Esquire
1992	Story
1993	The New Yorker
1994	Harper's Magazine
1995	Story
1996	Harper's Magazine
1997	The New Yorker
1998	The New Yorker
1999	Harper's Magazine
2000	The New Yorker
2001	Zoetrope: All-Story
2002	The New Yorker
2003	The New Yorker
2004	Esquire
2005	The Atlantic Monthly

General Excellence In New Media

1997	Money
1998	The Sporting News Online
1999	Cigar Aficionado
2000	BusinessWeek Online

General Excellence Online

(formerly General Excellence in New Media)

2001	U.S. News Online
2002	National Geographic Magazine Online
2003	Slate
2004	CNET News.com
2005	Style.com

Best Interactive Design

2001	SmartMoney.com

Essays and Criticism

1978	Esquire
1979	Life
1980	Natural History
1981	Time
1982	The Atlantic
1983	The American Lawyer
1984	The New Republic
1985	Boston Magazine
1986	The Sciences
1987	Outside
1988	Harper's Magazine
1989	Harper's Magazine
1990	Vanity Fair
1991	The Sciences
1992	The Nation
1993	The American Lawyer
1994	Harper's Magazine
1995	Harper's Magazine
1996	The New Yorker

1997	*The New Yorker*
1998	*The New Yorker*
1999	*The Atlantic Monthly*

Single Awards

1966	*Look*
1967	*Life*
1968	*Newsweek*
1969	*American Machinist*

Specialized Journalism

1970	*Philadelphia*
1971	*Rolling Stone*
1972	*Architectural Record*
1973	*Psychology Today*
1974	*Texas Monthly*
1975	*Medical Economics*
1976	*United Mine Workers Journal*
1977	*Architectural Record*
1978	*Scientific American*
1979	*National Journal*
1980	*IEEE Spectrum*

Visual Excellence

1970	*Look*
1971	*Vogue*
1972	*Esquire*
1973	*Horizon*
1974	*Newsweek*
1975	*Country Journal*
	National Lampoon

1976	*Horticulture*
1977	*Rolling Stone*
1978	*Architectural Digest*
1979	*Audubon*

Fiction and Belles Lettres

1970	*Redbook*
1971	*Esquire*
1972	*Mademoiselle*
1973	*The Atlantic Monthly*
1974	*The New Yorker*
1975	*Redbook*
1976	*Essence*
1977	*Mother Jones*

Service to the Individual

1974	*Sports Illustrated*
1975	*Esquire*
1976	*Modern Medicine*
1977	*Harper's Magazine*
1978	*Newsweek*
1979	*The American Journal of Nursing*
1980	*Saturday Review*
1982	*Philadelphia*
1983	*Sunset*
1984	*New York*
1985	*The Washingtonian*

Special Awards

| 1976 | *Time* |
| 1989 | Robert E. Kenyon Jr. |

ASME Board of Directors, 2004–2005

American Society of Magazine Editors
Mission Statement

ASME is the professional organization for editors of magazines edited and published in the United States.

ASME's mission is to:

- Bring magazine editors together for networking

- Uphold editorial integrity

- Encourage and reward outstanding and innovative achievement in the creation of magazines and their content

- Disseminate useful information on magazine editing to magazine staff members and others

- Attract talented young people to magazine editorial work

- Defend magazines against external pressures

- Speak out on public policy issues, particularly those pertaining to the First Amendment; and to acquaint the general public with the work of magazine editors and the special character of magazines as a channel of communication

ASME was founded in 1963 and currently has more than 850 members nationwide.